Snow White with the Red Hair

KIDUKI

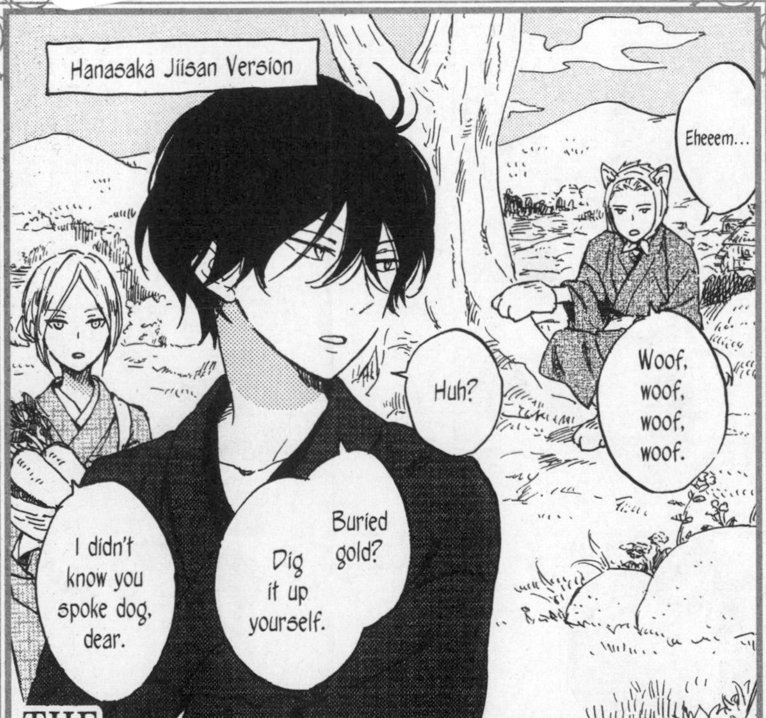
Hanasaka Jiisan Version
Eheeem...
Woof, woof, woof, woof.
Huh?
Buried gold?
Dig it up yourself.
I didn't know you spoke dog, dear.
THE END

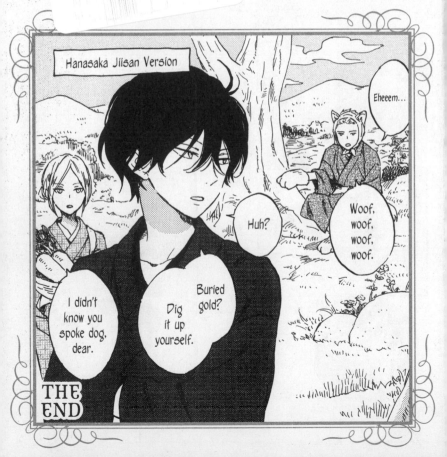

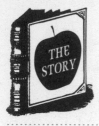

THE STORY

Shirayuki was born with beautiful hair as red as apples, but when her rare hair earns her unwanted attention from the notorious prince Raj, she's forced to flee her home. A young man named Zen helps her in the forest of the neighboring kingdom, Clarines, and it turns out he is that kingdom's second prince! Shirayuki decides to accompany Zen back to Wistal, the capital city of Clarines.

Shirayuki has met all manner of people since becoming a court herbalist, and her relationship with Zen continues to grow, as the two have finally made their feelings known to each other.

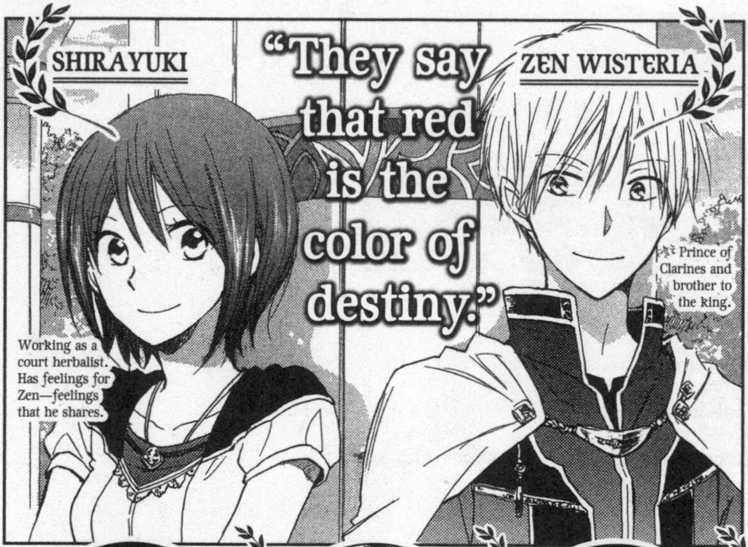
SHIRAYUKI
"They say that red is the color of destiny."
ZEN WISTERIA
Prince of Clarines and brother to the king.
Working as a court herbalist. Has feelings for Zen—feelings that he shares.

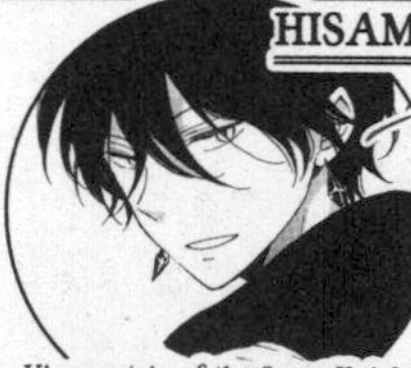
HISAME

Vice-captain of the Sereg Knights and second son of Count Rougis. He and Mistuhide get along like cats and dogs.

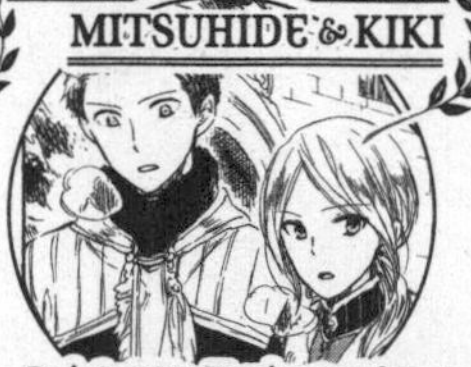
MITSUHIDE & KIKI

Zen's knights. They're good friends who share a strong bond.

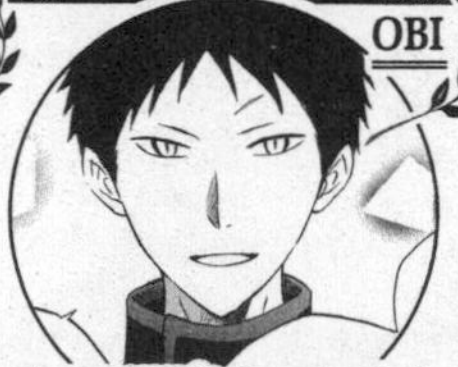
OBI

Former assassin. Currently, Zen's knight. Served as Shirayuki's bodyguard for part of her stay in Lilias.

After becoming a full-fledged court herbalist, Shirayuki takes a work trip to the northern city of Lilias with her boss, Ryu. When a mysterious illness starts spreading, they put their skills to use and figure out what's causing it.

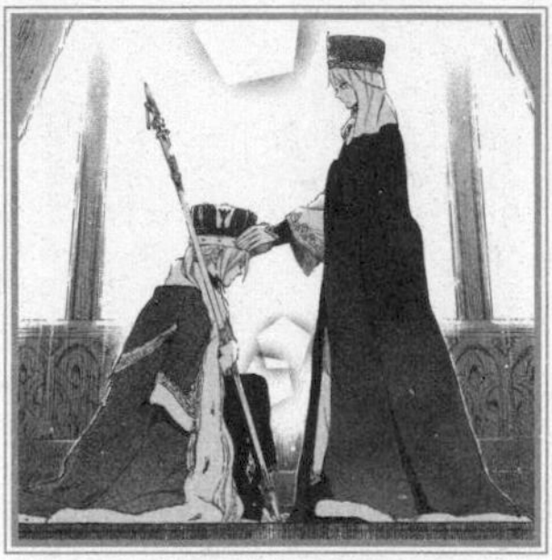

Once back in Wistal, Shirayuki and Ryu are ordered to return to Lilias by the newly crowned king Izana. But this time, it's no mere business trip—it's a personnel transfer for two whole years. Once there, the pair endeavor to bolster their herbalism skills and knowledge as they work with colleagues to neutralize the toxin of the glowing orimmallys—the same plant that caused the earlier outbreak.

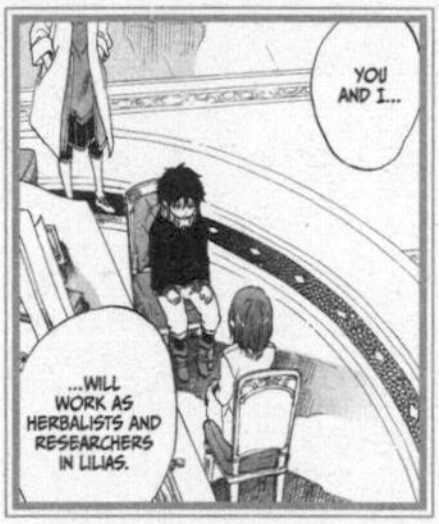
YOU AND I...
...WILL WORK AS HERBALISTS AND RESEARCHERS IN LILIAS.

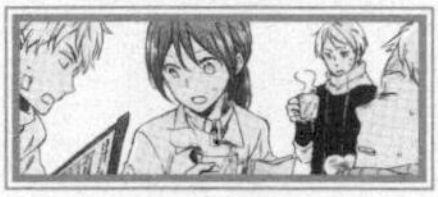

While struggling to figure out how to retain the glowing properties of the seeds once the toxin is removed, they enlist the help of a scholar who specializes in light and heat—the wunderock expert Rata Forzeno. Laborious experimentation leads to an understanding of how to amplify the glowing properties, and at long last the team breeds a new toxin-free strain of the plant that glows just as much as the original.

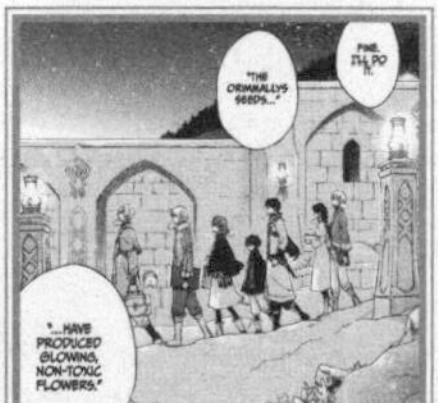
FINE. I'LL DO IT.
"THE ORIMMALLYS SEEDS..."
"...HAVE PRODUCED GLOWING, NON-TOXIC FLOWERS."

Meanwhile, Izana has dispatched Zen and his crew to the Sereg Knight Base, where twins from the powerful northern House Bergat have enlisted. Soon after their arrival, word spreads that Kiki's potential suitors are being attacked one after the other, and apparently Mistuhide is the prime suspect?!

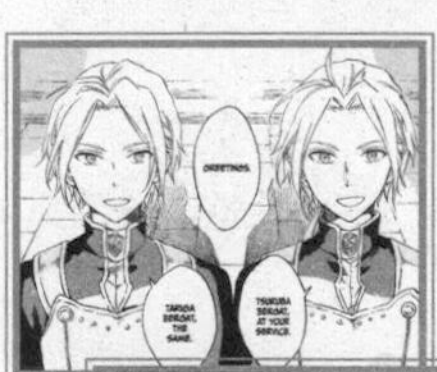
GREETINGS.
AT YOUR SERVICE.
THE SAME.

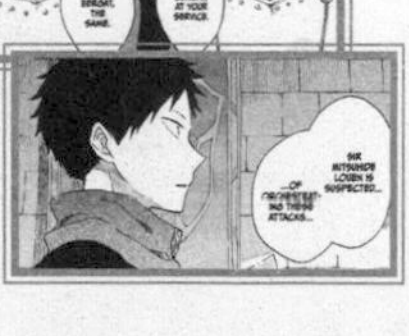
SIR MITSUHIDE LOUEN IS SUSPECTED...
...OF ORCHESTRATING THESE ATTACKS...

VOLUME 17
TABLE of CONTENTS

Chapter 78 ·· 5

Chapter 79 ·· 35

Chapter 80 ·· 67

Chapter 81 ·· 97

Chapter 82 ··· 127

Chapter 83 ··· 159

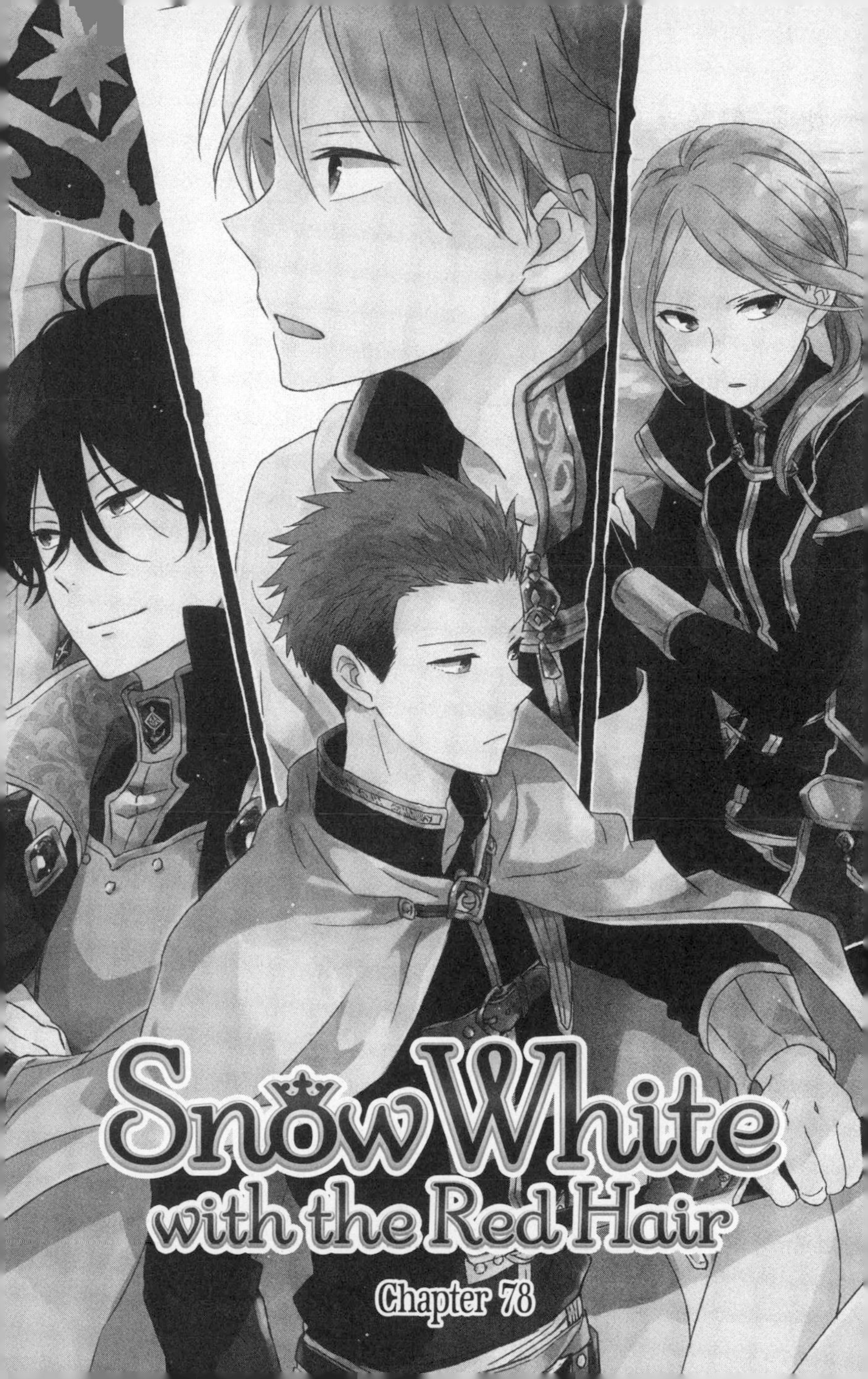
Snow White
with the Red Hair
Chapter 78

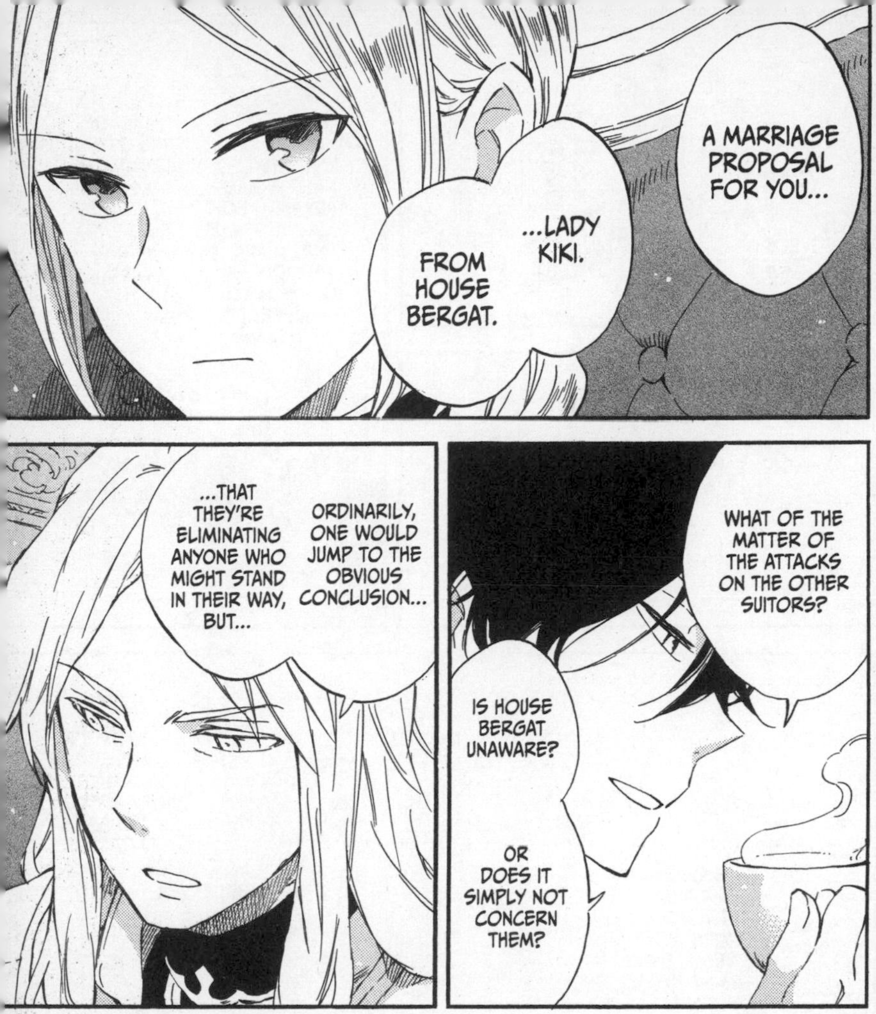
A MARRIAGE PROPOSAL FOR YOU...
...LADY KIKI.
FROM HOUSE BERGAT.
WHAT OF THE MATTER OF THE ATTACKS ON THE OTHER SUITORS?
IS HOUSE BERGAT UNAWARE?
OR DOES IT SIMPLY NOT CONCERN THEM?
ORDINARILY, ONE WOULD JUMP TO THE OBVIOUS CONCLUSION...
...THAT THEY'RE ELIMINATING ANYONE WHO MIGHT STAND IN THEIR WAY, BUT...

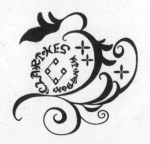

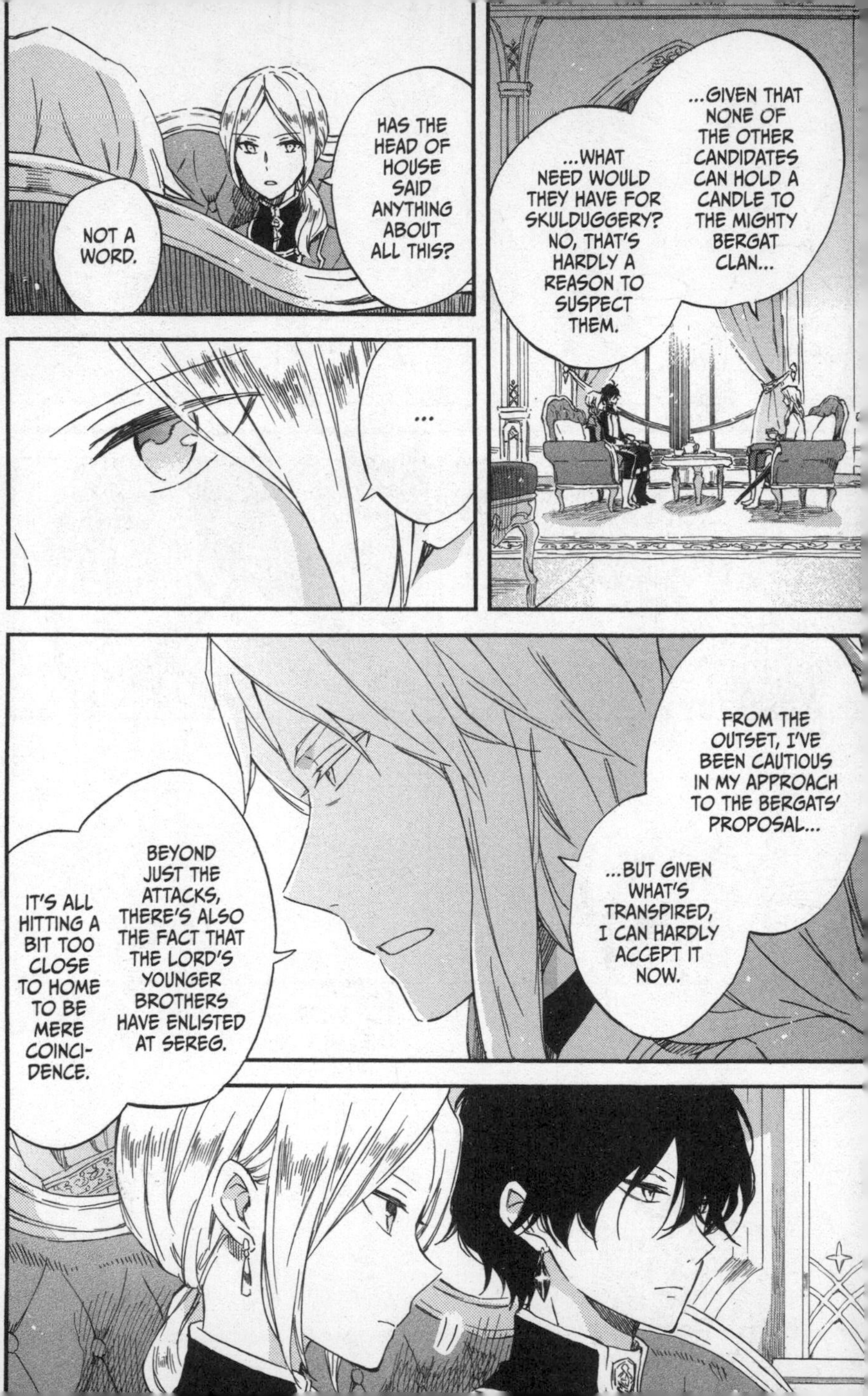
...GIVEN THAT NONE OF THE OTHER CANDIDATES CAN HOLD A CANDLE TO THE MIGHTY BERGAT CLAN...
...WHAT NEED WOULD THEY HAVE FOR SKULDUGGERY? NO, THAT'S HARDLY A REASON TO SUSPECT THEM.
HAS THE HEAD OF HOUSE SAID ANYTHING ABOUT ALL THIS?
NOT A WORD.
...
FROM THE OUTSET, I'VE BEEN CAUTIOUS IN MY APPROACH TO THE BERGATS' PROPOSAL...
...BUT GIVEN WHAT'S TRANSPIRED, I CAN HARDLY ACCEPT IT NOW.
BEYOND JUST THE ATTACKS, THERE'S ALSO THE FACT THAT THE LORD'S YOUNGER BROTHERS HAVE ENLISTED AT SEREG.
IT'S ALL HITTING A BIT TOO CLOSE TO HOME TO BE MERE COINCI-DENCE.

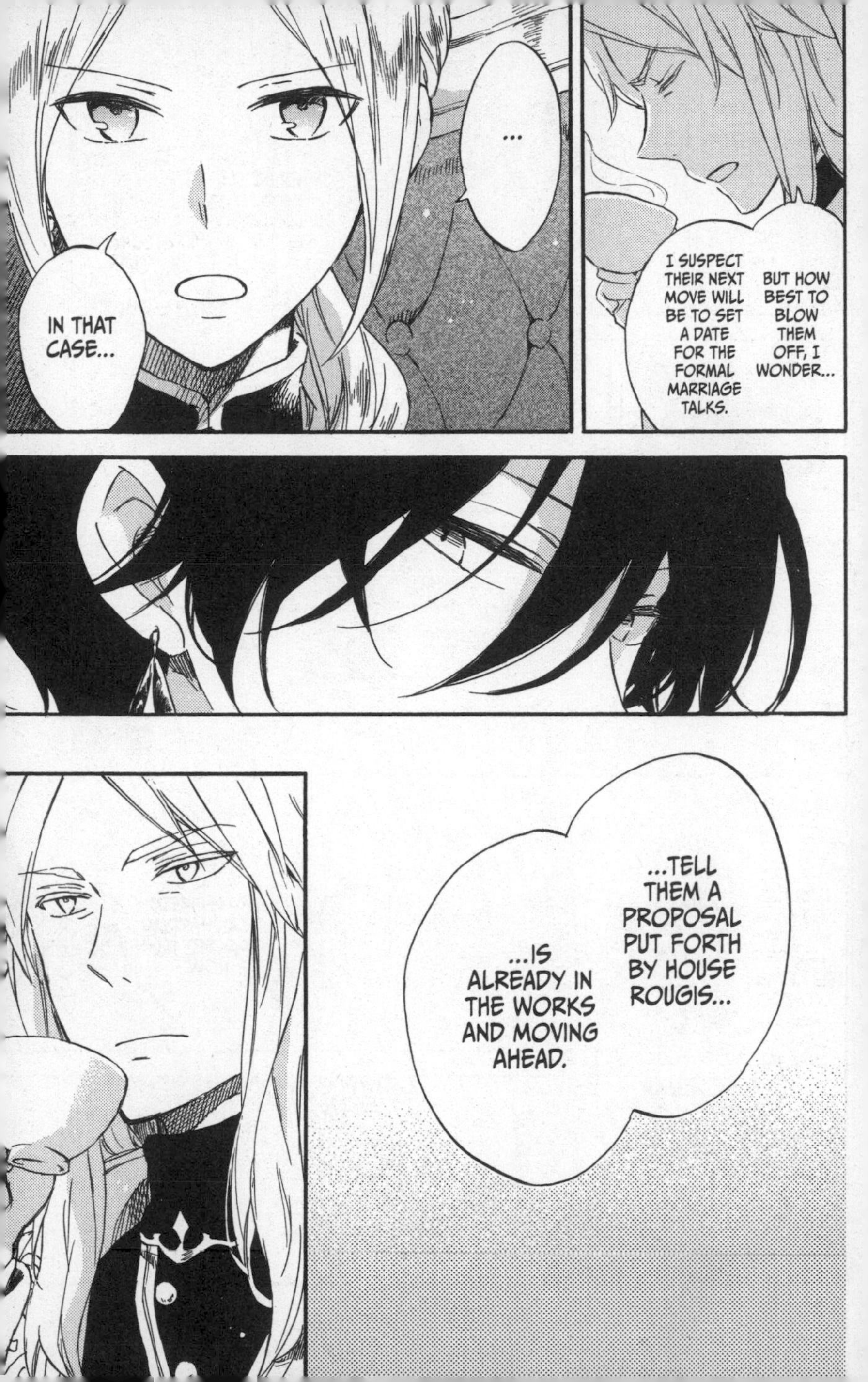

I SUSPECT THEIR NEXT MOVE WILL BE TO SET A DATE FOR THE FORMAL MARRIAGE TALKS.
BUT HOW BEST TO BLOW THEM OFF, I WONDER...
...
IN THAT CASE...
...TELL THEM A PROPOSAL PUT FORTH BY HOUSE ROUGIS...
...IS ALREADY IN THE WORKS AND MOVING AHEAD.

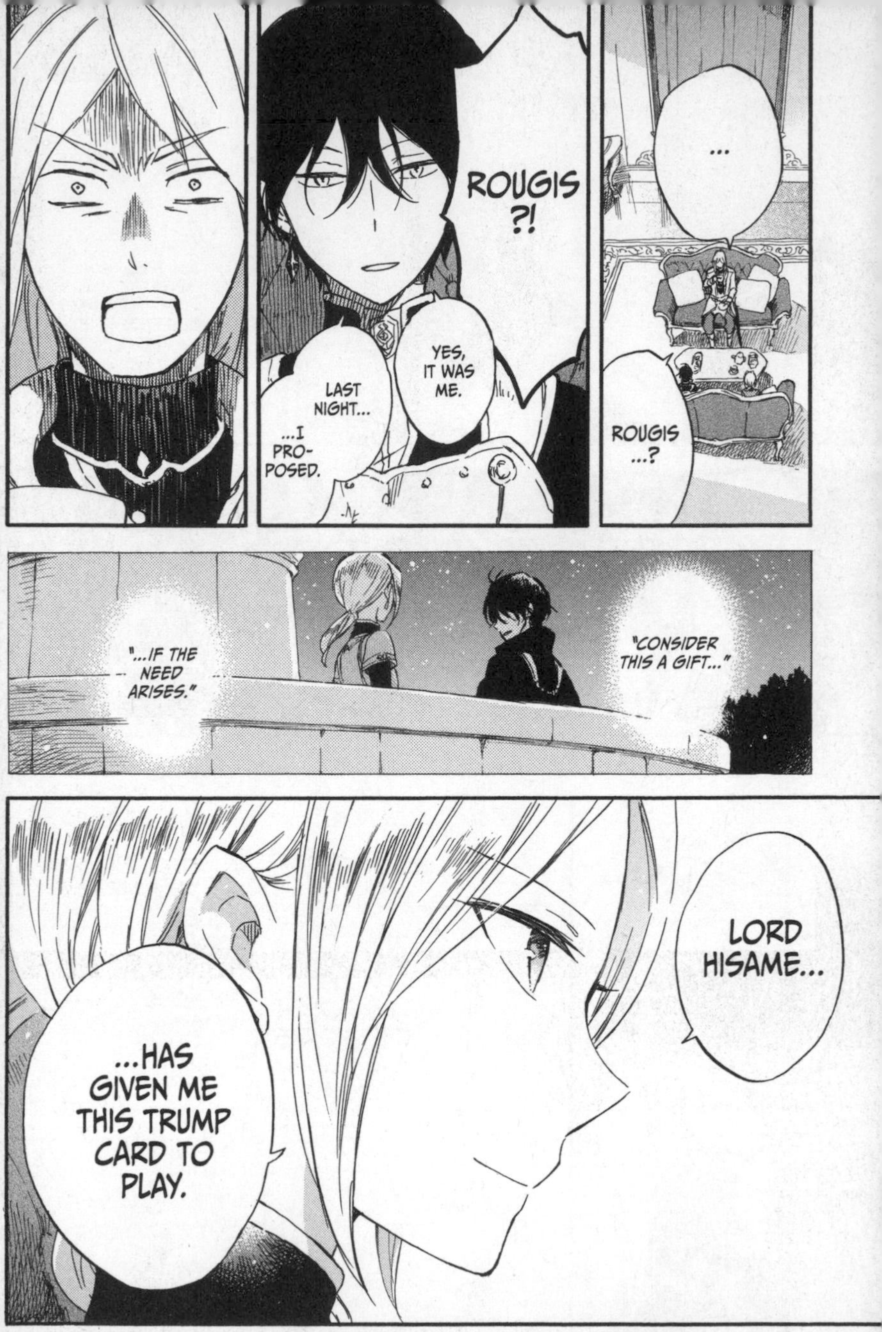
...
ROUGIS ...?
ROUGIS ?!
YES, IT WAS ME.
LAST NIGHT... ...I PROPOSED.
"CONSIDER THIS A GIFT..."
"...IF THE NEED ARISES."
LORD HISAME...
...HAS GIVEN ME THIS TRUMP CARD TO PLAY.

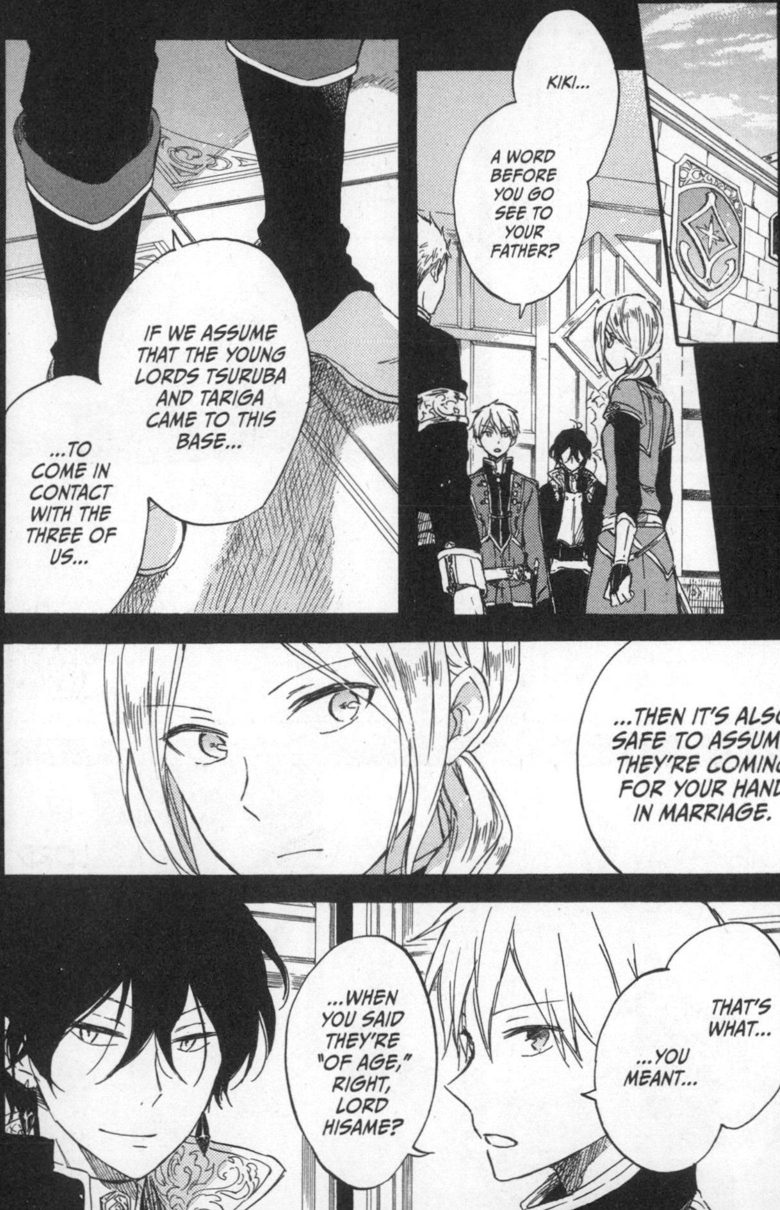
KIKI...
A WORD BEFORE YOU GO SEE TO YOUR FATHER?
IF WE ASSUME THAT THE YOUNG LORDS TSURUBA AND TARIGA CAME TO THIS BASE...
...TO COME IN CONTACT WITH THE THREE OF US...
...THEN IT'S ALSO SAFE TO ASSUME THEY'RE COMING FOR YOUR HAND IN MARRIAGE.
THAT'S WHAT...
...YOU MEANT...
...WHEN YOU SAID THEY'RE "OF AGE," RIGHT, LORD HISAME?

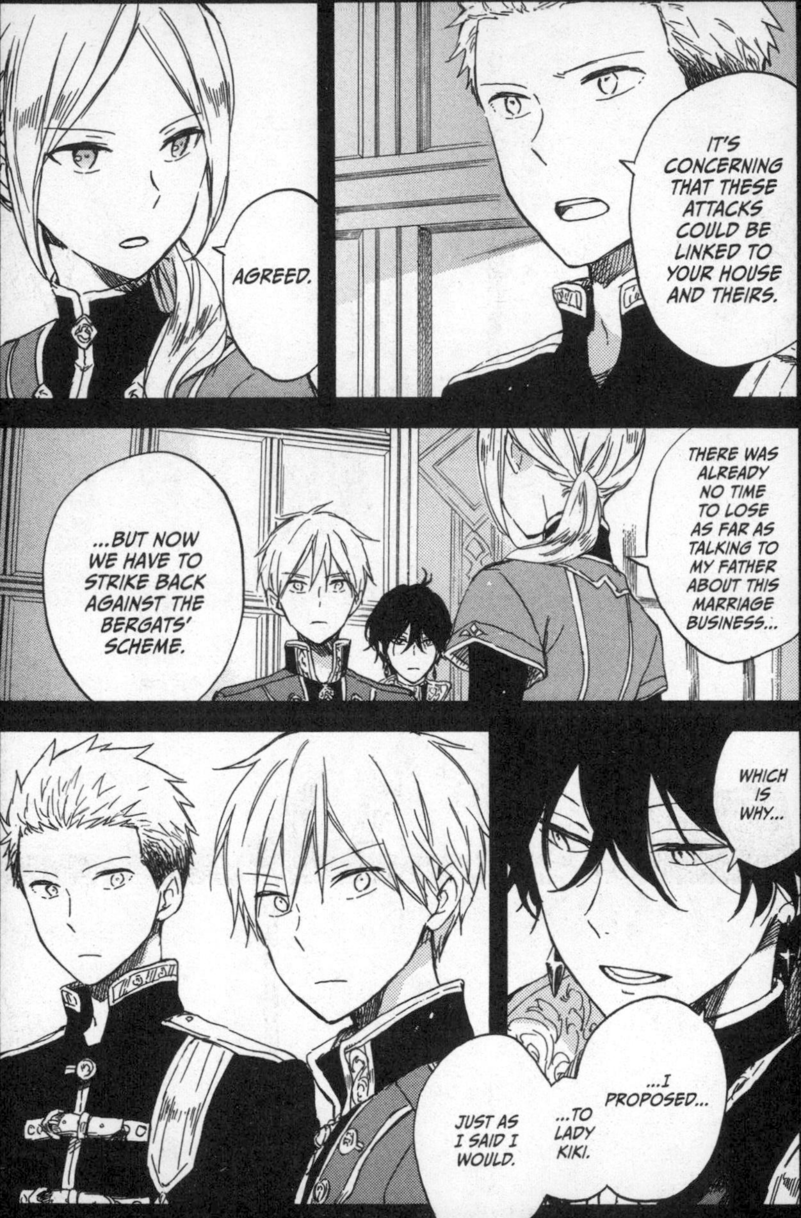
IT'S CONCERNING THAT THESE ATTACKS COULD BE LINKED TO YOUR HOUSE AND THEIRS.
AGREED.
THERE WAS ALREADY NO TIME TO LOSE AS FAR AS TALKING TO MY FATHER ABOUT THIS MARRIAGE BUSINESS...
...BUT NOW WE HAVE TO STRIKE BACK AGAINST THE BERGATS' SCHEME.
WHICH IS WHY...
...I PROPOSED...
...TO LADY KIKI.
JUST AS I SAID I WOULD.

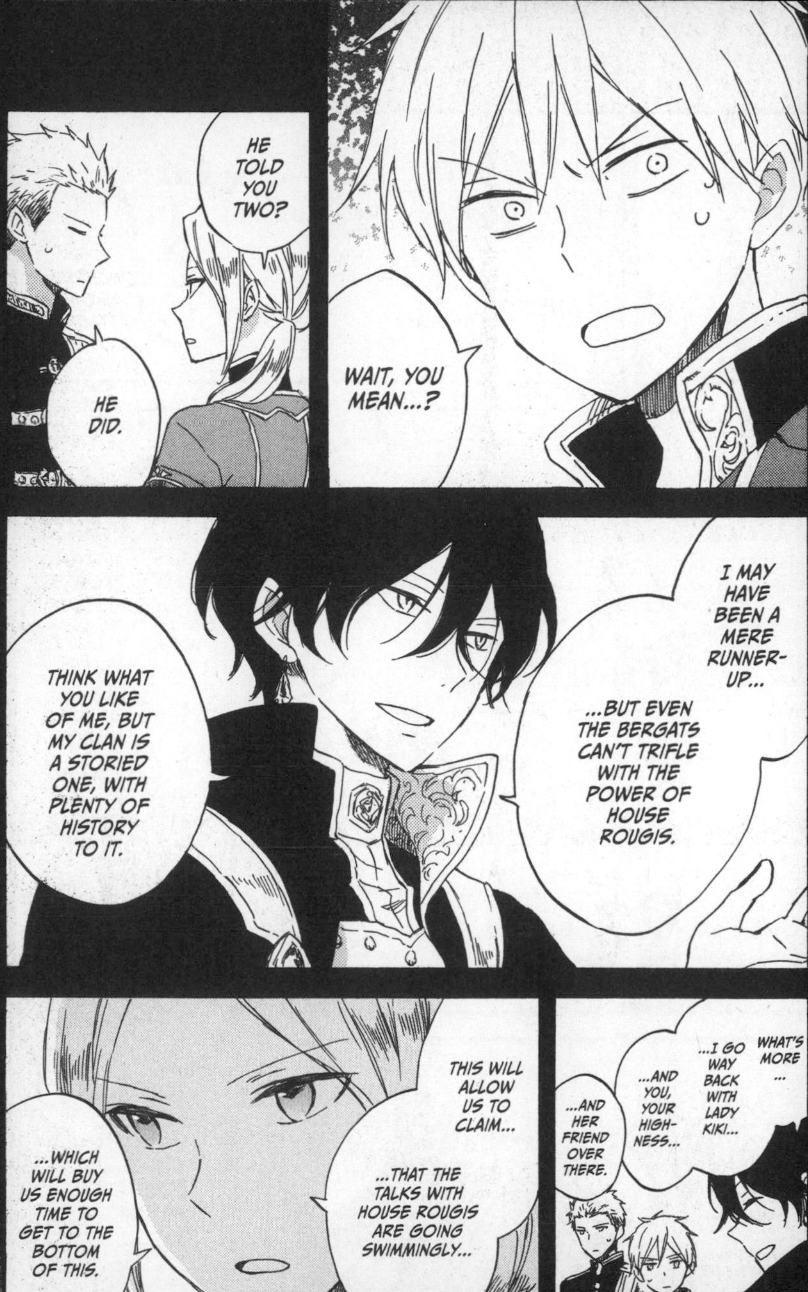
WAIT, YOU MEAN...?
HE TOLD YOU TWO?
HE DID.
I MAY HAVE BEEN A MERE RUNNER-UP...
...BUT EVEN THE BERGATS CAN'T TRIFLE WITH THE POWER OF HOUSE ROUGIS.
THINK WHAT YOU LIKE OF ME, BUT MY CLAN IS A STORIED ONE, WITH PLENTY OF HISTORY TO IT.
WHAT'S MORE...
...I GO WAY BACK WITH LADY KIKI...
...AND YOU, YOUR HIGHNESS...
...AND HER FRIEND OVER THERE.
THIS WILL ALLOW US TO CLAIM...
...THAT THE TALKS WITH HOUSE ROUGIS ARE GOING SWIMMINGLY...
...WHICH WILL BUY US ENOUGH TIME TO GET TO THE BOTTOM OF THIS.

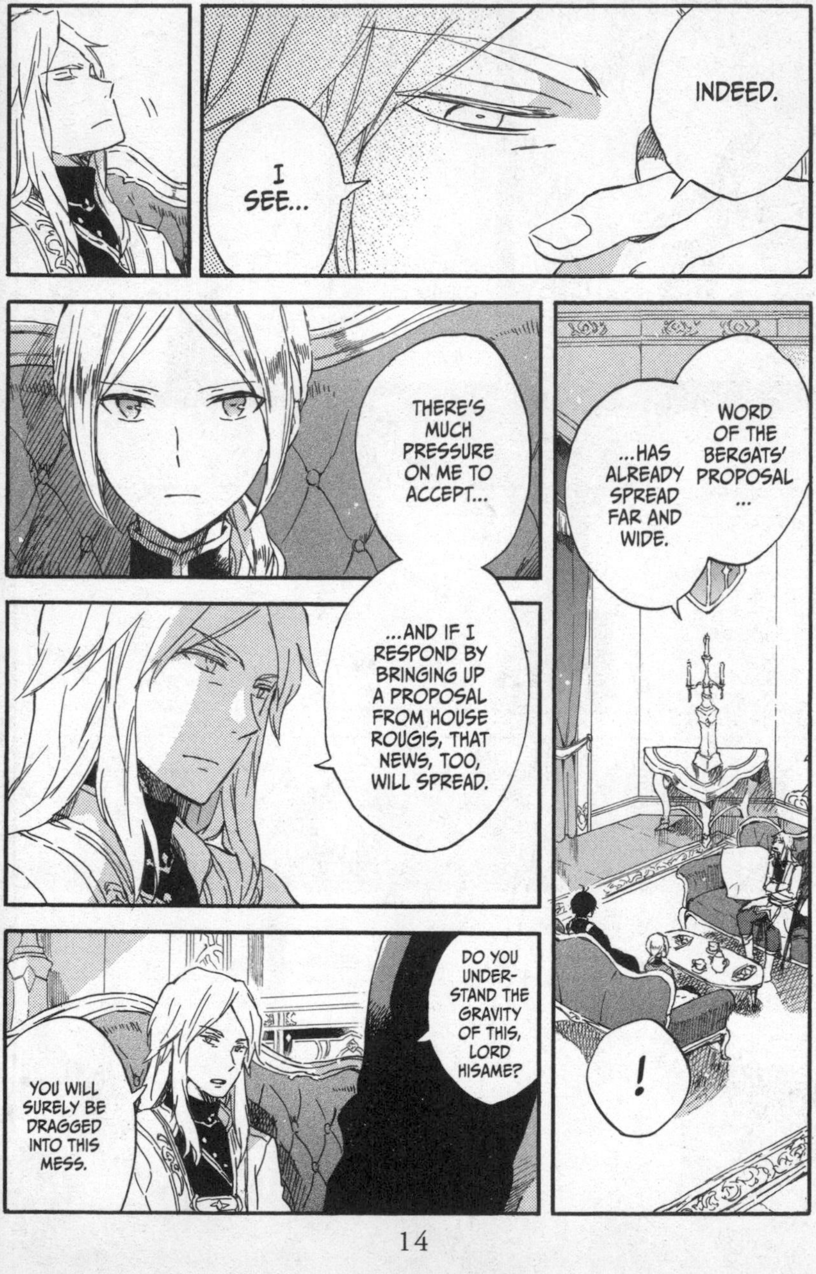
INDEED.
I SEE...
WORD OF THE BERGATS' PROPOSAL ...
...HAS ALREADY SPREAD FAR AND WIDE.
!
THERE'S MUCH PRESSURE ON ME TO ACCEPT...
...AND IF I RESPOND BY BRINGING UP A PROPOSAL FROM HOUSE ROUGIS, THAT NEWS, TOO, WILL SPREAD.
DO YOU UNDERSTAND THE GRAVITY OF THIS, LORD HISAME?
YOU WILL SURELY BE DRAGGED INTO THIS MESS.

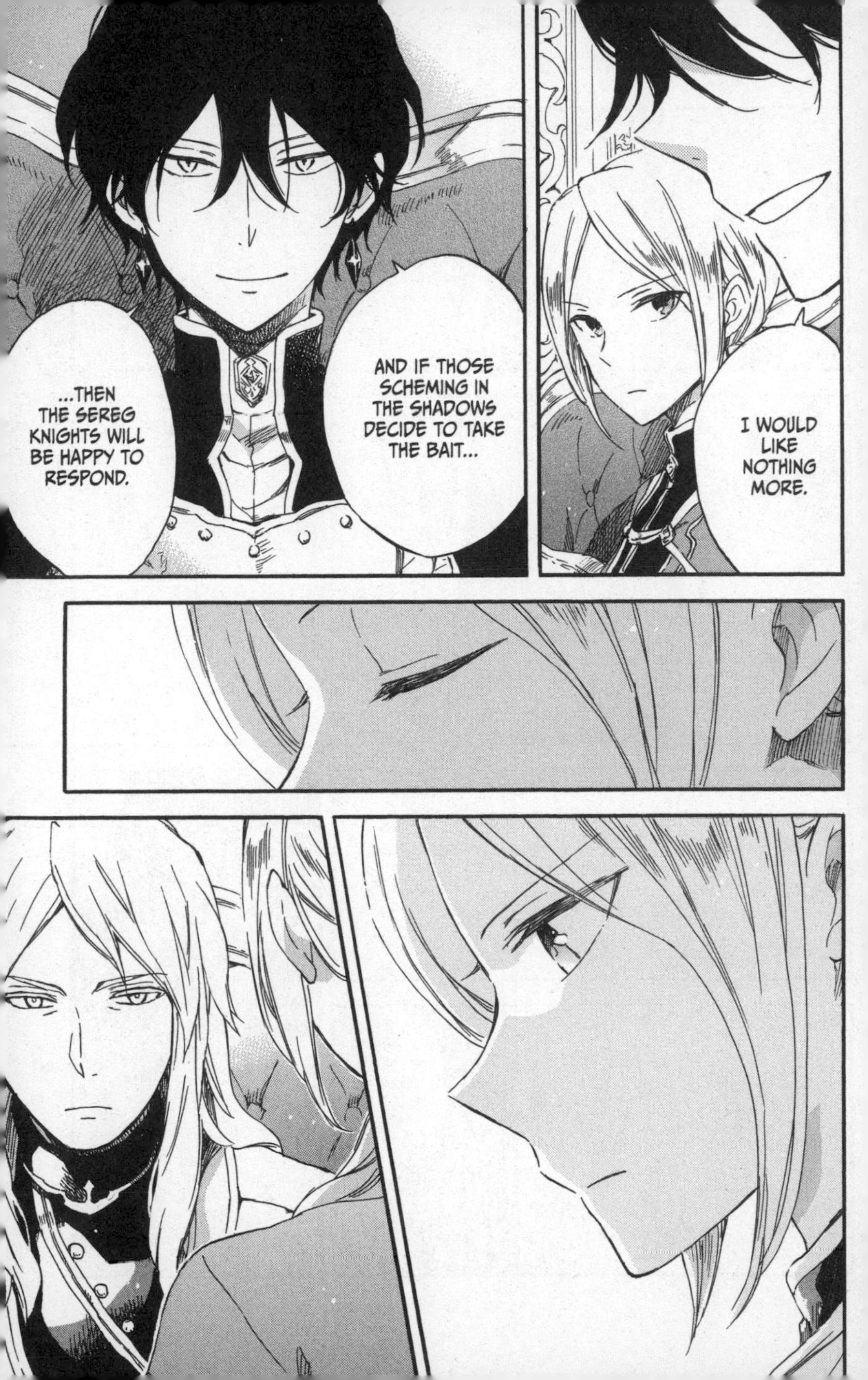
I WOULD LIKE NOTHING MORE.
AND IF THOSE SCHEMING IN THE SHADOWS DECIDE TO TAKE THE BAIT...
...THEN THE SEREG KNIGHTS WILL BE HAPPY TO RESPOND.

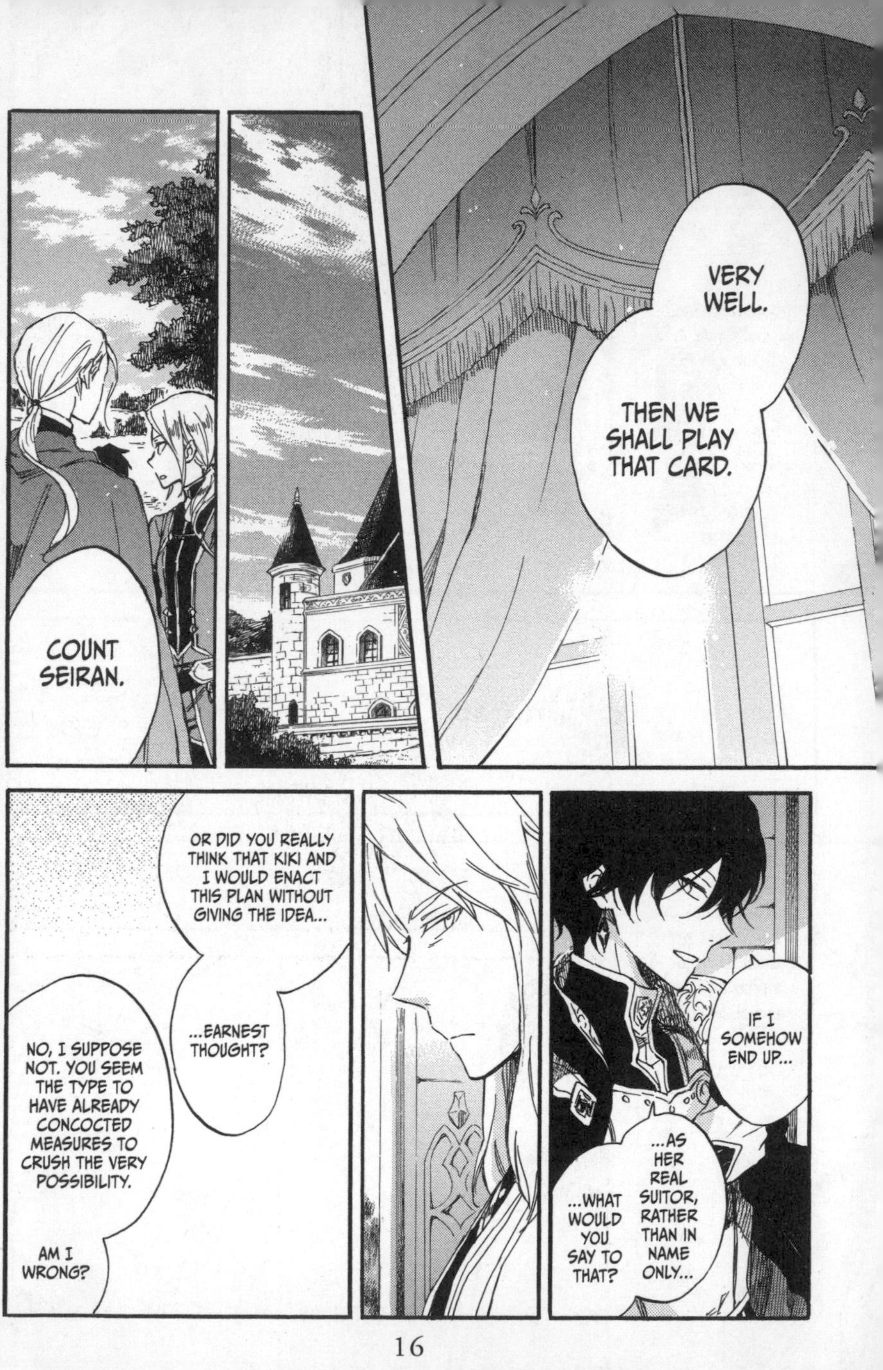
VERY WELL.
THEN WE SHALL PLAY THAT CARD.
COUNT SEIRAN.
IF I SOMEHOW END UP...
...AS HER REAL SUITOR, RATHER THAN IN NAME ONLY...
...WHAT WOULD YOU SAY TO THAT?
OR DID YOU REALLY THINK THAT KIKI AND I WOULD ENACT THIS PLAN WITHOUT GIVING THE IDEA...
...EARNEST THOUGHT?
NO, I SUPPOSE NOT. YOU SEEM THE TYPE TO HAVE ALREADY CONCOCTED MEASURES TO CRUSH THE VERY POSSIBILITY.
AM I WRONG?

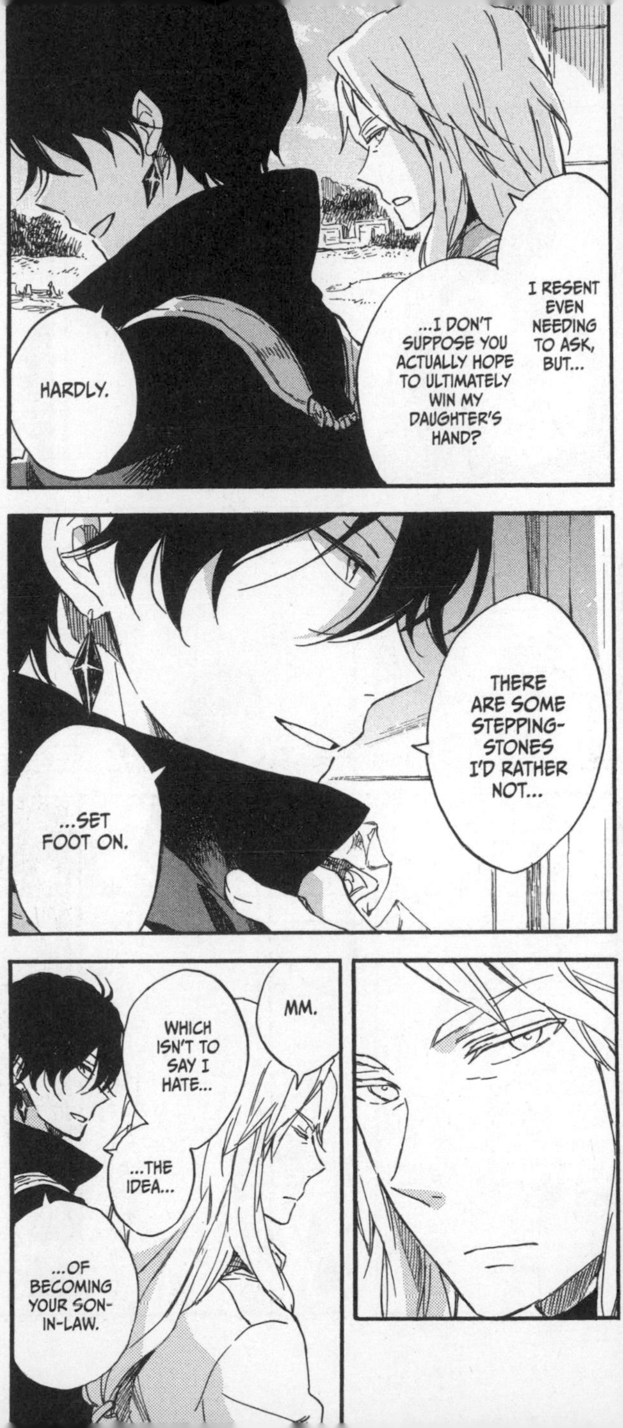
I RESENT EVEN NEEDING TO ASK, BUT...
...I DON'T SUPPOSE YOU ACTUALLY HOPE TO ULTIMATELY WIN MY DAUGHTER'S HAND?
HARDLY.
THERE ARE SOME STEPPING-STONES I'D RATHER NOT...
...SET FOOT ON.
MM.
WHICH ISN'T TO SAY I HATE...
...THE IDEA...
...OF BECOMING YOUR SON-IN-LAW.

1

GREETINGS

Hello, everyone. It's me, Sorata Akiduki. Thank you for picking up volume 17 of Snow White with the Red Hair.

It seems 2017 is in full swing, huh? And can you believe it? My first book release of the year just so happens to be volume 17! 2017! Volume 17! It makes it so much easier to remember this occasion!

Perfect!

Please tell everyone you know.

Anyhow, I hope our five heroes get to sit down for a relaxing meal sooner or later.

Let's dive into volume 17.

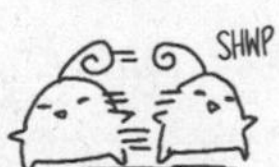
SHWP
SHWP

Hidden Art: Twinsies

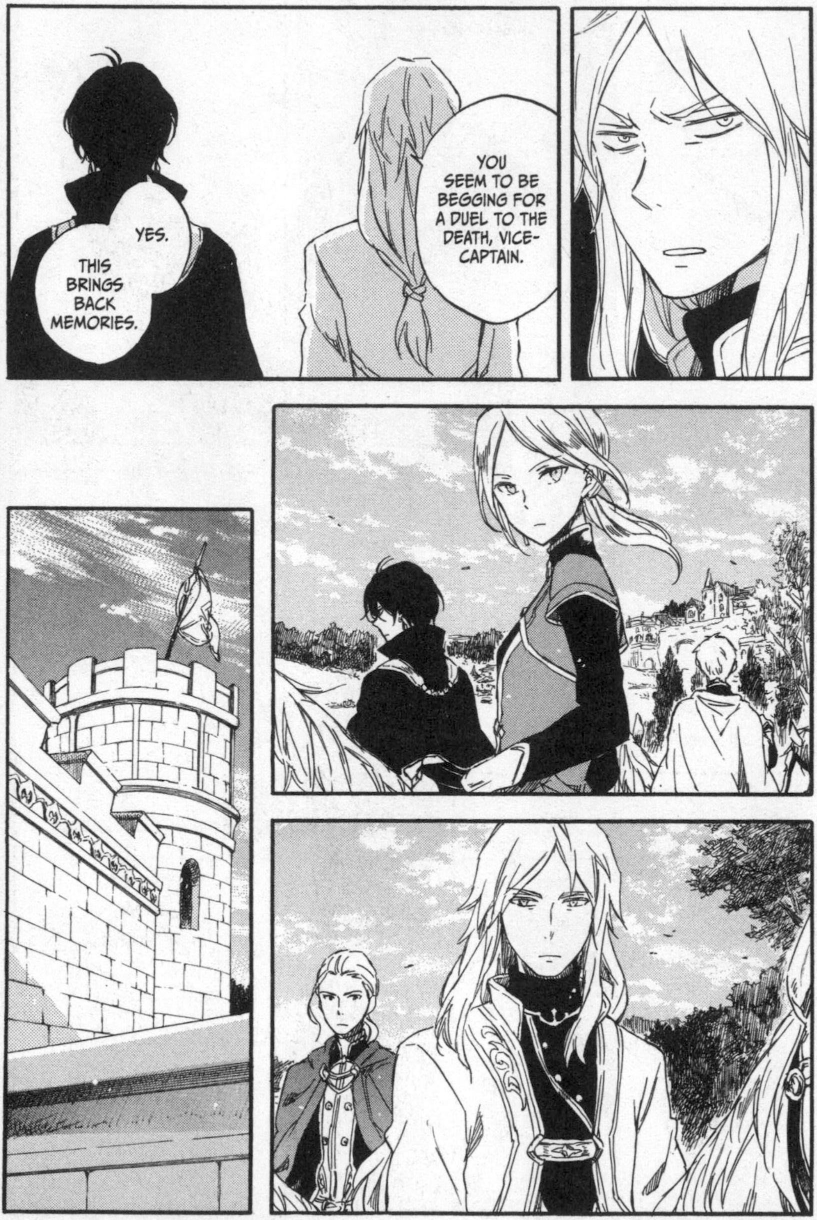
YOU SEEM TO BE BEGGING FOR A DUEL TO THE DEATH, VICE-CAPTAIN.
YES.
THIS BRINGS BACK MEMORIES.

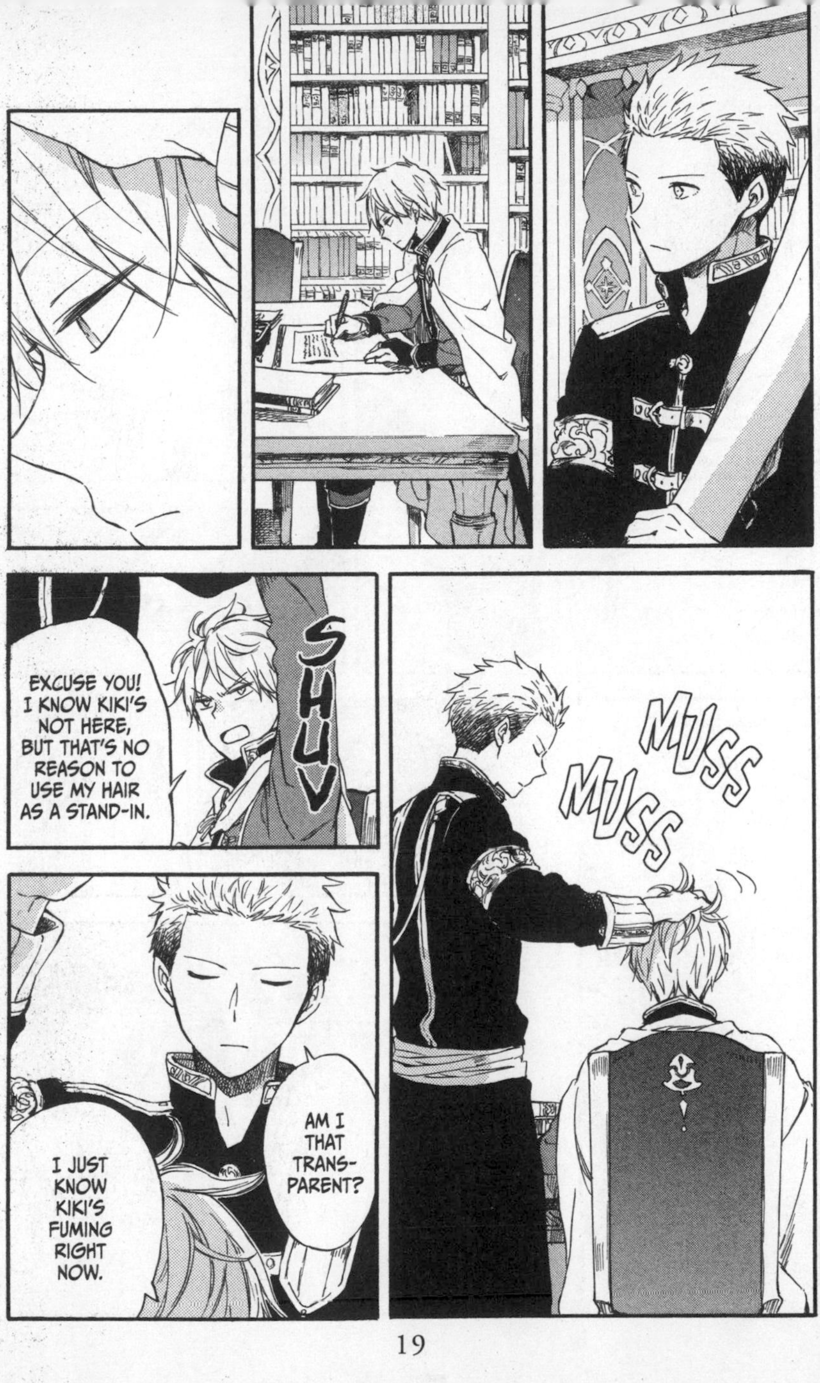
MUSS
MUSS
SHUV
EXCUSE YOU! I KNOW KIKI'S NOT HERE, BUT THAT'S NO REASON TO USE MY HAIR AS A STAND-IN.
AM I THAT TRANS-PARENT?
I JUST KNOW KIKI'S FUMING RIGHT NOW.

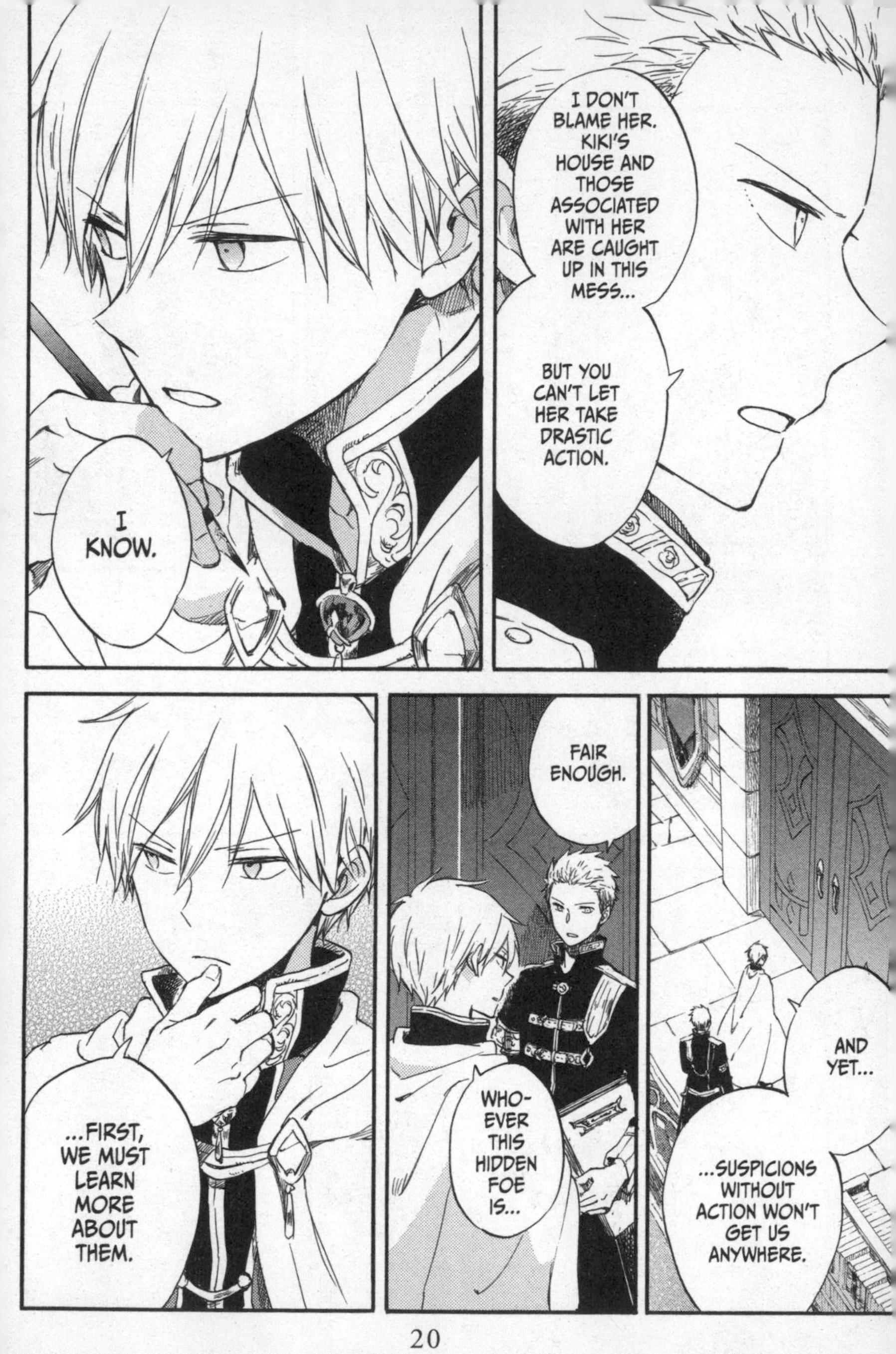
I DON'T BLAME HER. KIKI'S HOUSE AND THOSE ASSOCIATED WITH HER ARE CAUGHT UP IN THIS MESS...
BUT YOU CAN'T LET HER TAKE DRASTIC ACTION.
I KNOW.
AND YET...
...SUSPICIONS WITHOUT ACTION WON'T GET US ANYWHERE.
FAIR ENOUGH.
WHO-EVER THIS HIDDEN FOE IS...
...FIRST, WE MUST LEARN MORE ABOUT THEM.

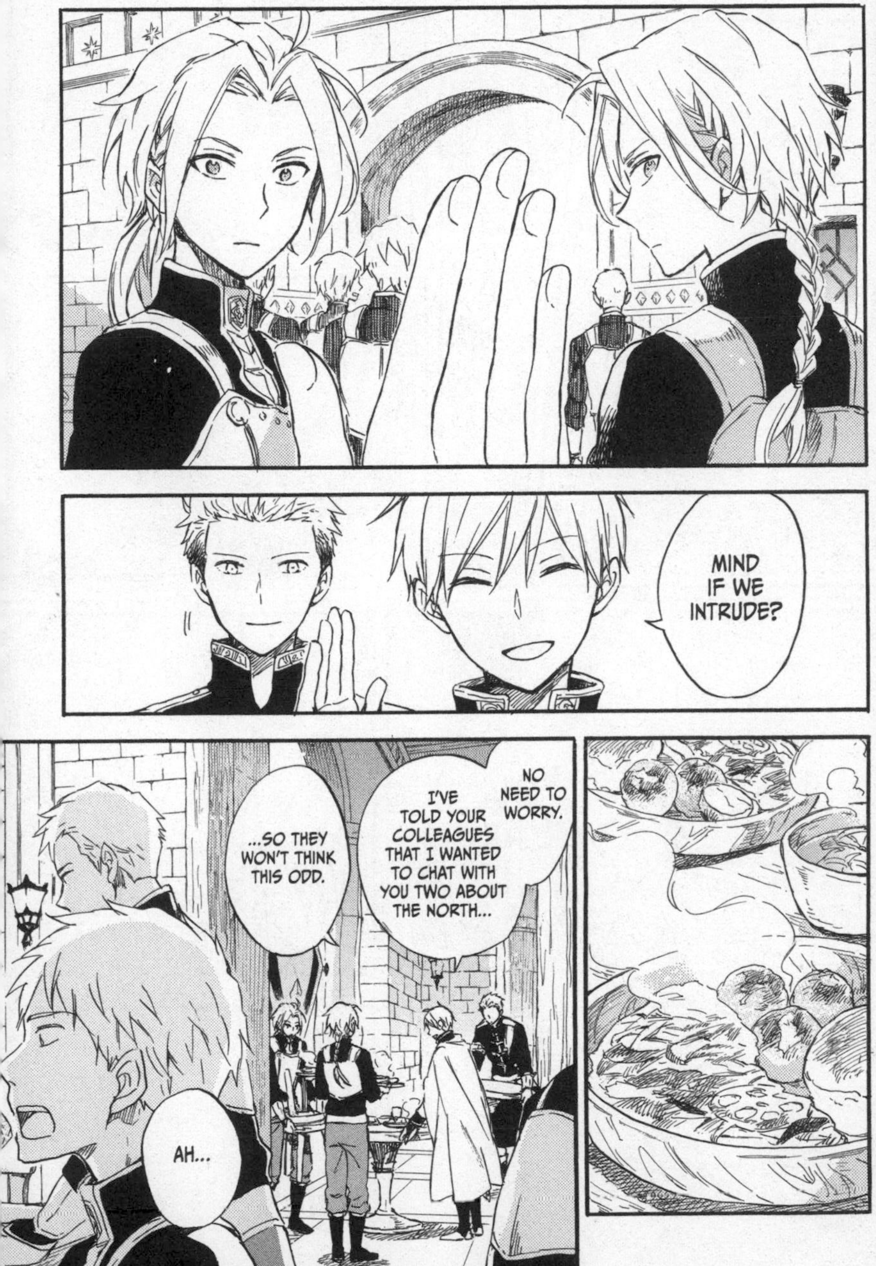
MIND IF WE INTRUDE?
NO NEED TO WORRY.
I'VE TOLD YOUR COLLEAGUES THAT I WANTED TO CHAT WITH YOU TWO ABOUT THE NORTH...
...SO THEY WON'T THINK THIS ODD.
AH...

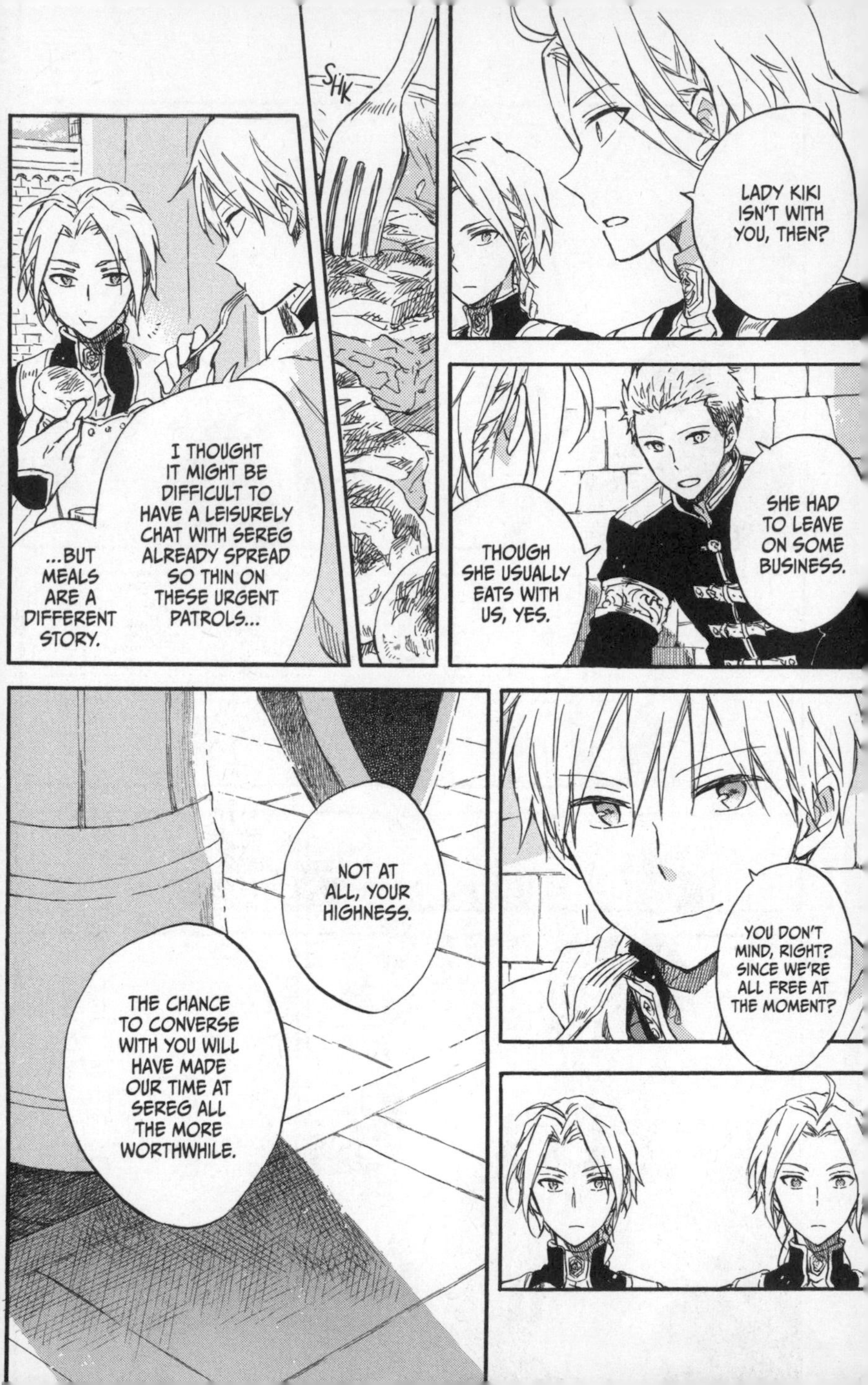
LADY KIKI ISN'T WITH YOU, THEN?
SHE HAD TO LEAVE ON SOME BUSINESS.
THOUGH SHE USUALLY EATS WITH US, YES.
SHK
I THOUGHT IT MIGHT BE DIFFICULT TO HAVE A LEISURELY CHAT WITH SEREG ALREADY SPREAD SO THIN ON THESE URGENT PATROLS...
...BUT MEALS ARE A DIFFERENT STORY.
YOU DON'T MIND, RIGHT? SINCE WE'RE ALL FREE AT THE MOMENT?
NOT AT ALL, YOUR HIGHNESS.
THE CHANCE TO CONVERSE WITH YOU WILL HAVE MADE OUR TIME AT SEREG ALL THE MORE WORTHWHILE.

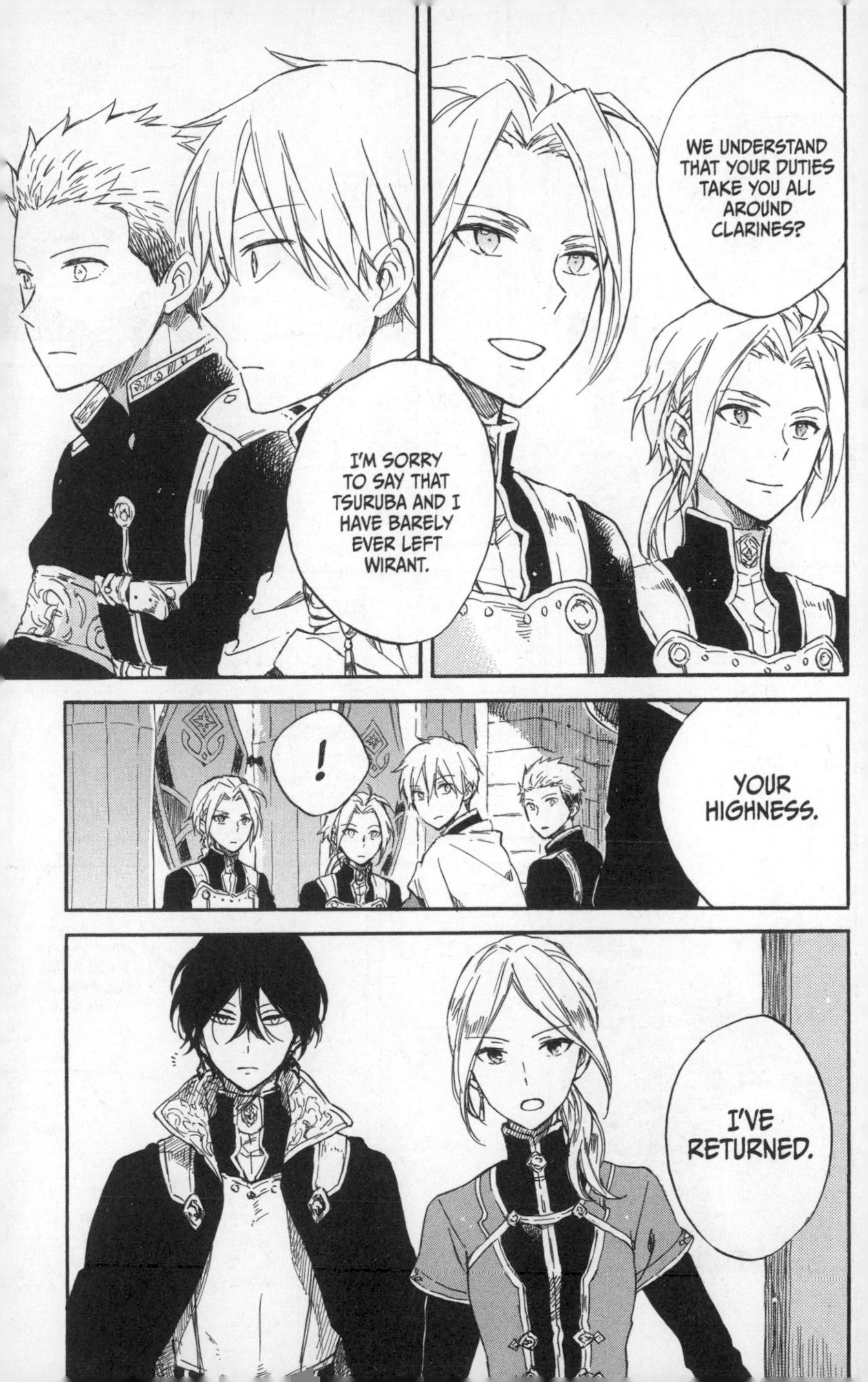
WE UNDERSTAND THAT YOUR DUTIES TAKE YOU ALL AROUND CLARINES?
I'M SORRY TO SAY THAT TSURUBA AND I HAVE BARELY EVER LEFT WIRANT.
YOUR HIGHNESS.
!
I'VE RETURNED.

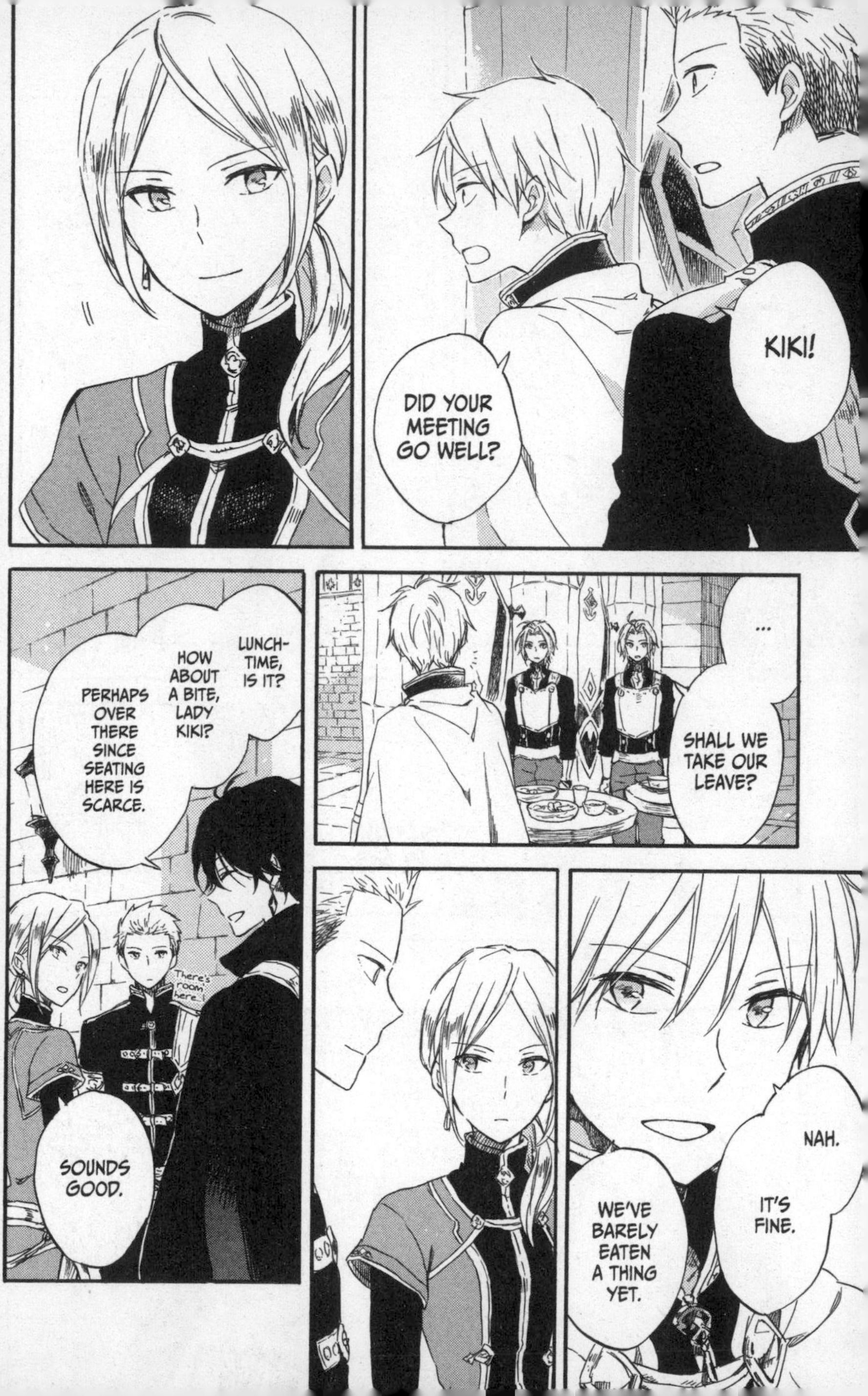
KIKI!
DID YOUR MEETING GO WELL?
...
SHALL WE TAKE OUR LEAVE?
NAH.
IT'S FINE.
WE'VE BARELY EATEN A THING YET.
LUNCH-TIME, IS IT?
HOW ABOUT A BITE, LADY KIKI?
PERHAPS OVER THERE SINCE SEATING HERE IS SCARCE.
There's room here...
SOUNDS GOOD.

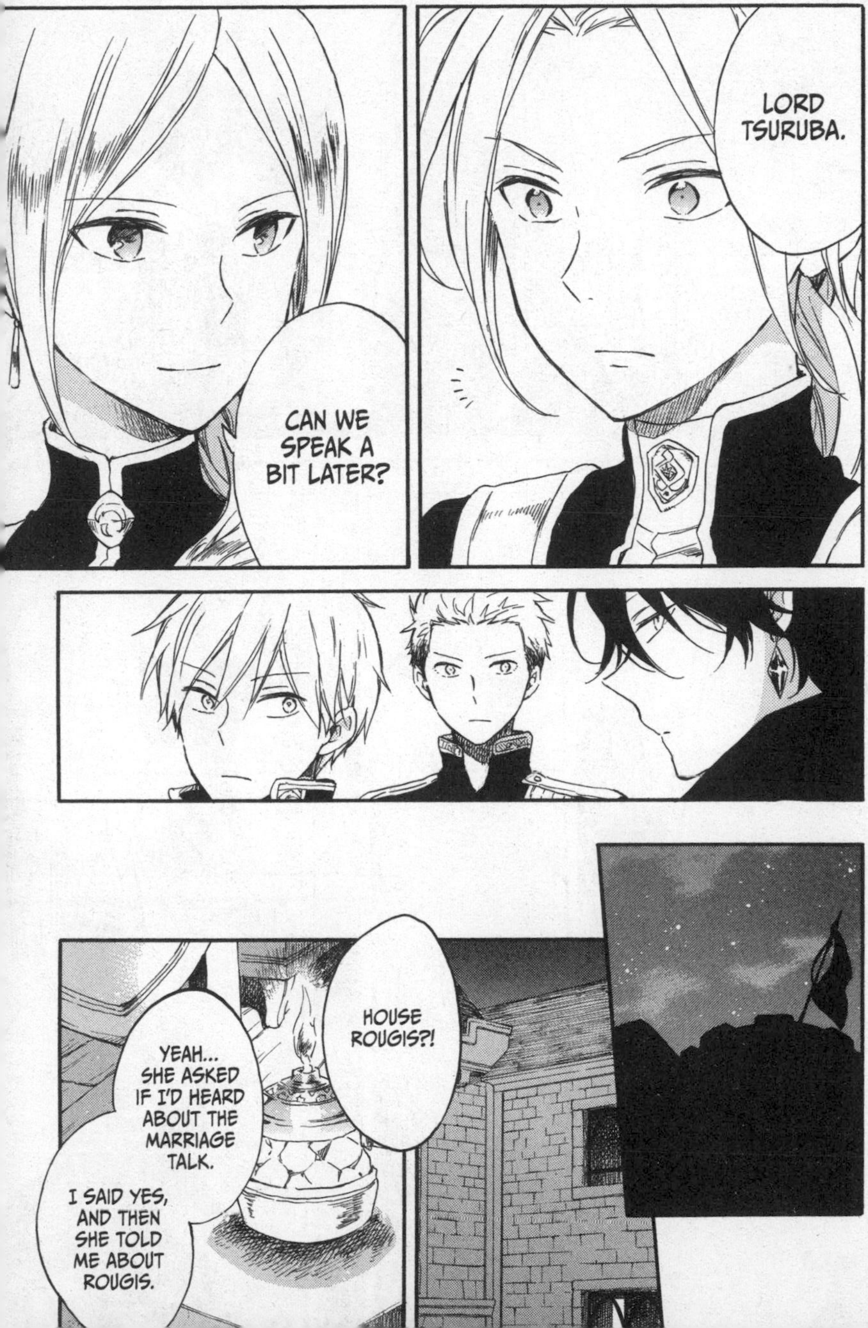
LORD TSURUBA.
CAN WE SPEAK A BIT LATER?
HOUSE ROUGIS?!
YEAH... SHE ASKED IF I'D HEARD ABOUT THE MARRIAGE TALK.
I SAID YES, AND THEN SHE TOLD ME ABOUT ROUGIS.

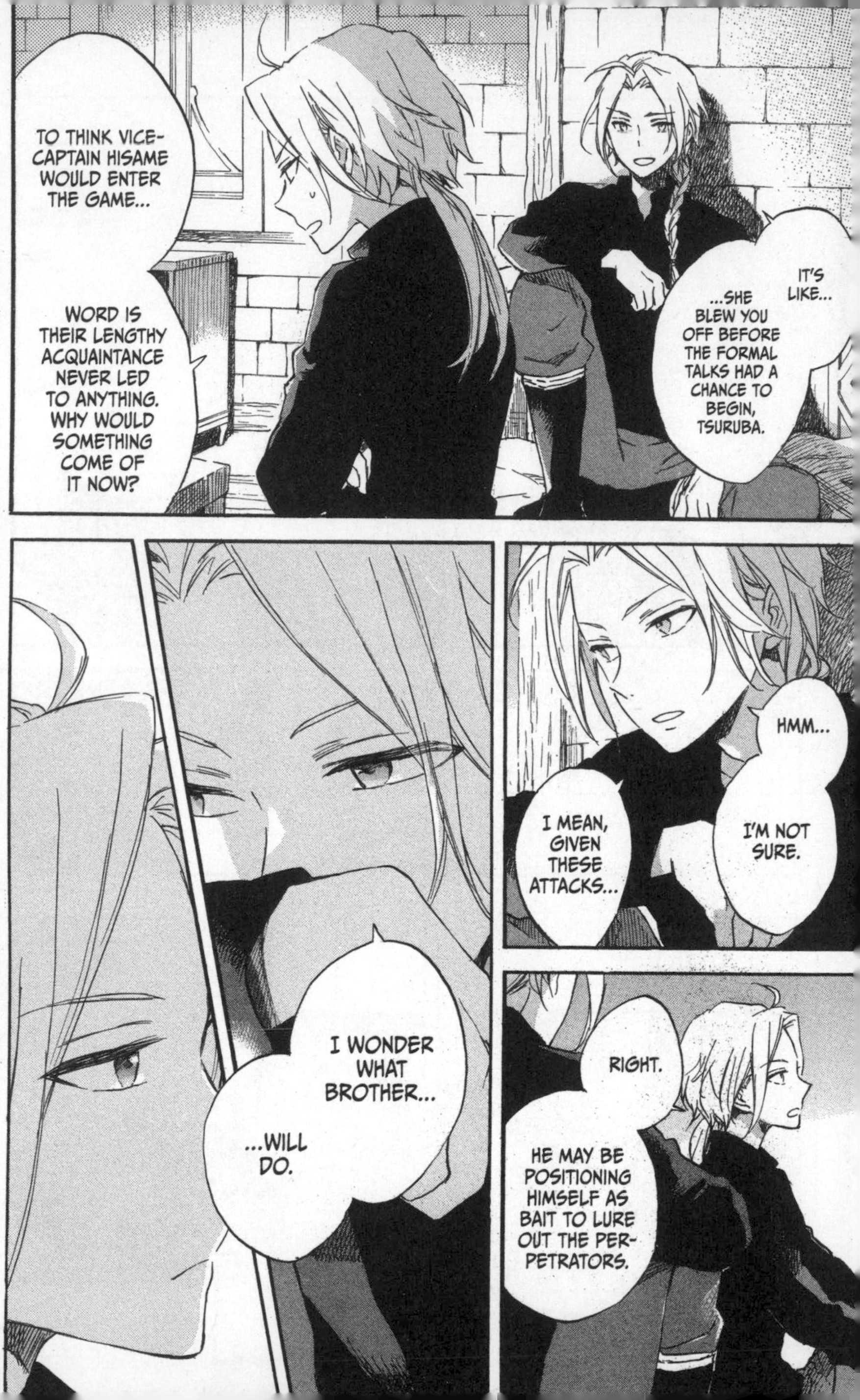
IT'S LIKE...
...SHE BLEW YOU OFF BEFORE THE FORMAL TALKS HAD A CHANCE TO BEGIN, TSURUBA.
TO THINK VICE-CAPTAIN HISAME WOULD ENTER THE GAME...
WORD IS THEIR LENGTHY ACQUAINTANCE NEVER LED TO ANYTHING. WHY WOULD SOMETHING COME OF IT NOW?
HMM...
I'M NOT SURE.
I MEAN, GIVEN THESE ATTACKS...
RIGHT.
HE MAY BE POSITIONING HIMSELF AS BAIT TO LURE OUT THE PER-PETRATORS.
I WONDER WHAT BROTHER...
...WILL DO.

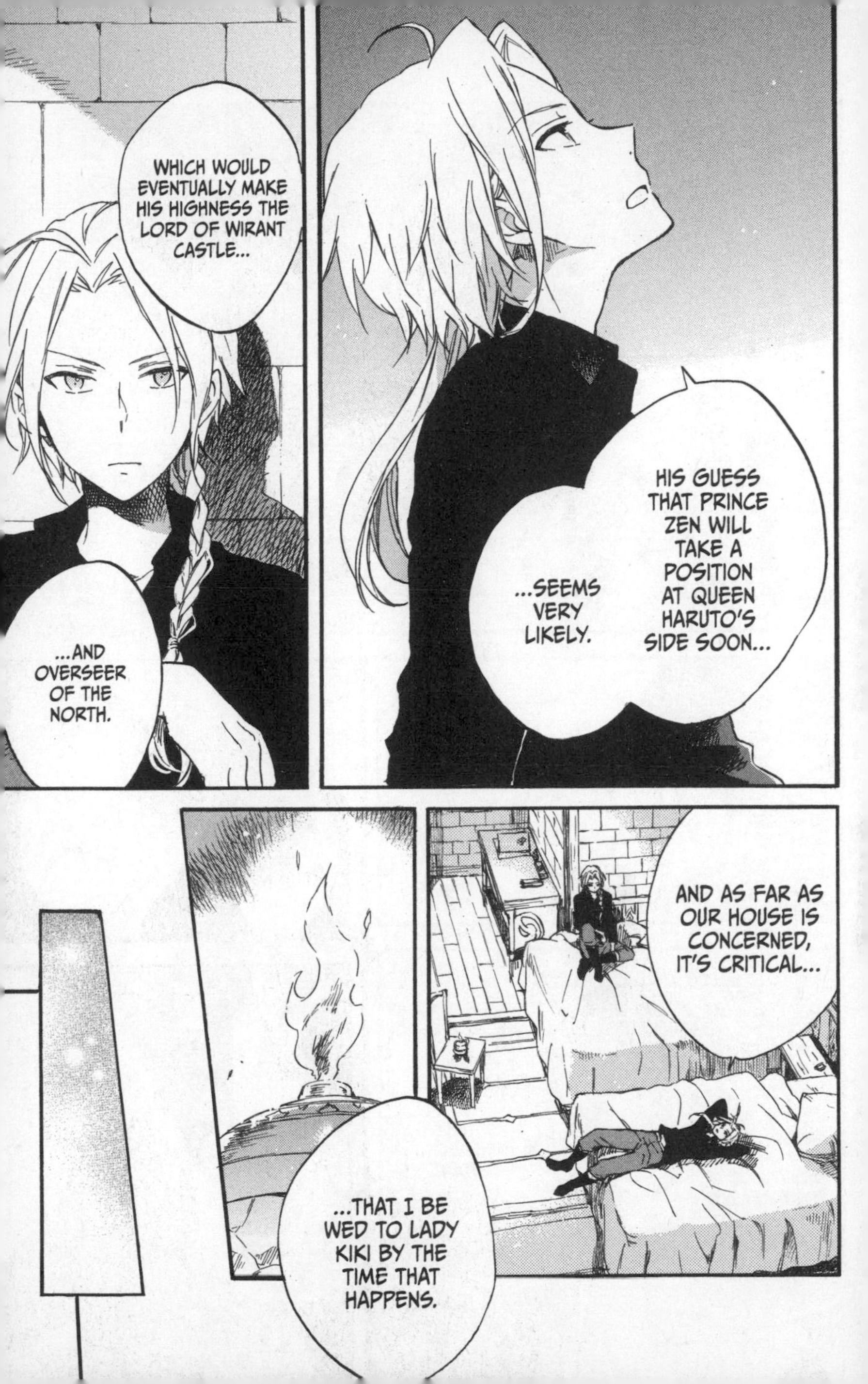
HIS GUESS THAT PRINCE ZEN WILL TAKE A POSITION AT QUEEN HARUTO'S SIDE SOON...
...SEEMS VERY LIKELY.
WHICH WOULD EVENTUALLY MAKE HIS HIGHNESS THE LORD OF WIRANT CASTLE...
...AND OVERSEER OF THE NORTH.
AND AS FAR AS OUR HOUSE IS CONCERNED, IT'S CRITICAL...
...THAT I BE WED TO LADY KIKI BY THE TIME THAT HAPPENS.

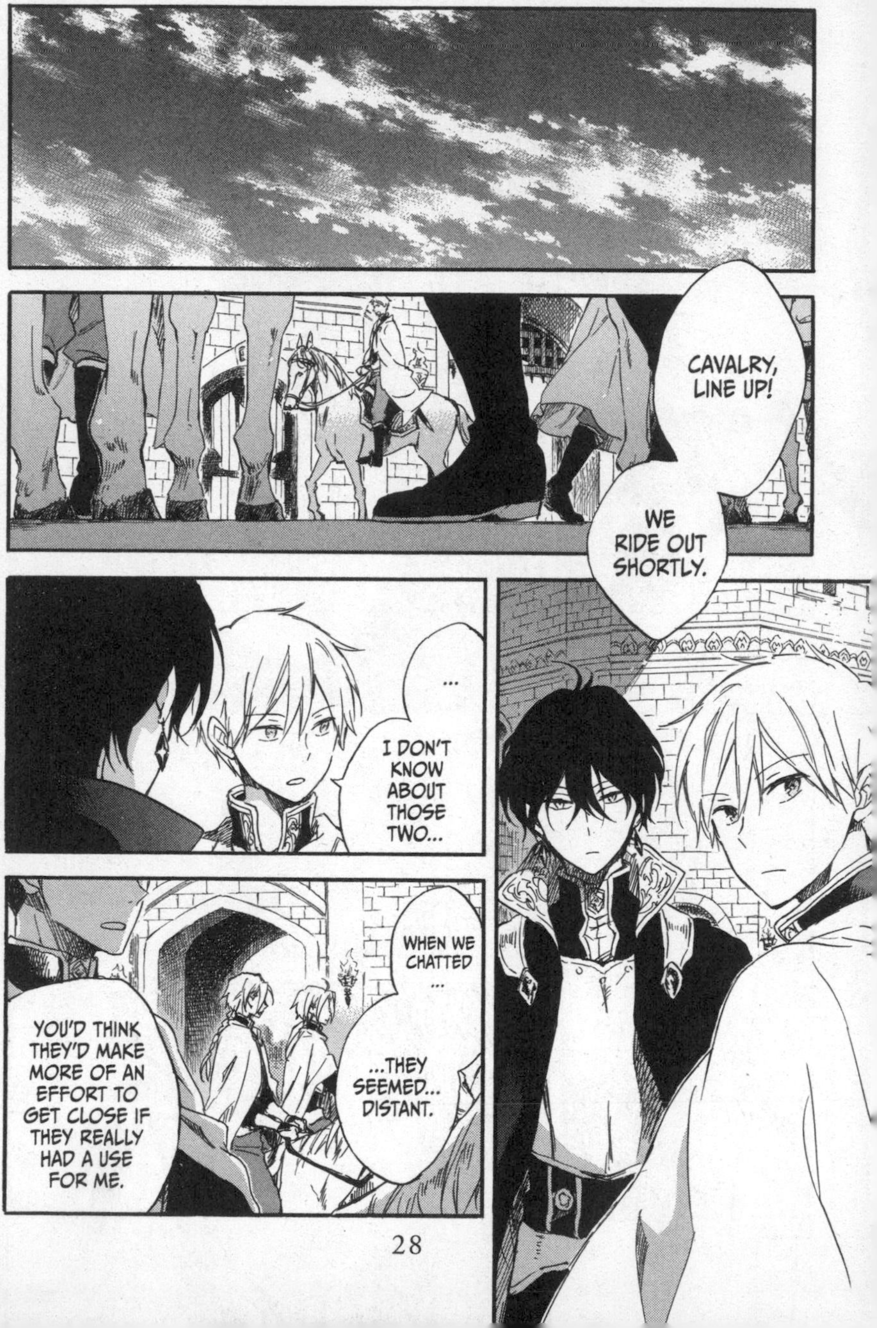
CAVALRY, LINE UP!
WE RIDE OUT SHORTLY.
...
I DON'T KNOW ABOUT THOSE TWO...
WHEN WE CHATTED...
...THEY SEEMED... DISTANT.
YOU'D THINK THEY'D MAKE MORE OF AN EFFORT TO GET CLOSE IF THEY REALLY HAD A USE FOR ME.

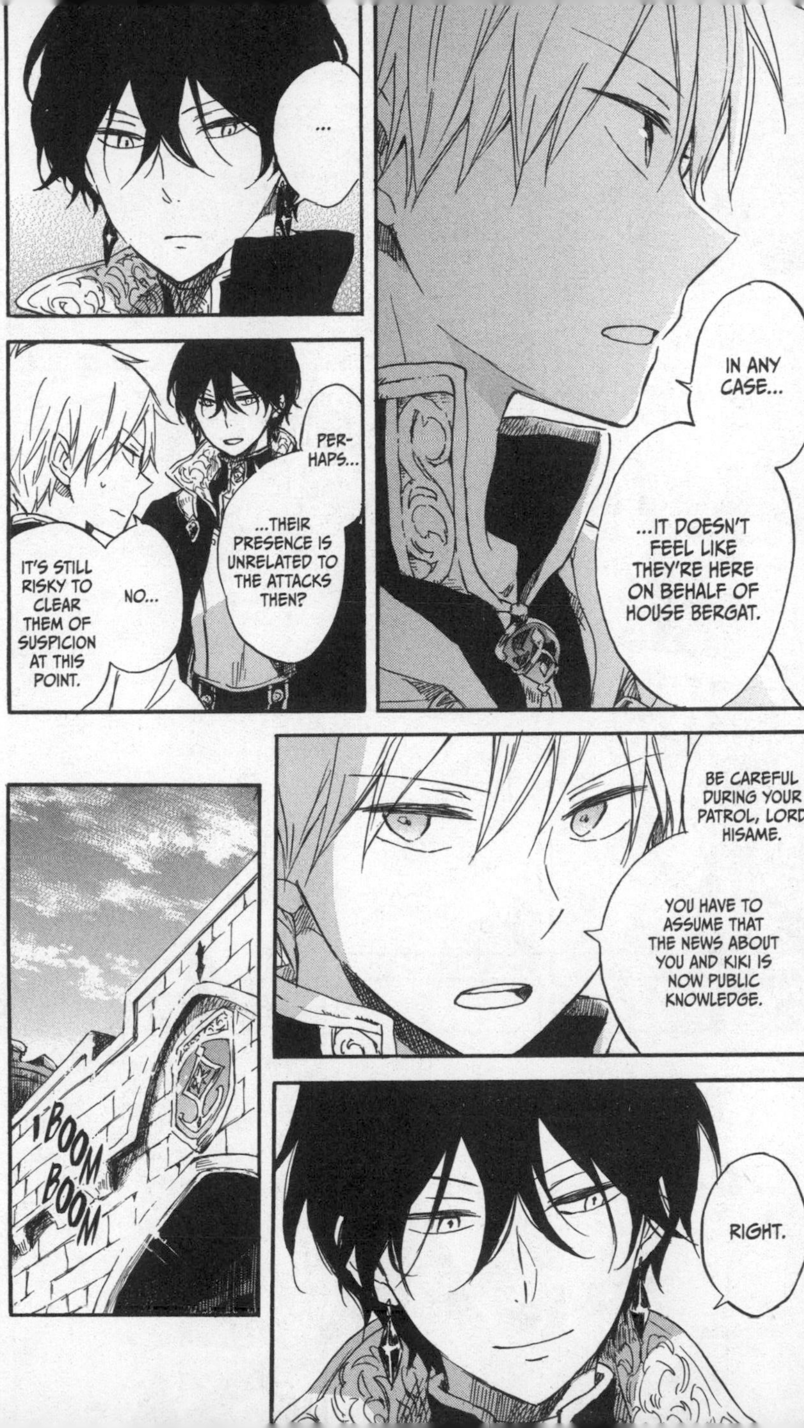
IN ANY CASE...
...IT DOESN'T FEEL LIKE THEY'RE HERE ON BEHALF OF HOUSE BERGAT.
...
PER-HAPS...
...THEIR PRESENCE IS UNRELATED TO THE ATTACKS THEN?
NO...
IT'S STILL RISKY TO CLEAR THEM OF SUSPICION AT THIS POINT.
BE CAREFUL DURING YOUR PATROL, LORD HISAME.
YOU HAVE TO ASSUME THAT THE NEWS ABOUT YOU AND KIKI IS NOW PUBLIC KNOWLEDGE.
RIGHT.
BOOM BOOM

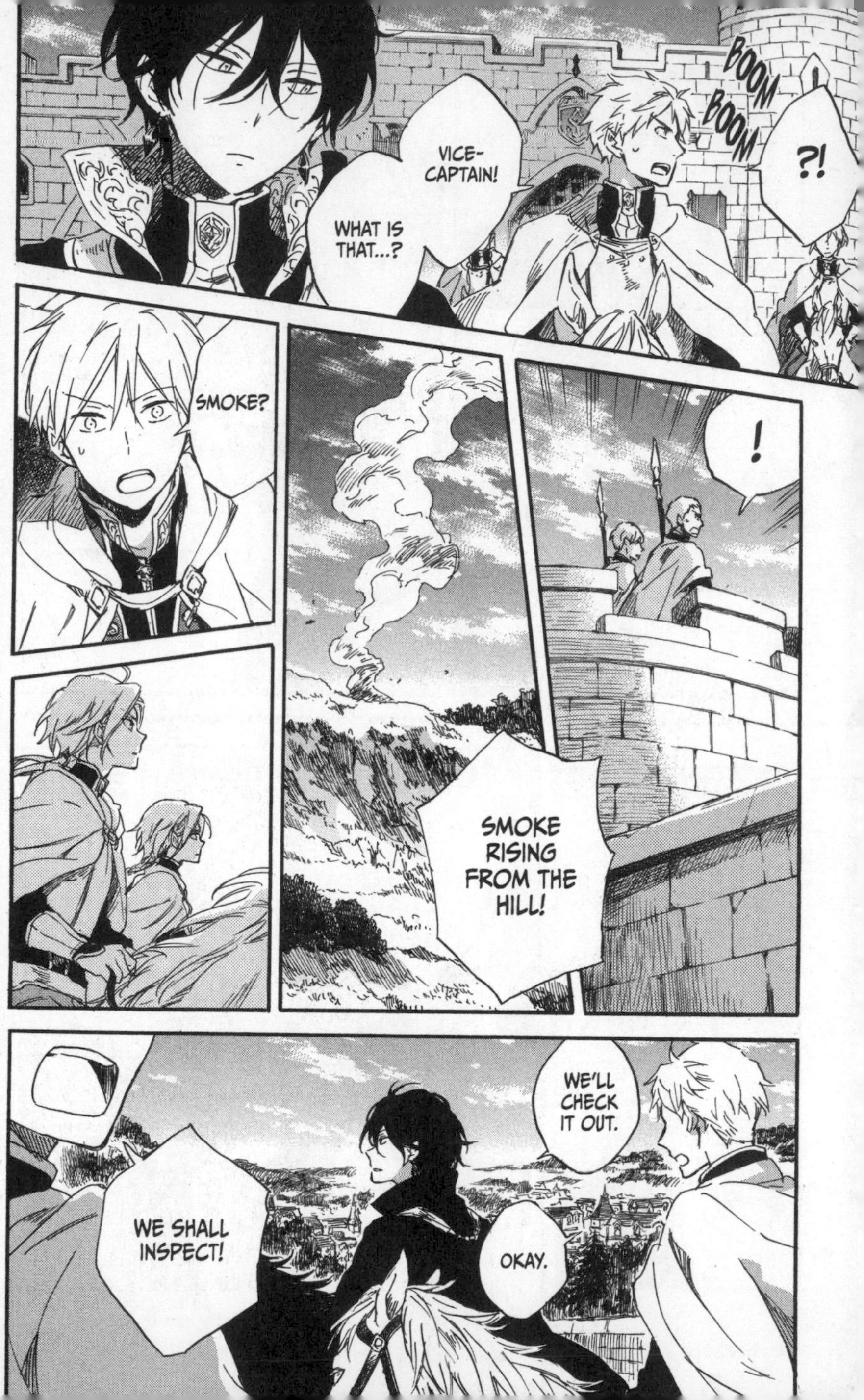
?!
BOOM
BOOM
VICE-CAPTAIN!
WHAT IS THAT...?
!
SMOKE RISING FROM THE HILL!
SMOKE?
WE'LL CHECK IT OUT.
OKAY.
WE SHALL INSPECT!

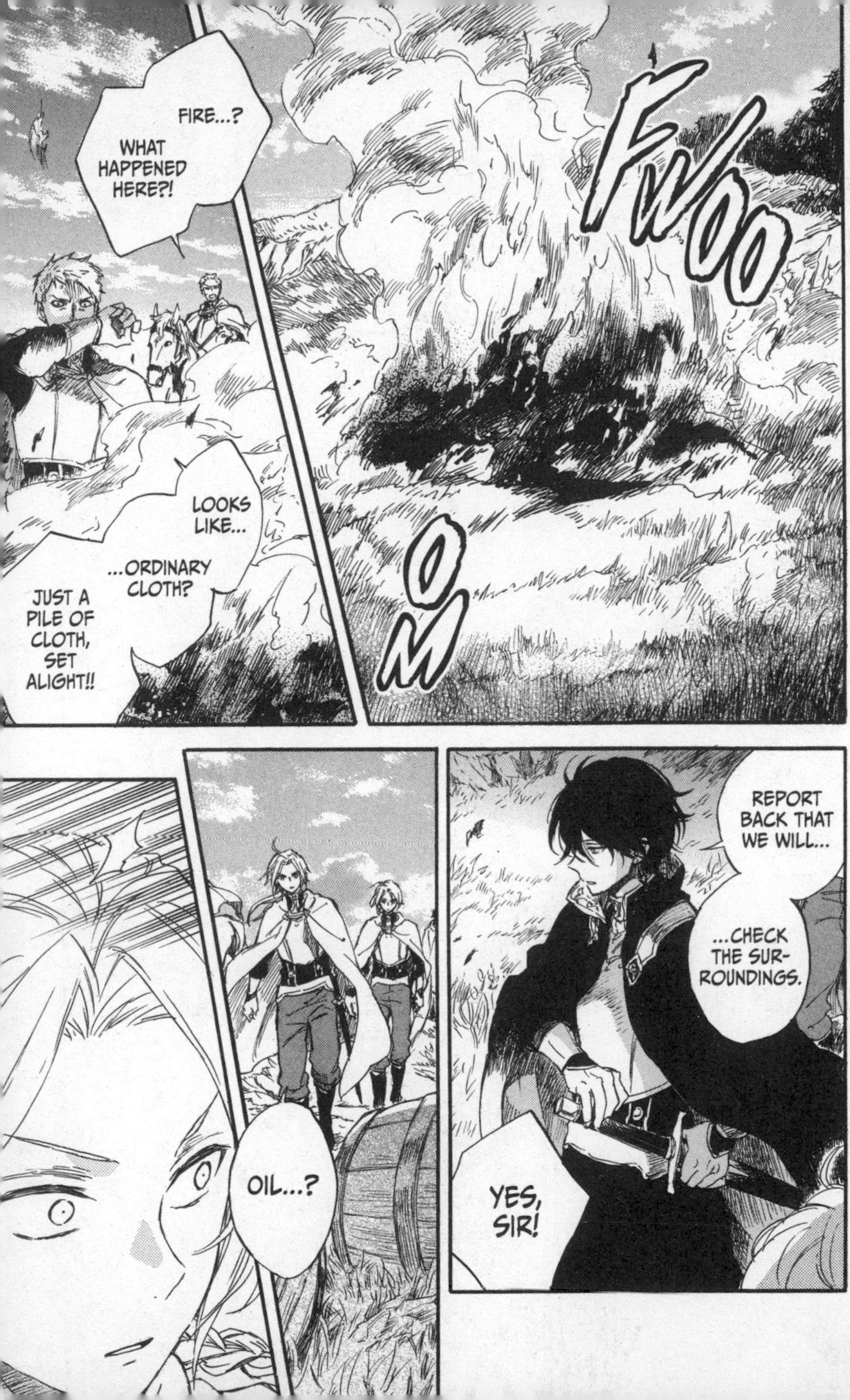
FWOO
FIRE...?
WHAT HAPPENED HERE?!
LOOKS LIKE...
...ORDINARY CLOTH?
JUST A PILE OF CLOTH, SET ALIGHT!!
REPORT BACK THAT WE WILL...
...CHECK THE SUR-ROUNDINGS.
YES, SIR!
OIL...?

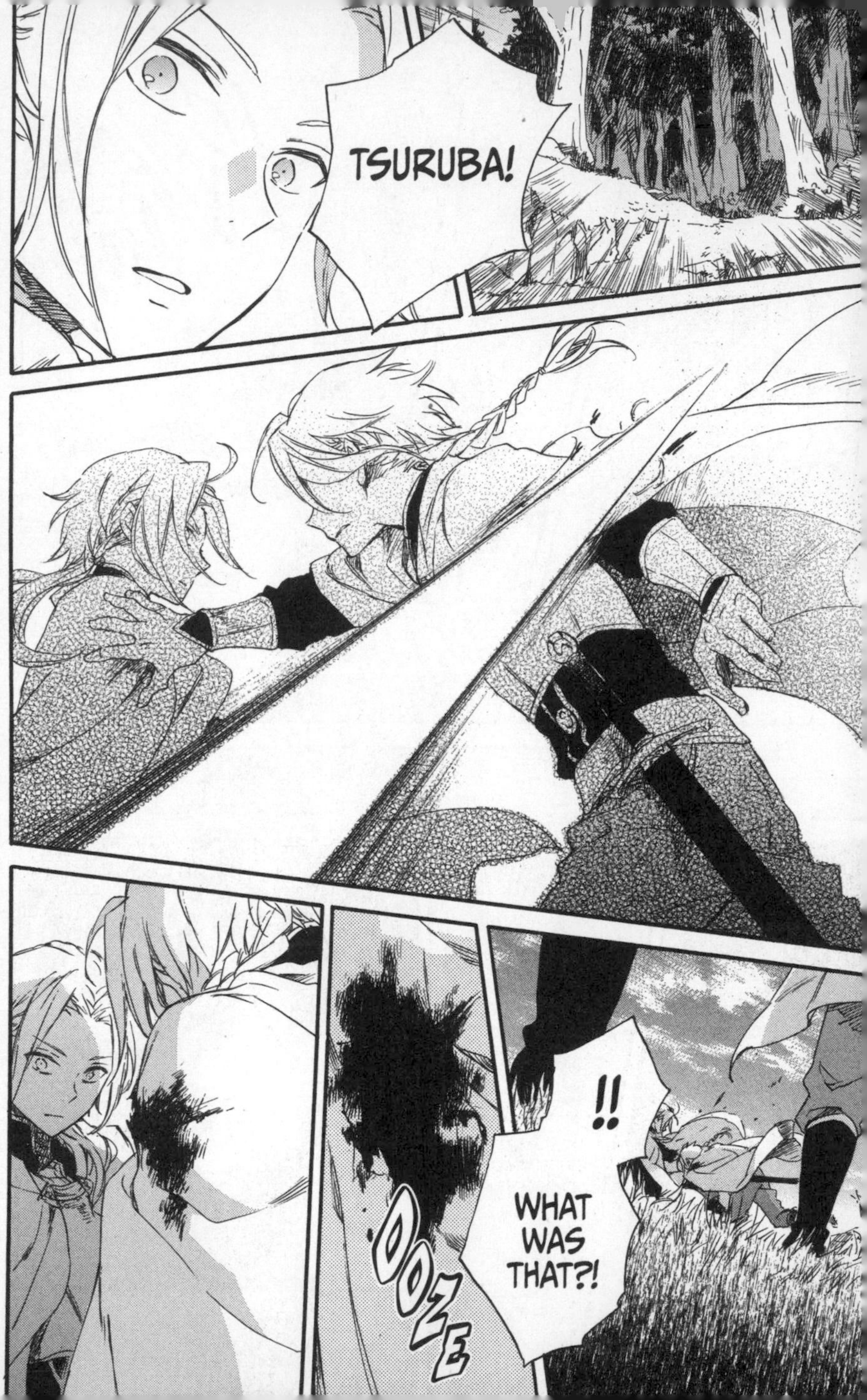
TSURUBA!
!!
WHAT WAS THAT?!
OOZE

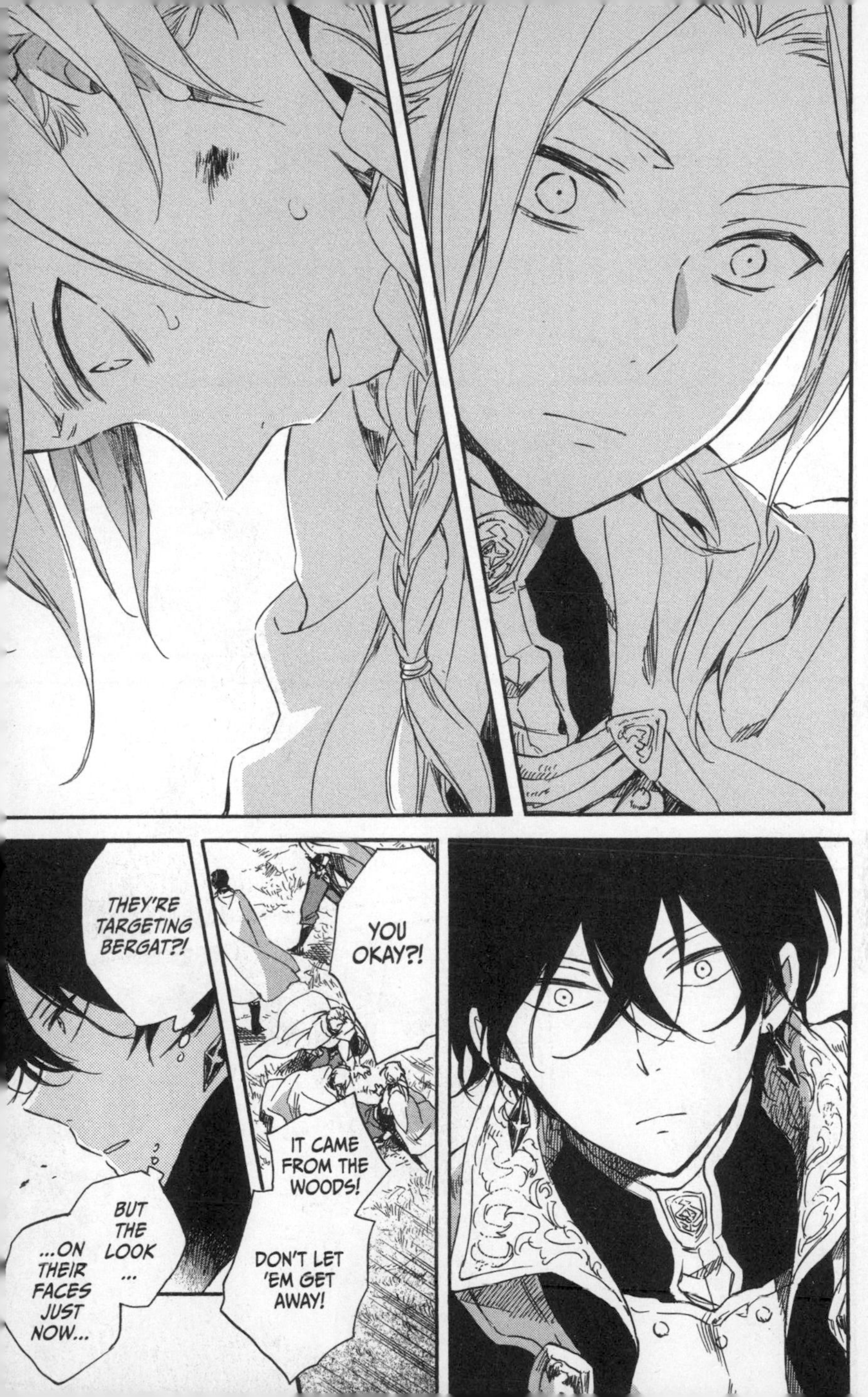
YOU OKAY?!
IT CAME FROM THE WOODS!
DON'T LET 'EM GET AWAY!
THEY'RE TARGETING BERGAT?!
BUT THE LOOK ...
...ON THEIR FACES JUST NOW...

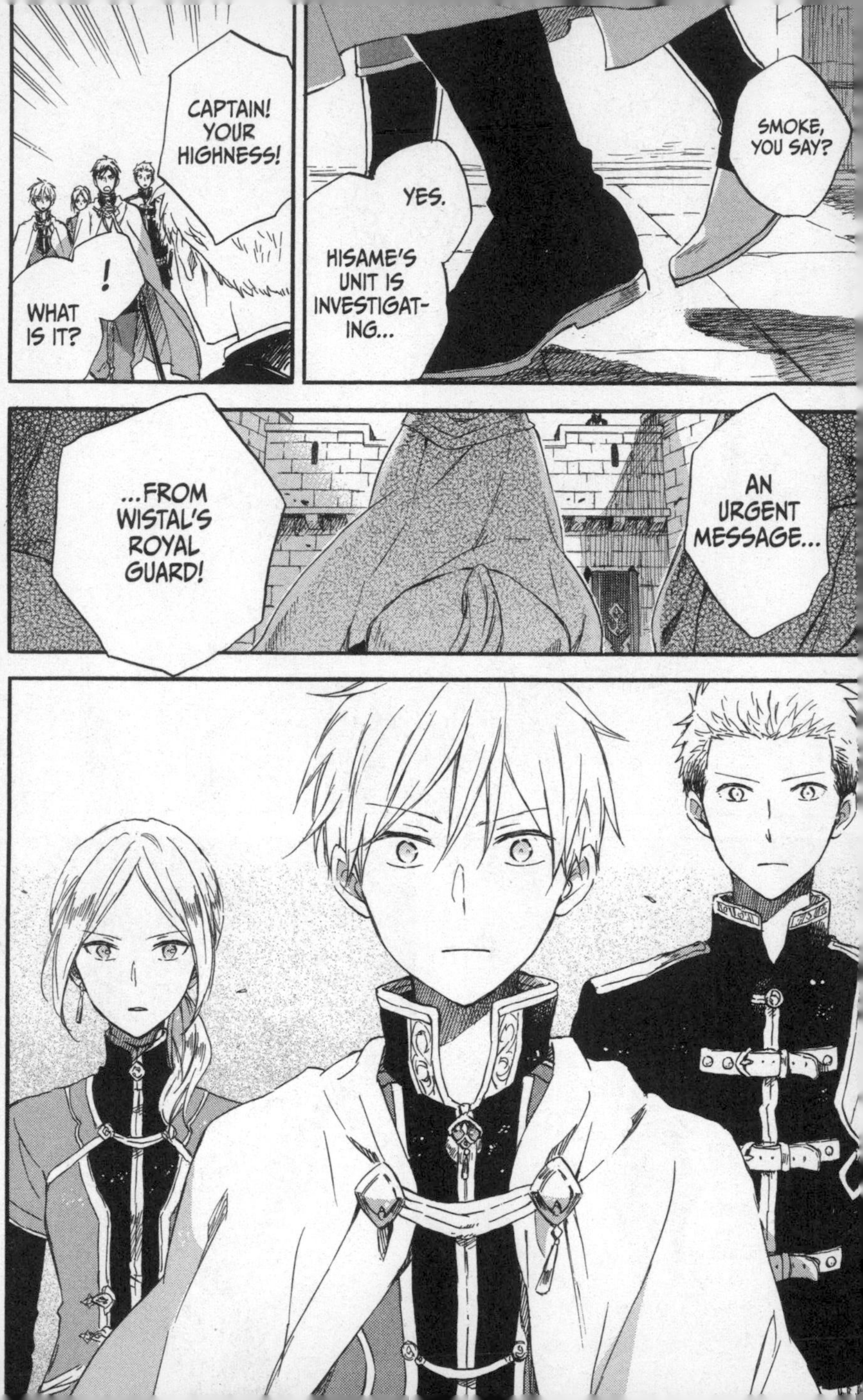
SMOKE, YOU SAY?
YES.
HISAME'S UNIT IS INVESTIGAT-ING...
CAPTAIN! YOUR HIGHNESS!
!
WHAT IS IT?
AN URGENT MESSAGE...
...FROM WISTAL'S ROYAL GUARD!

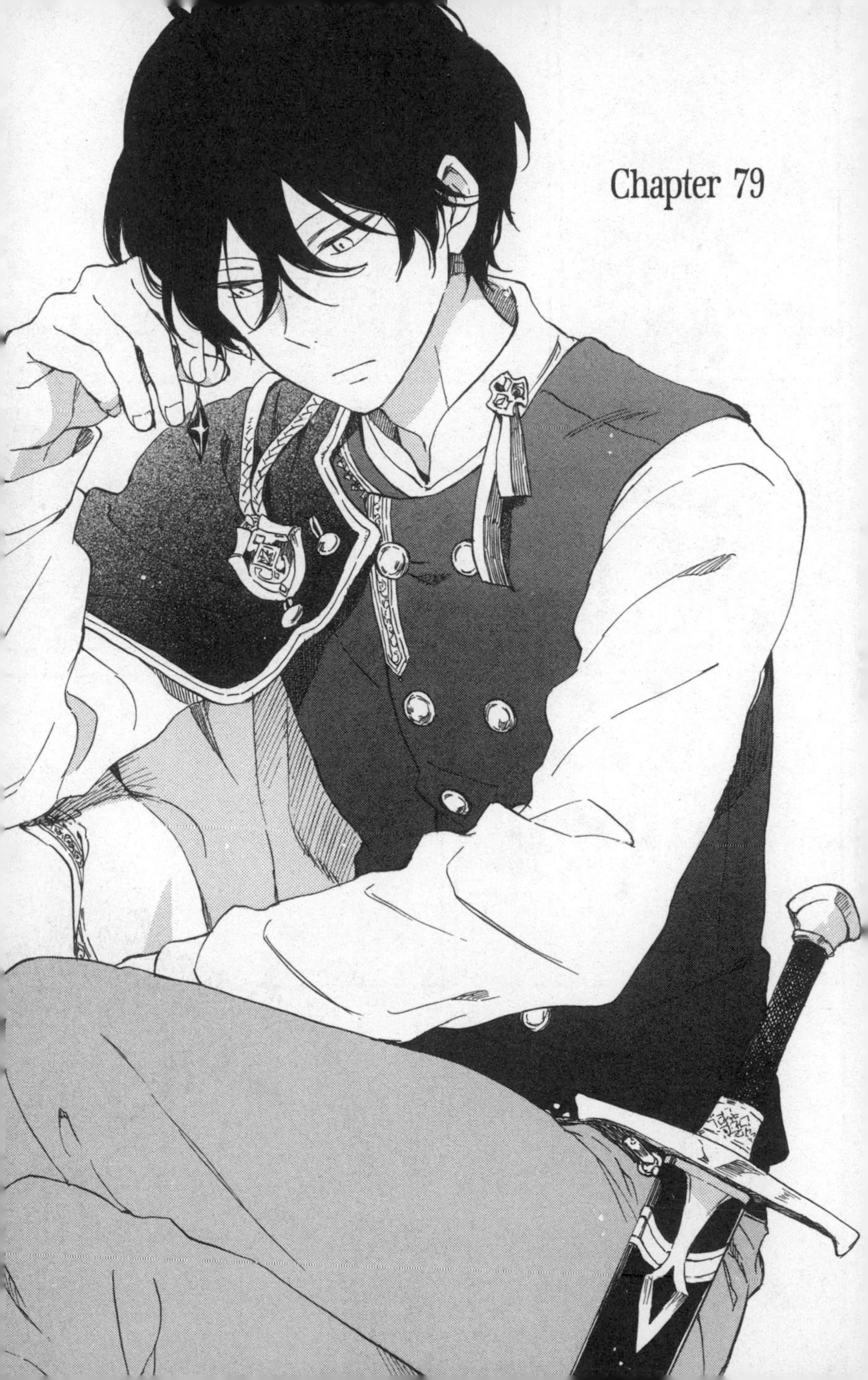
Chapter 79

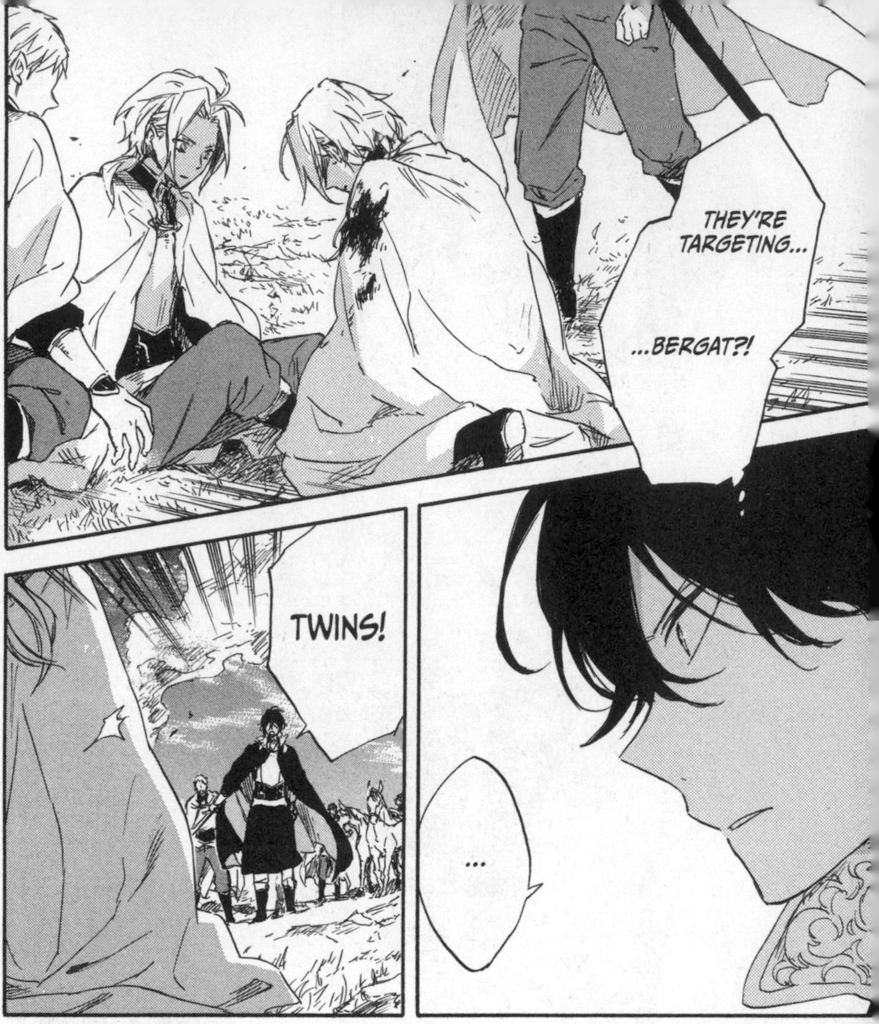
THEY'RE TARGETING...
...BERGAT?!
...
TWINS!

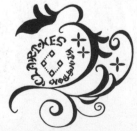

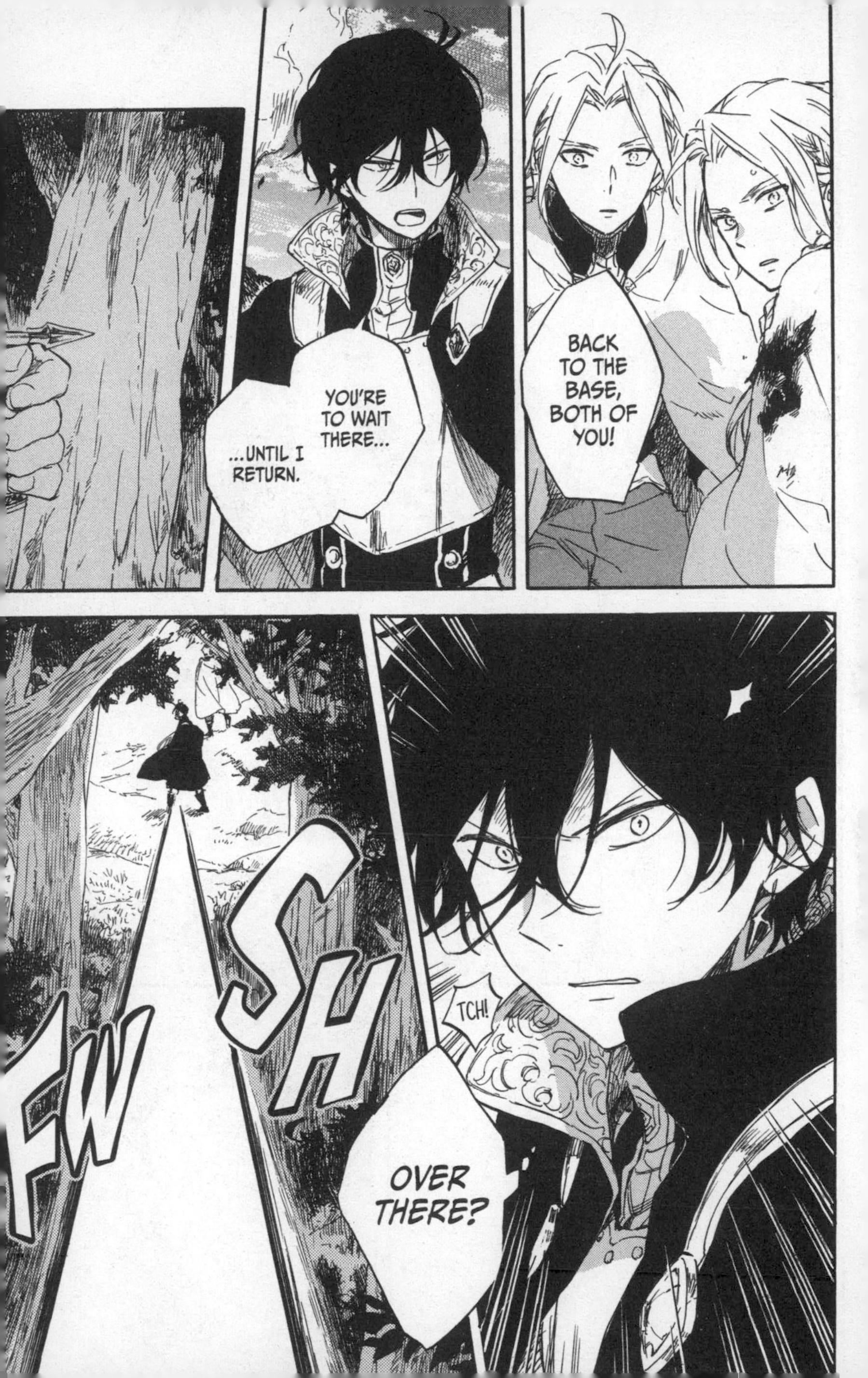
BACK TO THE BASE, BOTH OF YOU!
YOU'RE TO WAIT THERE...
...UNTIL I RETURN.
TCH!
OVER THERE?
SH
FW

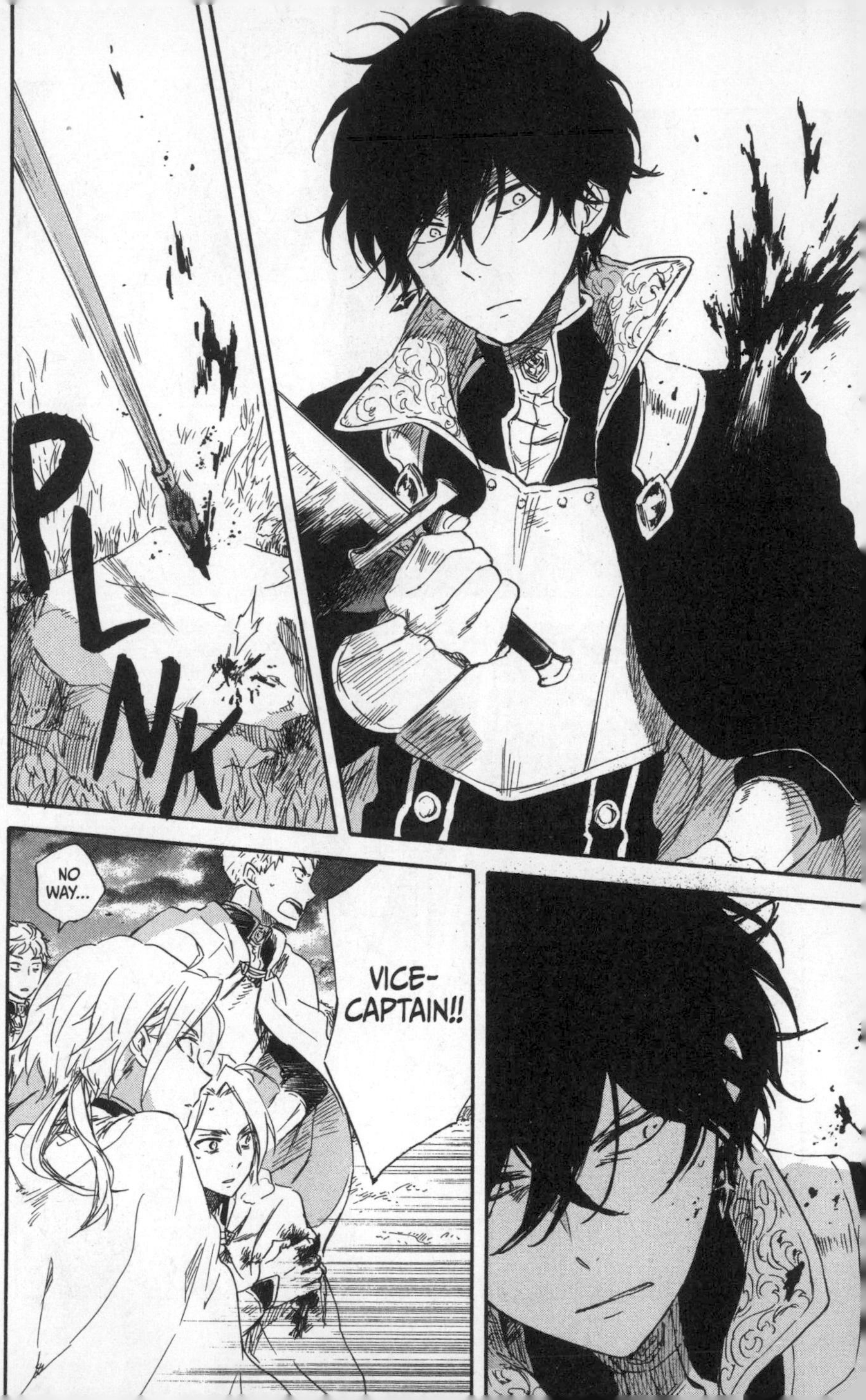
PLNK
VICE-CAPTAIN!!
NO WAY...

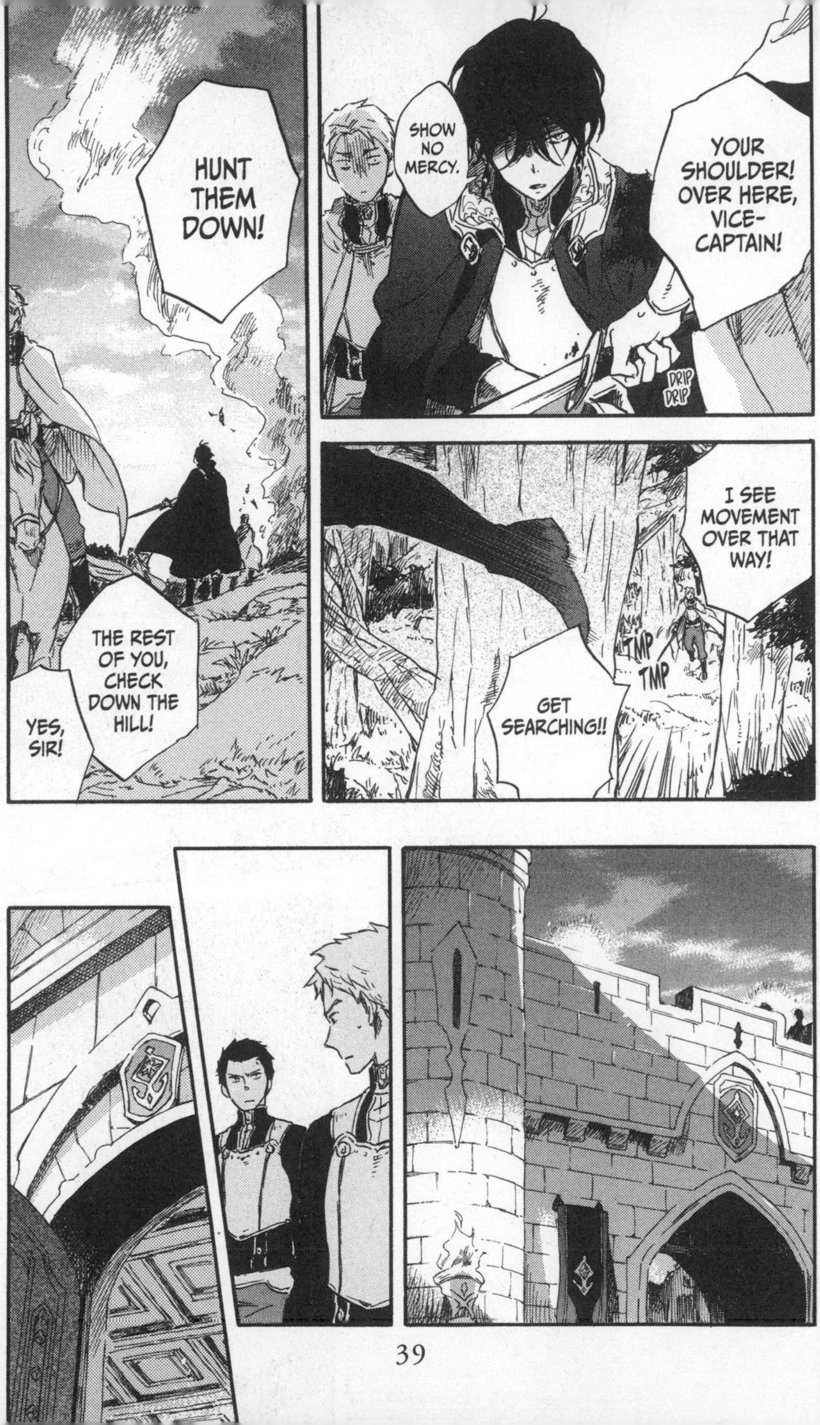
YOUR SHOULDER! OVER HERE, VICE-CAPTAIN!
SHOW NO MERCY.
DRIP DRIP
I SEE MOVEMENT OVER THAT WAY!
TMP TMP
GET SEARCHING!!
HUNT THEM DOWN!
THE REST OF YOU, CHECK DOWN THE HILL!
YES, SIR!

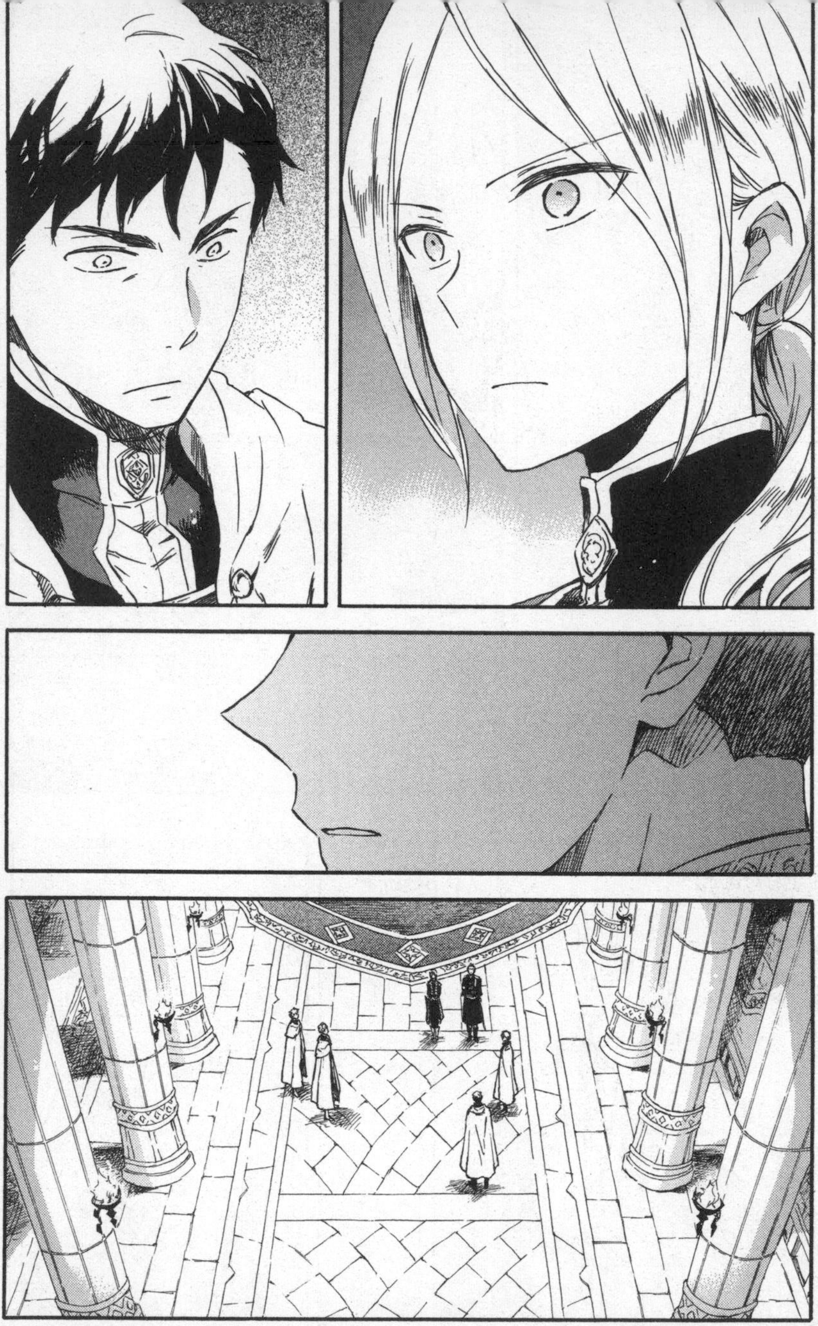

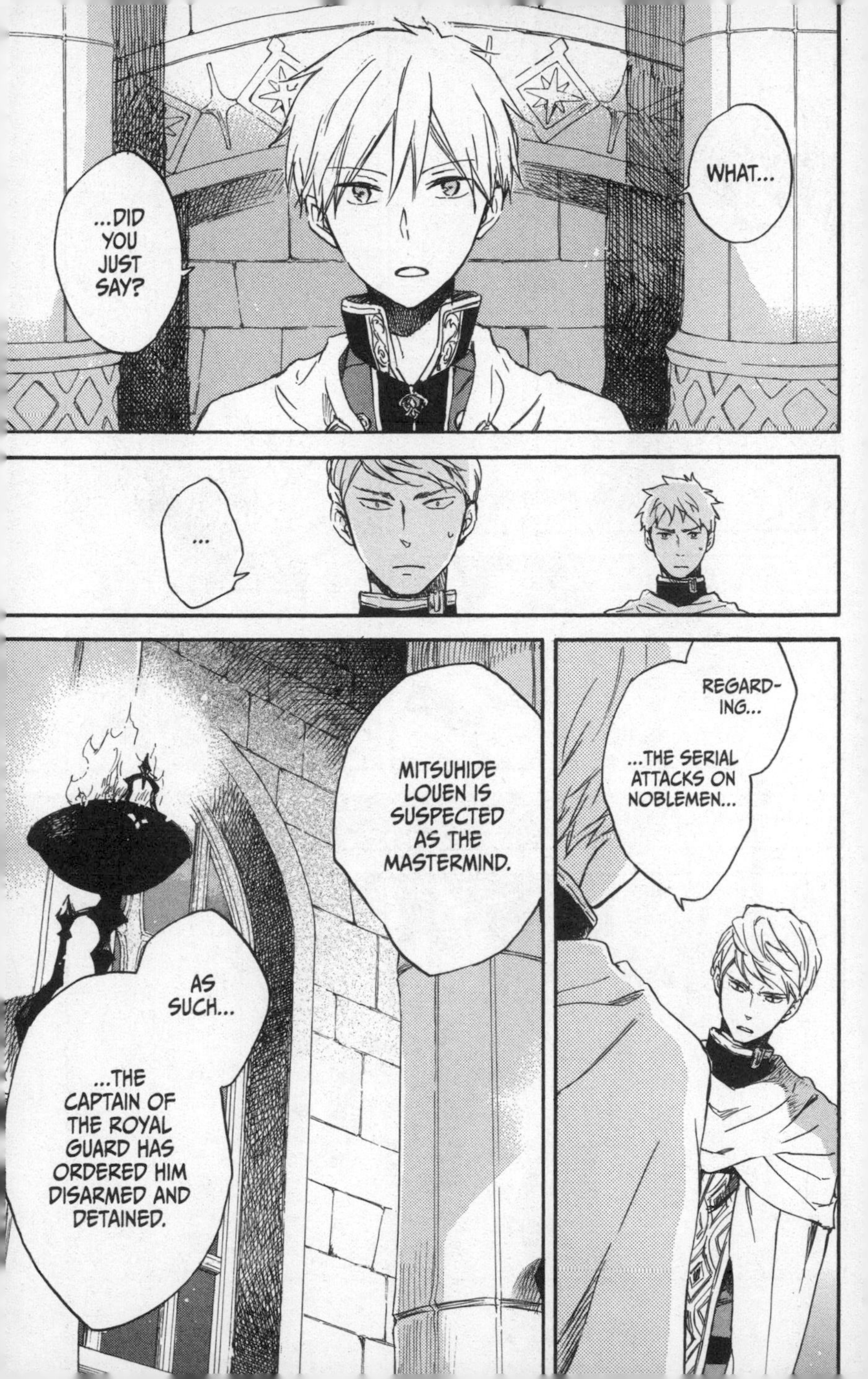
WHAT...
...DID YOU JUST SAY?
...
REGARDING...
...THE SERIAL ATTACKS ON NOBLEMEN...
MITSUHIDE LOUEN IS SUSPECTED AS THE MASTERMIND.
AS SUCH...
...THE CAPTAIN OF THE ROYAL GUARD HAS ORDERED HIM DISARMED AND DETAINED.

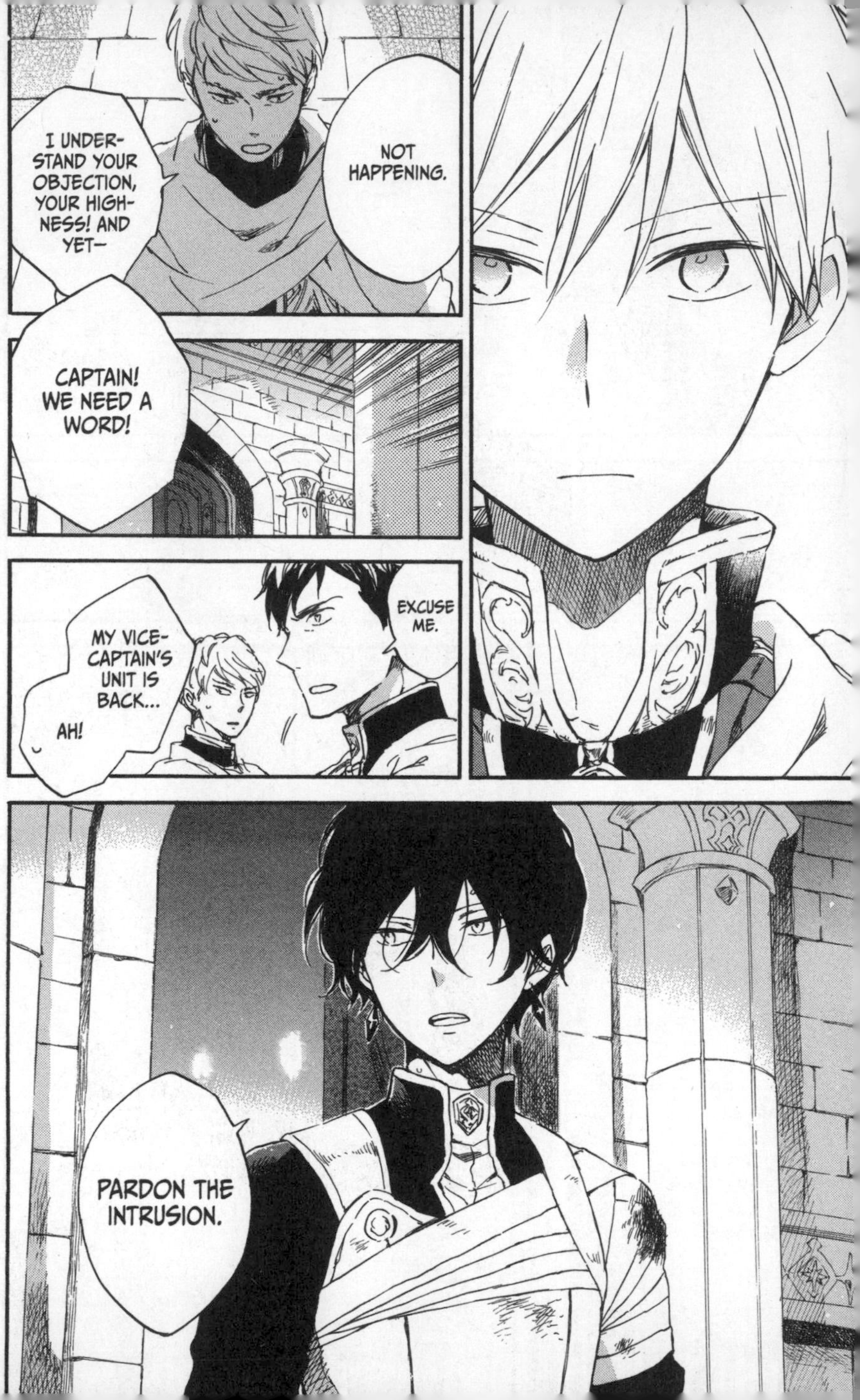
NOT HAPPENING.
I UNDERSTAND YOUR OBJECTION, YOUR HIGHNESS! AND YET—
CAPTAIN! WE NEED A WORD!
EXCUSE ME.
MY VICE-CAPTAIN'S UNIT IS BACK...
AH!
PARDON THE INTRUSION.

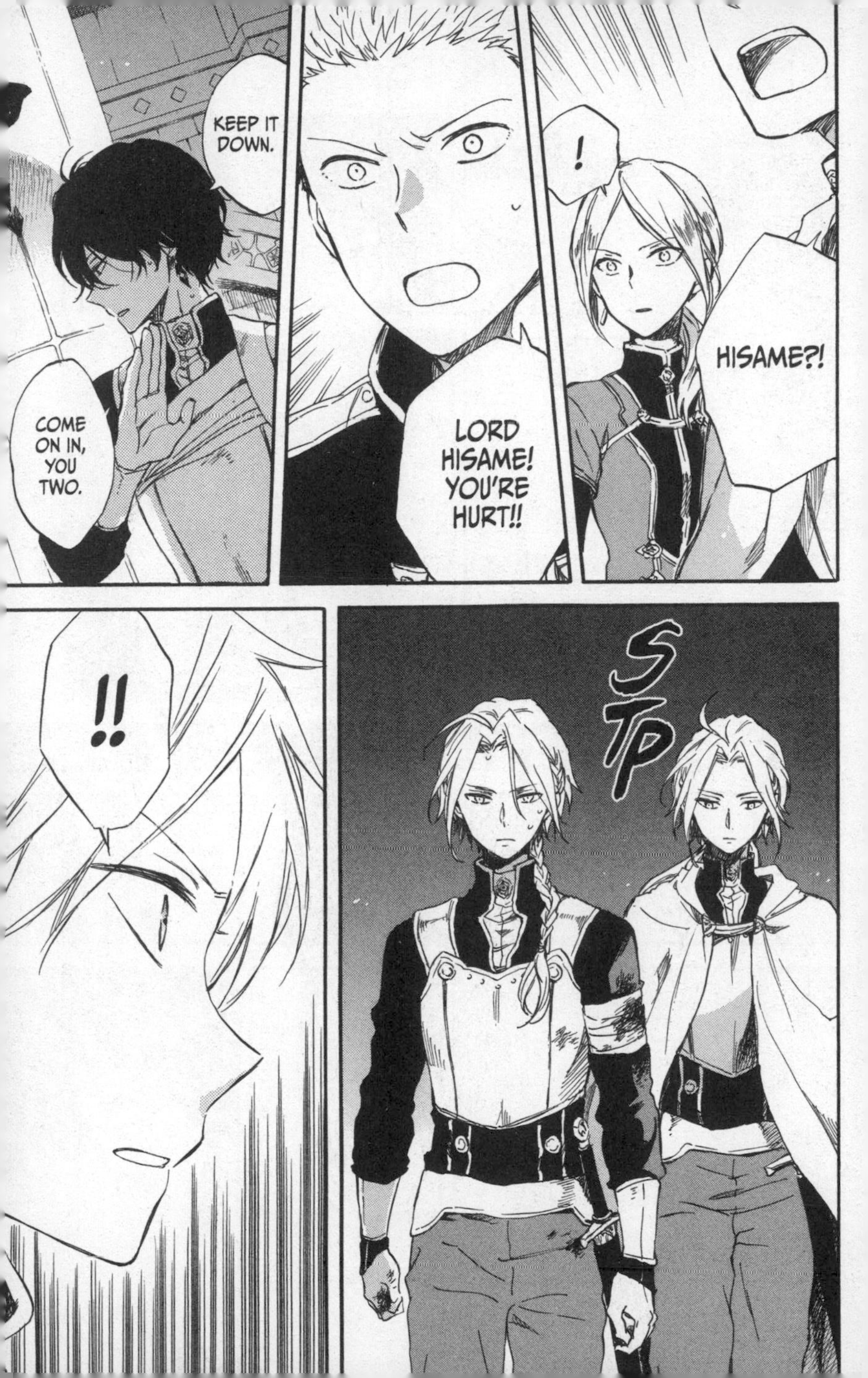
HISAME?!
!
LORD HISAME! YOU'RE HURT!!
KEEP IT DOWN.
COME ON IN, YOU TWO.
STP
!!

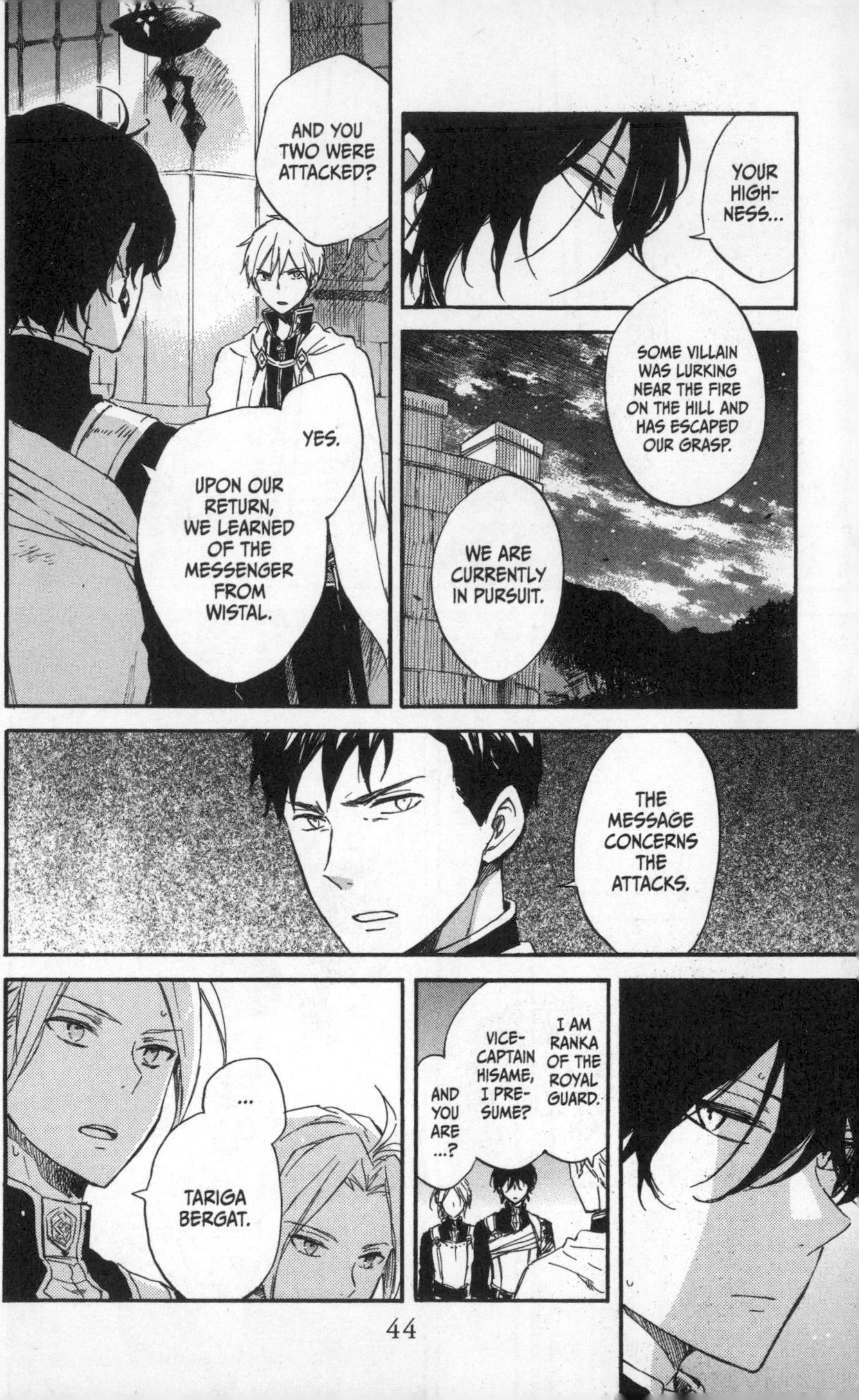
YOUR HIGHNESS...
SOME VILLAIN WAS LURKING NEAR THE FIRE ON THE HILL AND HAS ESCAPED OUR GRASP.
WE ARE CURRENTLY IN PURSUIT.
AND YOU TWO WERE ATTACKED?
YES.
UPON OUR RETURN, WE LEARNED OF THE MESSENGER FROM WISTAL.
THE MESSAGE CONCERNS THE ATTACKS.
I AM RANKA OF THE ROYAL GUARD.
VICE-CAPTAIN HISAME, I PRESUME?
AND YOU ARE ...?
...
TARIGA BERGAT.

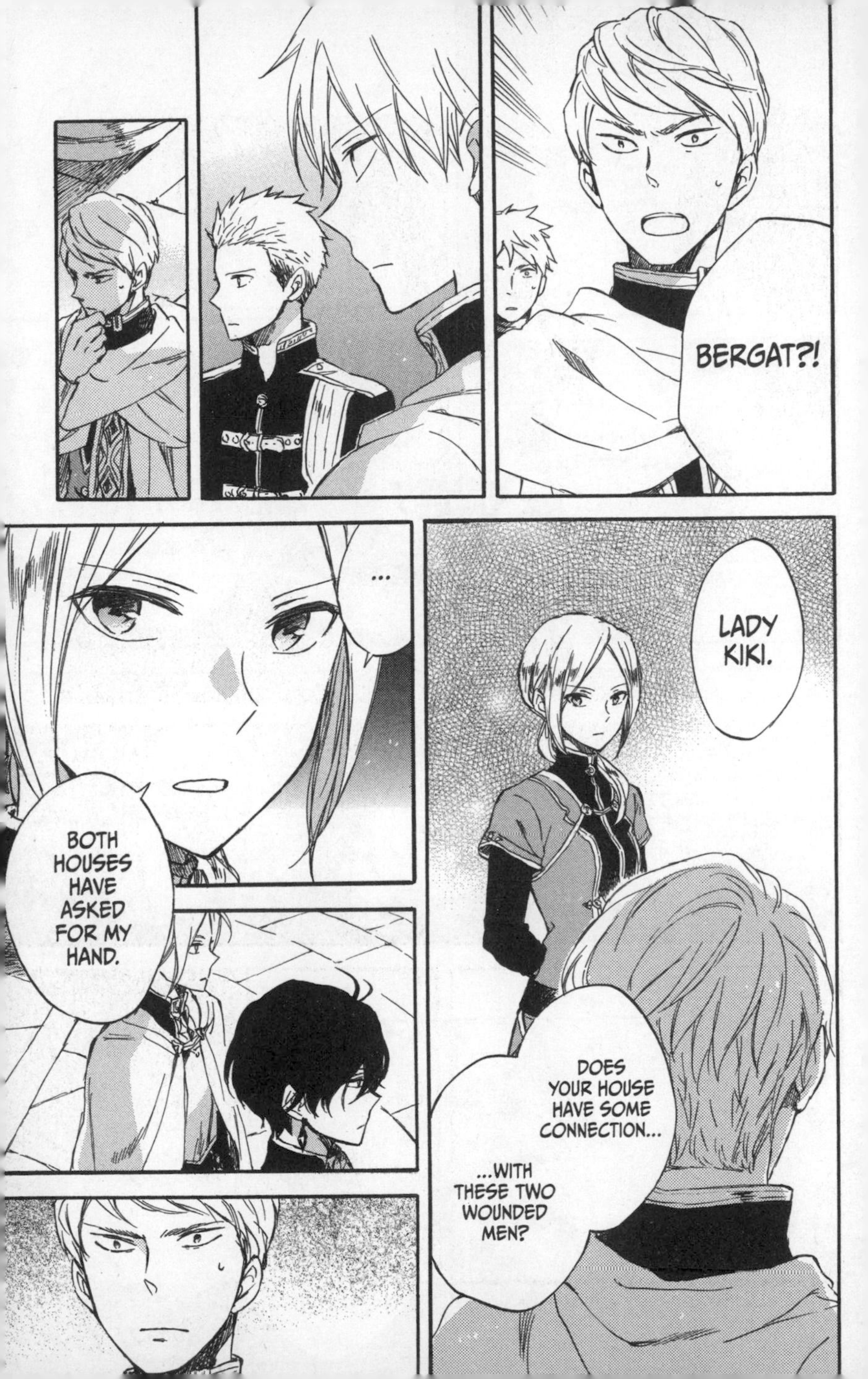
BERGAT?!
LADY KIKI.
DOES YOUR HOUSE HAVE SOME CONNECTION...
...WITH THESE TWO WOUNDED MEN?
...
BOTH HOUSES HAVE ASKED FOR MY HAND.

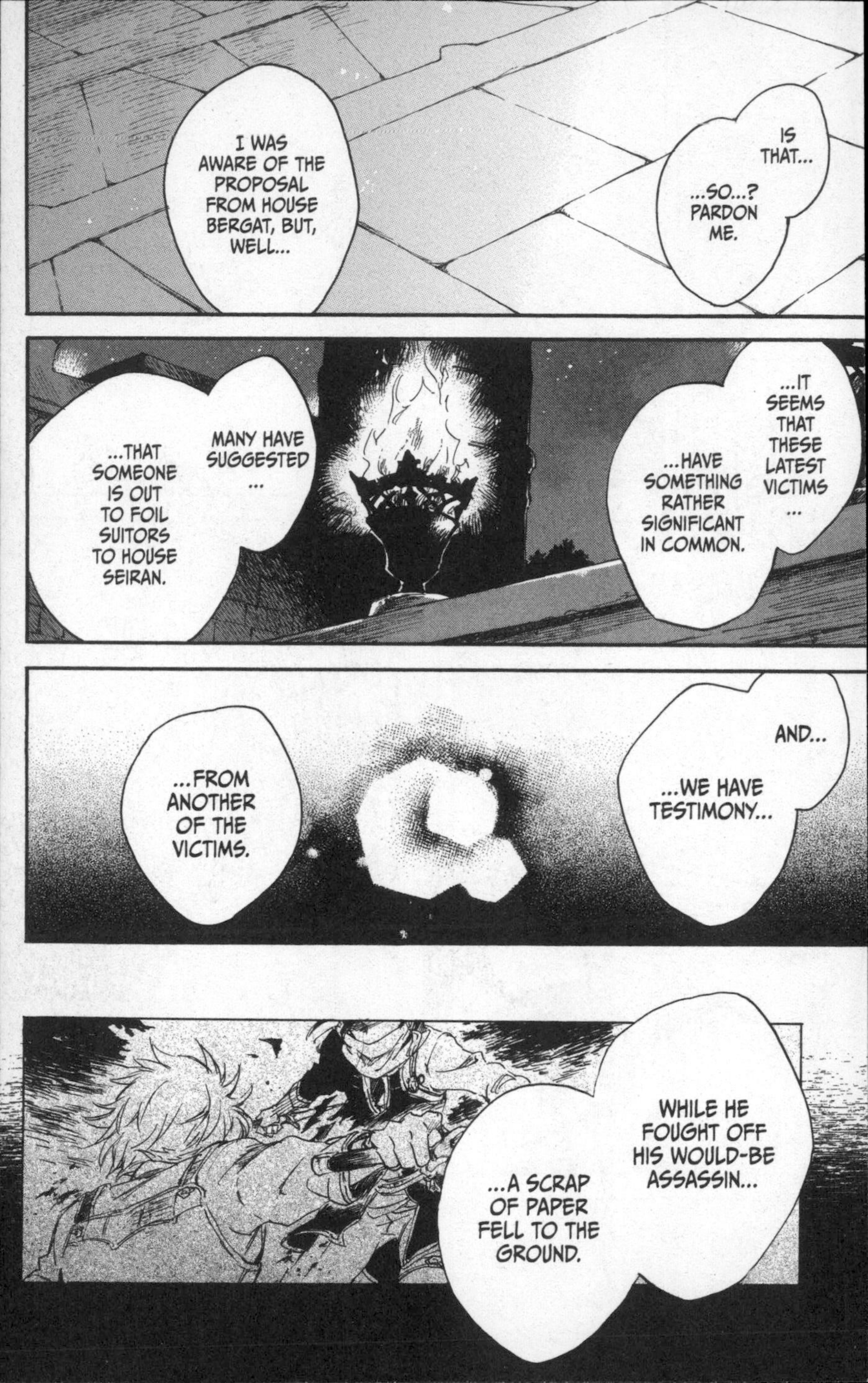
IS THAT...
...SO...? PARDON ME.
I WAS AWARE OF THE PROPOSAL FROM HOUSE BERGAT, BUT, WELL...
...IT SEEMS THAT THESE LATEST VICTIMS...
...HAVE SOMETHING RATHER SIGNIFICANT IN COMMON.
MANY HAVE SUGGESTED...
...THAT SOMEONE IS OUT TO FOIL SUITORS TO HOUSE SEIRAN.
AND...
...WE HAVE TESTIMONY...
...FROM ANOTHER OF THE VICTIMS.
WHILE HE FOUGHT OFF HIS WOULD-BE ASSASSIN...
...A SCRAP OF PAPER FELL TO THE GROUND.

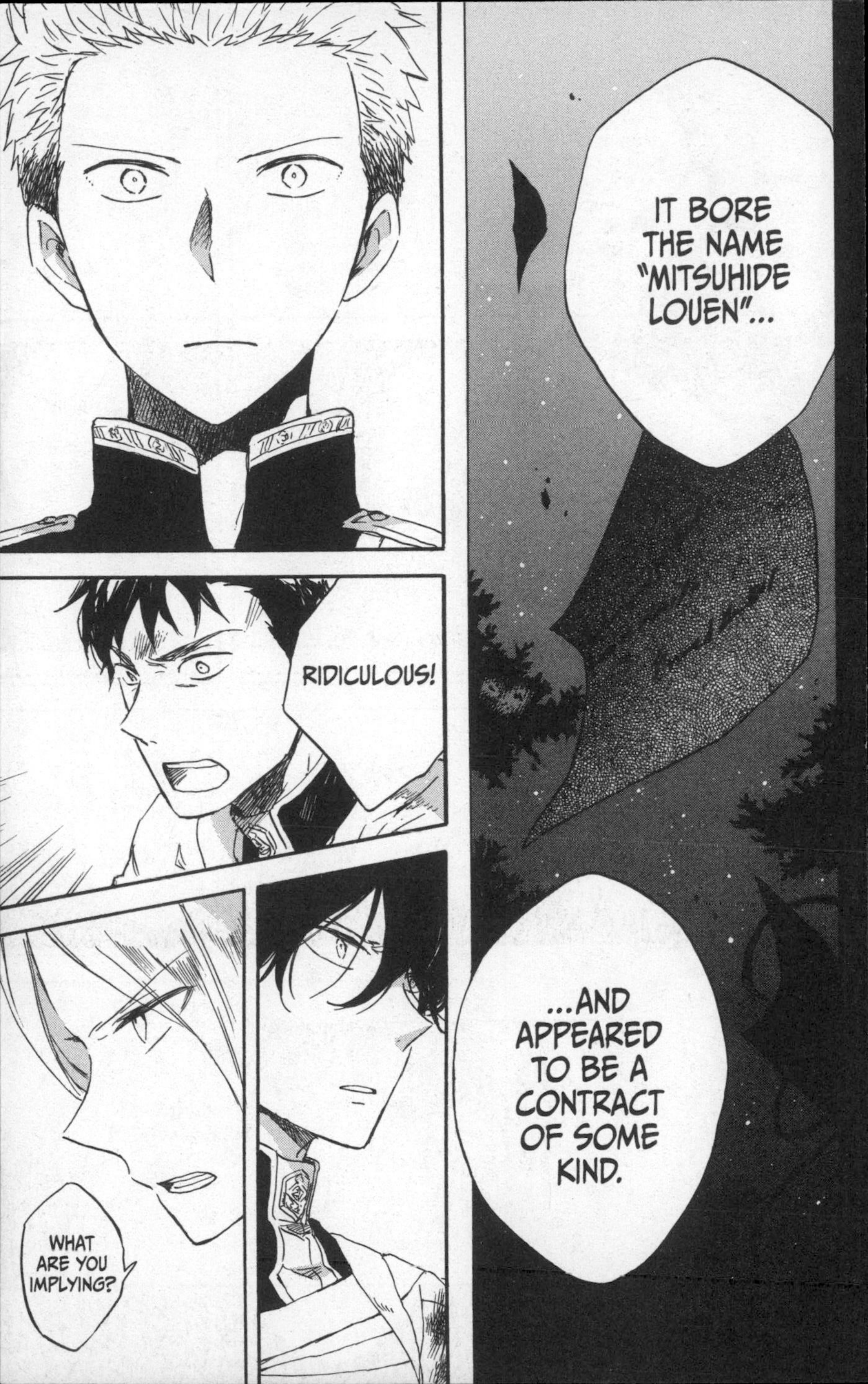
IT BORE THE NAME "MITSUHIDE LOUEN"...
...AND APPEARED TO BE A CONTRACT OF SOME KIND.
RIDICULOUS!
WHAT ARE YOU IMPLYING?

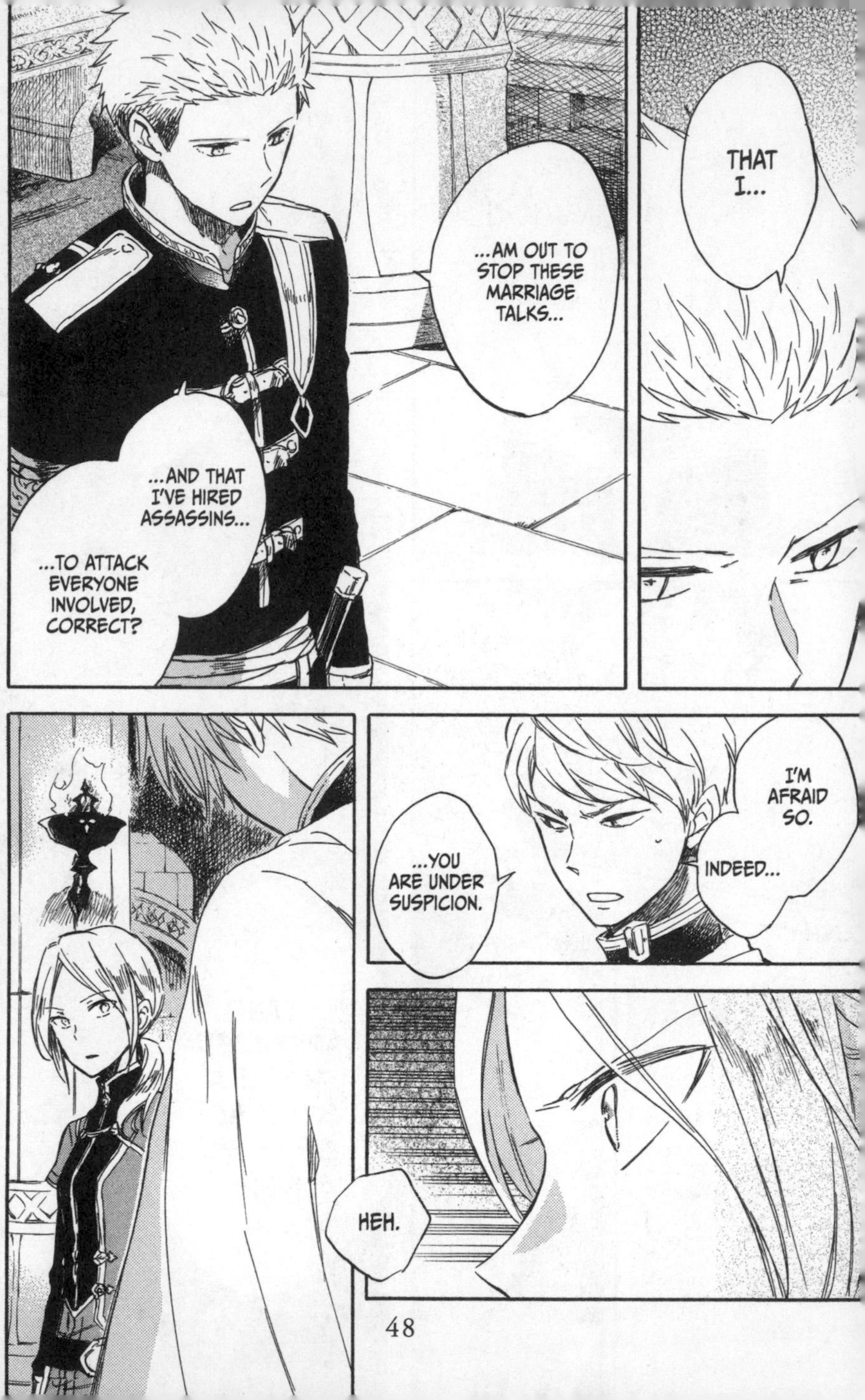
THAT I...
...AM OUT TO STOP THESE MARRIAGE TALKS...
...AND THAT I'VE HIRED ASSASSINS...
...TO ATTACK EVERYONE INVOLVED, CORRECT?
I'M AFRAID SO.
INDEED...
...YOU ARE UNDER SUSPICION.
HEH.

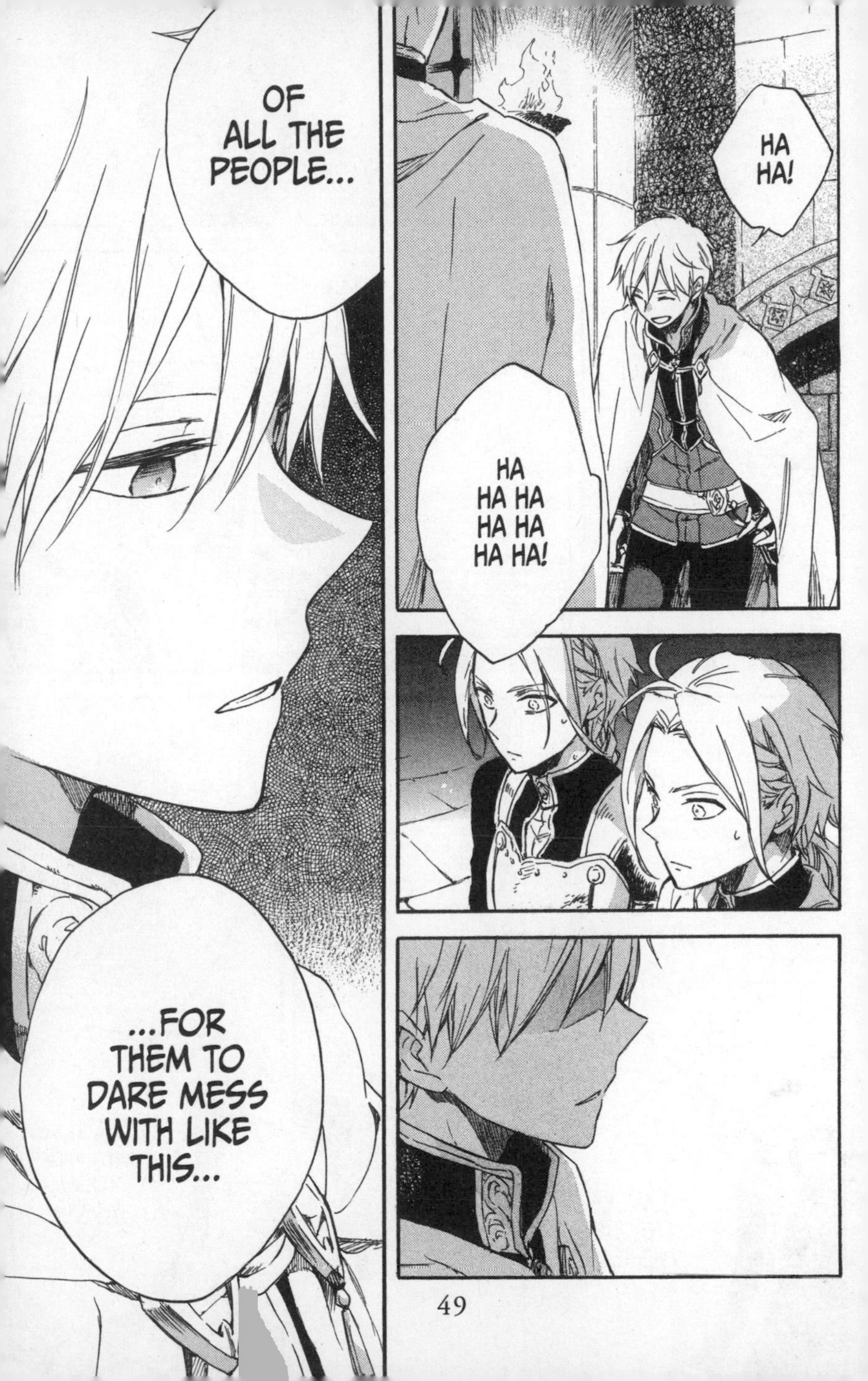
HA HA!
HA HA HA HA HA HA HA!
OF ALL THE PEOPLE...
...FOR THEM TO DARE MESS WITH LIKE THIS...

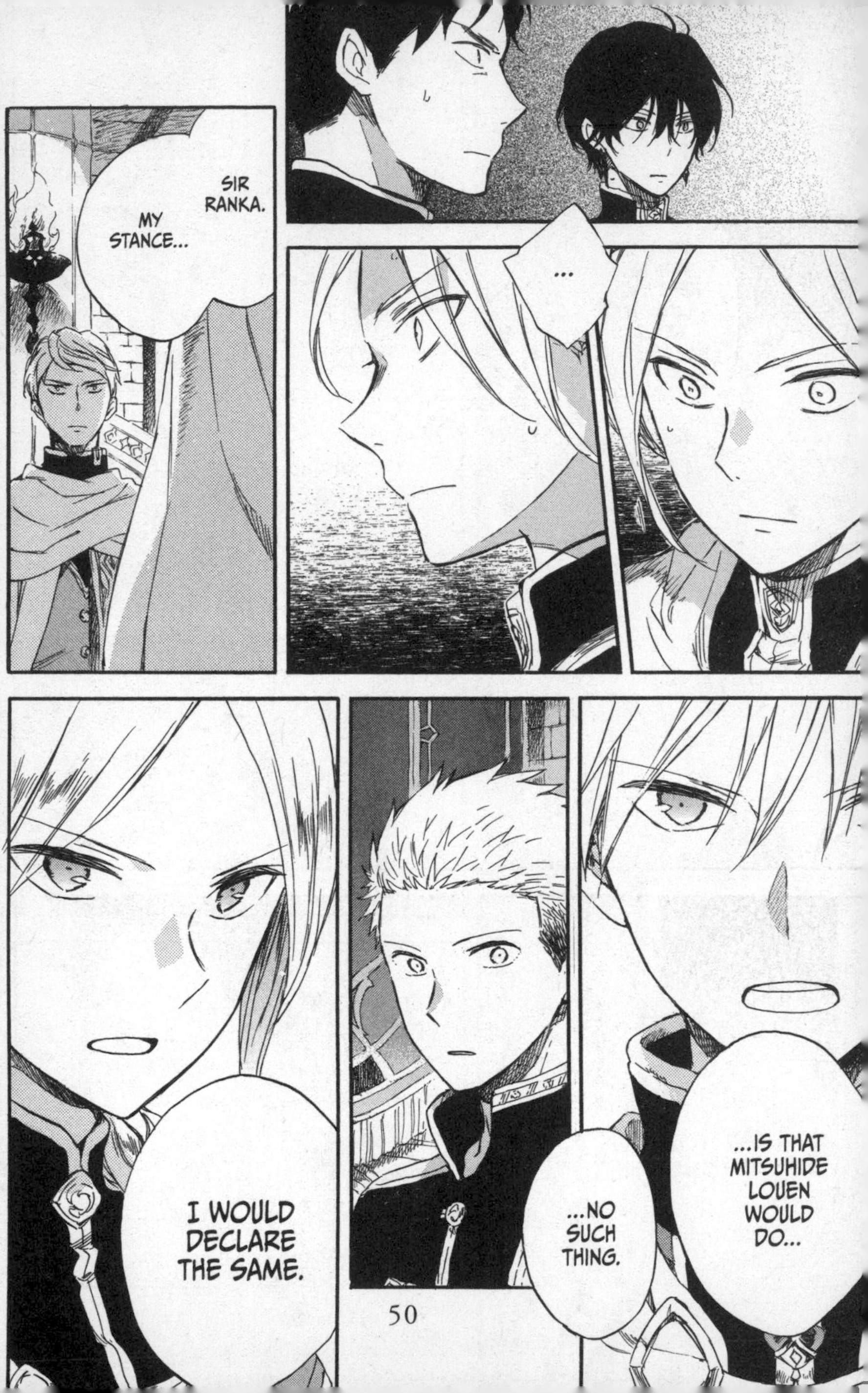
...
SIR RANKA.
MY STANCE...
...IS THAT MITSUHIDE LOUEN WOULD DO...
...NO SUCH THING.
I WOULD DECLARE THE SAME.

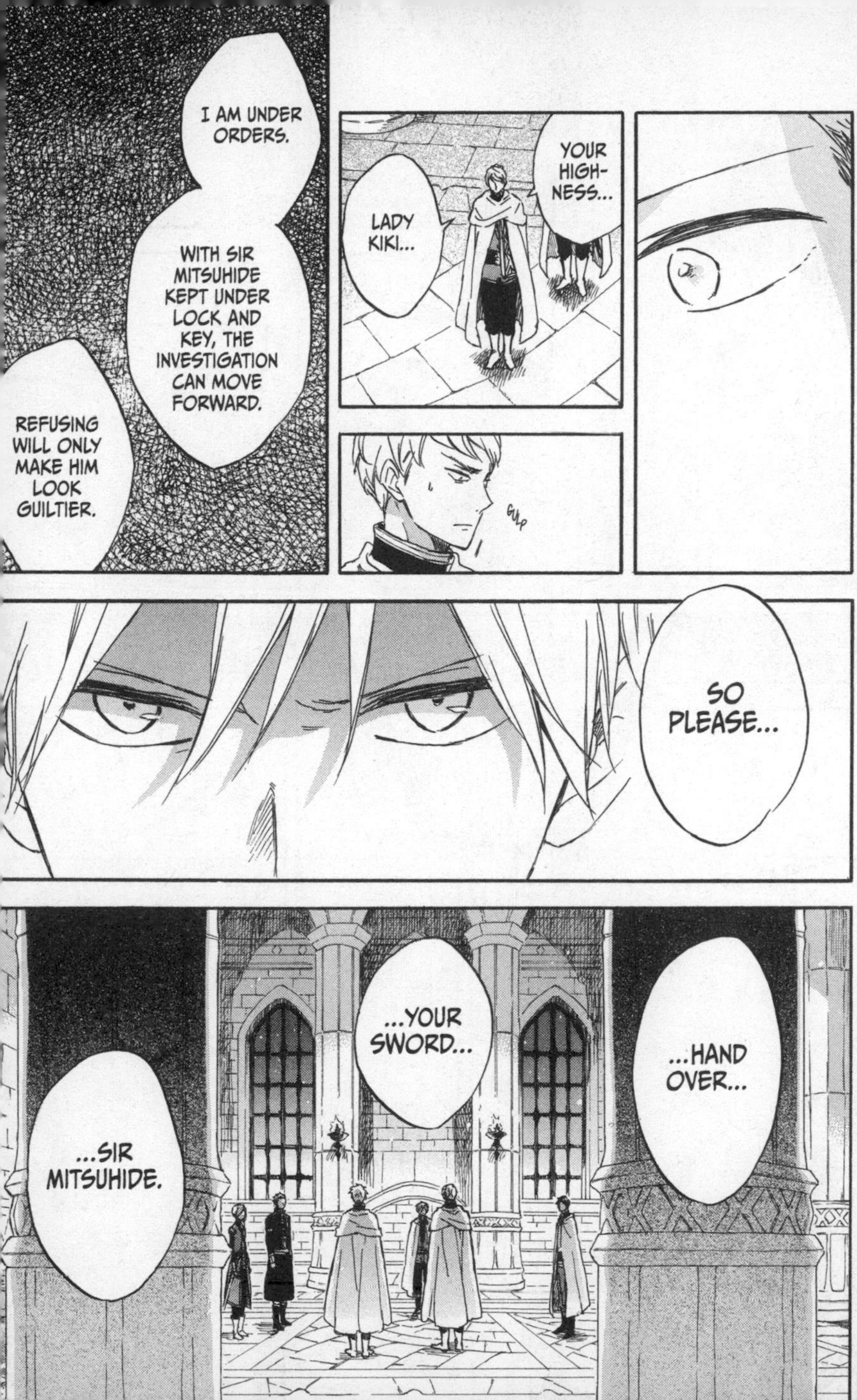
YOUR HIGHNESS...
LADY KIKI...
GULP
I AM UNDER ORDERS.
WITH SIR MITSUHIDE KEPT UNDER LOCK AND KEY, THE INVESTIGATION CAN MOVE FORWARD.
REFUSING WILL ONLY MAKE HIM LOOK GUILTIER.
SO PLEASE...
...HAND OVER...
...YOUR SWORD...
...SIR MITSUHIDE.

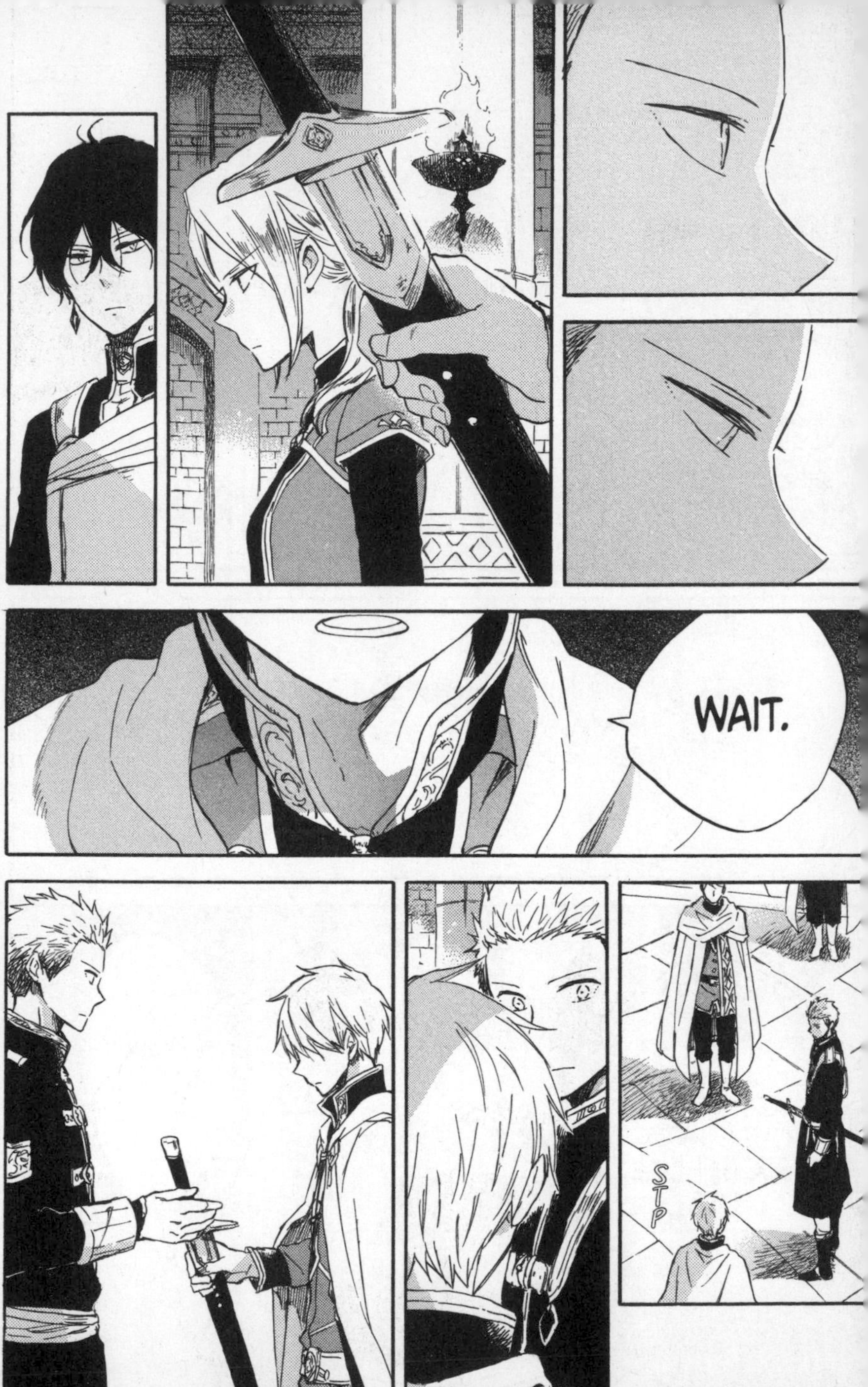
WAIT.
STP

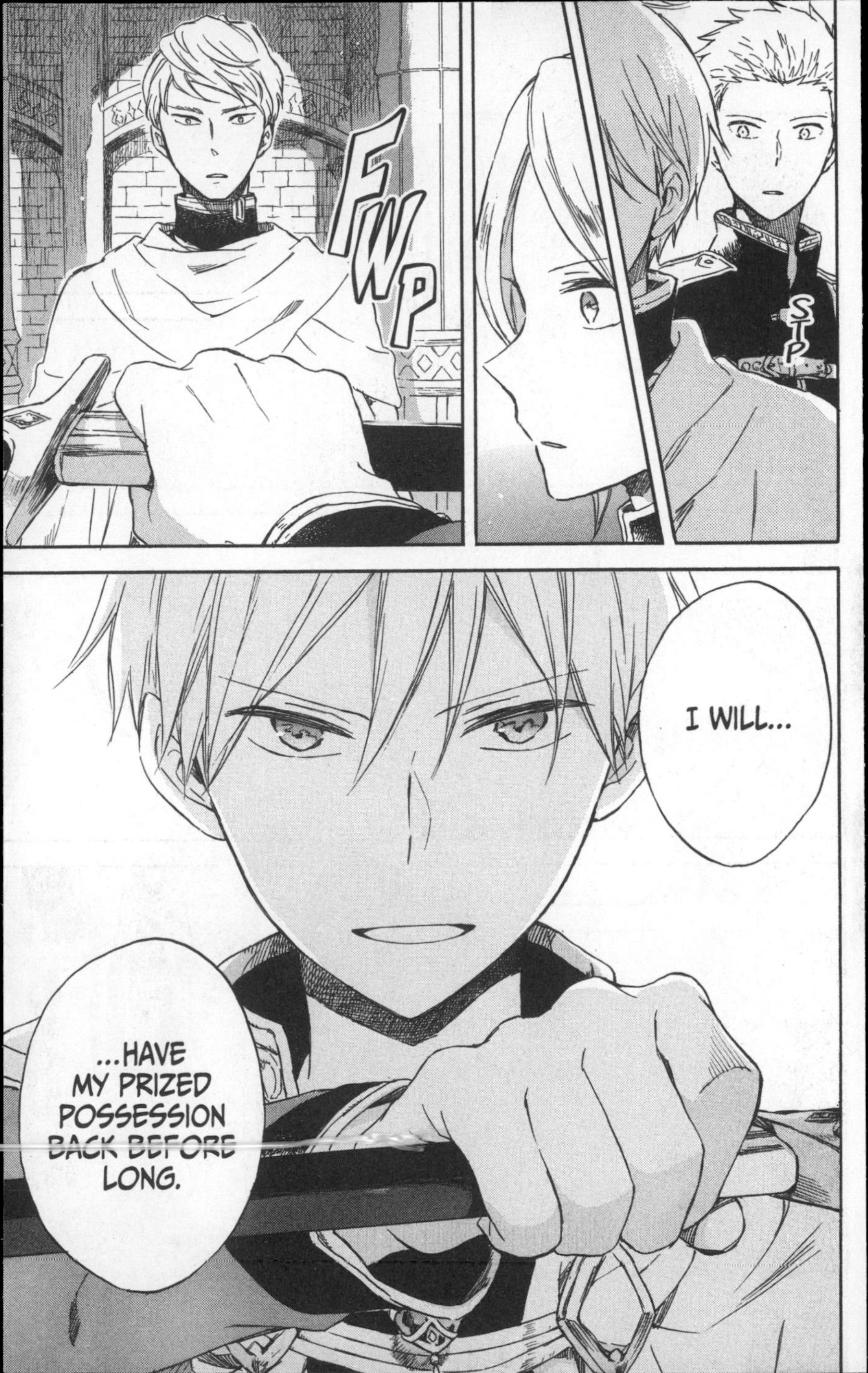
STIP
FWP
I WILL...
...HAVE MY PRIZED POSSESSION BACK BEFORE LONG.

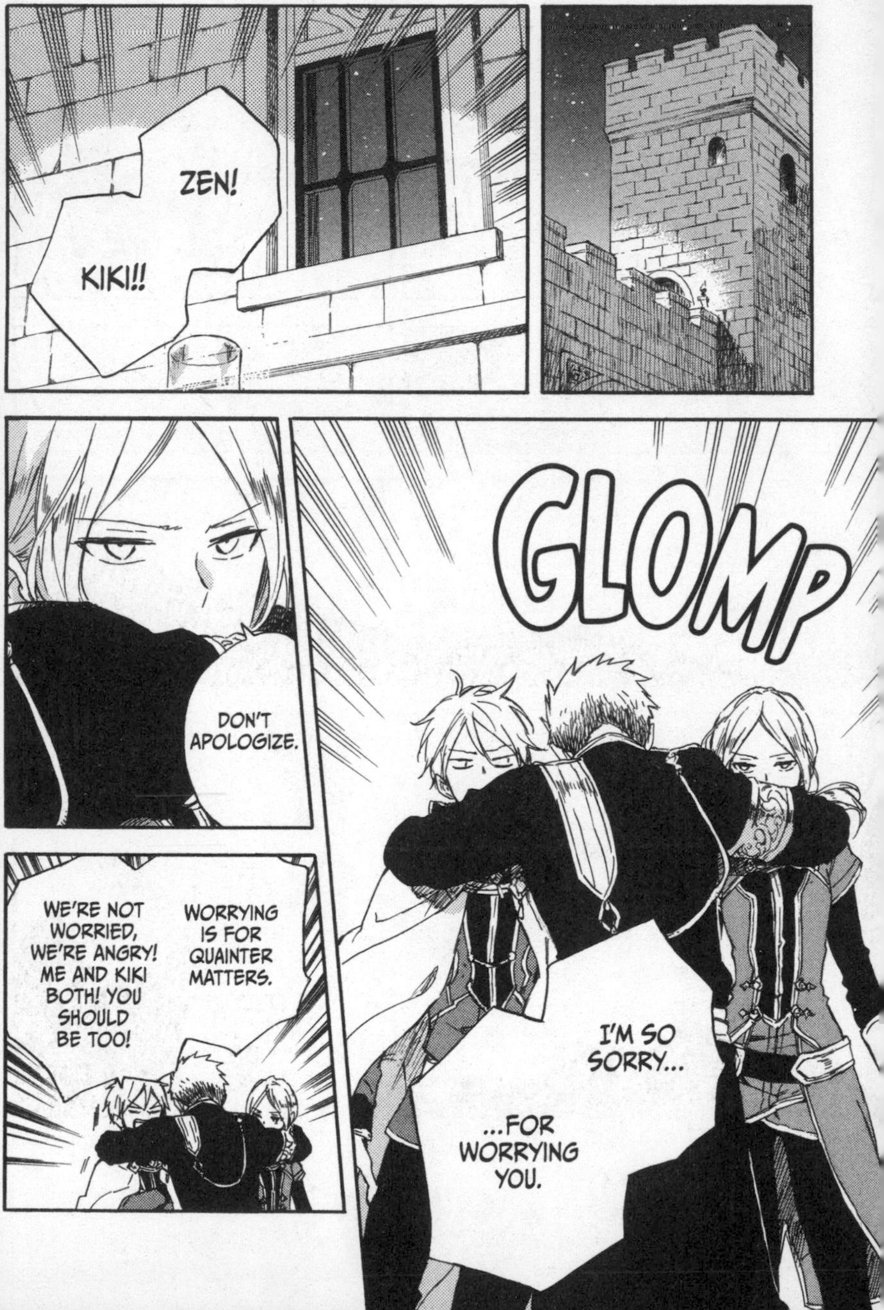
ZEN!
KIKI!!
GLOMP
I'M SO SORRY...
...FOR WORRYING YOU.
DON'T APOLOGIZE.
WORRYING IS FOR QUAINTER MATTERS.
WE'RE NOT WORRIED, WE'RE ANGRY! ME AND KIKI BOTH! YOU SHOULD BE TOO!

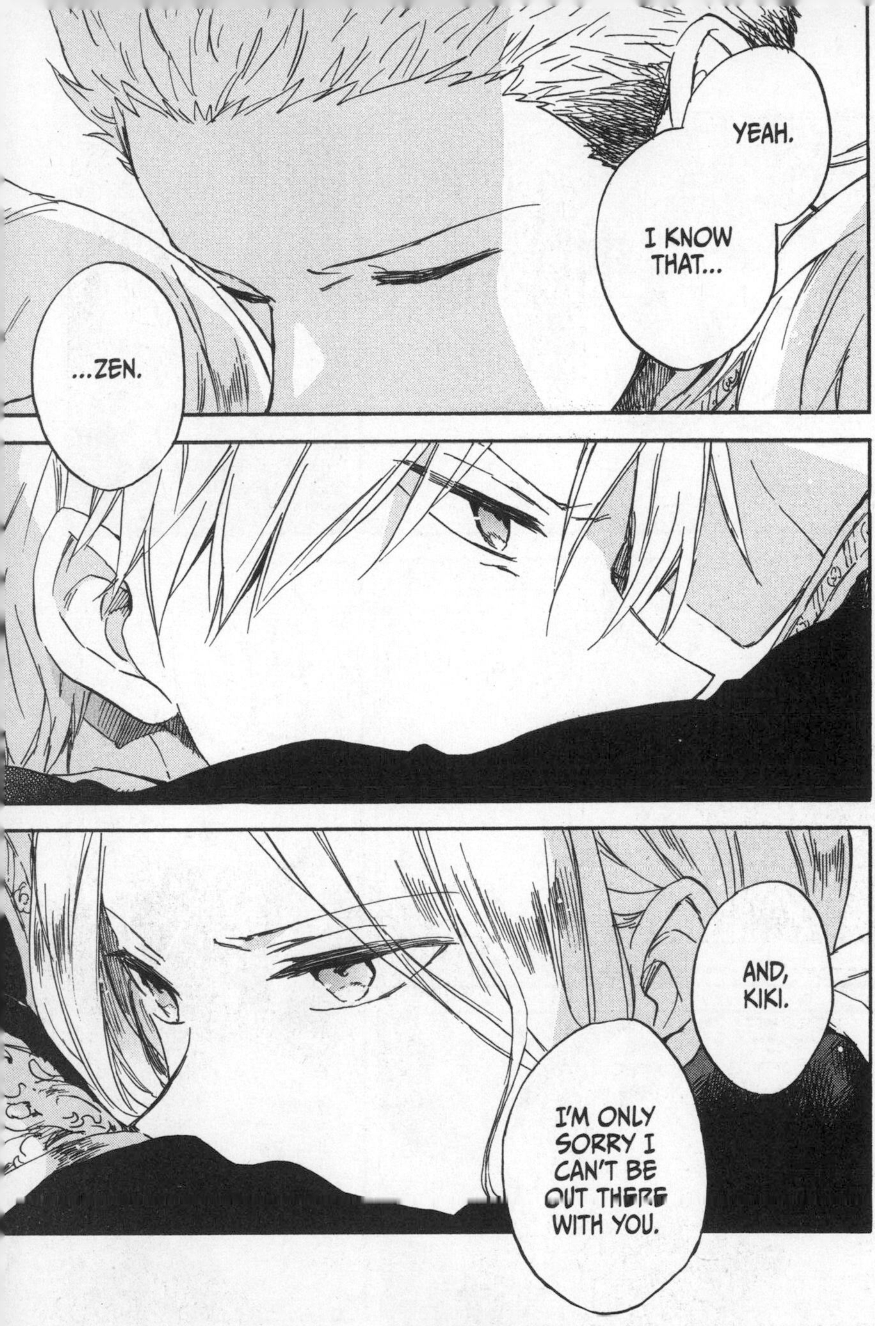
YEAH.
I KNOW THAT...
...ZEN.
AND, KIKI.
I'M ONLY SORRY I CAN'T BE OUT THERE WITH YOU.

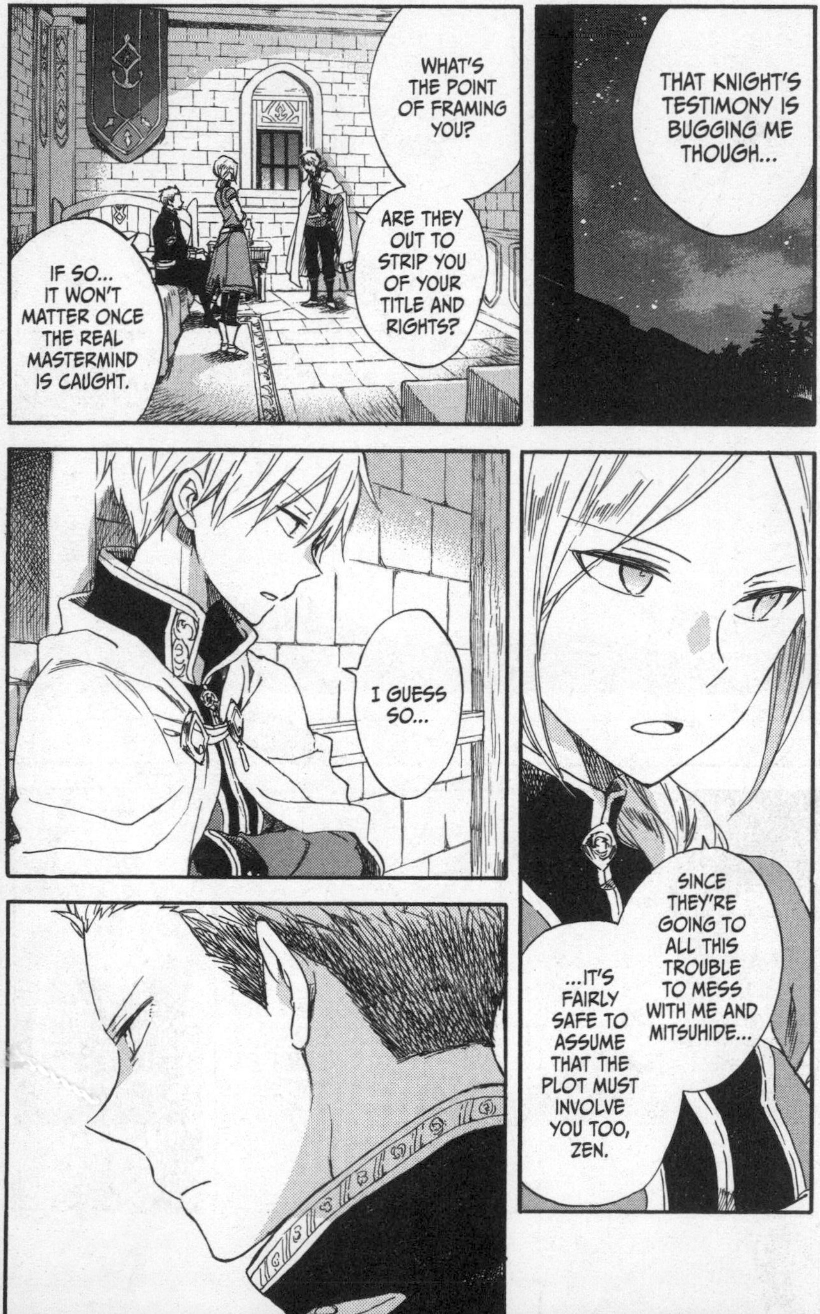
THAT KNIGHT'S TESTIMONY IS BUGGING ME THOUGH...
WHAT'S THE POINT OF FRAMING YOU?
ARE THEY OUT TO STRIP YOU OF YOUR TITLE AND RIGHTS?
IF SO... IT WON'T MATTER ONCE THE REAL MASTERMIND IS CAUGHT.
SINCE THEY'RE GOING TO ALL THIS TROUBLE TO MESS WITH ME AND MITSUHIDE...
...IT'S FAIRLY SAFE TO ASSUME THAT THE PLOT MUST INVOLVE YOU TOO, ZEN.
I GUESS SO...

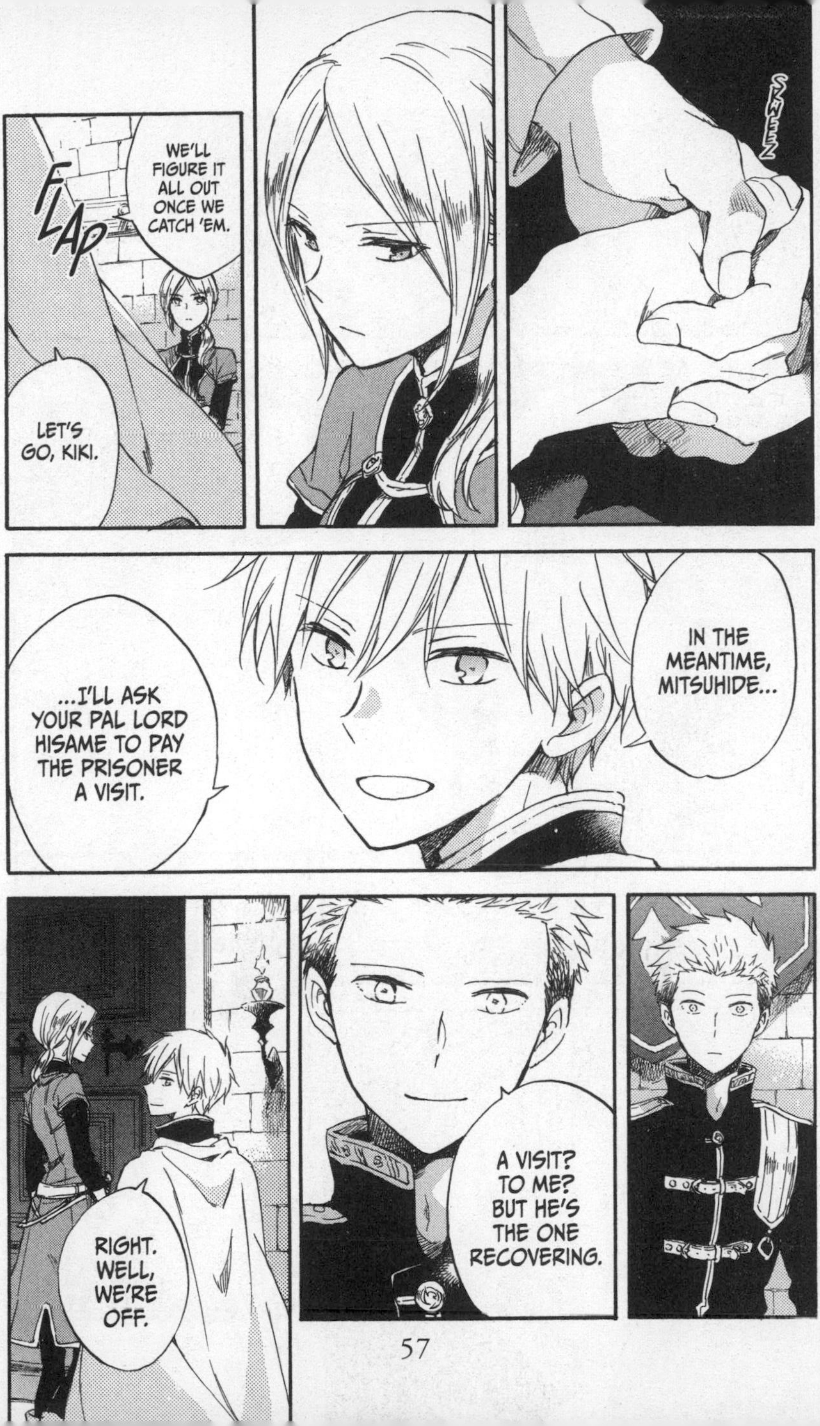
SKWEEZ
WE'LL FIGURE IT ALL OUT ONCE WE CATCH 'EM.
FLAP
LET'S GO, KIKI.
IN THE MEANTIME, MITSUHIDE...
...I'LL ASK YOUR PAL LORD HISAME TO PAY THE PRISONER A VISIT.
A VISIT? TO ME? BUT HE'S THE ONE RECOVERING.
RIGHT. WELL, WE'RE OFF.

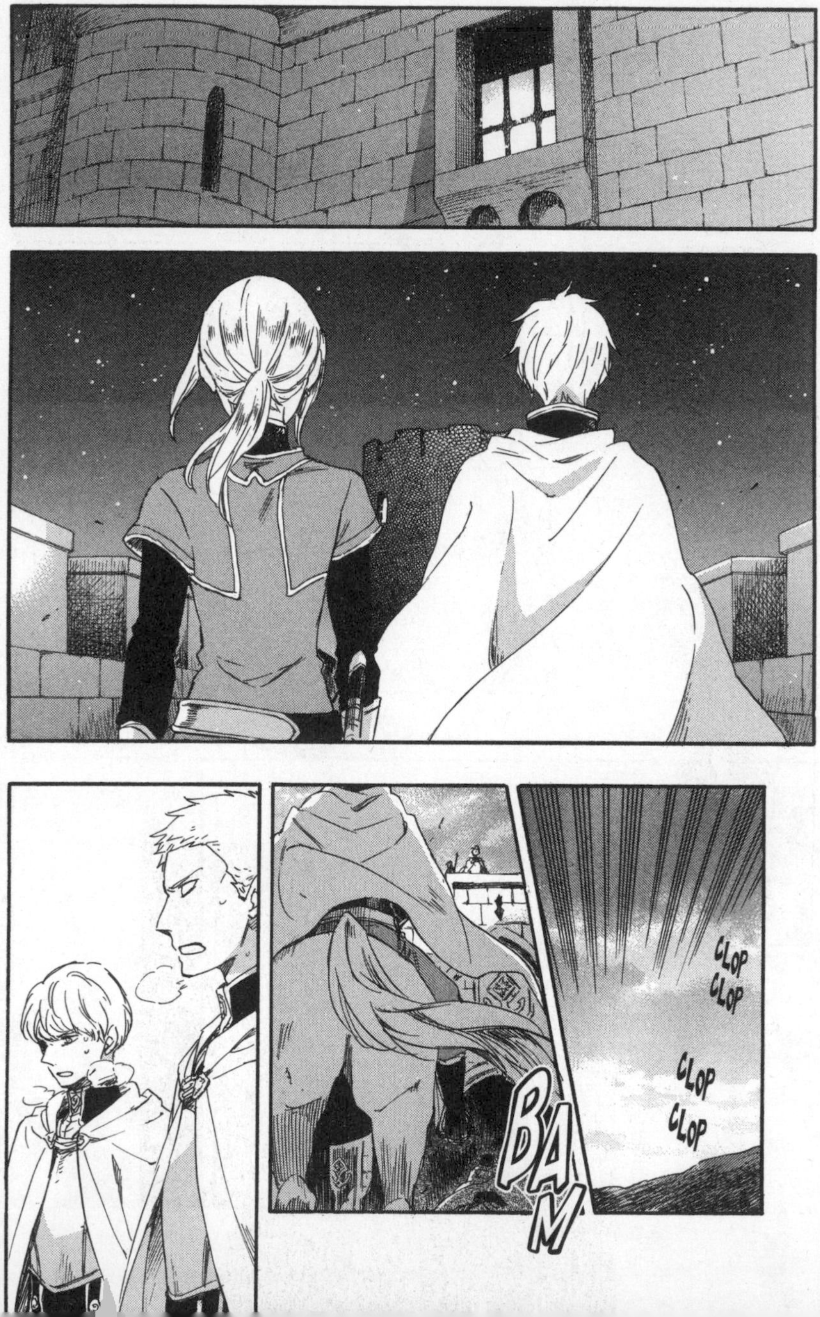
CLOP CLOP
CLOP CLOP
BAM

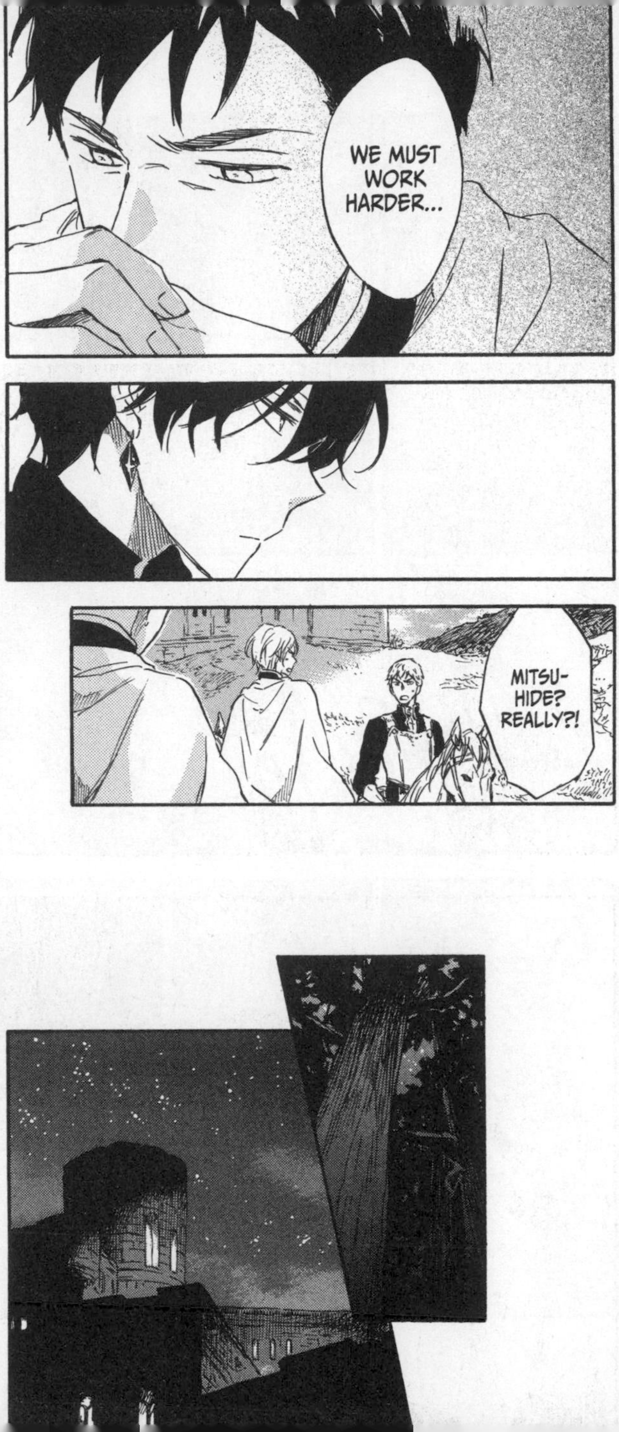
WE MUST WORK HARDER...
MITSU-HIDE? REALLY?!

2

Rata Forzeno at age 20

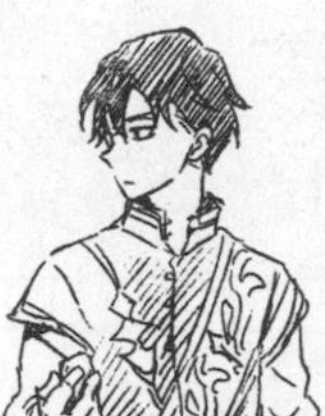

I'm quitting this knight gig.

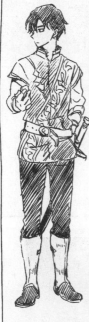

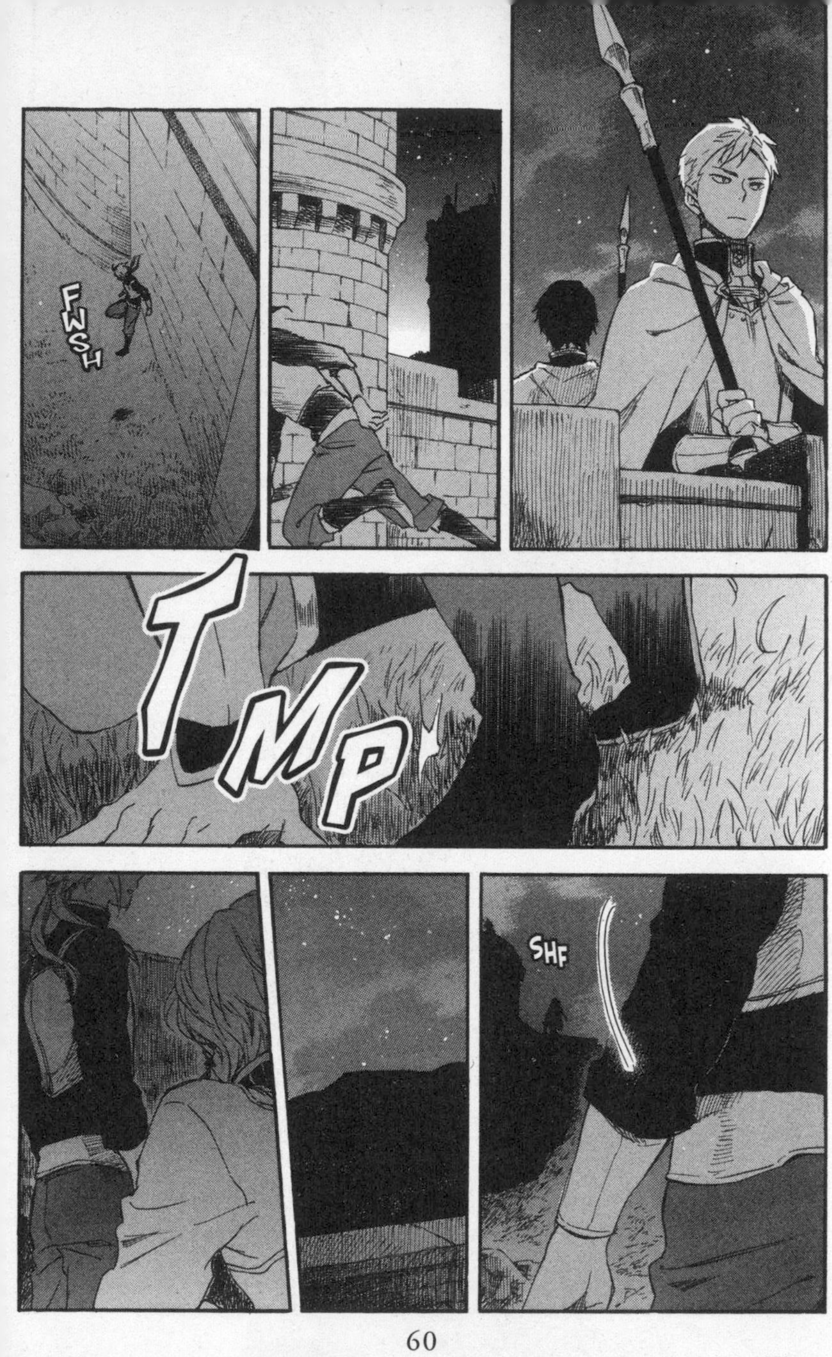
FWSH
TMP
SHF

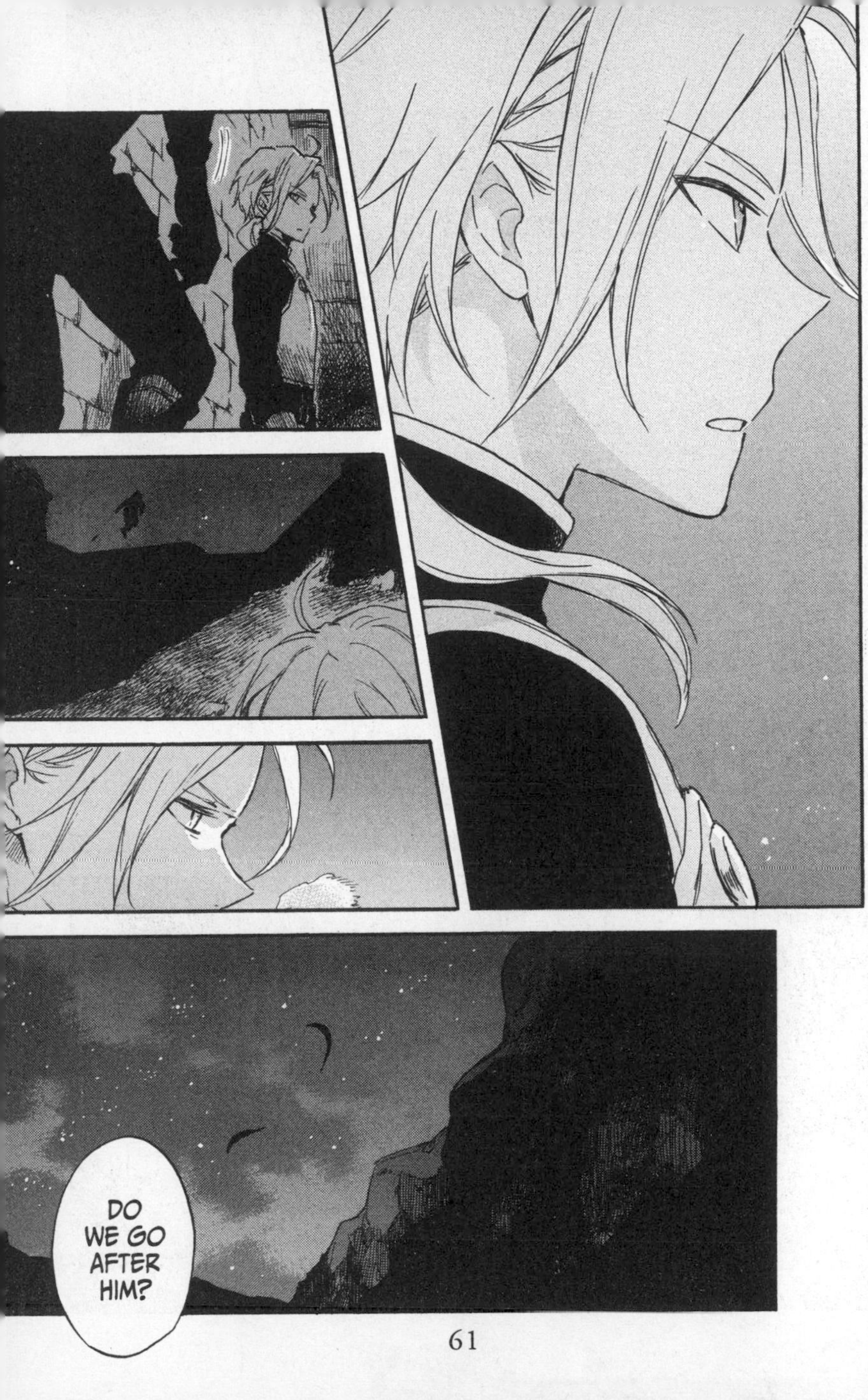
DO WE GO AFTER HIM?

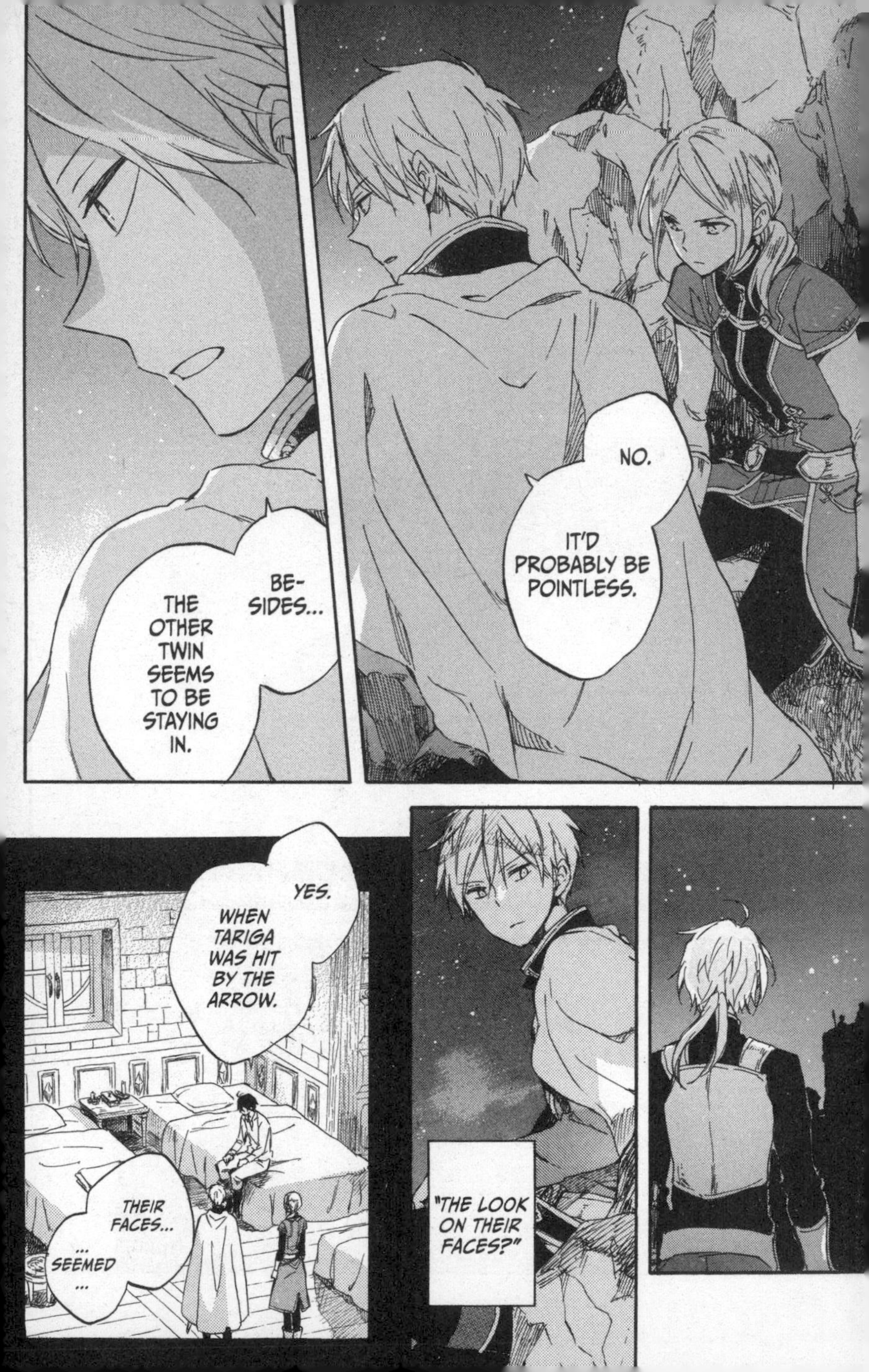
NO.
IT'D PROBABLY BE POINTLESS.
BE-SIDES...
THE OTHER TWIN SEEMS TO BE STAYING IN.
"THE LOOK ON THEIR FACES?"
YES.
WHEN TARIGA WAS HIT BY THE ARROW.
THEIR FACES...
...SEEMED ...

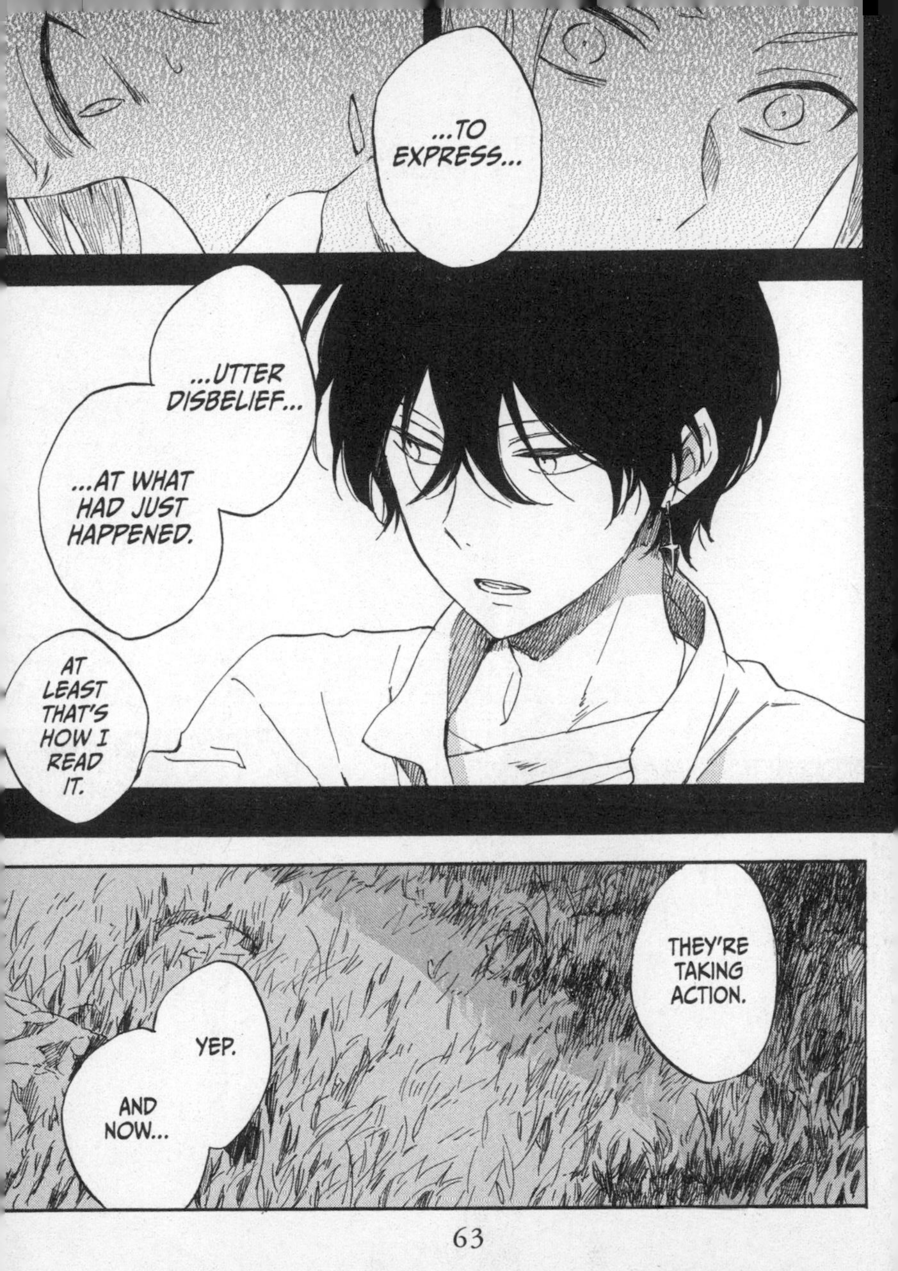
...TO EXPRESS...
...UTTER DISBELIEF...
...AT WHAT HAD JUST HAPPENED.
AT LEAST THAT'S HOW I READ IT.
THEY'RE TAKING ACTION.
YEP.
AND NOW...

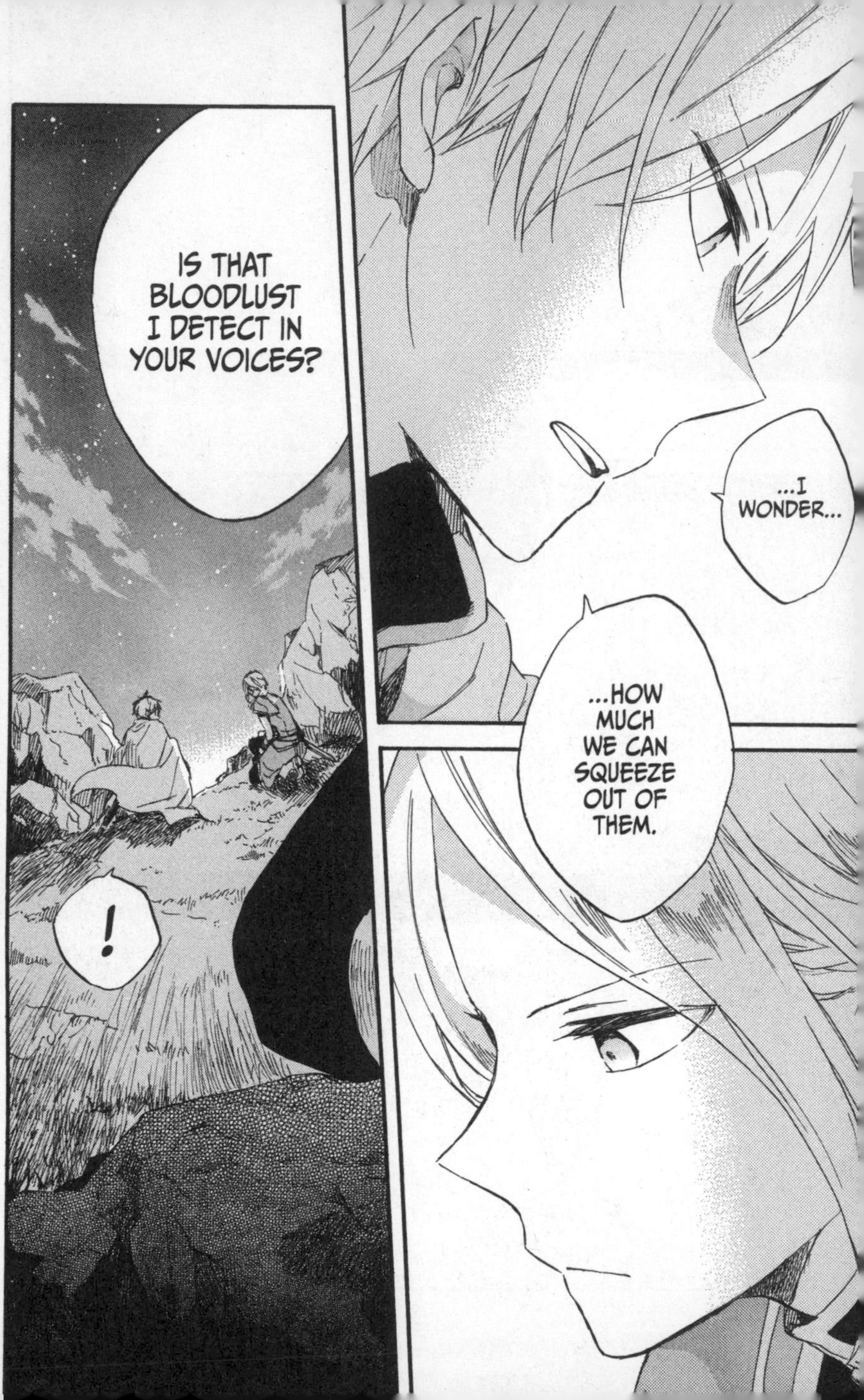
...I WONDER...
...HOW MUCH WE CAN SQUEEZE OUT OF THEM.
IS THAT BLOODLUST I DETECT IN YOUR VOICES?
!

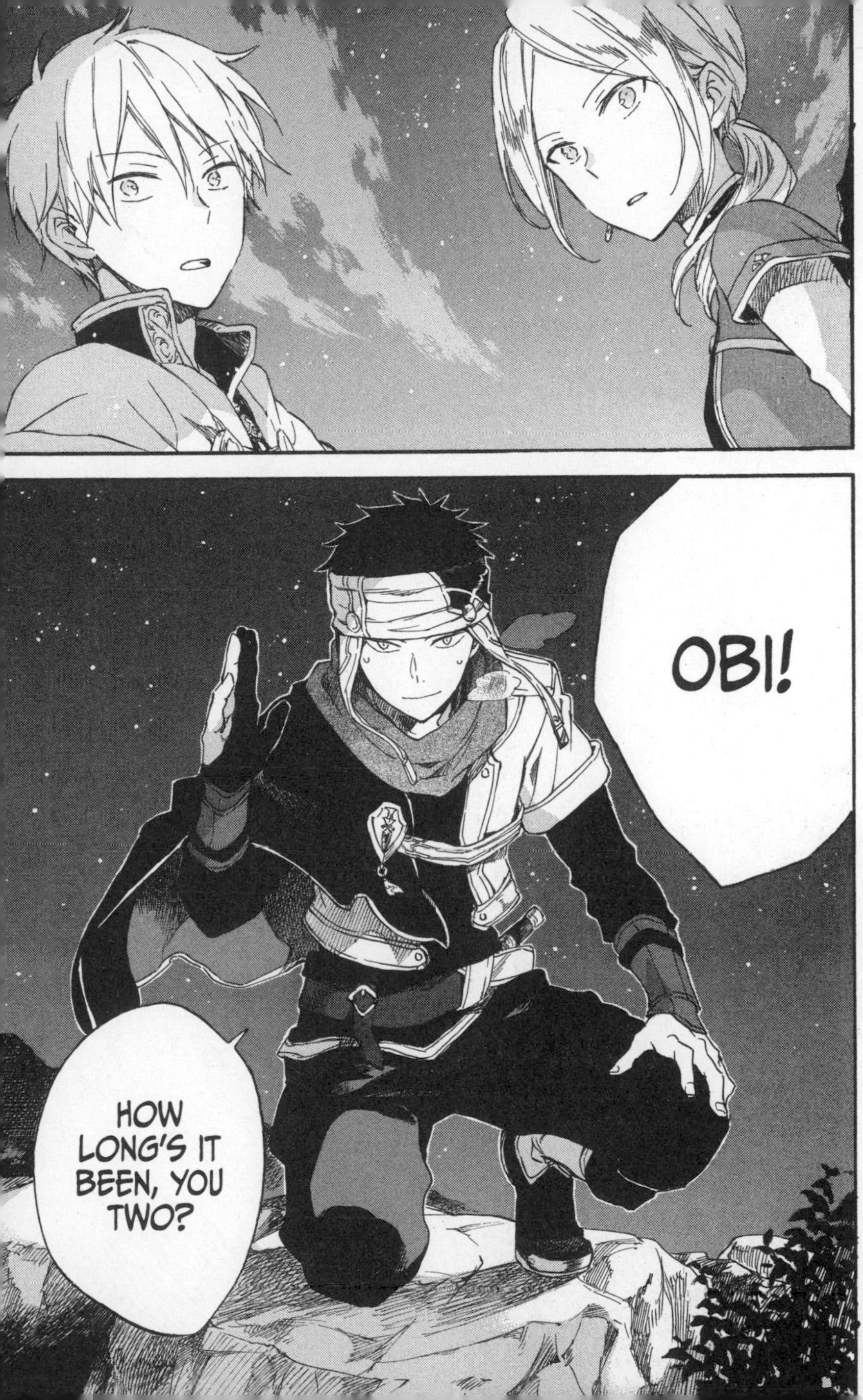
OBI!
HOW LONG'S IT BEEN, YOU TWO?

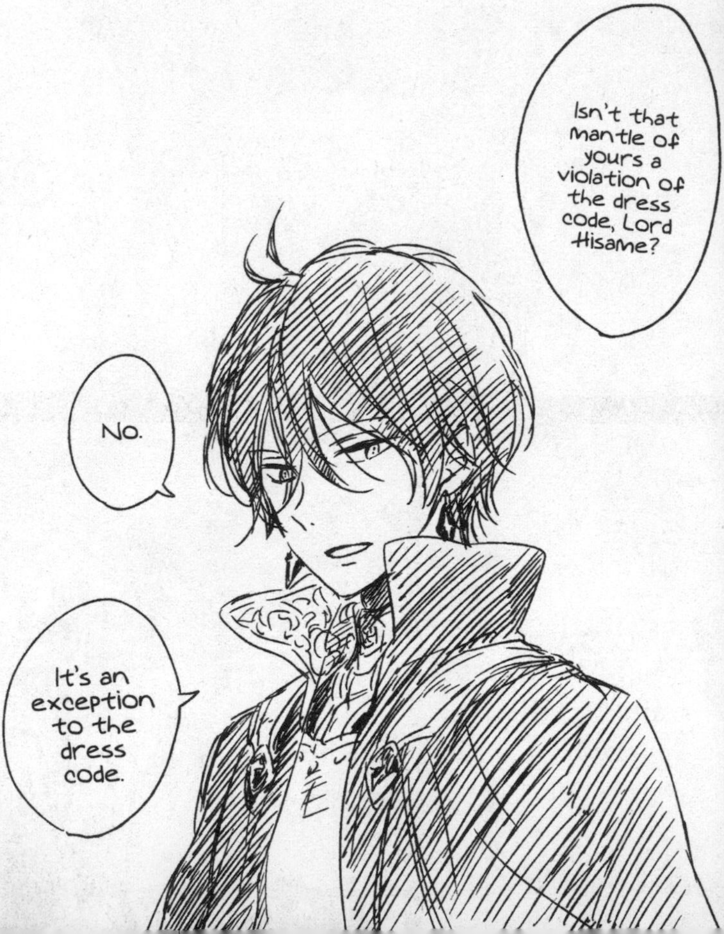
Isn't that mantle of yours a violation of the dress code, Lord Hisame?
No.
It's an exception to the dress code.

Chapter 80

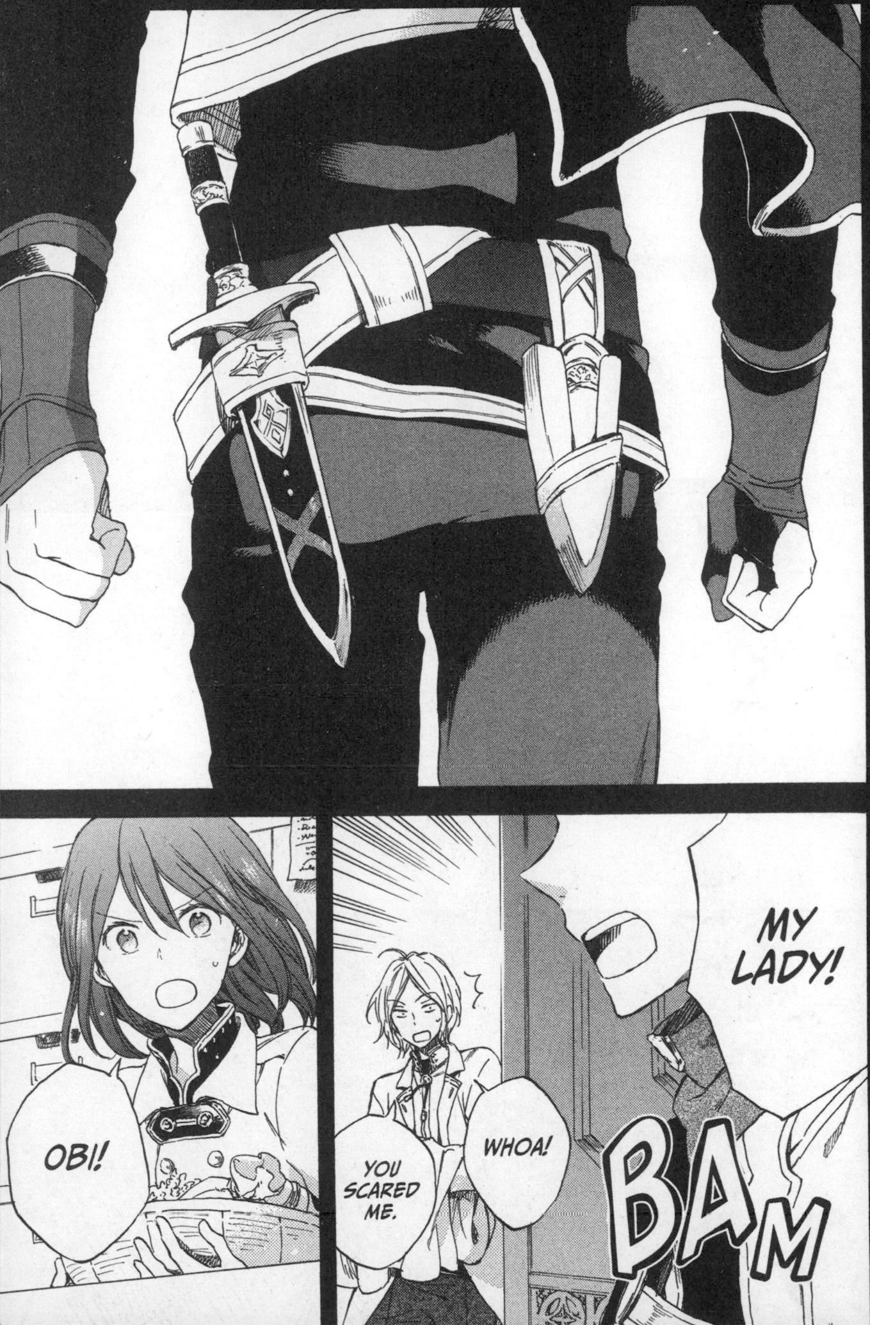
MY LADY!
BAM
WHOA!
YOU SCARED ME.
OBI!

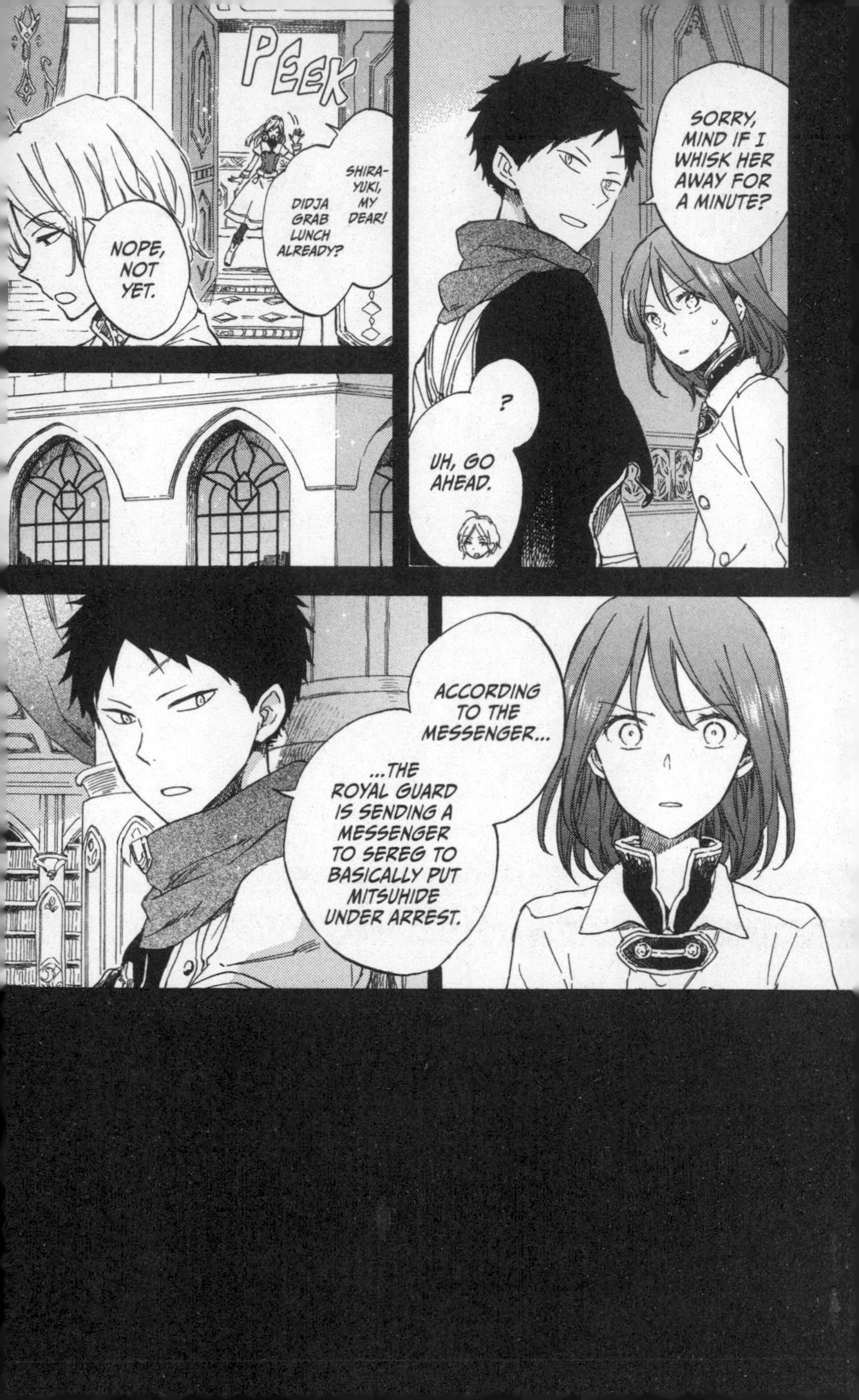
SORRY, MIND IF I WHISK HER AWAY FOR A MINUTE?
?
UH, GO AHEAD.
PEEK
SHIRA-YUKI, MY DEAR!
DIDJA GRAB LUNCH ALREADY?
NOPE, NOT YET.
ACCORDING TO THE MESSENGER...
...THE ROYAL GUARD IS SENDING A MESSENGER TO SEREG TO BASICALLY PUT MITSUHIDE UNDER ARREST.

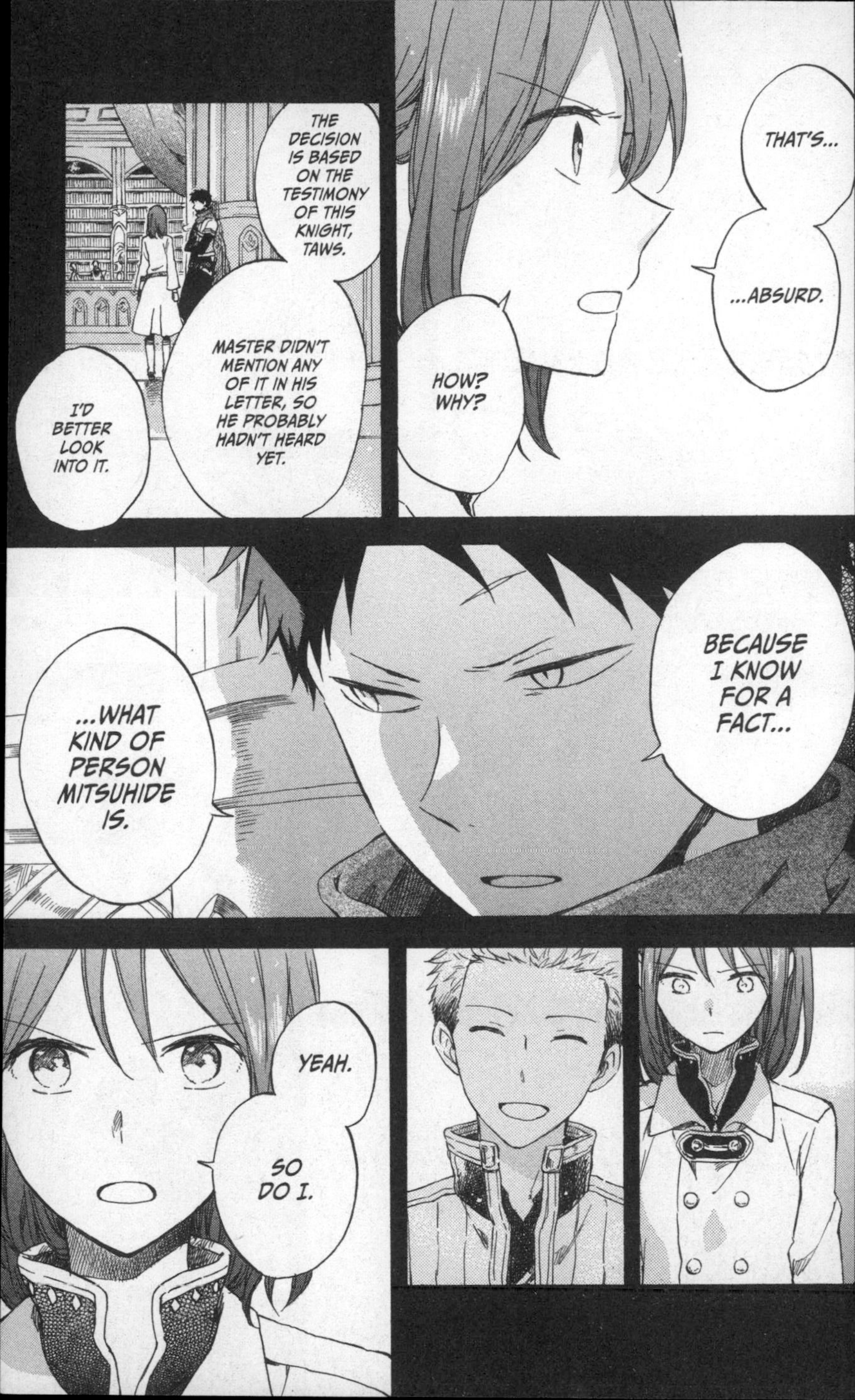
THAT'S...
...ABSURD.
HOW? WHY?
THE DECISION IS BASED ON THE TESTIMONY OF THIS KNIGHT, TAWS.
MASTER DIDN'T MENTION ANY OF IT IN HIS LETTER, SO HE PROBABLY HADN'T HEARD YET.
I'D BETTER LOOK INTO IT.
BECAUSE I KNOW FOR A FACT...
...WHAT KIND OF PERSON MITSUHIDE IS.
YEAH.
SO DO I.

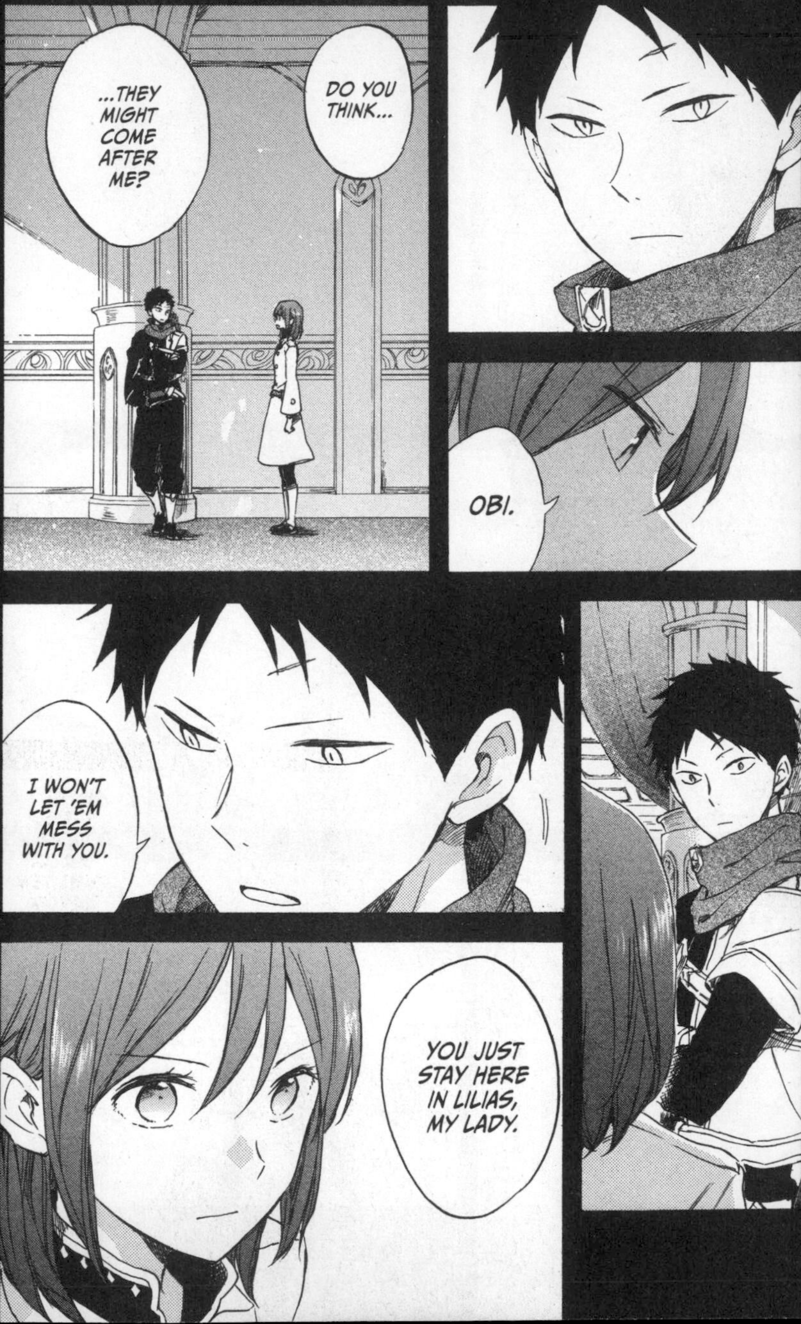
OBI.
DO YOU THINK...
...THEY MIGHT COME AFTER ME?
I WON'T LET 'EM MESS WITH YOU.
YOU JUST STAY HERE IN LILIAS, MY LADY.

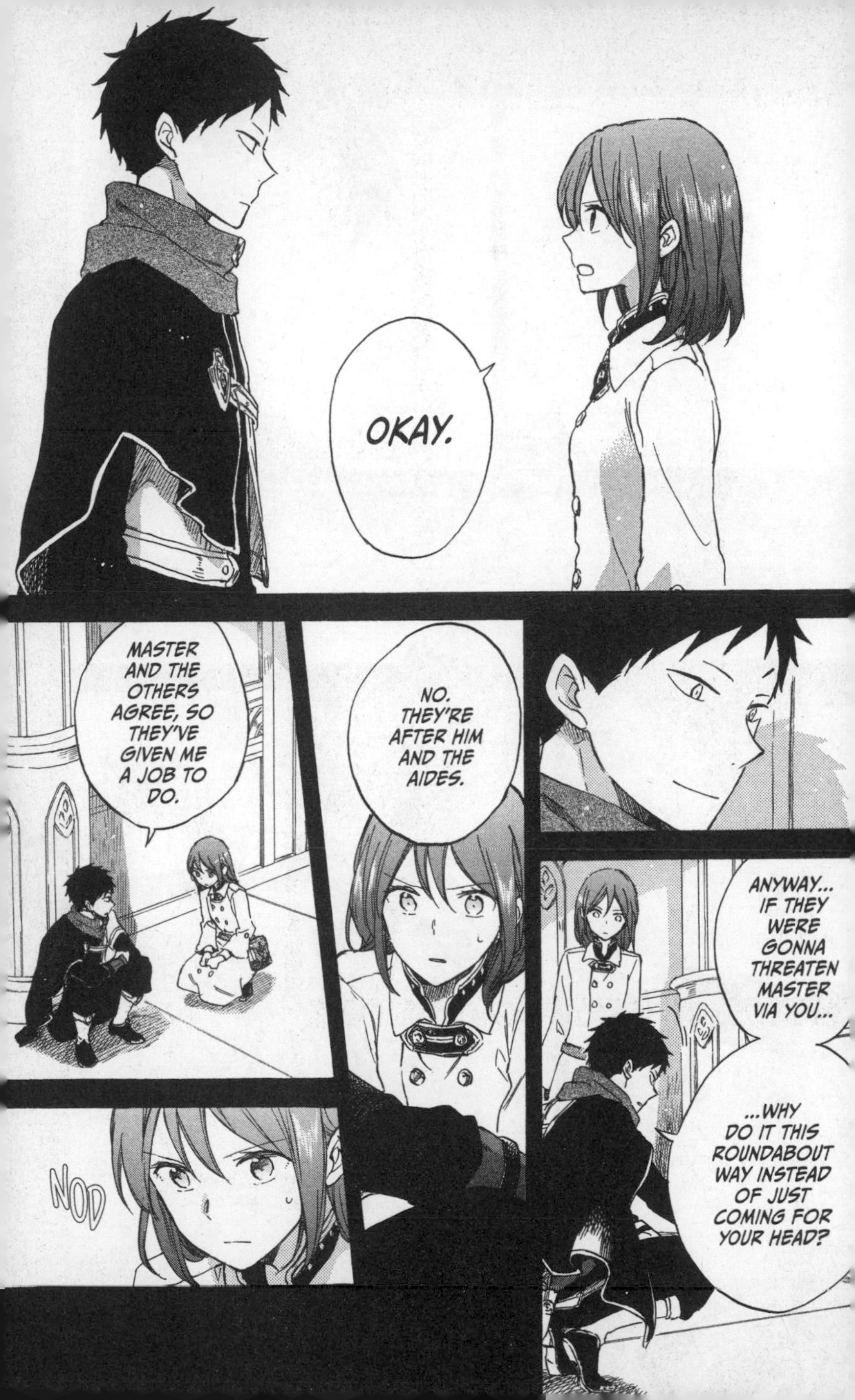
OKAY.
NO. THEY'RE AFTER HIM AND THE AIDES.
MASTER AND THE OTHERS AGREE, SO THEY'VE GIVEN ME A JOB TO DO.
ANYWAY... IF THEY WERE GONNA THREATEN MASTER VIA YOU...
...WHY DO IT THIS ROUNDABOUT WAY INSTEAD OF JUST COMING FOR YOUR HEAD?
NOD

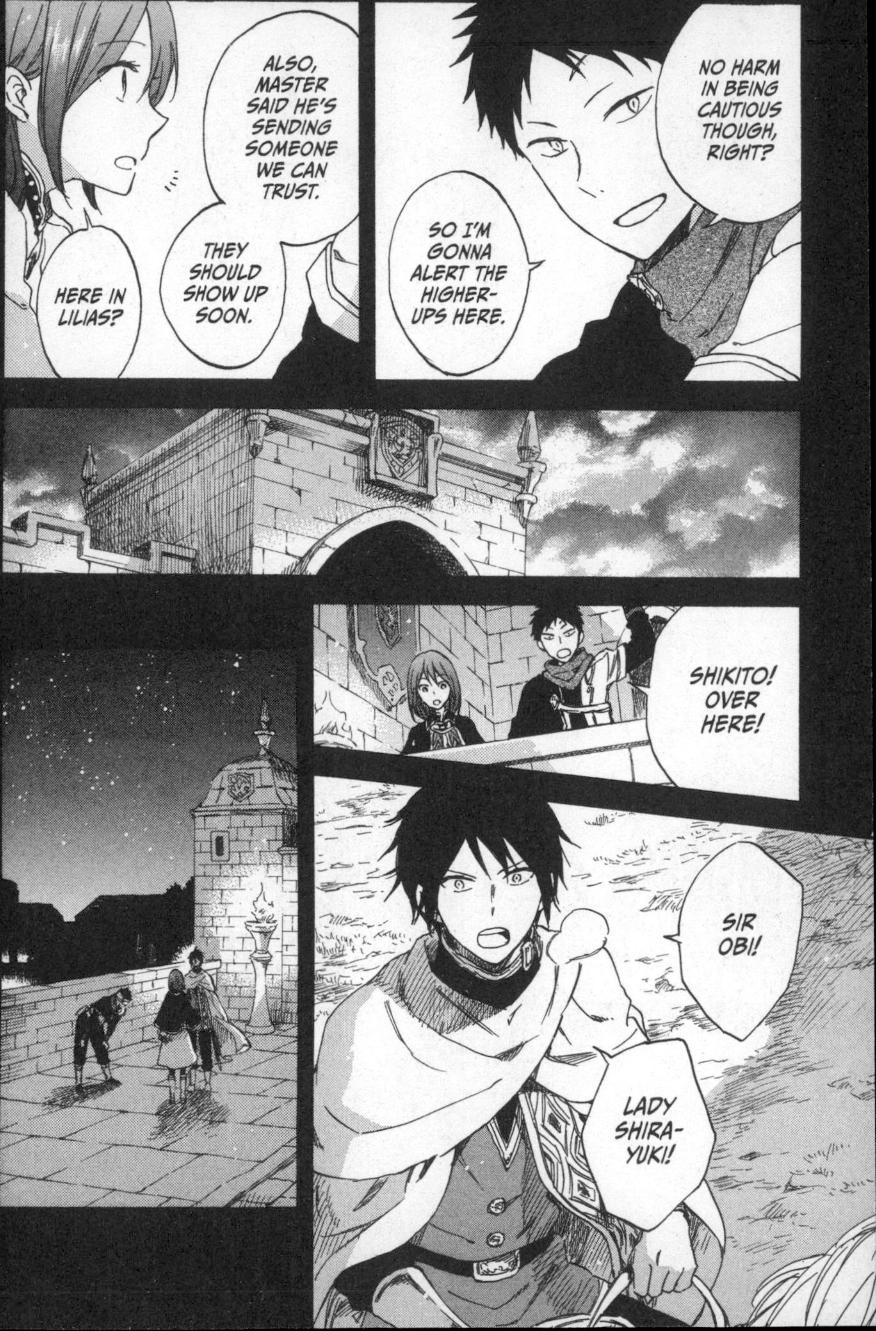
NO HARM IN BEING CAUTIOUS THOUGH, RIGHT?
SO I'M GONNA ALERT THE HIGHER-UPS HERE.
ALSO, MASTER SAID HE'S SENDING SOMEONE WE CAN TRUST.
THEY SHOULD SHOW UP SOON.
HERE IN LILIAS?
SHIKITO! OVER HERE!
SIR OBI!
LADY SHIRA-YUKI!

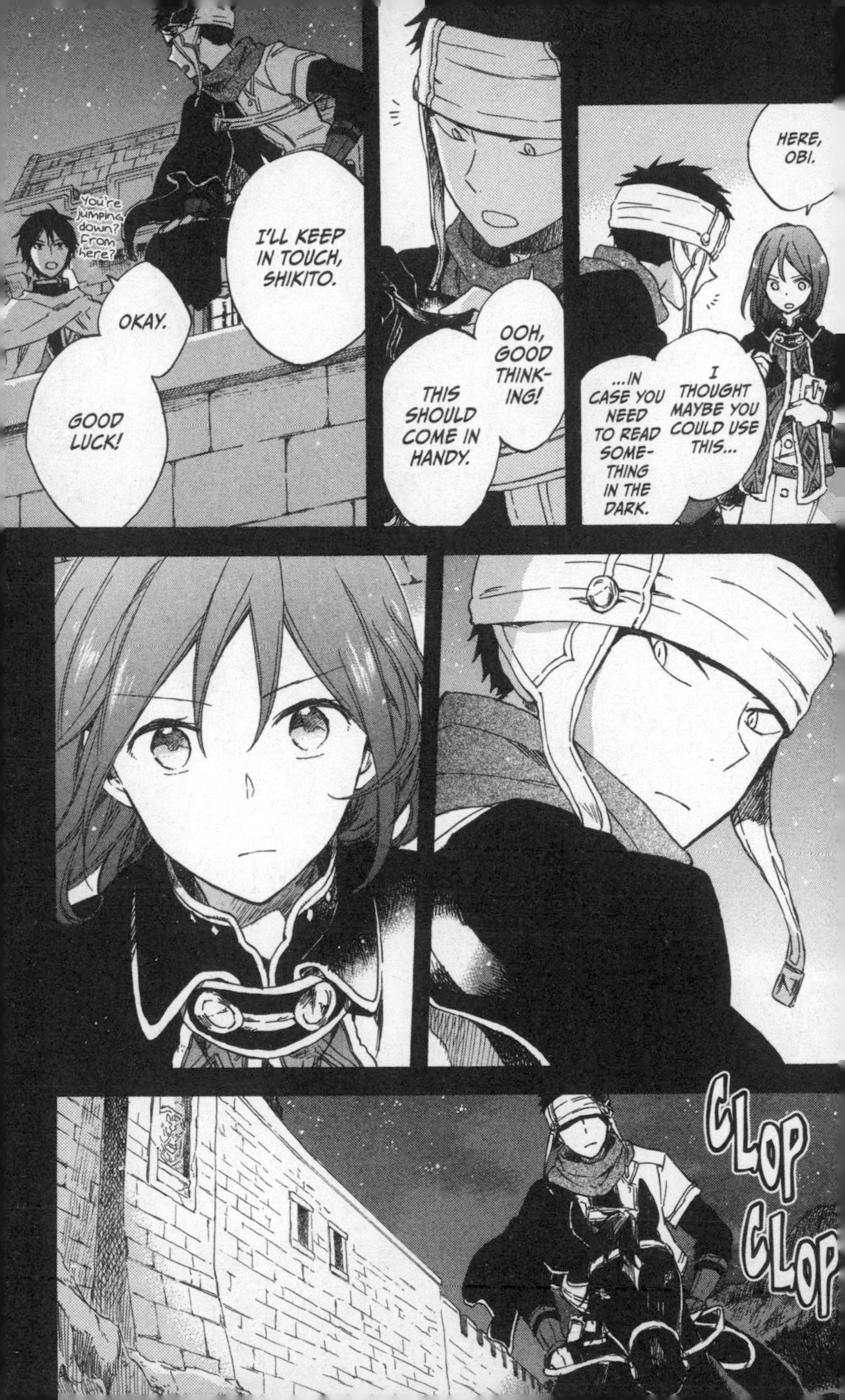
HERE, OBI.
I THOUGHT MAYBE YOU COULD USE THIS...
...IN CASE YOU NEED TO READ SOME-THING IN THE DARK.
OOH, GOOD THINK-ING!
THIS SHOULD COME IN HANDY.
I'LL KEEP IN TOUCH, SHIKITO.
You're jumping down? From here?
OKAY.
GOOD LUCK!
CLOP
CLOP

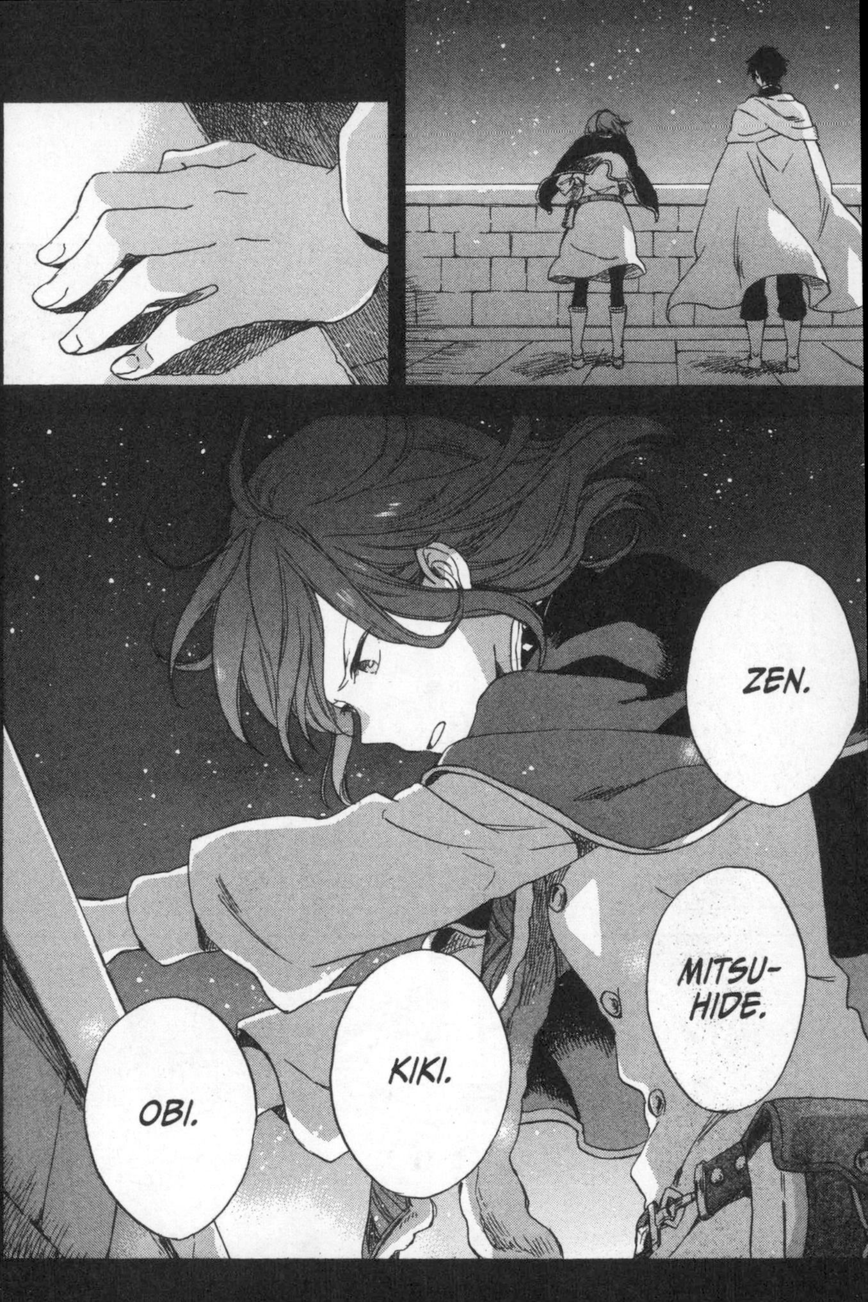
ZEN.
MITSU-HIDE.
KIKI.
OBI.

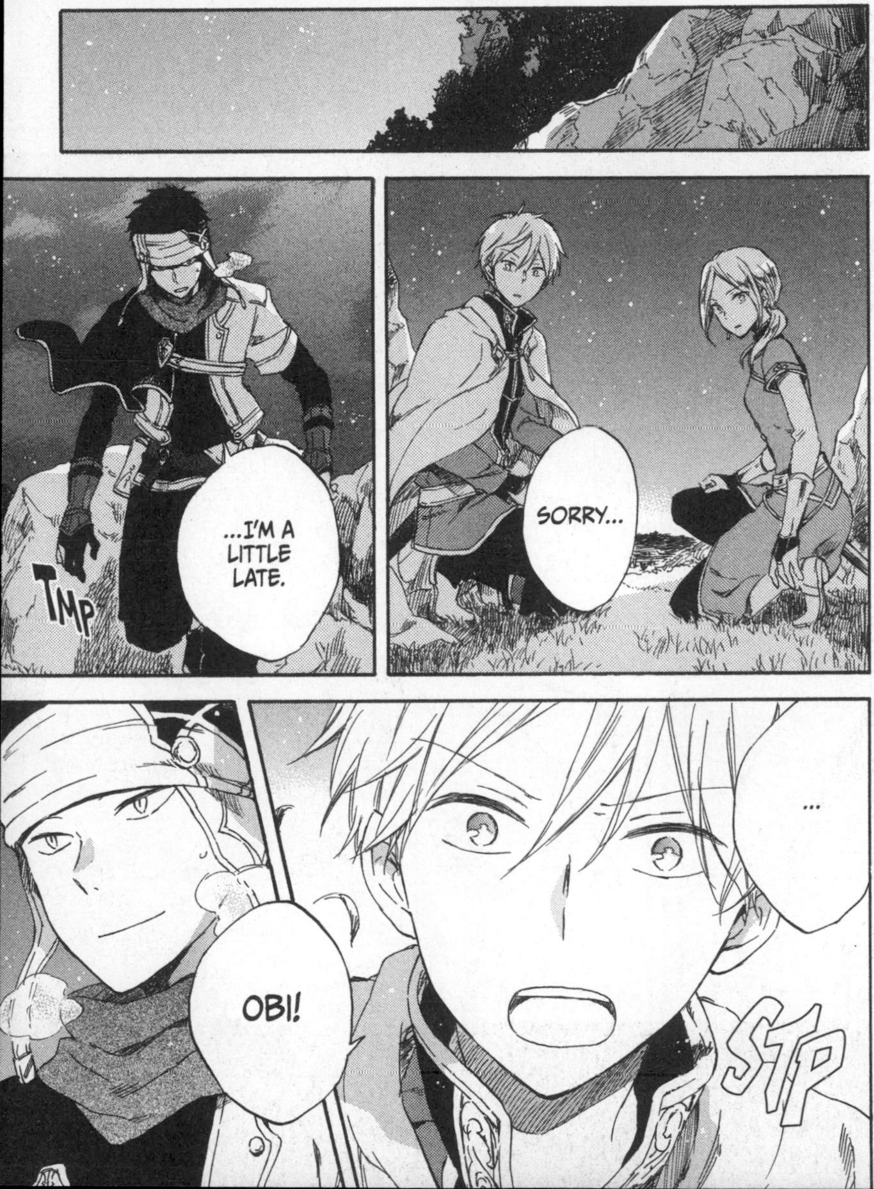
SORRY...
...I'M A LITTLE LATE.
TMP
...
STP
OBI!

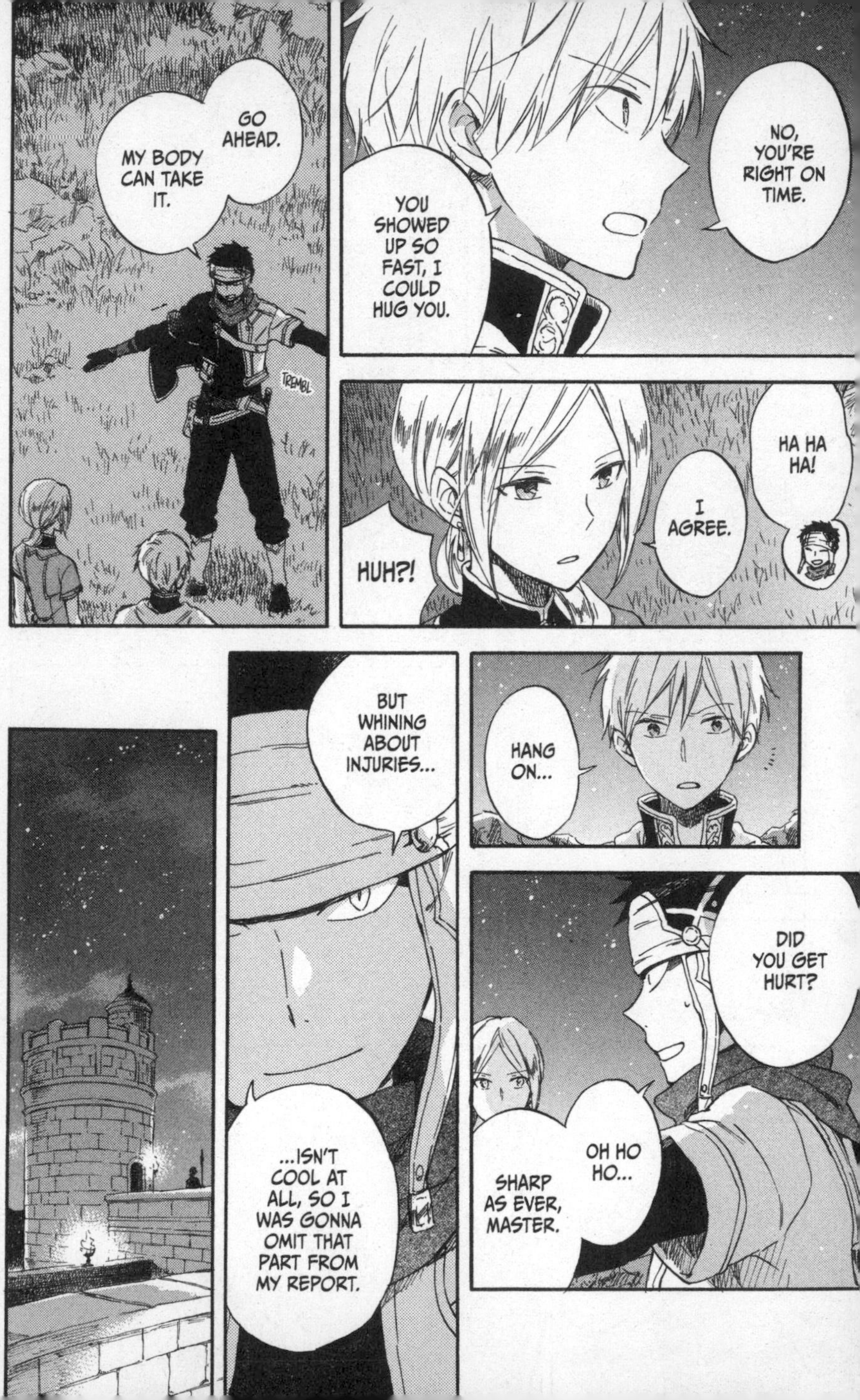
NO, YOU'RE RIGHT ON TIME.
YOU SHOWED UP SO FAST, I COULD HUG YOU.
HA HA HA!
I AGREE.
HUH?!
GO AHEAD.
MY BODY CAN TAKE IT.
TREMBL
HANG ON...
DID YOU GET HURT?
OH HO HO...
SHARP AS EVER, MASTER.
BUT WHINING ABOUT INJURIES...
...ISN'T COOL AT ALL, SO I WAS GONNA OMIT THAT PART FROM MY REPORT.

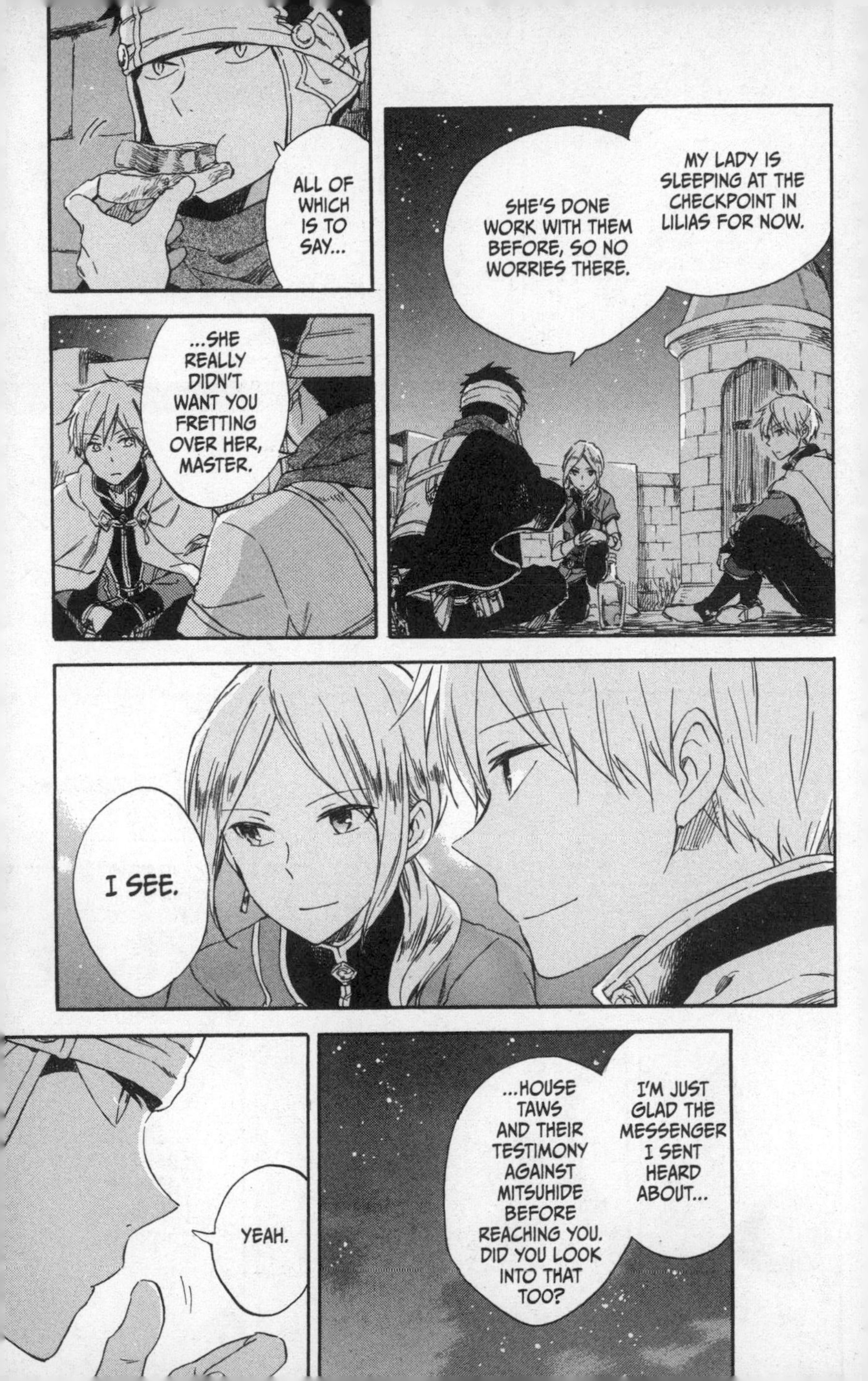
MY LADY IS SLEEPING AT THE CHECKPOINT IN LILIAS FOR NOW.
SHE'S DONE WORK WITH THEM BEFORE, SO NO WORRIES THERE.
ALL OF WHICH IS TO SAY...
...SHE REALLY DIDN'T WANT YOU FRETTING OVER HER, MASTER.
I SEE.
I'M JUST GLAD THE MESSENGER I SENT HEARD ABOUT...
...HOUSE TAWS AND THEIR TESTIMONY AGAINST MITSUHIDE BEFORE REACHING YOU. DID YOU LOOK INTO THAT TOO?
YEAH.

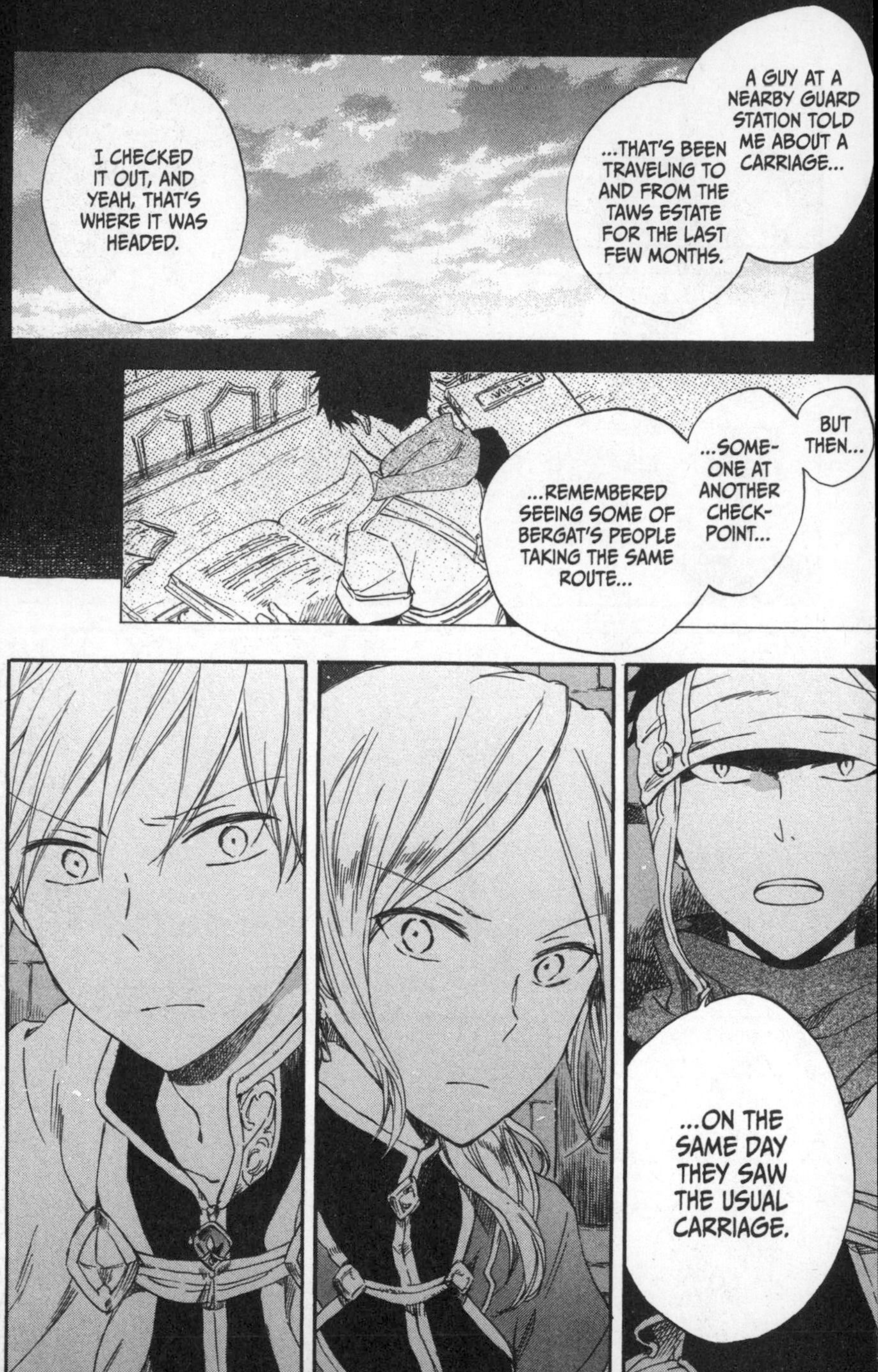
A GUY AT A NEARBY GUARD STATION TOLD ME ABOUT A CARRIAGE...
...THAT'S BEEN TRAVELING TO AND FROM THE TAWS ESTATE FOR THE LAST FEW MONTHS.
I CHECKED IT OUT, AND YEAH, THAT'S WHERE IT WAS HEADED.
BUT THEN...
...SOME-ONE AT ANOTHER CHECK-POINT...
...REMEMBERED SEEING SOME OF BERGAT'S PEOPLE TAKING THE SAME ROUTE...
...ON THE SAME DAY THEY SAW THE USUAL CARRIAGE.

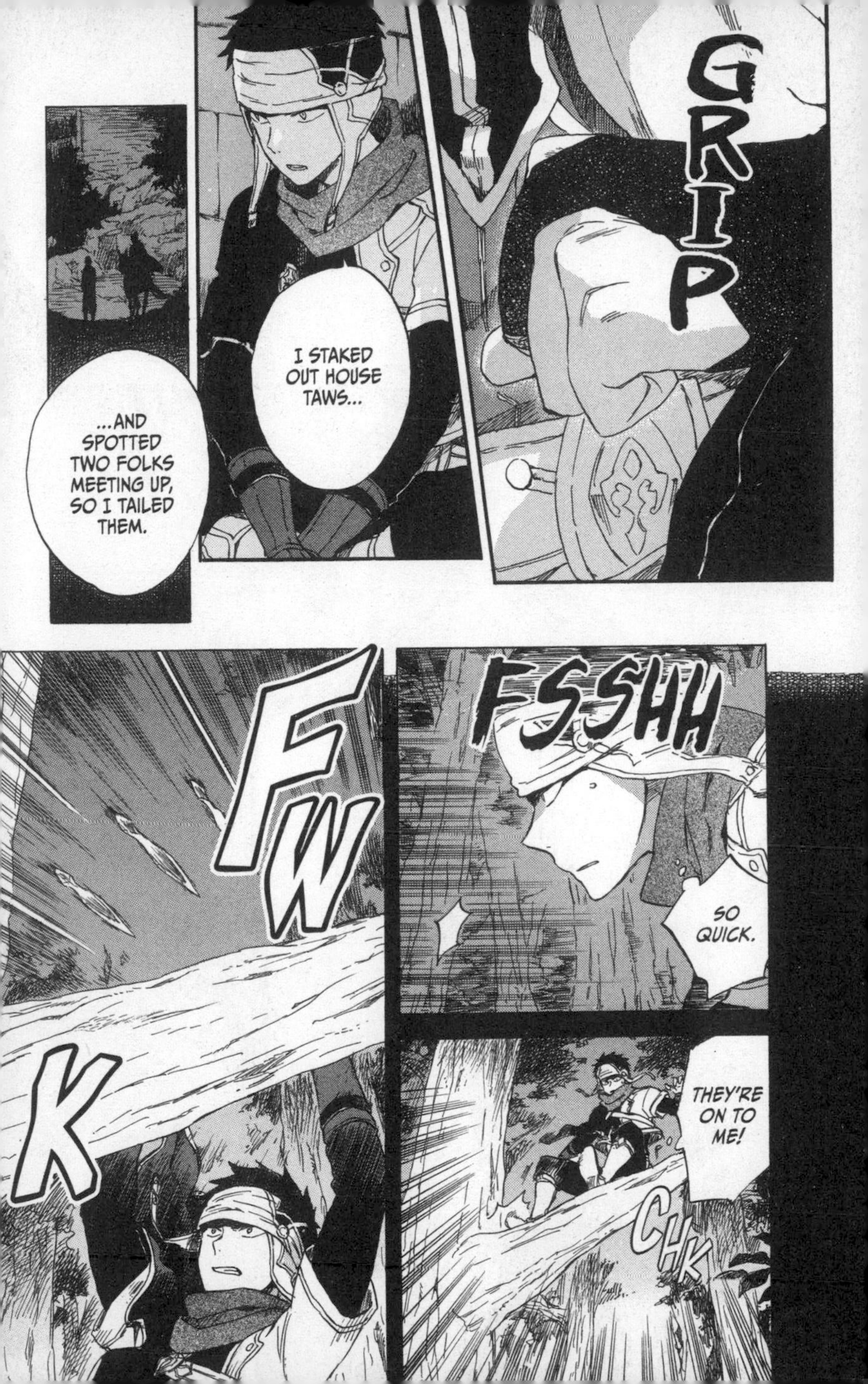
GRIP
I STAKED OUT HOUSE TAWS...
...AND SPOTTED TWO FOLKS MEETING UP, SO I TAILED THEM.
FSSHH
SO QUICK.
THEY'RE ON TO ME!
CHK
FWK

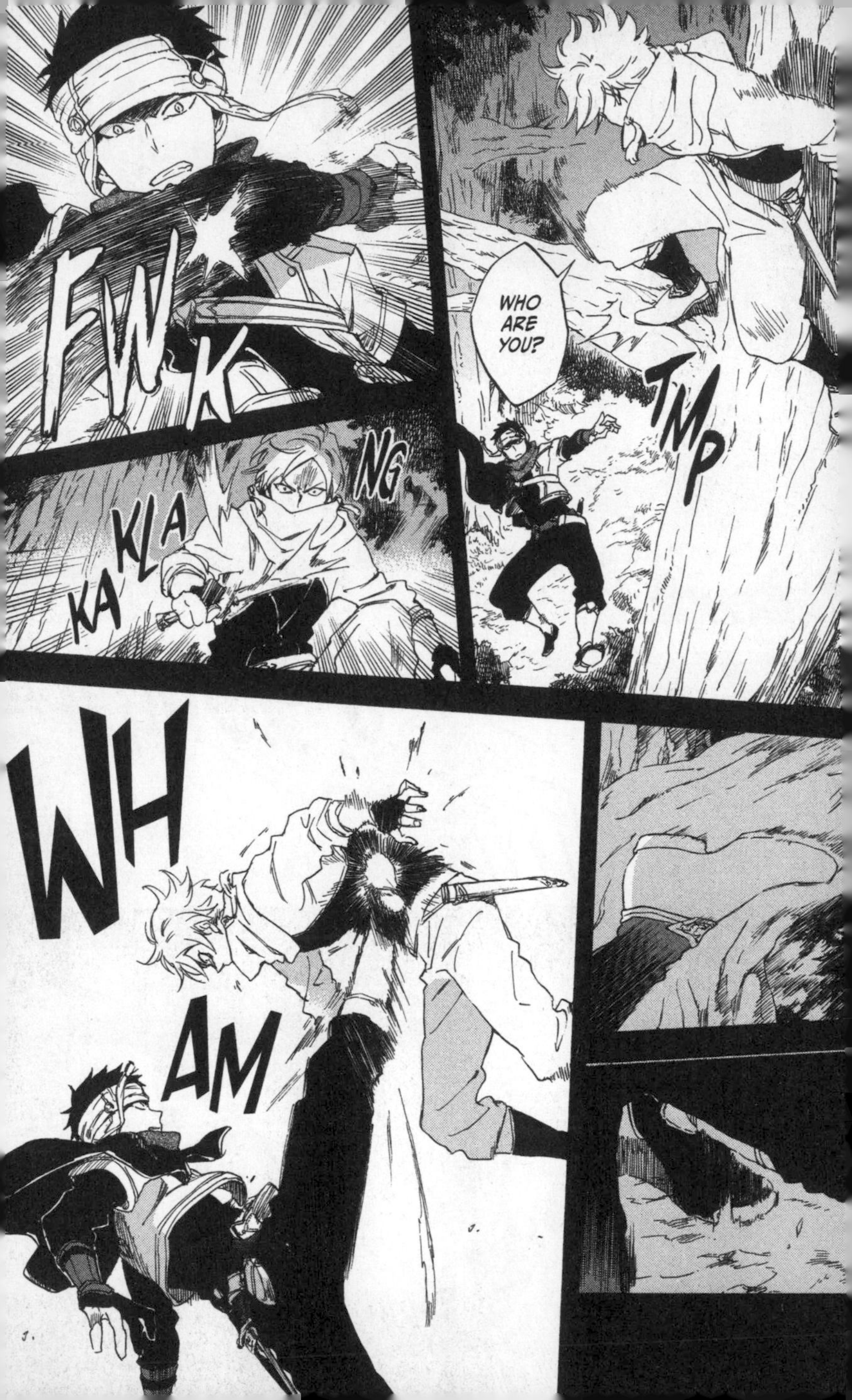
WHO ARE YOU?
TMP
FWK
KAKLANG
WHAM

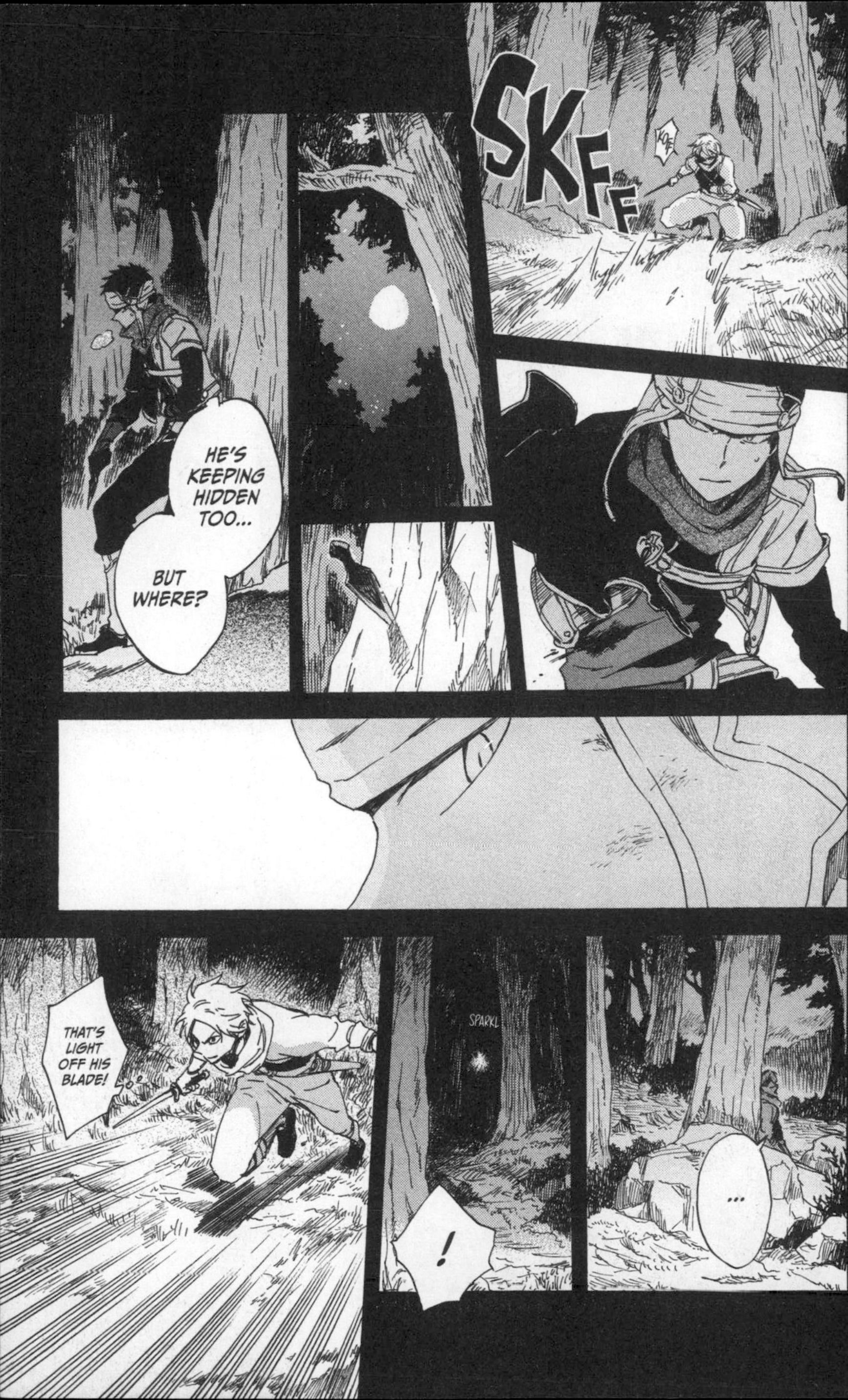
KOFF
SKFF
HE'S KEEPING HIDDEN TOO...
BUT WHERE?
...
SPARKL
!
THAT'S LIGHT OFF HIS BLADE!

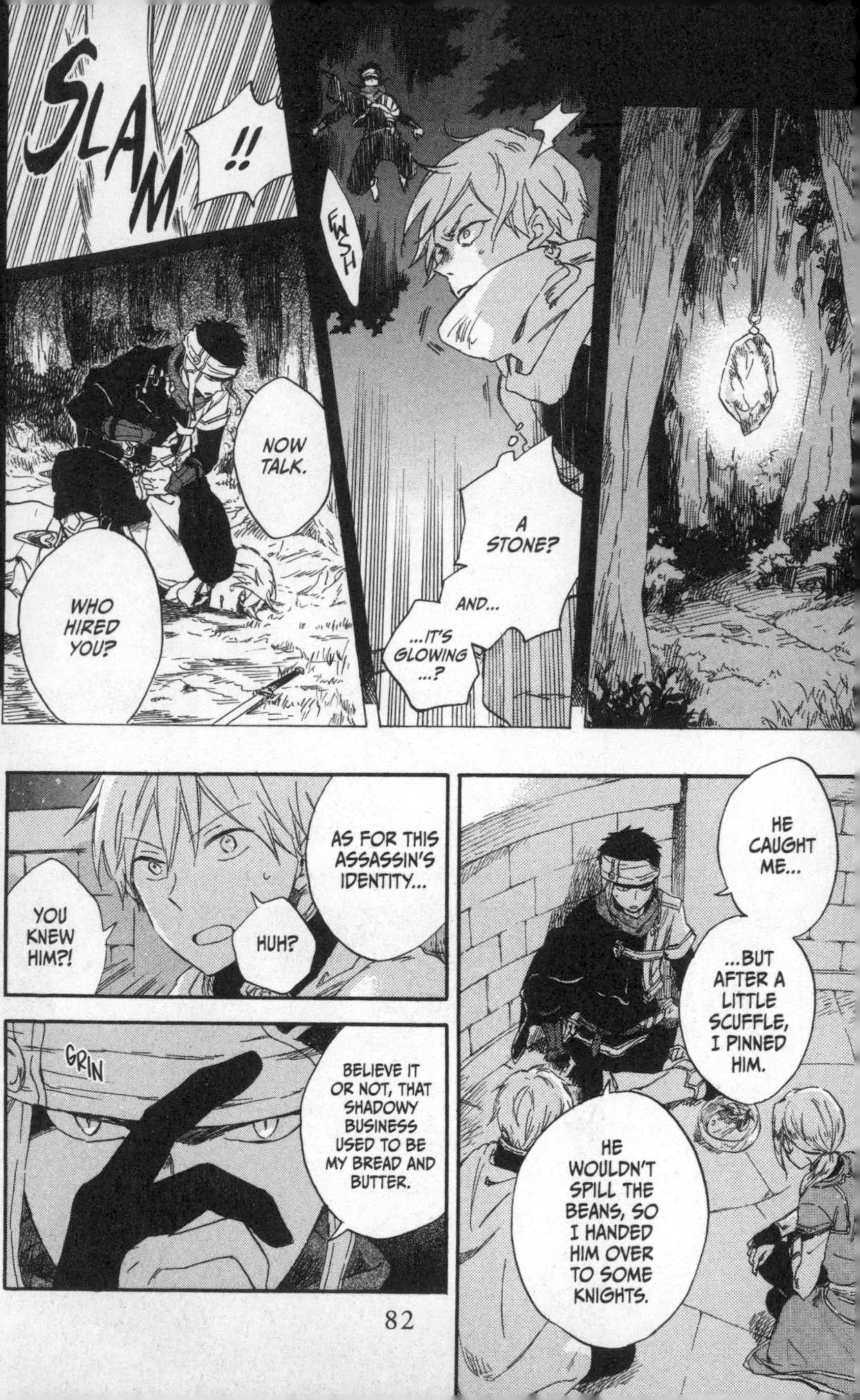
FWSH
A STONE?
AND...
...IT'S GLOWING...?
SLAM
!!
NOW TALK.
WHO HIRED YOU?
HE CAUGHT ME...
...BUT AFTER A LITTLE SCUFFLE, I PINNED HIM.
HE WOULDN'T SPILL THE BEANS, SO I HANDED HIM OVER TO SOME KNIGHTS.
AS FOR THIS ASSASSIN'S IDENTITY...
HUH?
YOU KNEW HIM?!
GRIN
BELIEVE IT OR NOT, THAT SHADOWY BUSINESS USED TO BE MY BREAD AND BUTTER.

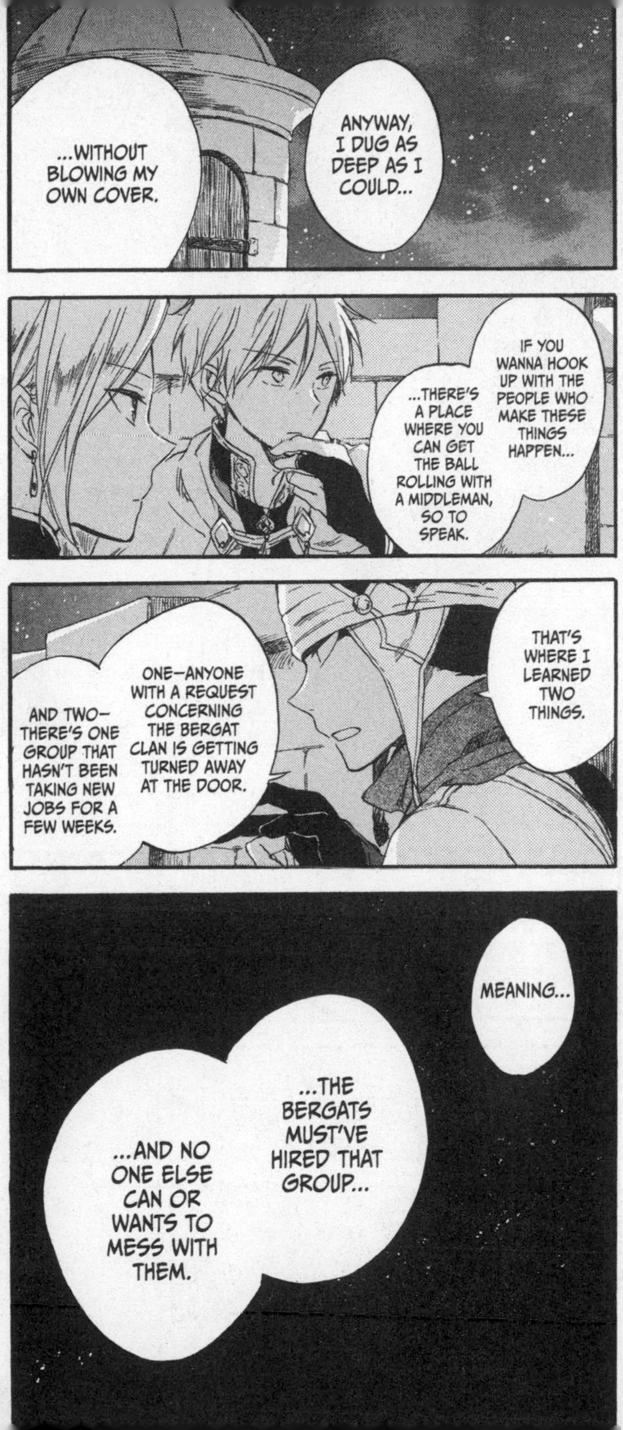
ANYWAY, I DUG AS DEEP AS I COULD...
...WITHOUT BLOWING MY OWN COVER.
IF YOU WANNA HOOK UP WITH THE PEOPLE WHO MAKE THESE THINGS HAPPEN...
...THERE'S A PLACE WHERE YOU CAN GET THE BALL ROLLING WITH A MIDDLEMAN, SO TO SPEAK.
THAT'S WHERE I LEARNED TWO THINGS.
ONE—ANYONE WITH A REQUEST CONCERNING THE BERGAT CLAN IS GETTING TURNED AWAY AT THE DOOR.
AND TWO—THERE'S ONE GROUP THAT HASN'T BEEN TAKING NEW JOBS FOR A FEW WEEKS.
MEANING...
...THE BERGATS MUST'VE HIRED THAT GROUP...
...AND NO ONE ELSE CAN OR WANTS TO MESS WITH THEM.

3

Haruka at age 24

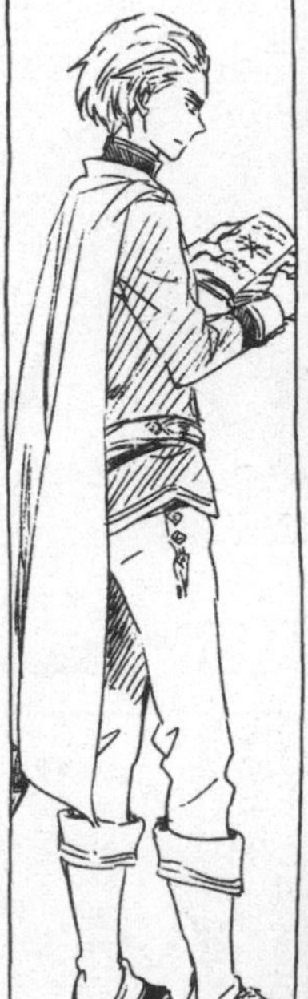

Queen Haruto gave him a collection of her poetry and told him it'd help him sleep well.

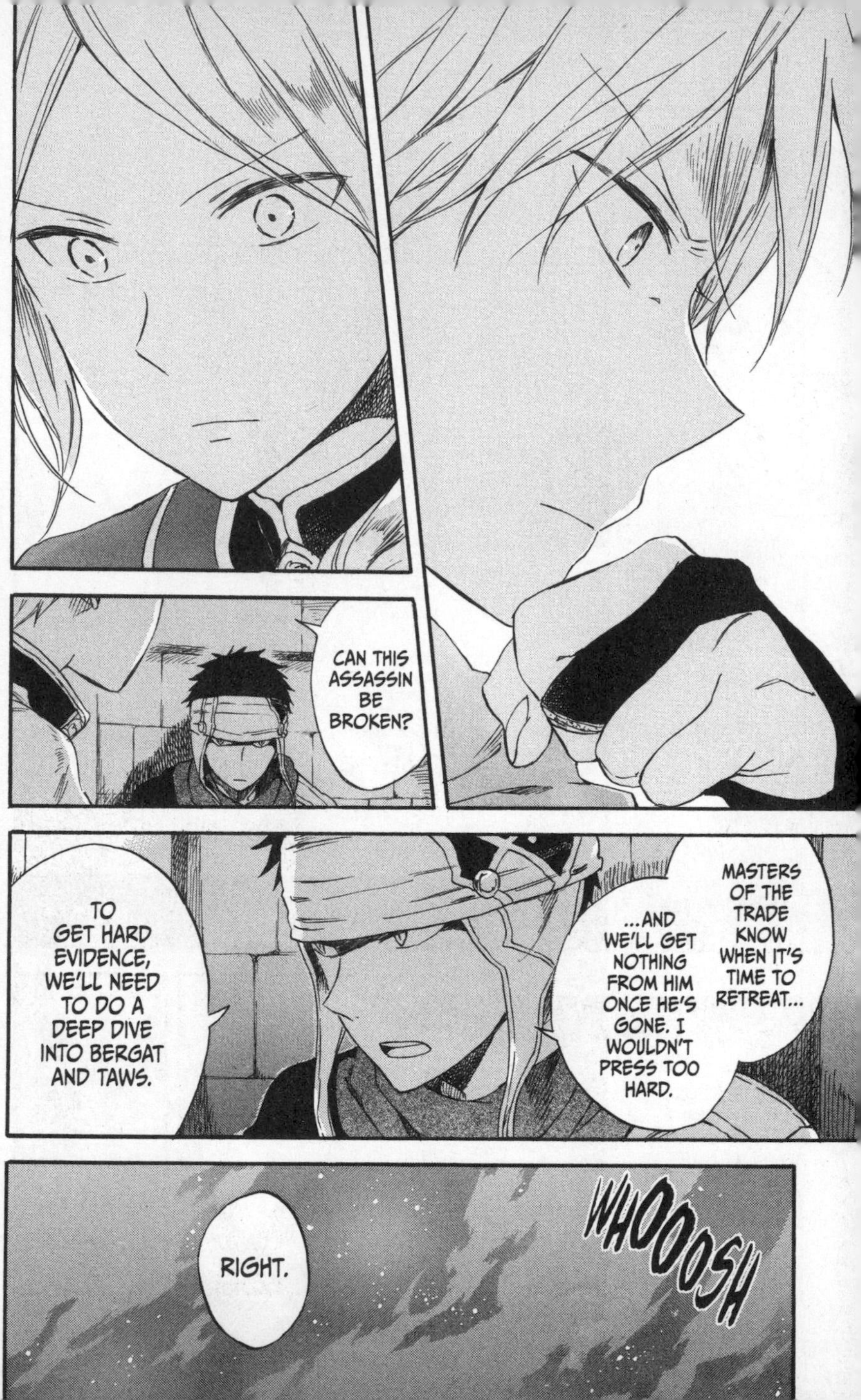
CAN THIS ASSASSIN BE BROKEN?
MASTERS OF THE TRADE KNOW WHEN IT'S TIME TO RETREAT...
...AND WE'LL GET NOTHING FROM HIM ONCE HE'S GONE. I WOULDN'T PRESS TOO HARD.
TO GET HARD EVIDENCE, WE'LL NEED TO DO A DEEP DIVE INTO BERGAT AND TAWS.
WHOOOSH
RIGHT.

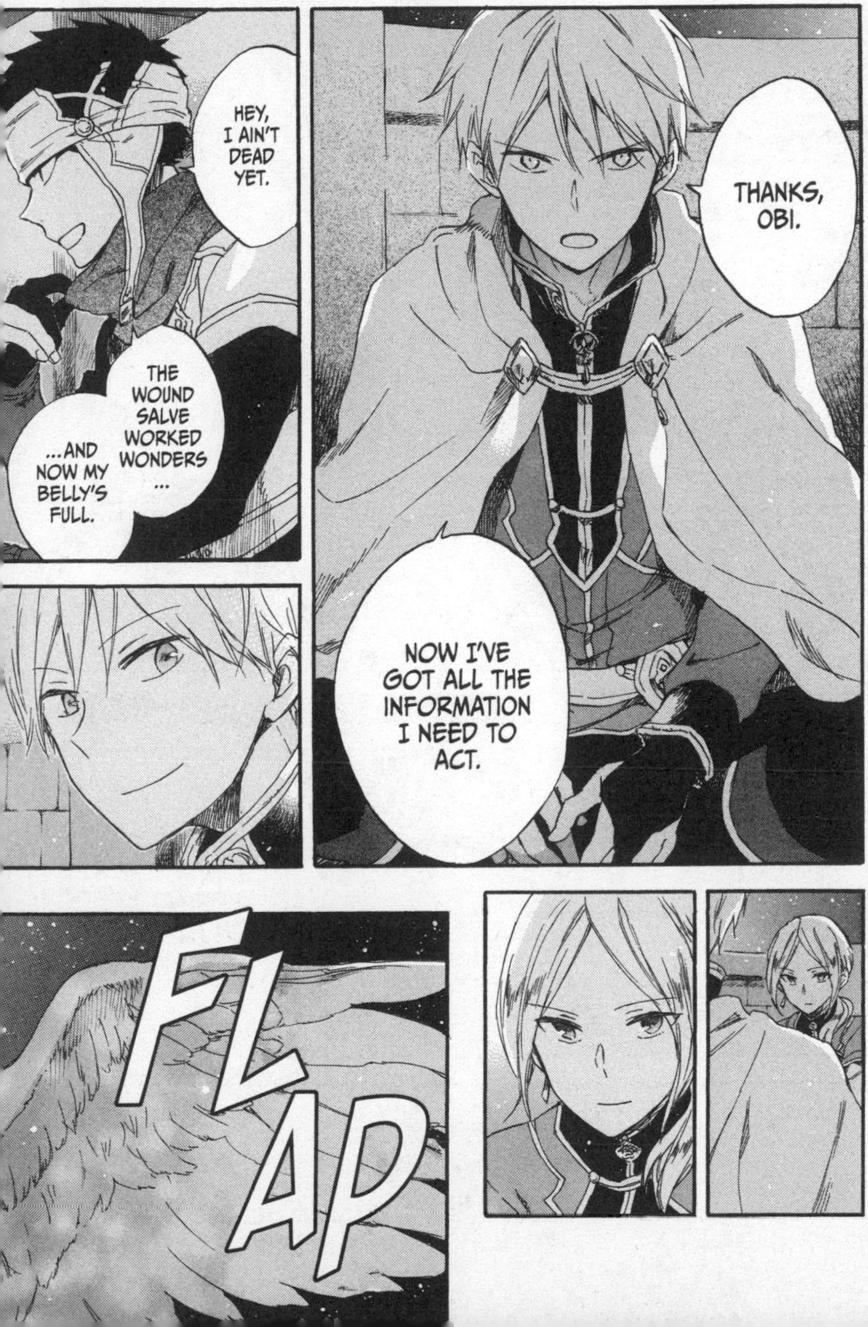
THANKS, OBI.
NOW I'VE GOT ALL THE INFORMATION I NEED TO ACT.
HEY, I AIN'T DEAD YET.
THE WOUND SALVE WORKED WONDERS...
...AND NOW MY BELLY'S FULL.
FLAP

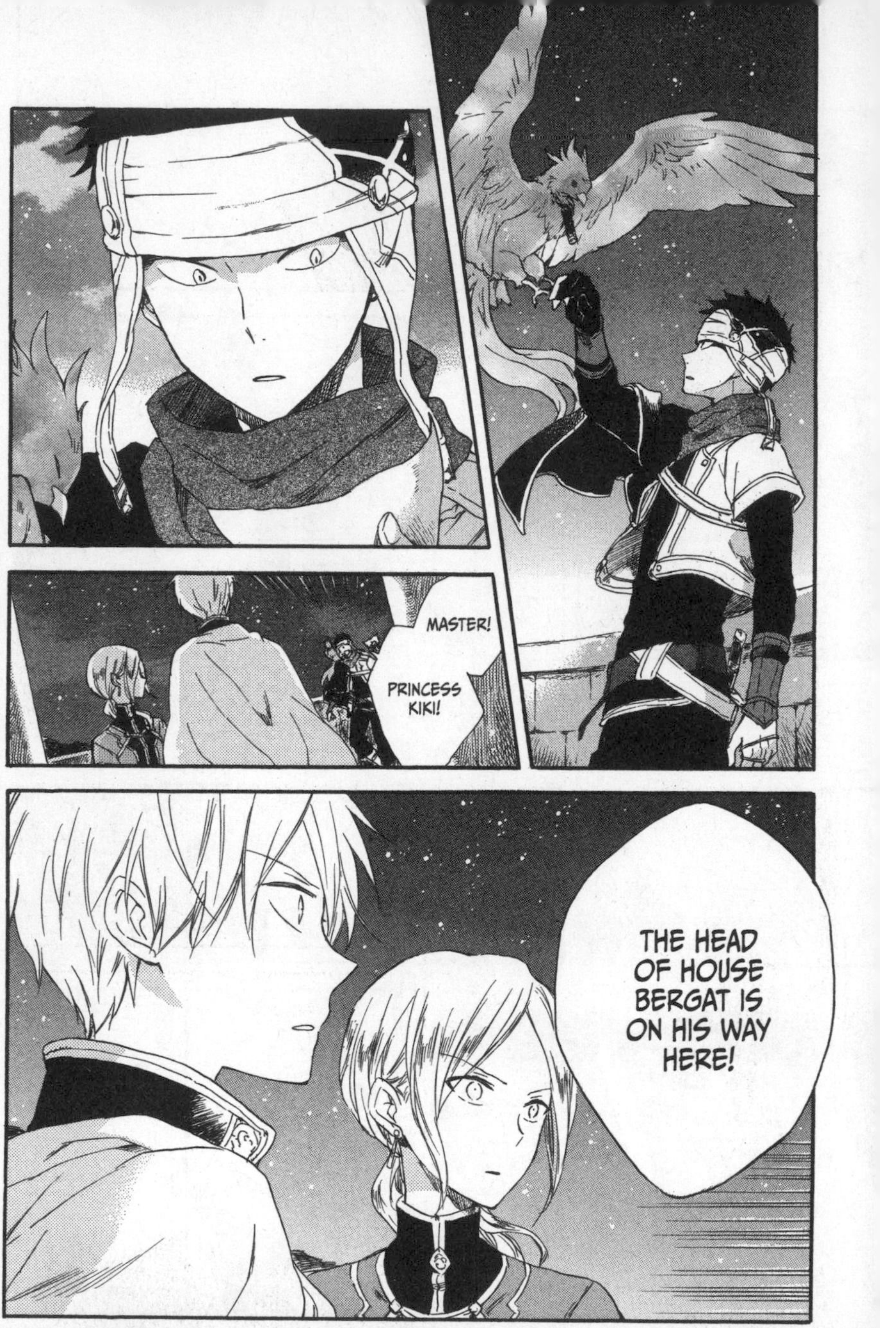
MASTER!
PRINCESS KIKI!
THE HEAD OF HOUSE BERGAT IS ON HIS WAY HERE!

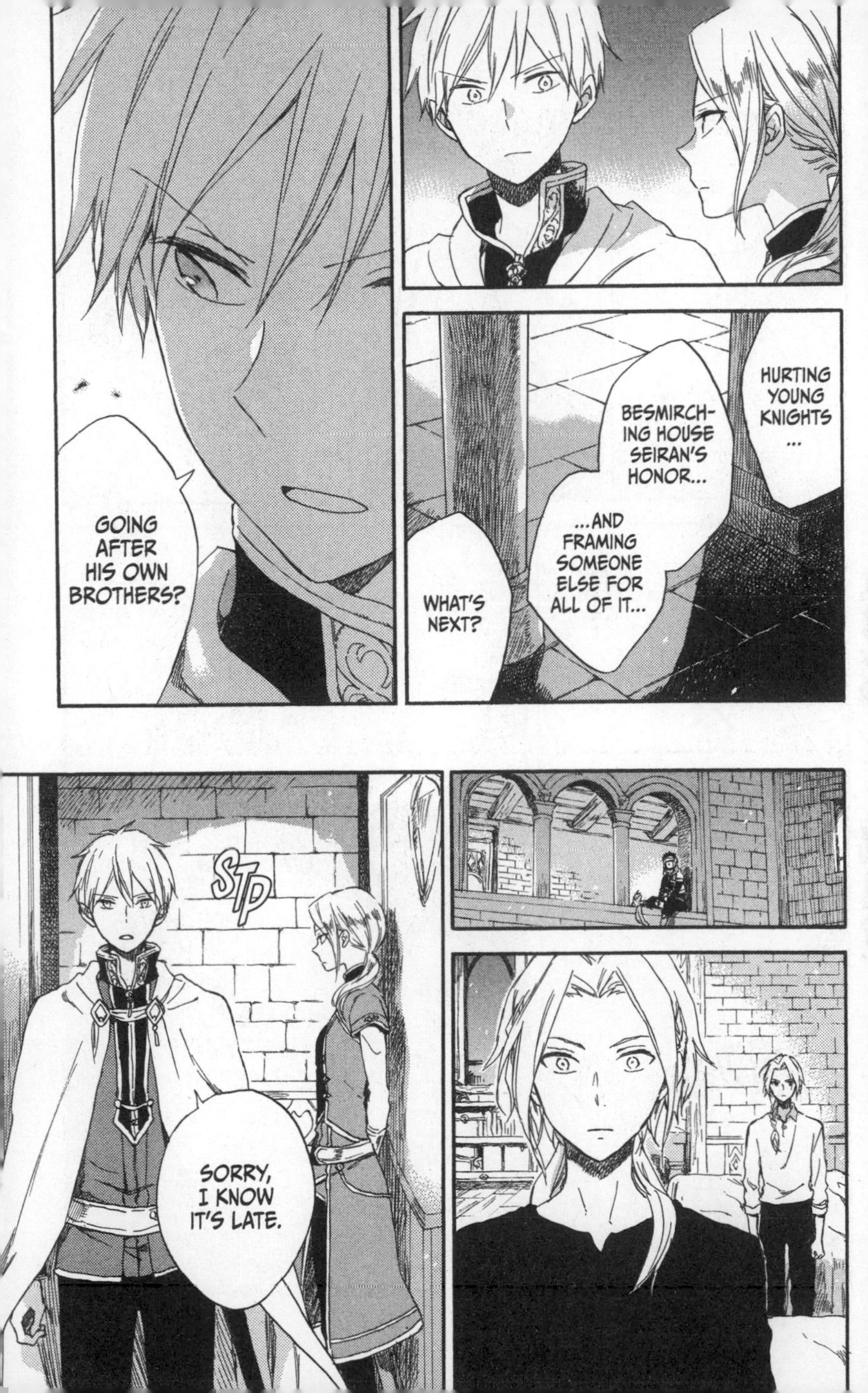
HURTING YOUNG KNIGHTS ...
BESMIRCHING HOUSE SEIRAN'S HONOR...
...AND FRAMING SOMEONE ELSE FOR ALL OF IT...
WHAT'S NEXT?
GOING AFTER HIS OWN BROTHERS?
STP
SORRY, I KNOW IT'S LATE.

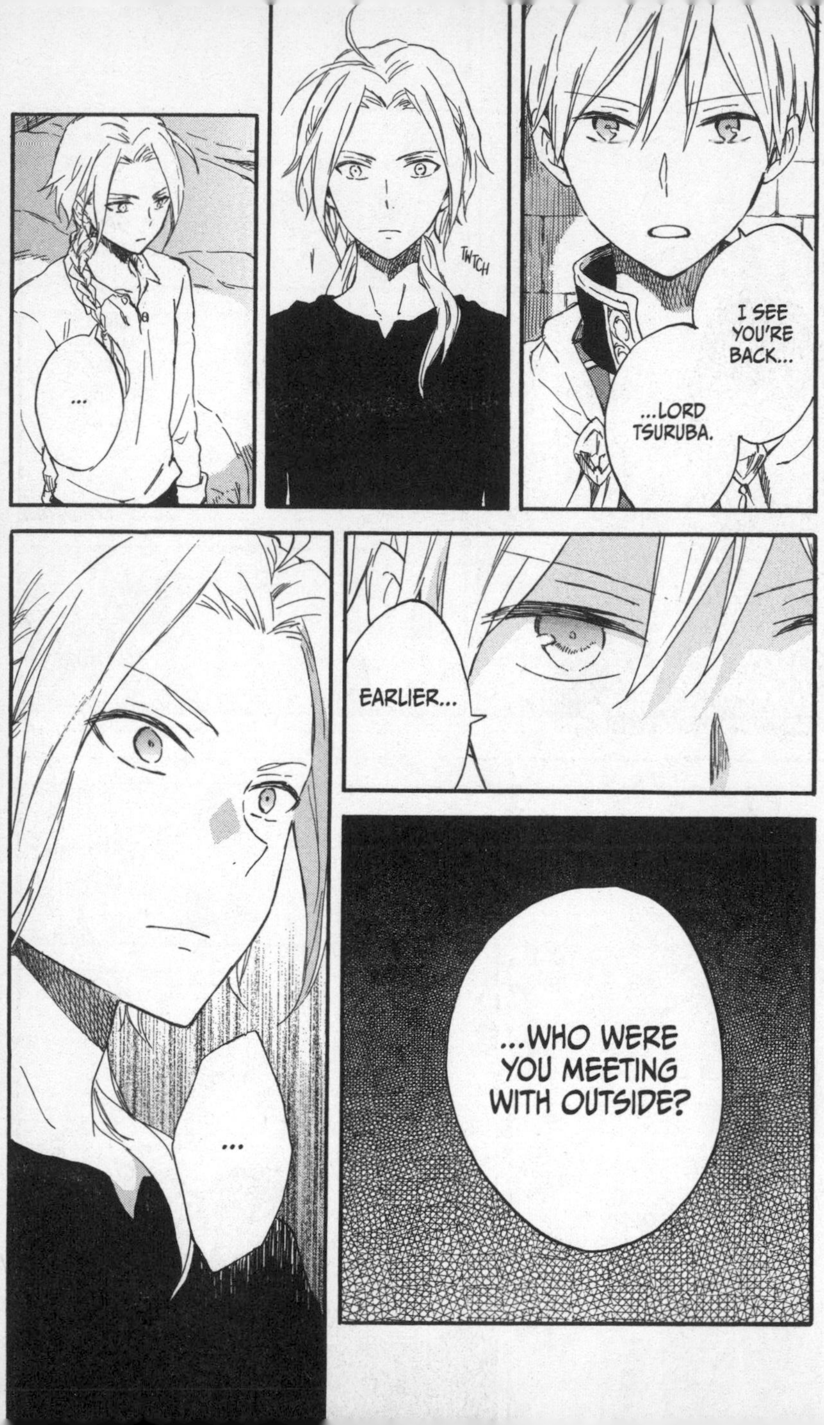
I SEE YOU'RE BACK...
...LORD TSURUBA.
TWTCH
...
EARLIER...
...WHO WERE YOU MEETING WITH OUTSIDE?
...

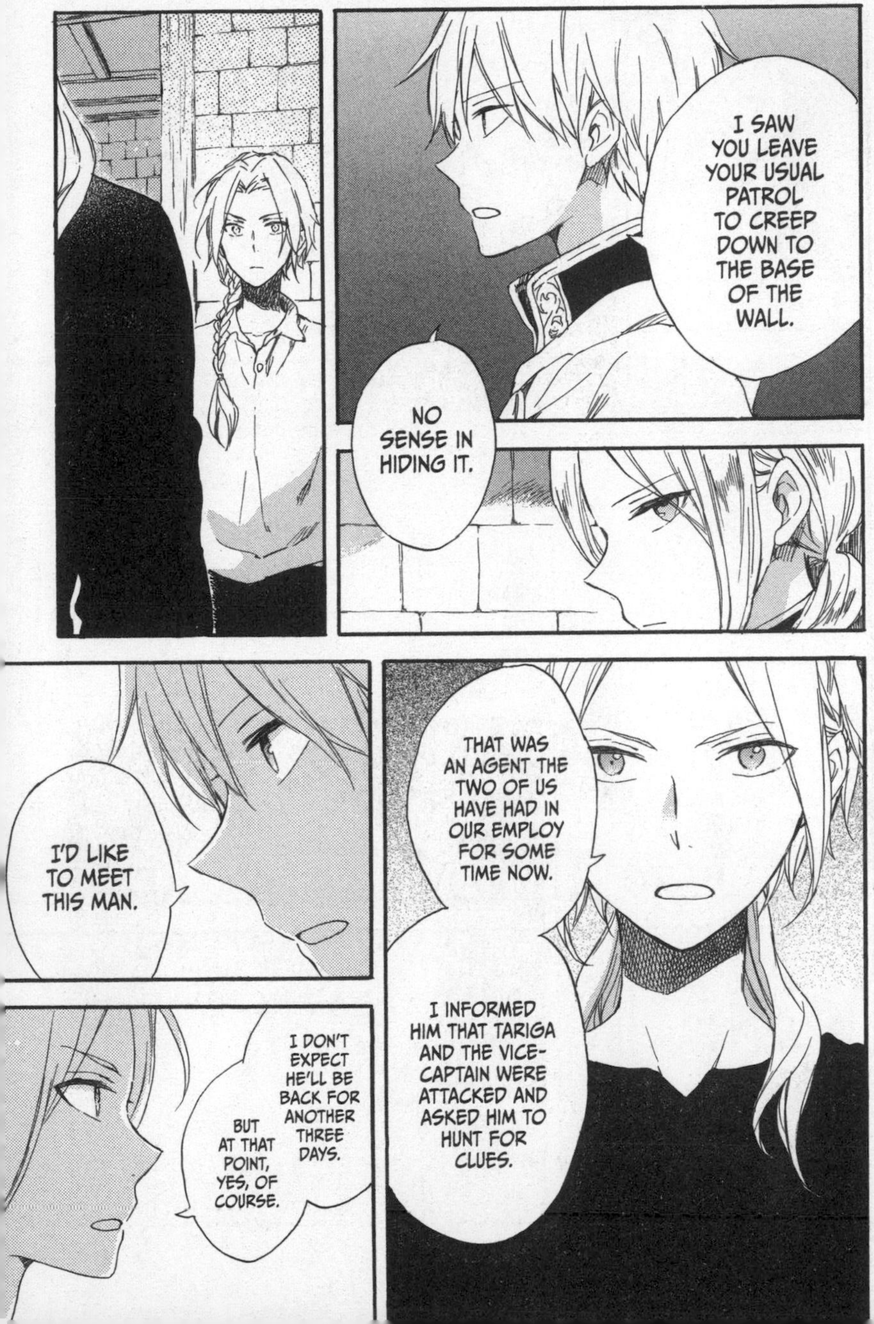
I SAW YOU LEAVE YOUR USUAL PATROL TO CREEP DOWN TO THE BASE OF THE WALL.
NO SENSE IN HIDING IT.
THAT WAS AN AGENT THE TWO OF US HAVE HAD IN OUR EMPLOY FOR SOME TIME NOW.
I INFORMED HIM THAT TARIGA AND THE VICE-CAPTAIN WERE ATTACKED AND ASKED HIM TO HUNT FOR CLUES.
I'D LIKE TO MEET THIS MAN.
I DON'T EXPECT HE'LL BE BACK FOR ANOTHER THREE DAYS.
BUT AT THAT POINT, YES, OF COURSE.

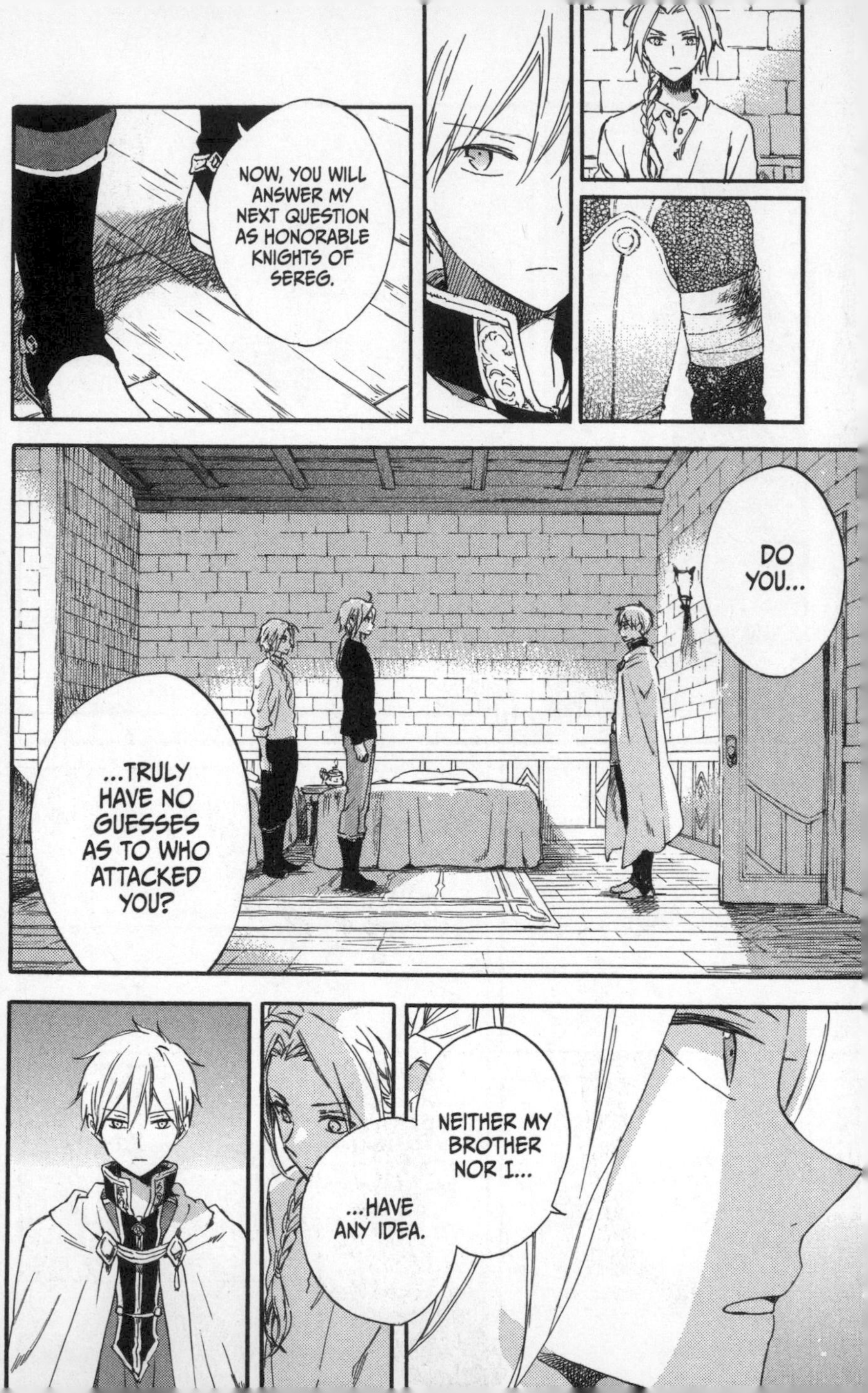
NOW, YOU WILL ANSWER MY NEXT QUESTION AS HONORABLE KNIGHTS OF SEREG.
DO YOU...
...TRULY HAVE NO GUESSES AS TO WHO ATTACKED YOU?
NEITHER MY BROTHER NOR I...
...HAVE ANY IDEA.

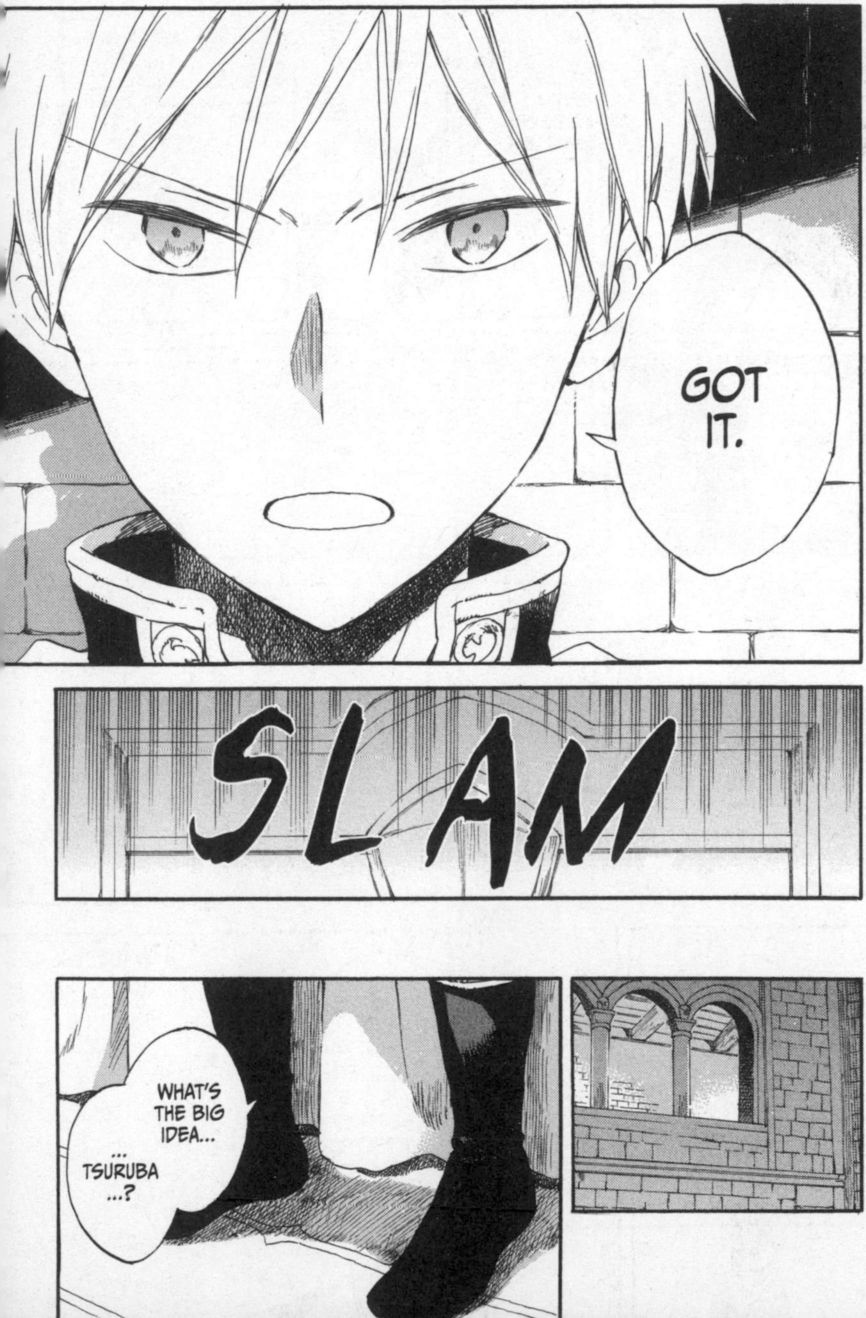
GOT IT.
SLAM
WHAT'S THE BIG IDEA...
... TSURUBA ...?

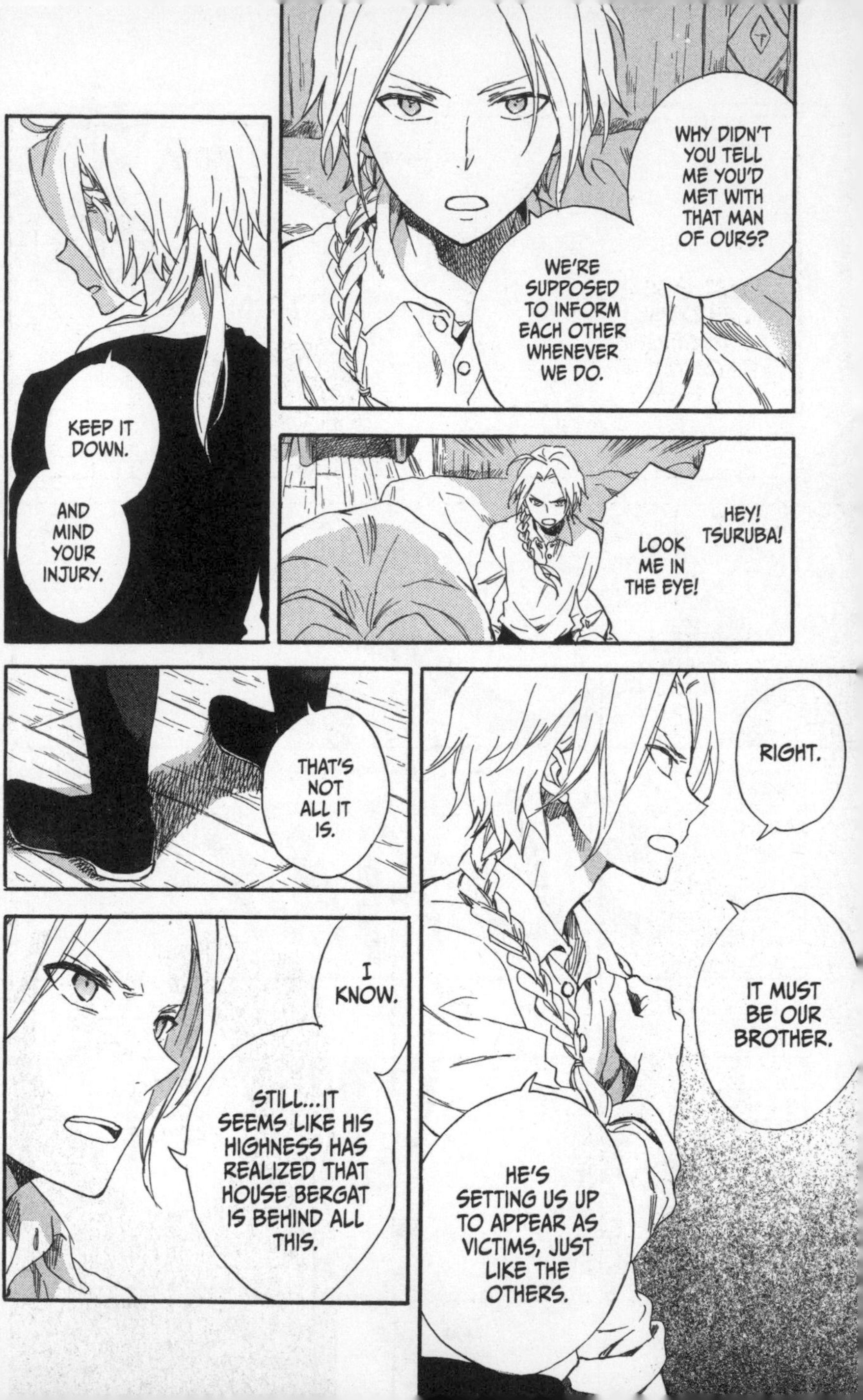
WHY DIDN'T YOU TELL ME YOU'D MET WITH THAT MAN OF OURS?
WE'RE SUPPOSED TO INFORM EACH OTHER WHENEVER WE DO.
HEY! TSURUBA!
LOOK ME IN THE EYE!
KEEP IT DOWN.
AND MIND YOUR INJURY.
RIGHT.
IT MUST BE OUR BROTHER.
HE'S SETTING US UP TO APPEAR AS VICTIMS, JUST LIKE THE OTHERS.
THAT'S NOT ALL IT IS.
I KNOW.
STILL...IT SEEMS LIKE HIS HIGHNESS HAS REALIZED THAT HOUSE BERGAT IS BEHIND ALL THIS.

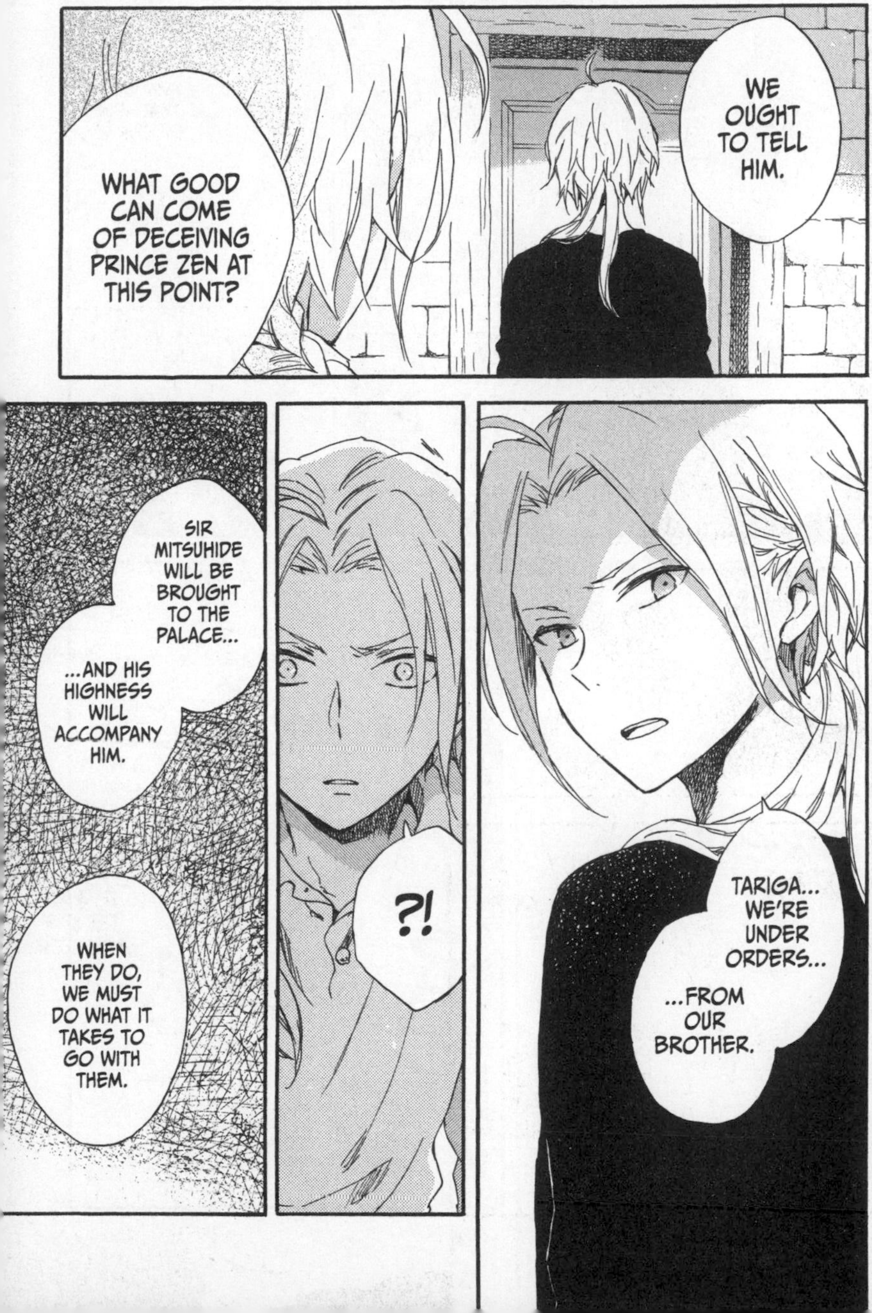
WE OUGHT TO TELL HIM.
WHAT GOOD CAN COME OF DECEIVING PRINCE ZEN AT THIS POINT?
TARIGA... WE'RE UNDER ORDERS...
...FROM OUR BROTHER.
?!
SIR MITSUHIDE WILL BE BROUGHT TO THE PALACE...
...AND HIS HIGHNESS WILL ACCOMPANY HIM.
WHEN THEY DO, WE MUST DO WHAT IT TAKES TO GO WITH THEM.

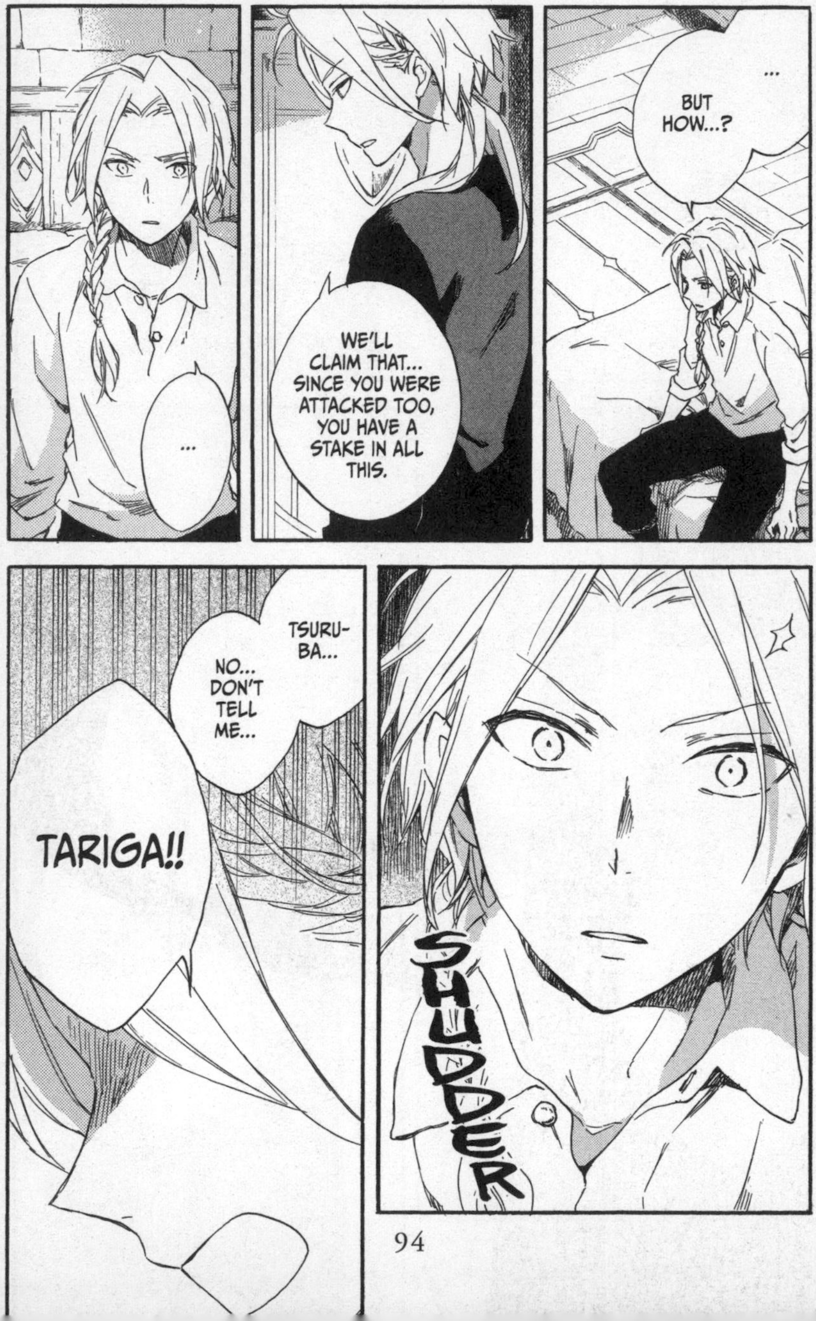
...
BUT HOW...?
WE'LL CLAIM THAT... SINCE YOU WERE ATTACKED TOO, YOU HAVE A STAKE IN ALL THIS.
...
SHUDDER
TSURU-BA...
NO... DON'T TELL ME...
TARIGA!!

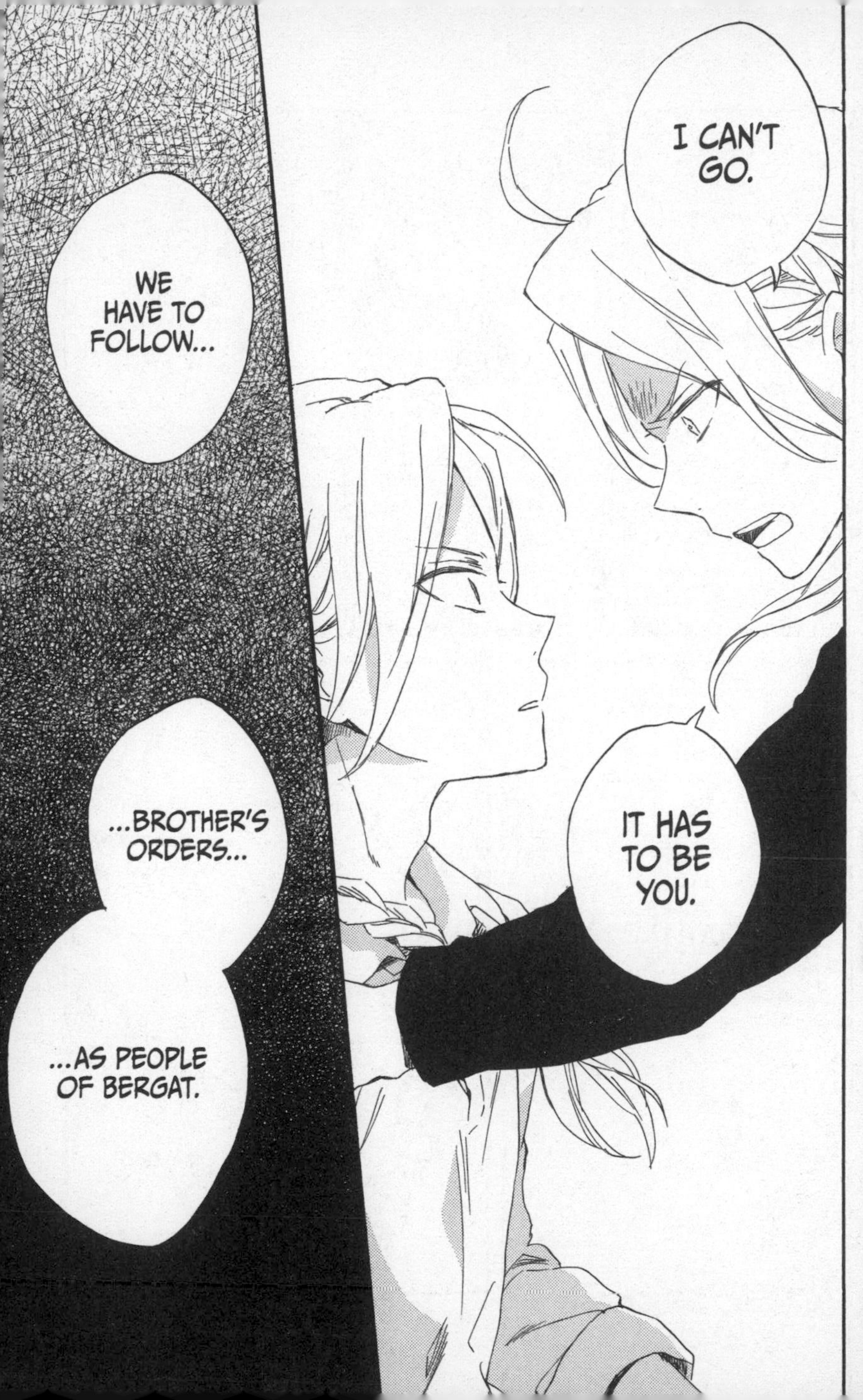
I CAN'T GO.
IT HAS TO BE YOU.
WE HAVE TO FOLLOW...
...BROTHER'S ORDERS...
...AS PEOPLE OF BERGAT.

Chapter 81

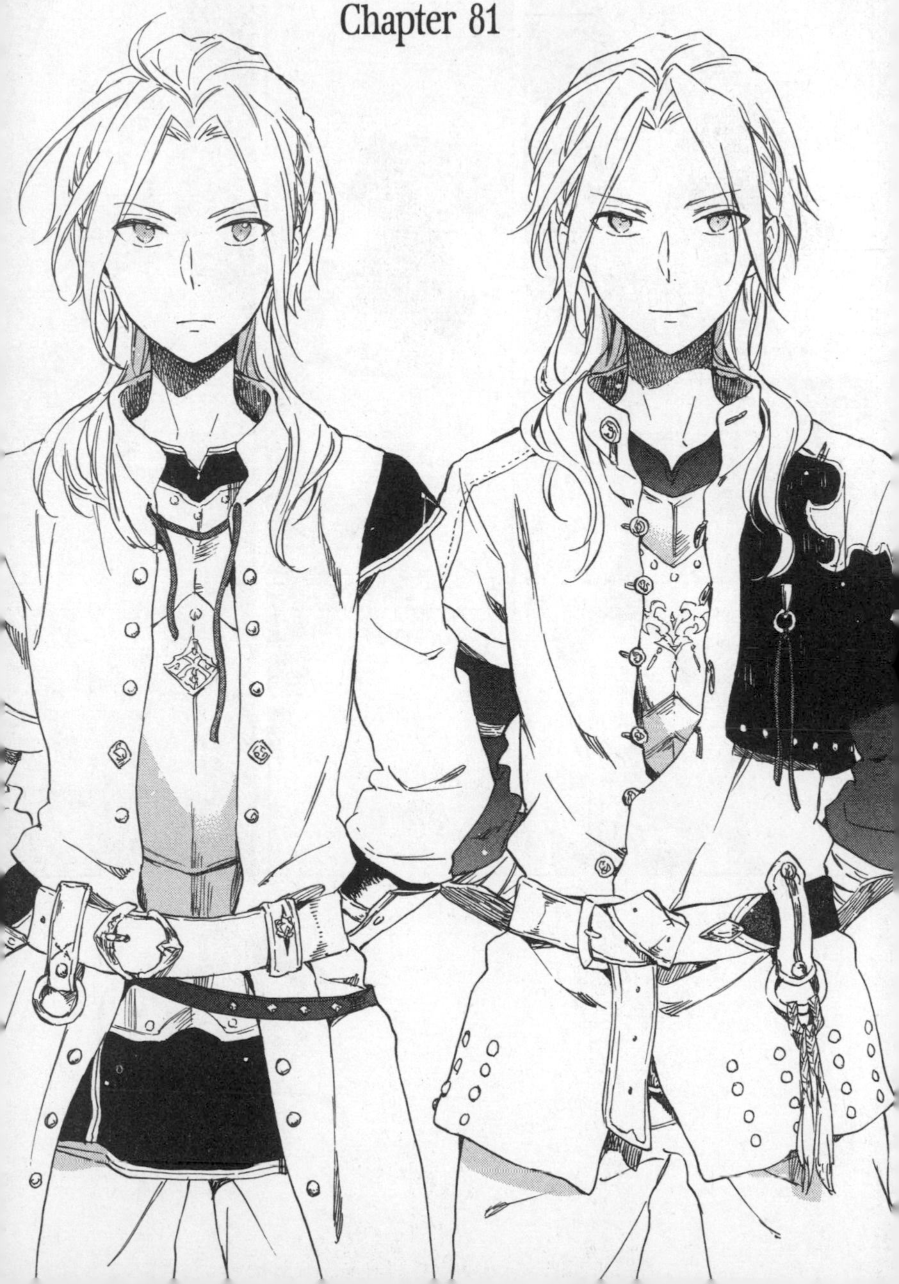

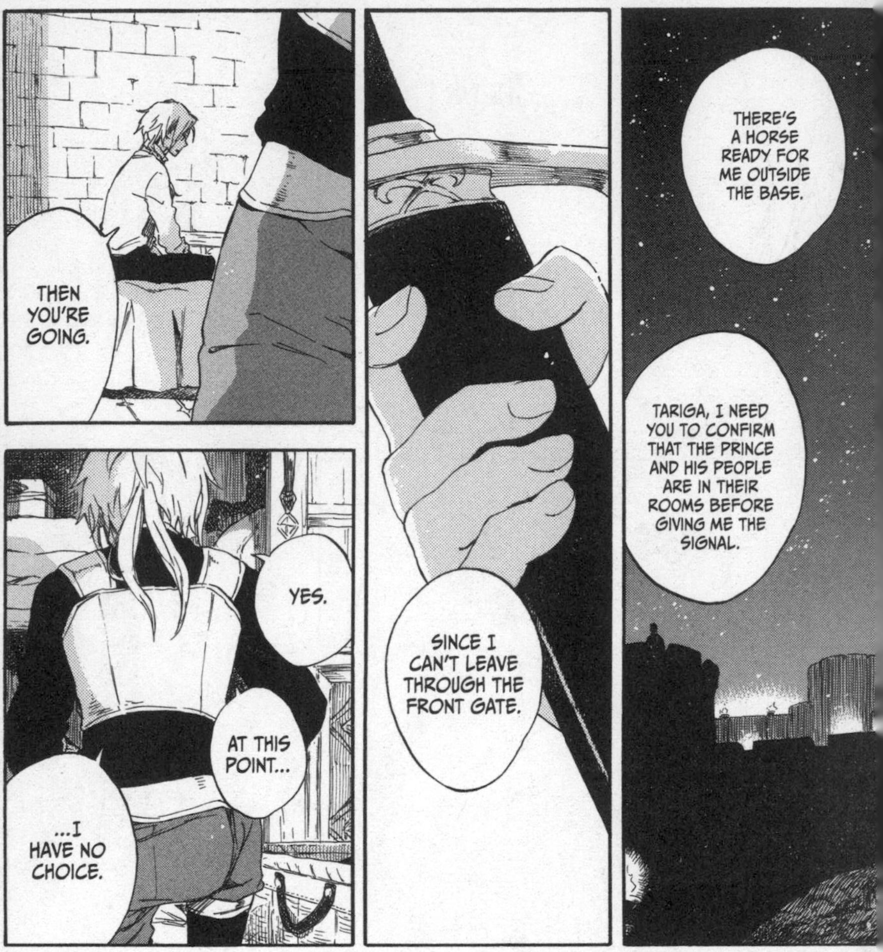
THERE'S A HORSE READY FOR ME OUTSIDE THE BASE.
TARIGA, I NEED YOU TO CONFIRM THAT THE PRINCE AND HIS PEOPLE ARE IN THEIR ROOMS BEFORE GIVING ME THE SIGNAL.
SINCE I CAN'T LEAVE THROUGH THE FRONT GATE.
THEN YOU'RE GOING.
YES.
AT THIS POINT...
...I HAVE NO CHOICE.

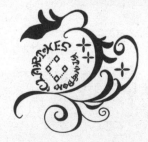

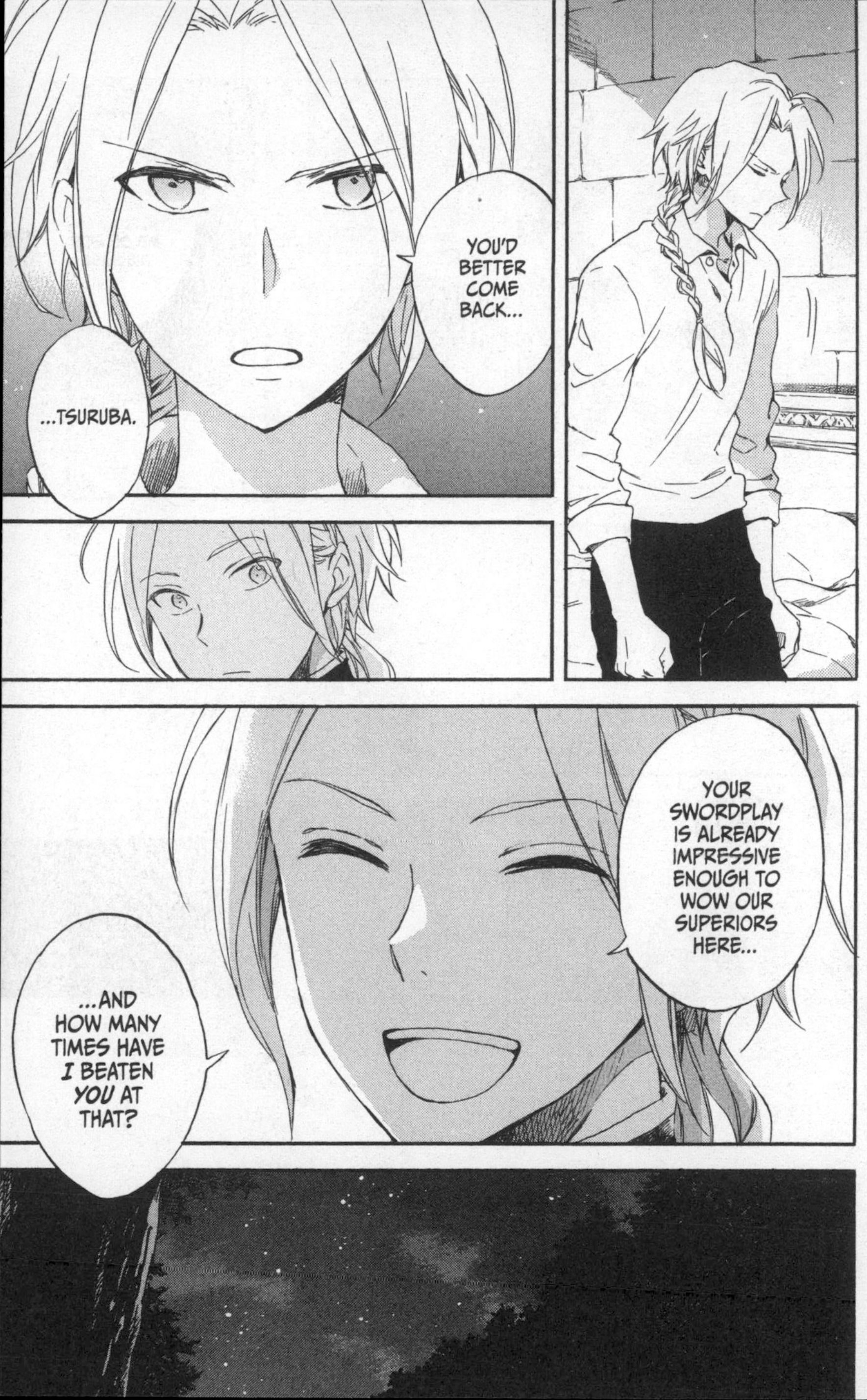
YOU'D BETTER COME BACK...
...TSURUBA.
YOUR SWORDPLAY IS ALREADY IMPRESSIVE ENOUGH TO WOW OUR SUPERIORS HERE...
...AND HOW MANY TIMES HAVE *I* BEATEN *YOU* AT THAT?

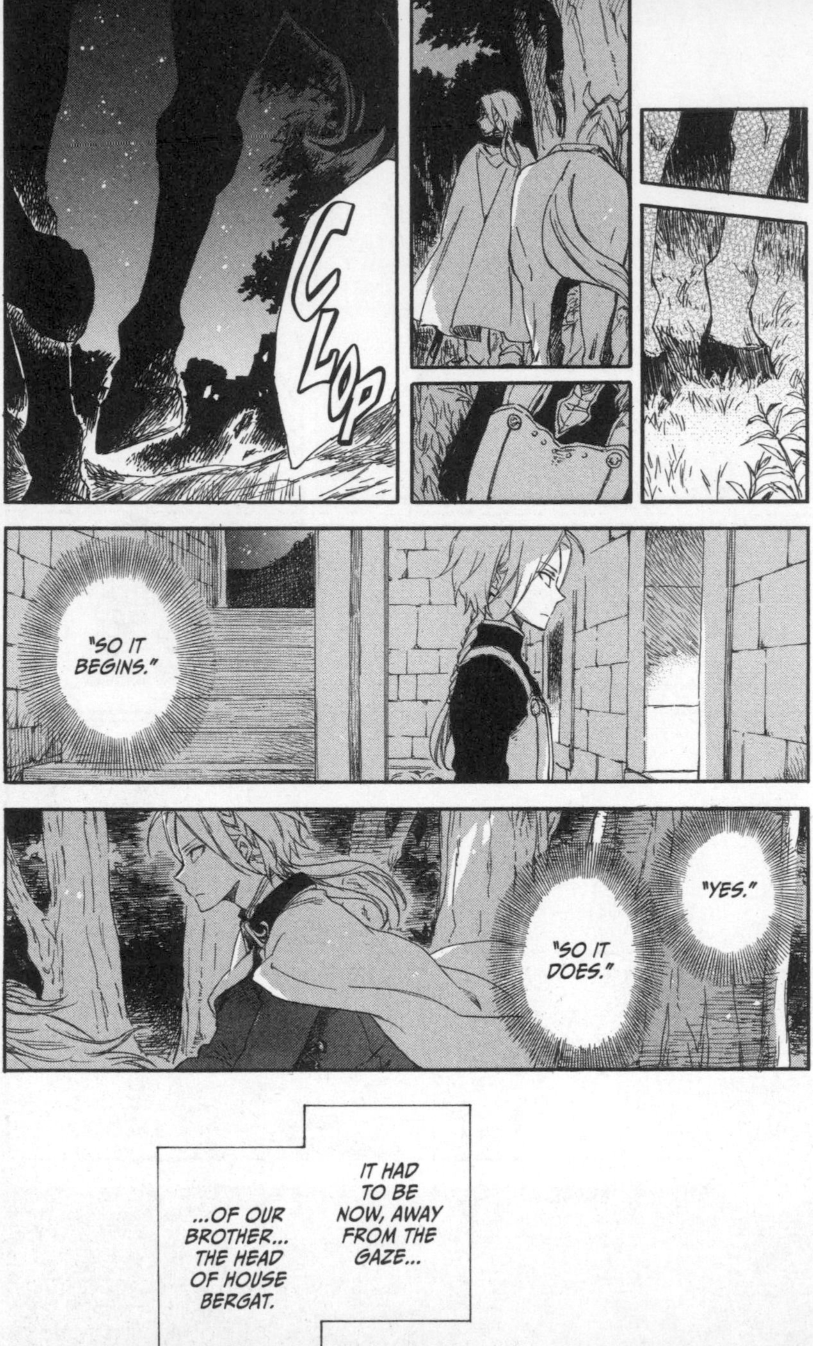
CLOP
"SO IT BEGINS."
"YES."
"SO IT DOES."
IT HAD TO BE NOW, AWAY FROM THE GAZE...
...OF OUR BROTHER... THE HEAD OF HOUSE BERGAT.

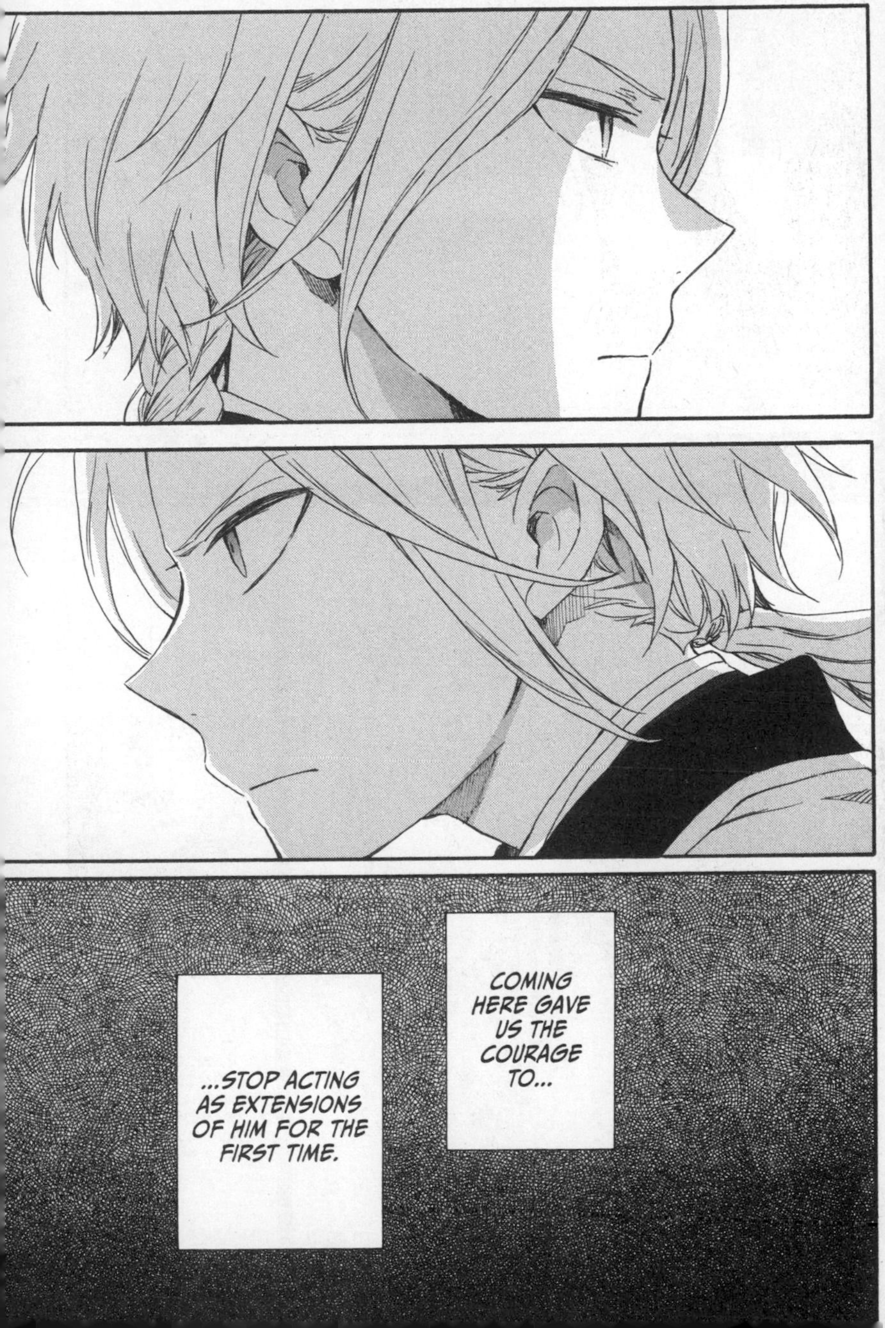
COMING HERE GAVE US THE COURAGE TO...
...STOP ACTING AS EXTENSIONS OF HIM FOR THE FIRST TIME.

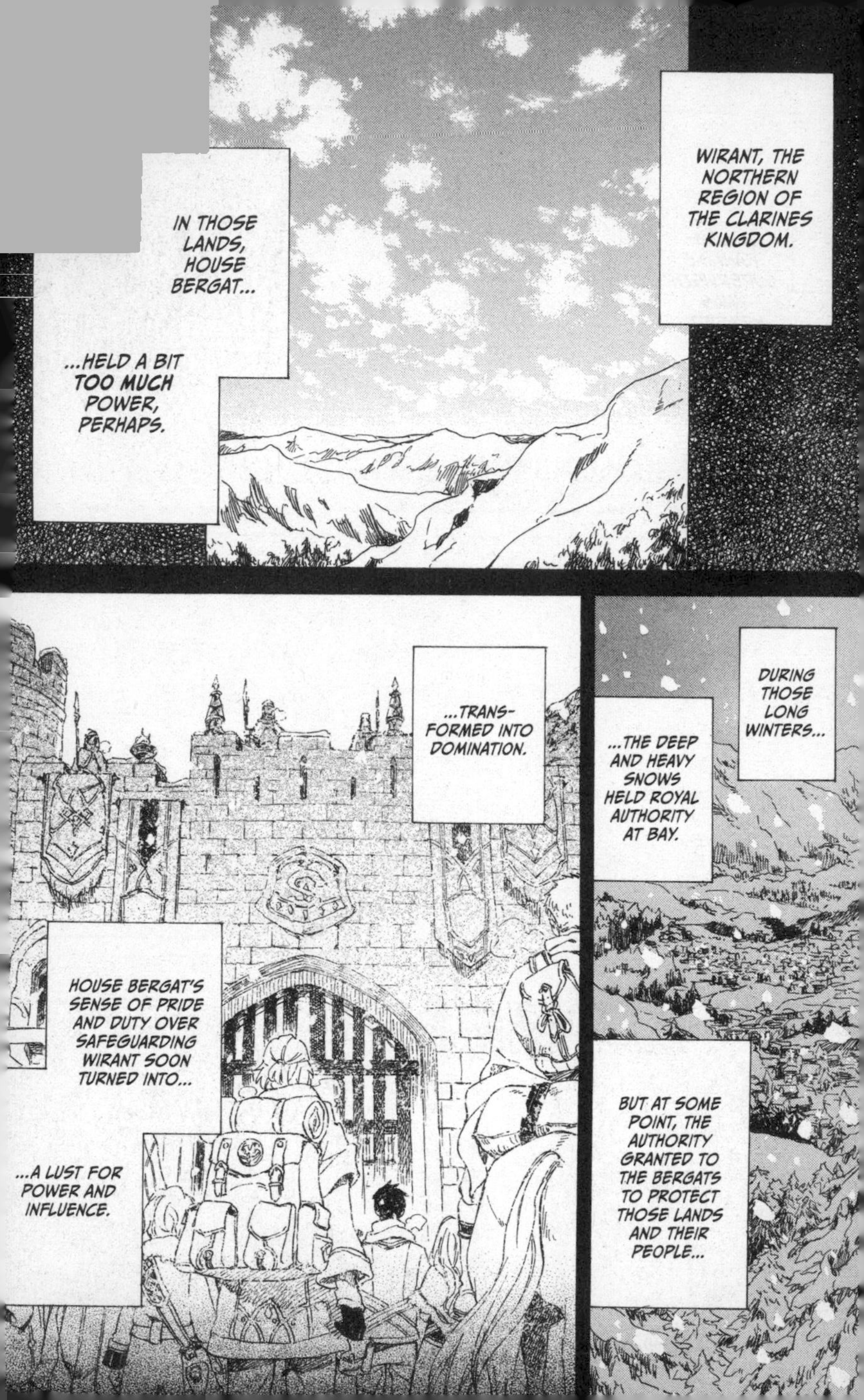
WIRANT, THE NORTHERN REGION OF THE CLARINES KINGDOM.
IN THOSE LANDS, HOUSE BERGAT...
...HELD A BIT TOO MUCH POWER, PERHAPS.
DURING THOSE LONG WINTERS...
...THE DEEP AND HEAVY SNOWS HELD ROYAL AUTHORITY AT BAY.
BUT AT SOME POINT, THE AUTHORITY GRANTED TO THE BERGATS TO PROTECT THOSE LANDS AND THEIR PEOPLE...
...TRANS-FORMED INTO DOMINATION.
HOUSE BERGAT'S SENSE OF PRIDE AND DUTY OVER SAFEGUARDING WIRANT SOON TURNED INTO...
...A LUST FOR POWER AND INFLUENCE.

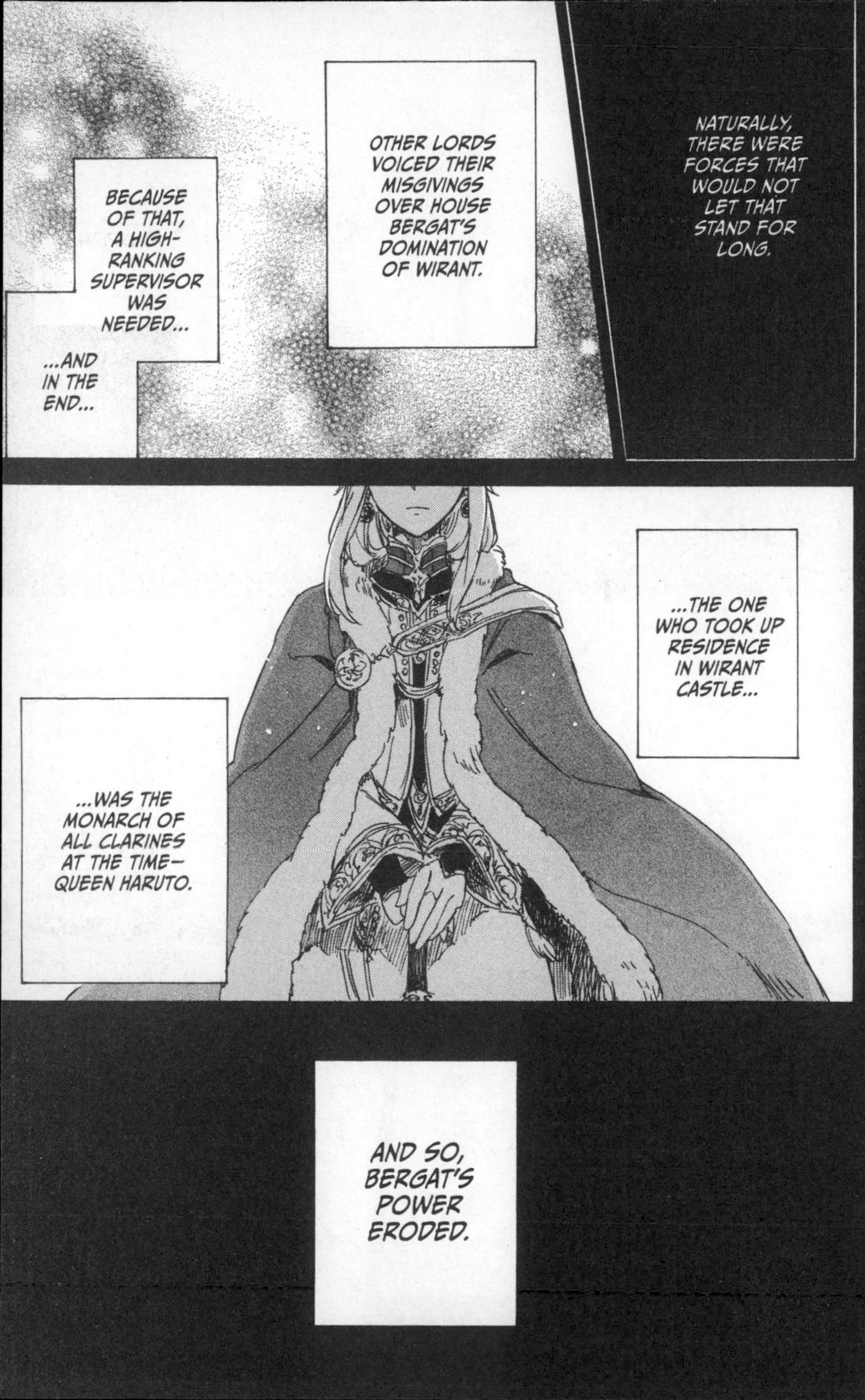
NATURALLY, THERE WERE FORCES THAT WOULD NOT LET THAT STAND FOR LONG.
OTHER LORDS VOICED THEIR MISGIVINGS OVER HOUSE BERGAT'S DOMINATION OF WIRANT.
BECAUSE OF THAT, A HIGH-RANKING SUPERVISOR WAS NEEDED...
...AND IN THE END...
...THE ONE WHO TOOK UP RESIDENCE IN WIRANT CASTLE...
...WAS THE MONARCH OF ALL CLARINES AT THE TIME—QUEEN HARUTO.
AND SO, BERGAT'S POWER ERODED.

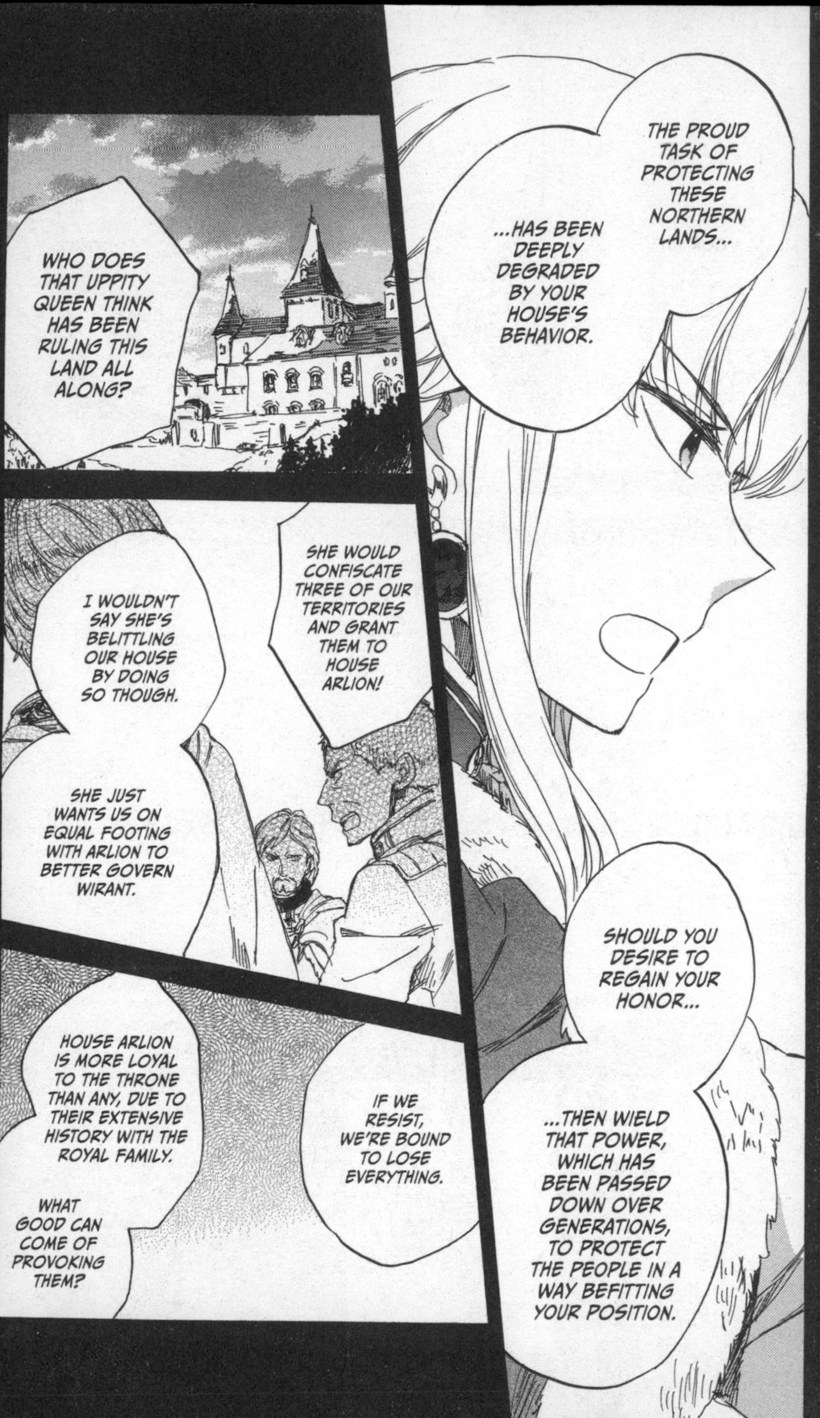
THE PROUD TASK OF PROTECTING THESE NORTHERN LANDS...
...HAS BEEN DEEPLY DEGRADED BY YOUR HOUSE'S BEHAVIOR.
SHOULD YOU DESIRE TO REGAIN YOUR HONOR...
...THEN WIELD THAT POWER, WHICH HAS BEEN PASSED DOWN OVER GENERATIONS, TO PROTECT THE PEOPLE IN A WAY BEFITTING YOUR POSITION.
WHO DOES THAT UPPITY QUEEN THINK HAS BEEN RULING THIS LAND ALL ALONG?
SHE WOULD CONFISCATE THREE OF OUR TERRITORIES AND GRANT THEM TO HOUSE ARLION!
I WOULDN'T SAY SHE'S BELITTLING OUR HOUSE BY DOING SO THOUGH.
SHE JUST WANTS US ON EQUAL FOOTING WITH ARLION TO BETTER GOVERN WIRANT.
IF WE RESIST, WE'RE BOUND TO LOSE EVERYTHING.
HOUSE ARLION IS MORE LOYAL TO THE THRONE THAN ANY, DUE TO THEIR EXTENSIVE HISTORY WITH THE ROYAL FAMILY.
WHAT GOOD CAN COME OF PROVOKING THEM?

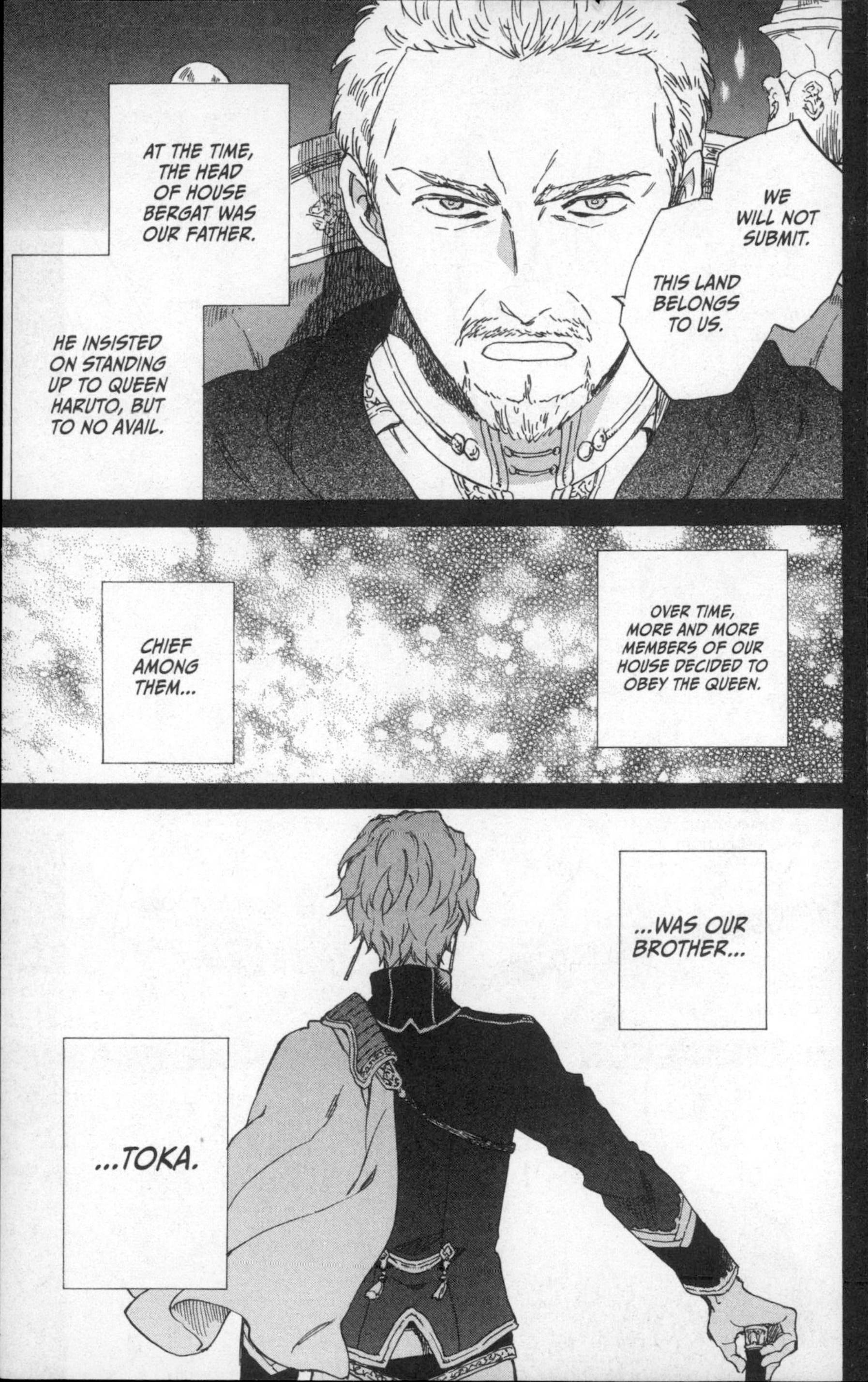

WE WILL NOT SUBMIT.
THIS LAND BELONGS TO US.
AT THE TIME, THE HEAD OF HOUSE BERGAT WAS OUR FATHER.
HE INSISTED ON STANDING UP TO QUEEN HARUTO, BUT TO NO AVAIL.
OVER TIME, MORE AND MORE MEMBERS OF OUR HOUSE DECIDED TO OBEY THE QUEEN.
CHIEF AMONG THEM...
...WAS OUR BROTHER...
...TOKA.

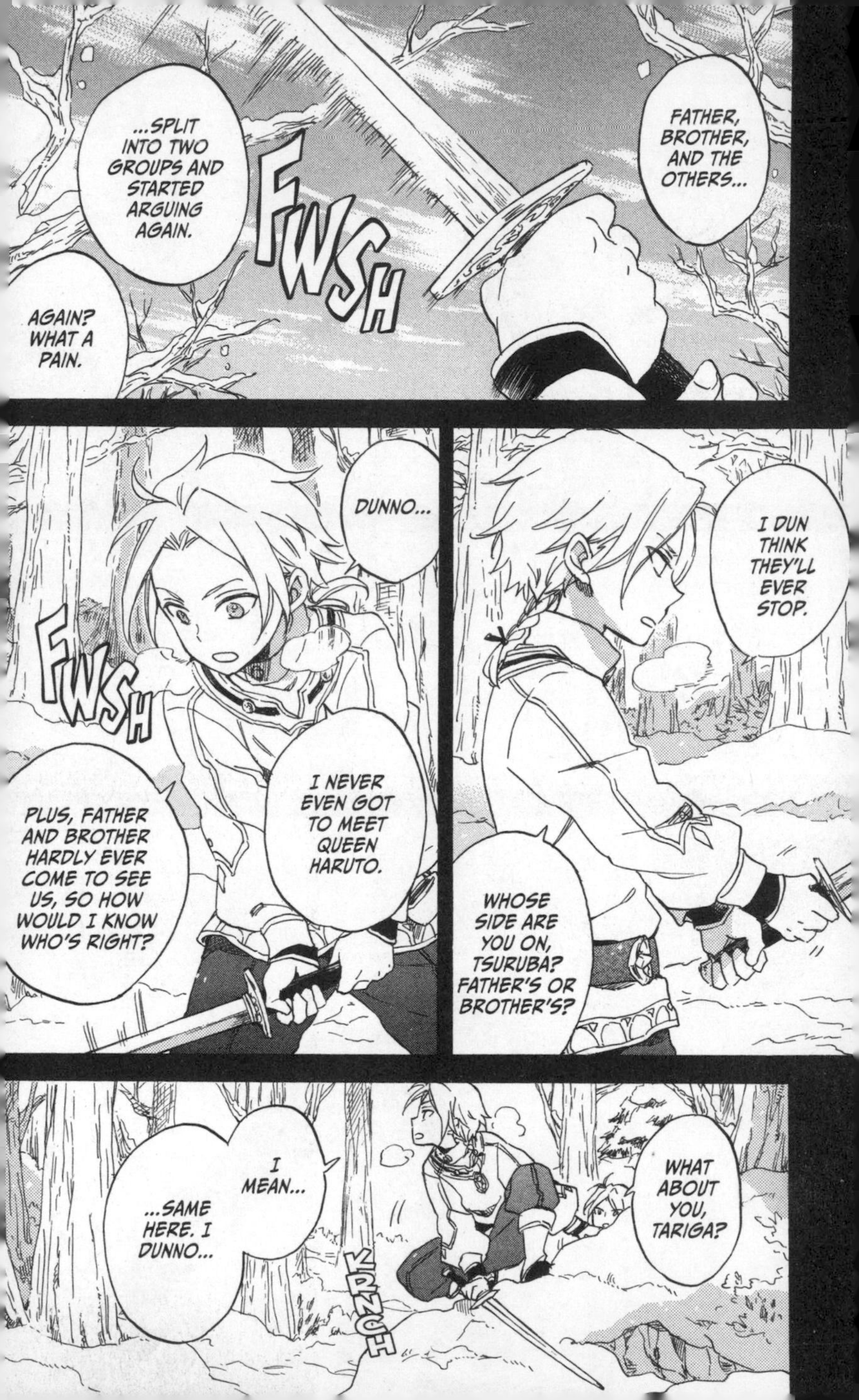

FATHER, BROTHER, AND THE OTHERS...
...SPLIT INTO TWO GROUPS AND STARTED ARGUING AGAIN.
FWSH
AGAIN? WHAT A PAIN.
I DUN THINK THEY'LL EVER STOP.
WHOSE SIDE ARE YOU ON, TSURUBA? FATHER'S OR BROTHER'S?
DUNNO...
FWSH
I NEVER EVEN GOT TO MEET QUEEN HARUTO.
PLUS, FATHER AND BROTHER HARDLY EVER COME TO SEE US, SO HOW WOULD I KNOW WHO'S RIGHT?
WHAT ABOUT YOU, TARIGA?
KRNCH
I MEAN...
...SAME HERE. I DUNNO...

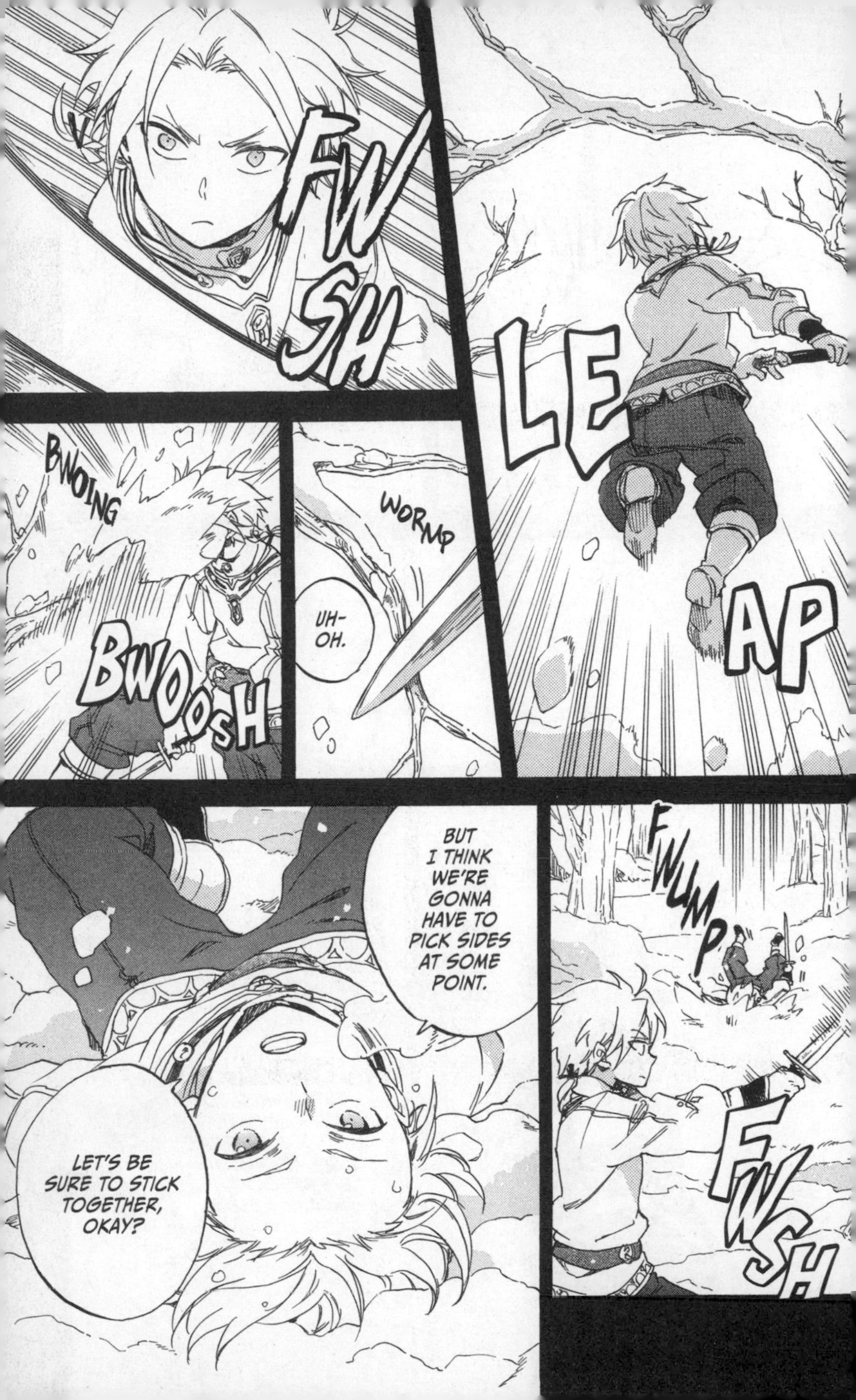
LEAP
FWSH
WORMP
UH-OH.
BWOING
BWOOSH
FWUMP
FWSH
BUT I THINK WE'RE GONNA HAVE TO PICK SIDES AT SOME POINT.
LET'S BE SURE TO STICK TOGETHER, OKAY?

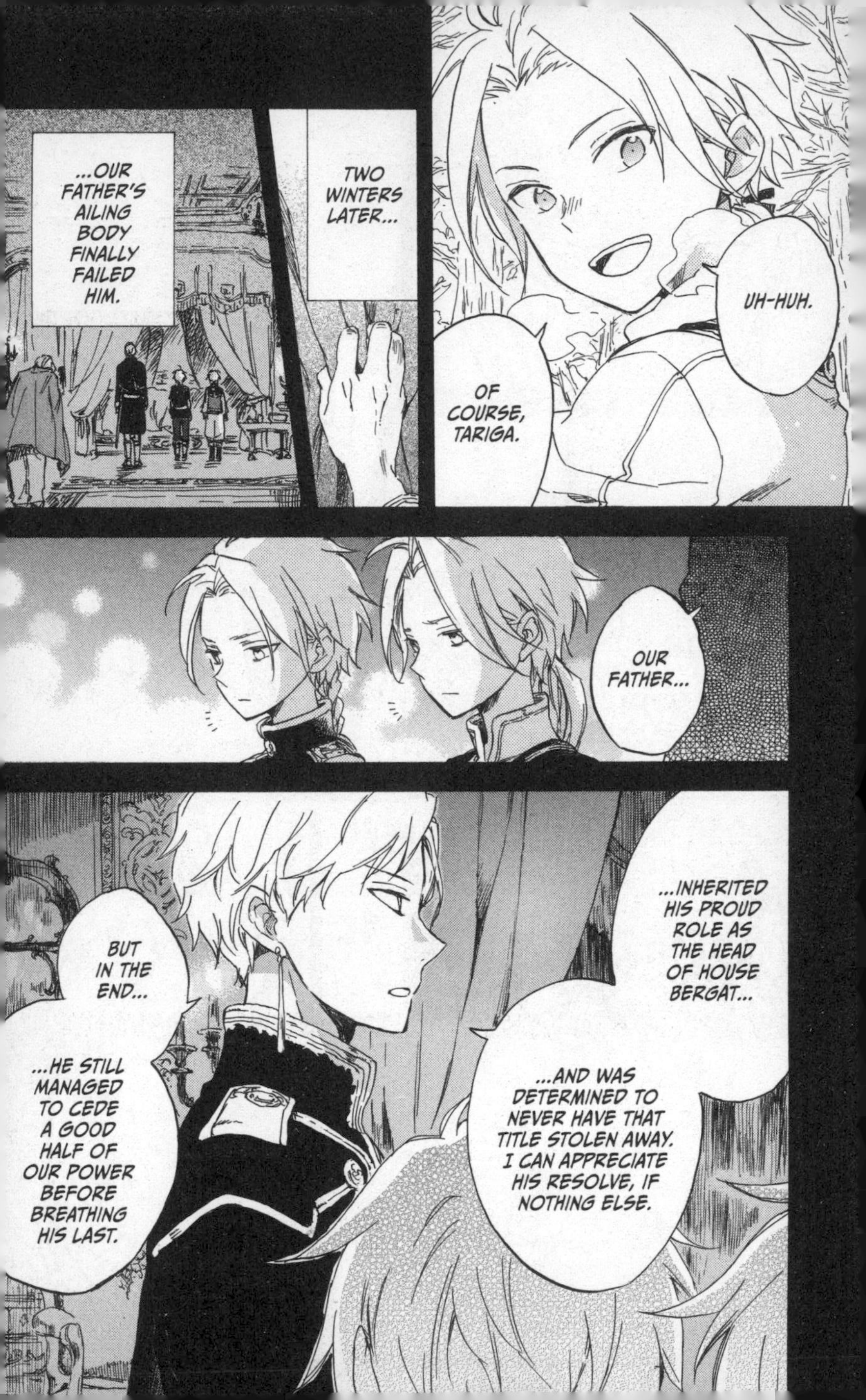
UH-HUH.
OF COURSE, TARIGA.
TWO WINTERS LATER...
...OUR FATHER'S AILING BODY FINALLY FAILED HIM.
OUR FATHER...
...INHERITED HIS PROUD ROLE AS THE HEAD OF HOUSE BERGAT...
...AND WAS DETERMINED TO NEVER HAVE THAT TITLE STOLEN AWAY. I CAN APPRECIATE HIS RESOLVE, IF NOTHING ELSE.
BUT IN THE END...
...HE STILL MANAGED TO CEDE A GOOD HALF OF OUR POWER BEFORE BREATHING HIS LAST.

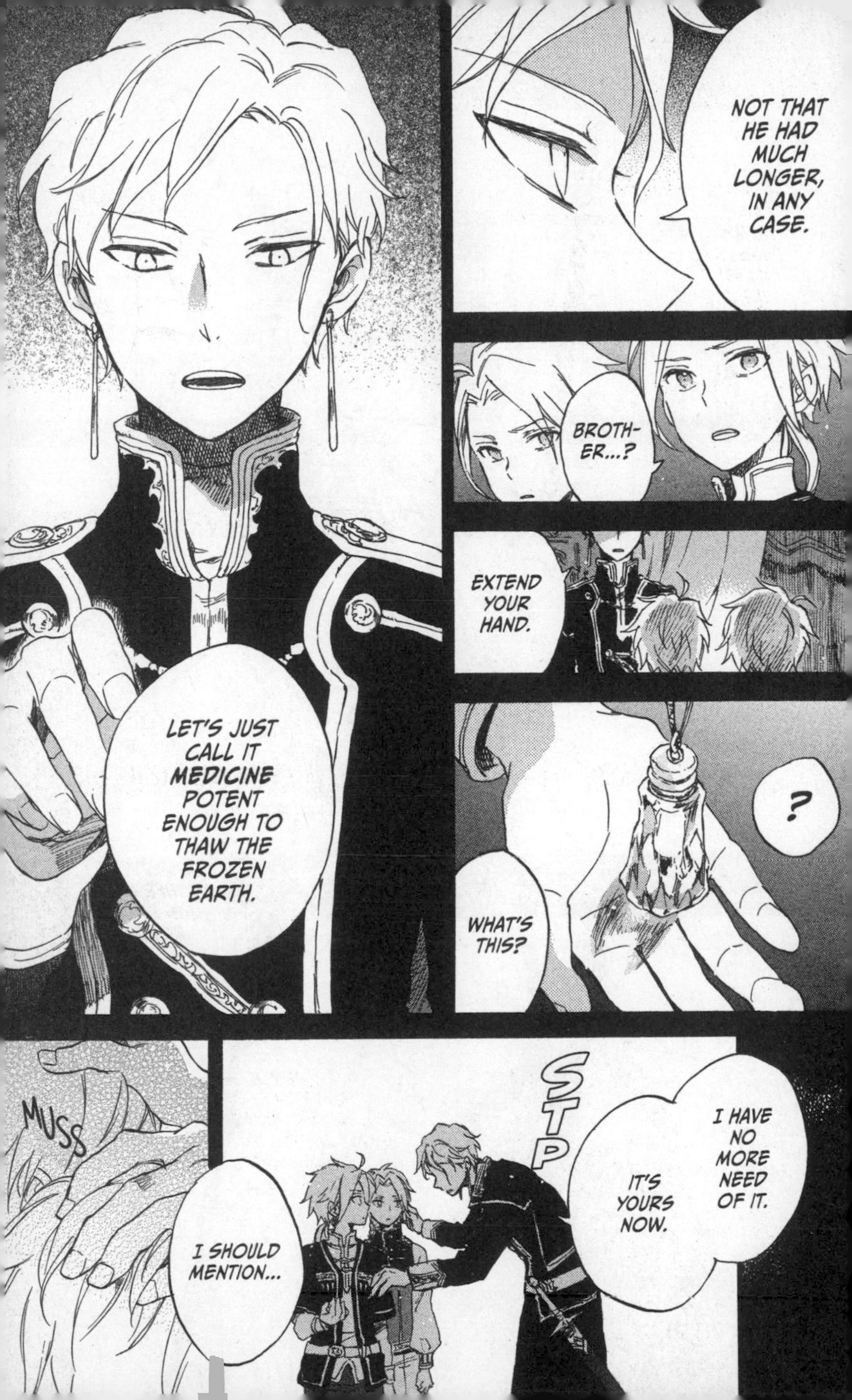
NOT THAT HE HAD MUCH LONGER, IN ANY CASE.
BROTHER...?
EXTEND YOUR HAND.
?
WHAT'S THIS?
LET'S JUST CALL IT MEDICINE POTENT ENOUGH TO THAW THE FROZEN EARTH.
STP
I HAVE NO MORE NEED OF IT.
IT'S YOURS NOW.
I SHOULD MENTION...
MUSS

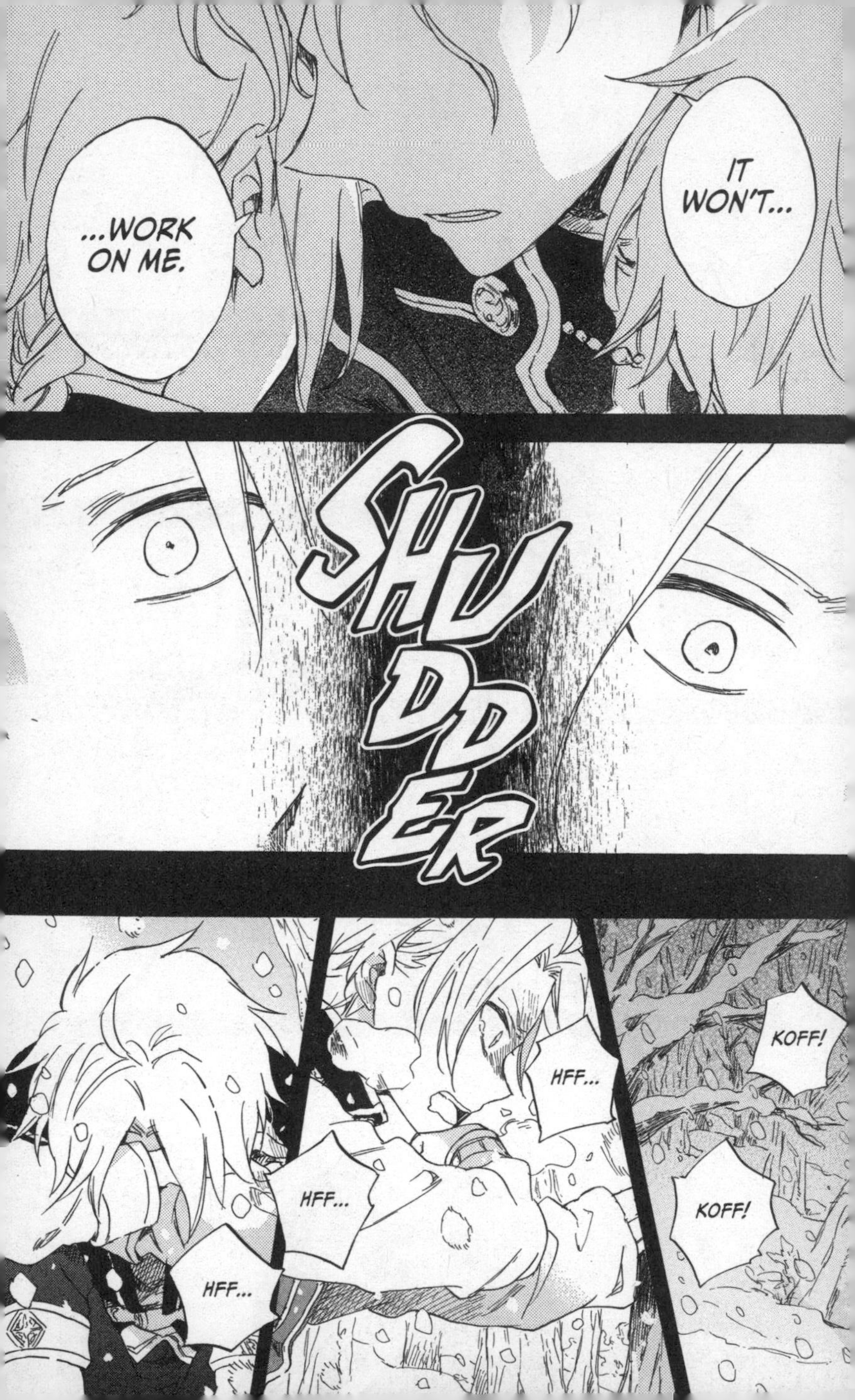
IT WON'T...
...WORK ON ME.
SHUDDER
KOFF!
HFF...
KOFF!
HFF...
HFF...

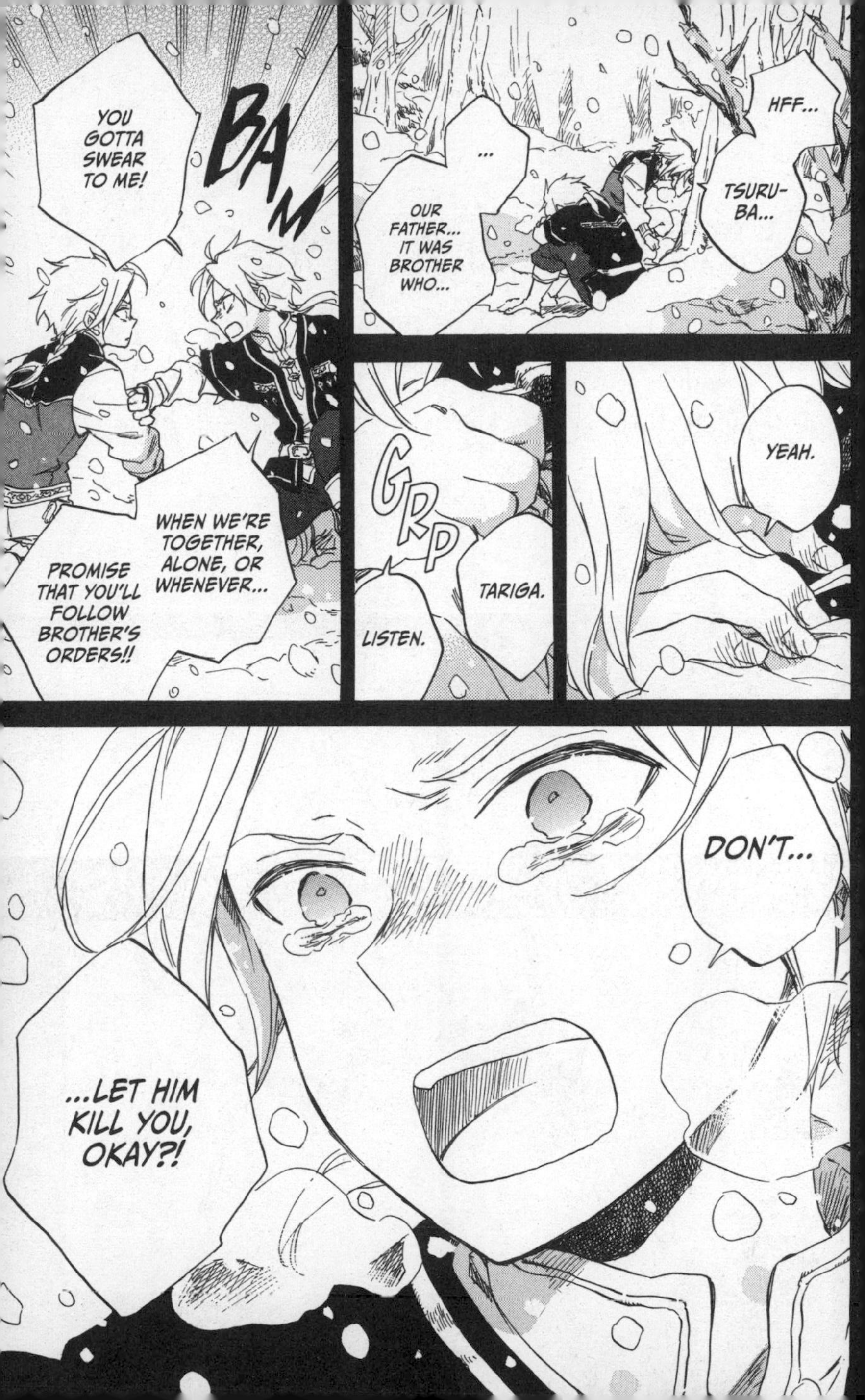
HFF...
TSURU-BA...
...
OUR FATHER... IT WAS BROTHER WHO...
YEAH.
GRP
TARIGA.
LISTEN.
BAM
YOU GOTTA SWEAR TO ME!
WHEN WE'RE TOGETHER, ALONE, OR WHENEVER...
PROMISE THAT YOU'LL FOLLOW BROTHER'S ORDERS!!
DON'T...
...LET HIM KILL YOU, OKAY?!

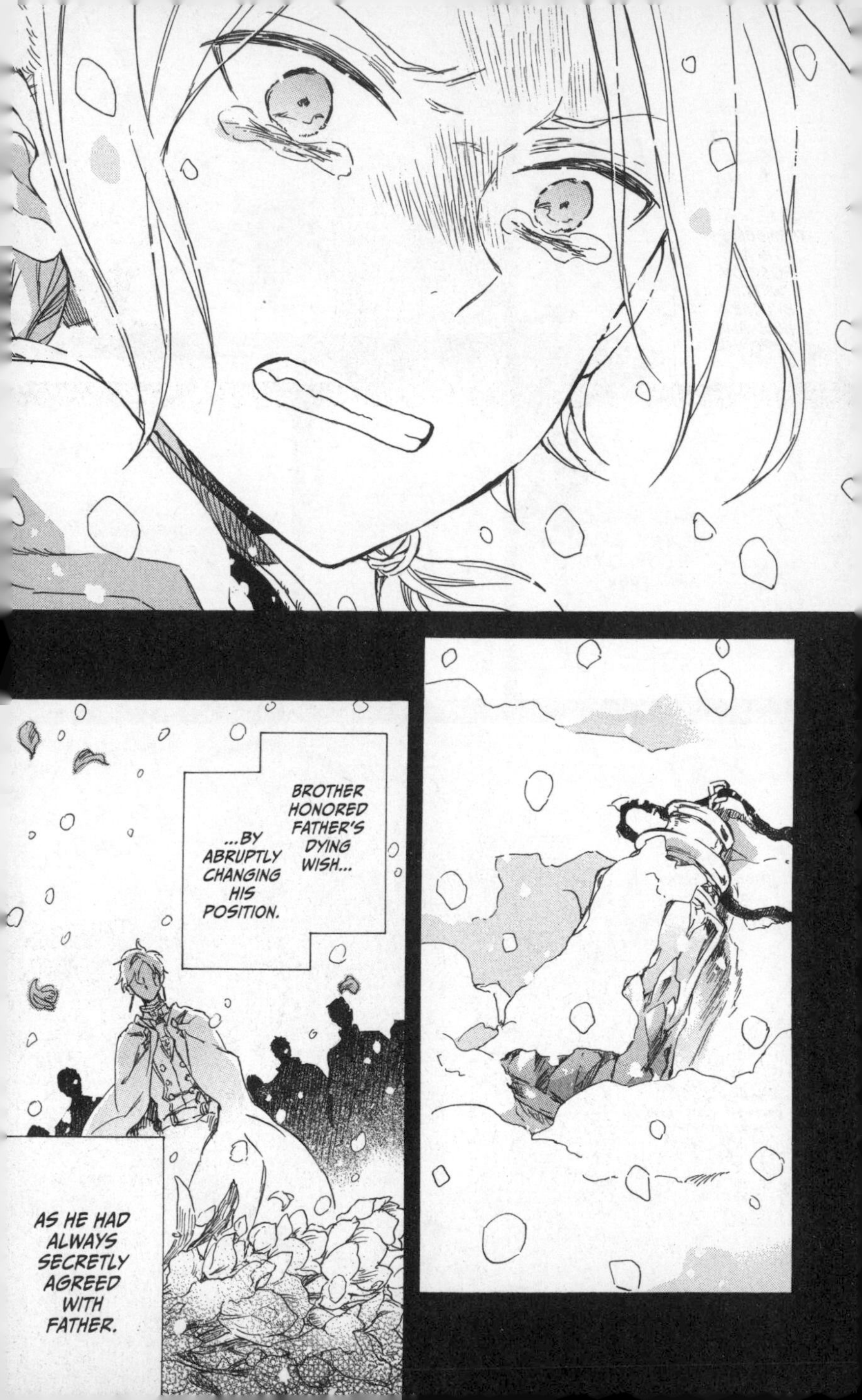
BROTHER HONORED FATHER'S DYING WISH...
...BY ABRUPTLY CHANGING HIS POSITION.
AS HE HAD ALWAYS SECRETLY AGREED WITH FATHER.

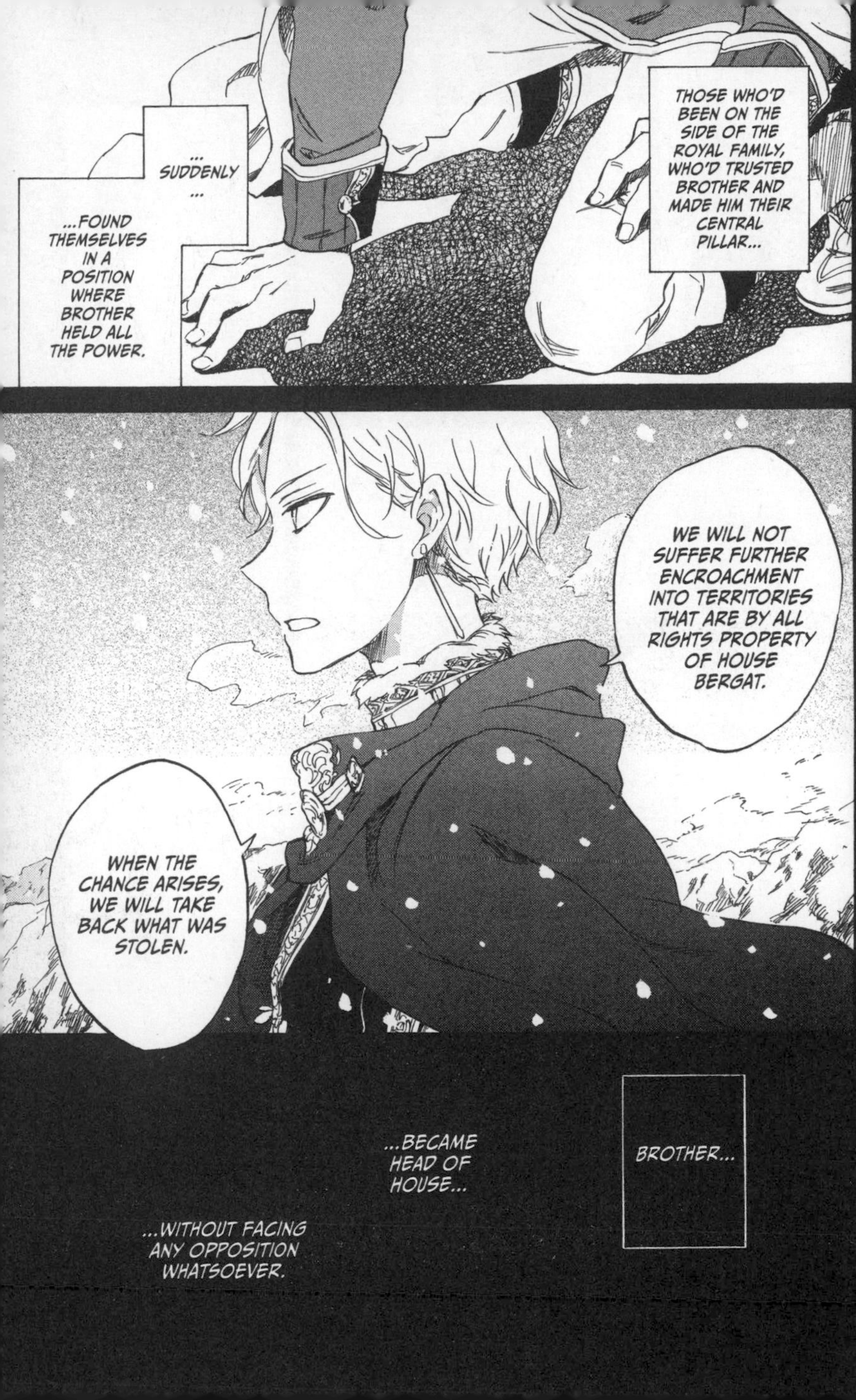
THOSE WHO'D BEEN ON THE SIDE OF THE ROYAL FAMILY, WHO'D TRUSTED BROTHER AND MADE HIM THEIR CENTRAL PILLAR...
...SUDDENLY...
...FOUND THEMSELVES IN A POSITION WHERE BROTHER HELD ALL THE POWER.
WE WILL NOT SUFFER FURTHER ENCROACHMENT INTO TERRITORIES THAT ARE BY ALL RIGHTS PROPERTY OF HOUSE BERGAT.
WHEN THE CHANCE ARISES, WE WILL TAKE BACK WHAT WAS STOLEN.
BROTHER...
...BECAME HEAD OF HOUSE...
...WITHOUT FACING ANY OPPOSITION WHATSOEVER.

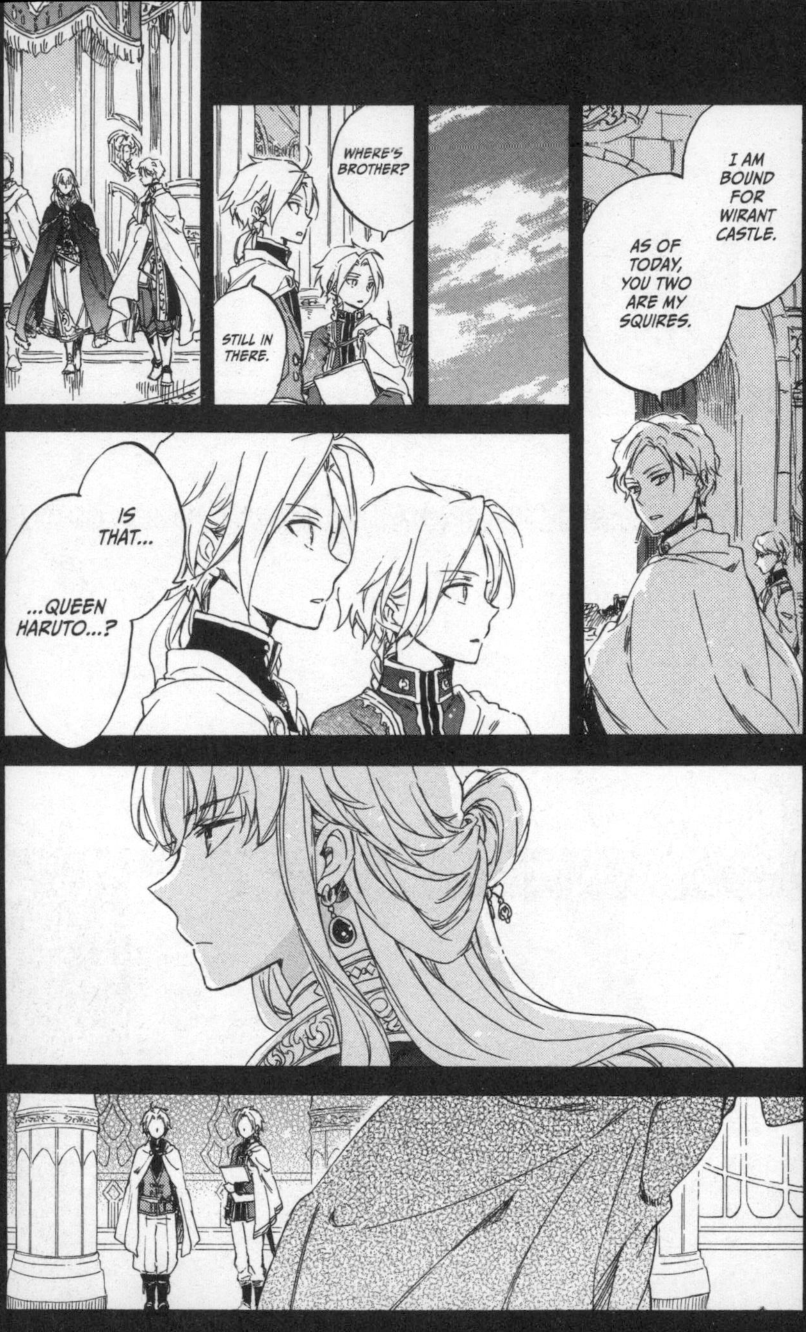
I AM BOUND FOR WIRANT CASTLE.
AS OF TODAY, YOU TWO ARE MY SQUIRES.
WHERE'S BROTHER?
STILL IN THERE.
IS THAT...
...QUEEN HARUTO...?

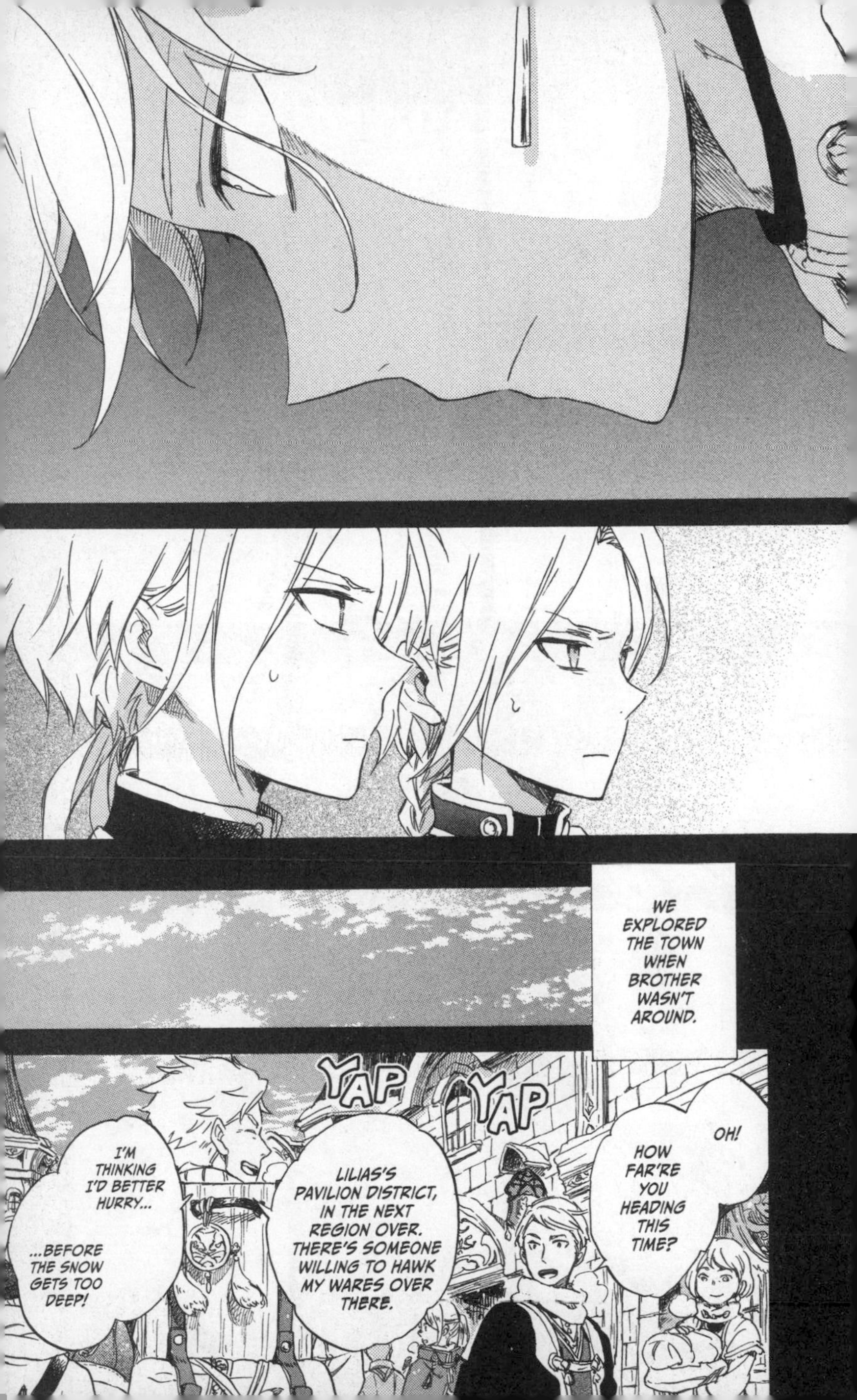
WE EXPLORED THE TOWN WHEN BROTHER WASN'T AROUND.
OH!
HOW FAR'RE YOU HEADING THIS TIME?
YAP YAP
LILIAS'S PAVILION DISTRICT, IN THE NEXT REGION OVER. THERE'S SOMEONE WILLING TO HAWK MY WARES OVER THERE.
I'M THINKING I'D BETTER HURRY...
...BEFORE THE SNOW GETS TOO DEEP!

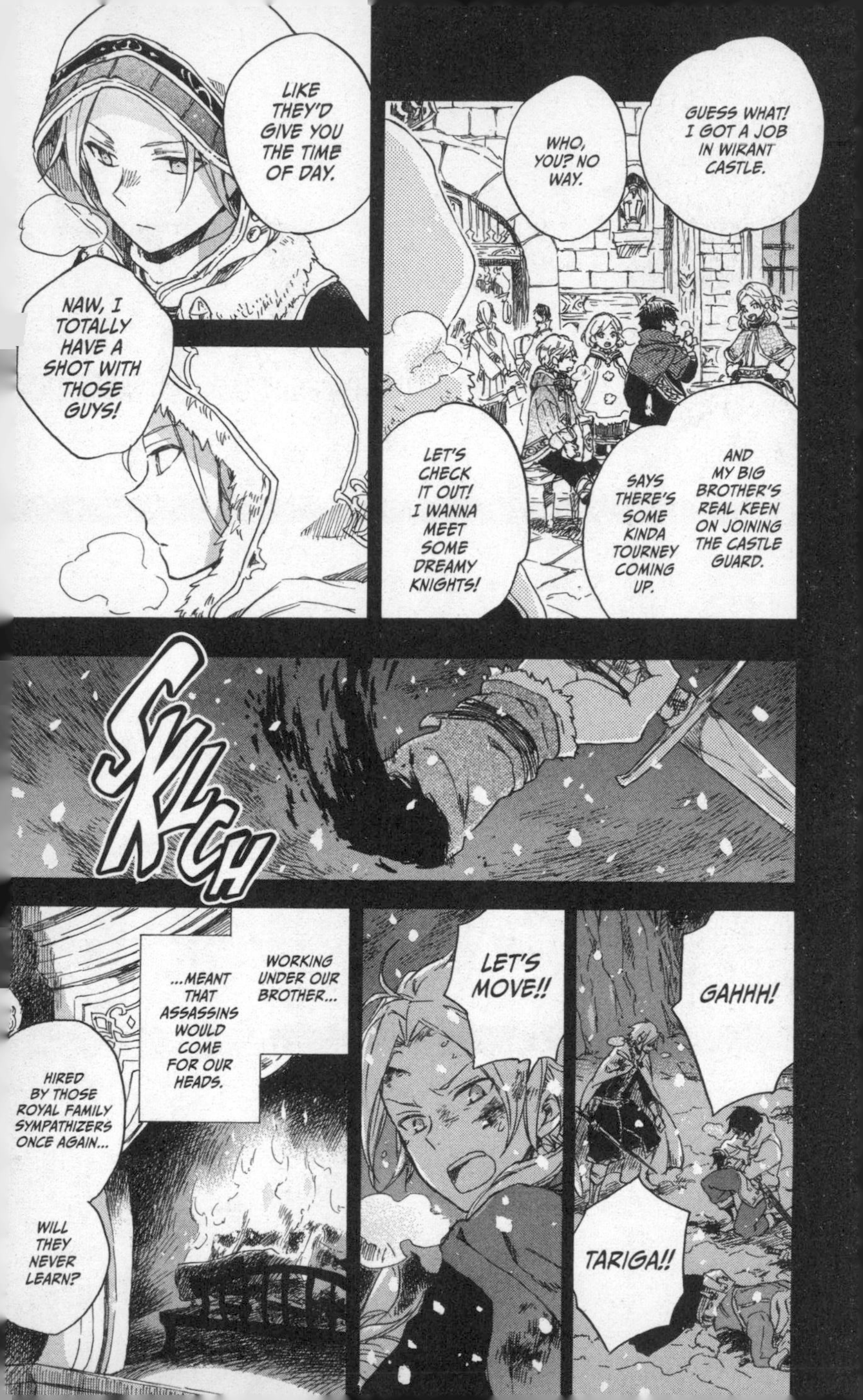
GUESS WHAT! I GOT A JOB IN WIRANT CASTLE.
WHO, YOU? NO WAY.
AND MY BIG BROTHER'S REAL KEEN ON JOINING THE CASTLE GUARD.
SAYS THERE'S SOME KINDA TOURNEY COMING UP.
LET'S CHECK IT OUT! I WANNA MEET SOME DREAMY KNIGHTS!
LIKE THEY'D GIVE YOU THE TIME OF DAY.
NAW, I TOTALLY HAVE A SHOT WITH THOSE GUYS!
SKLCH
GAHHH!
TARIGA!!
LET'S MOVE!!
WORKING UNDER OUR BROTHER...
...MEANT THAT ASSASSINS WOULD COME FOR OUR HEADS.
HIRED BY THOSE ROYAL FAMILY SYMPATHIZERS ONCE AGAIN...
WILL THEY NEVER LEARN?

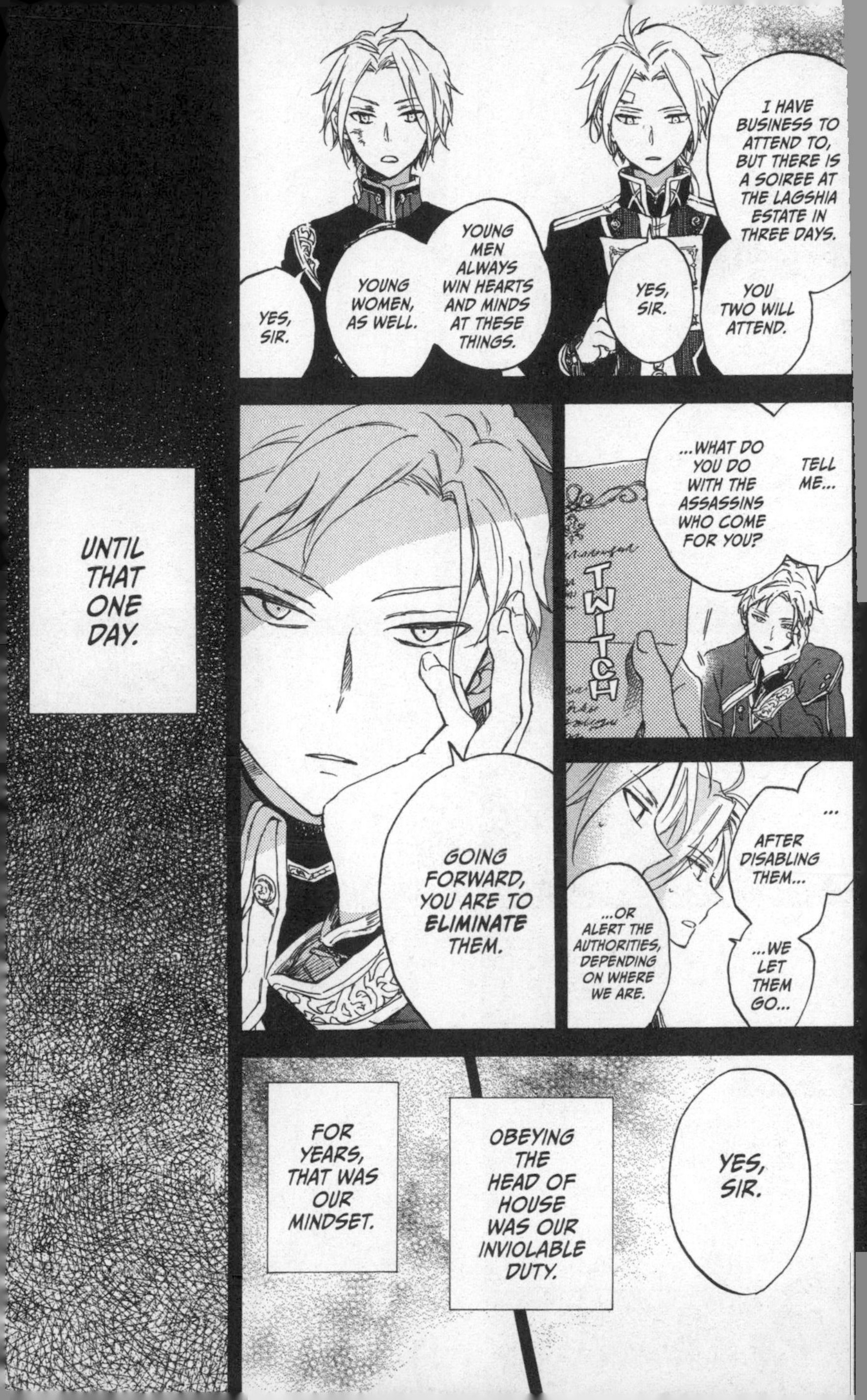
I HAVE BUSINESS TO ATTEND TO, BUT THERE IS A SOIREE AT THE LAGSHIA ESTATE IN THREE DAYS.
YOU TWO WILL ATTEND.
YES, SIR.
YOUNG MEN ALWAYS WIN HEARTS AND MINDS AT THESE THINGS.
YOUNG WOMEN, AS WELL.
YES, SIR.
TELL ME...
...WHAT DO YOU DO WITH THE ASSASSINS WHO COME FOR YOU?
TWITCH
...
AFTER DISABLING THEM...
...WE LET THEM GO...
...OR ALERT THE AUTHORITIES, DEPENDING ON WHERE WE ARE.
GOING FORWARD, YOU ARE TO ELIMINATE THEM.
YES, SIR.
OBEYING THE HEAD OF HOUSE WAS OUR INVIOLABLE DUTY.
FOR YEARS, THAT WAS OUR MINDSET.
UNTIL THAT ONE DAY.

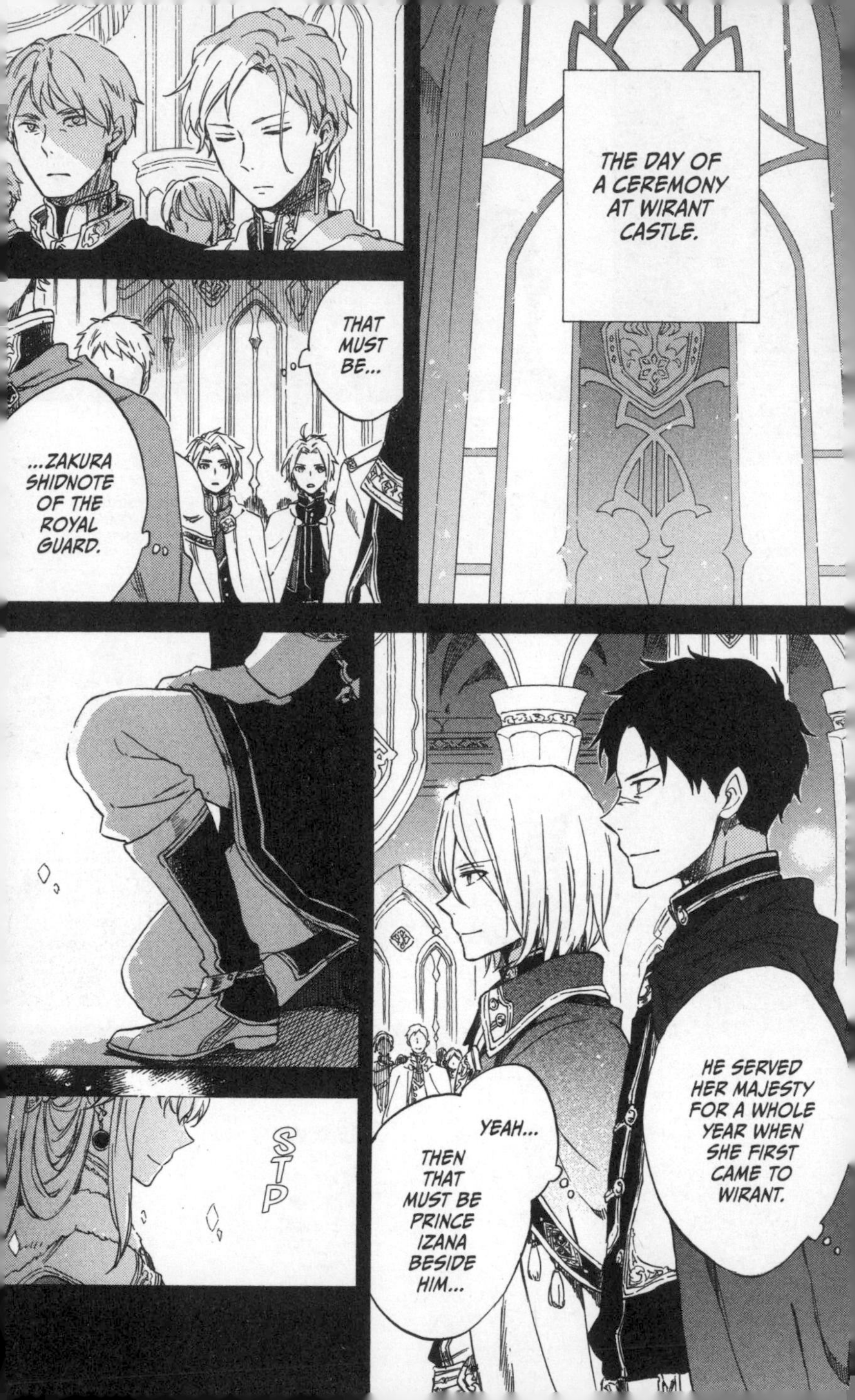
THE DAY OF A CEREMONY AT WIRANT CASTLE.
THAT MUST BE...
...ZAKURA SHIDNOTE OF THE ROYAL GUARD.
HE SERVED HER MAJESTY FOR A WHOLE YEAR WHEN SHE FIRST CAME TO WIRANT.
YEAH...
THEN THAT MUST BE PRINCE IZANA BESIDE HIM...
STP

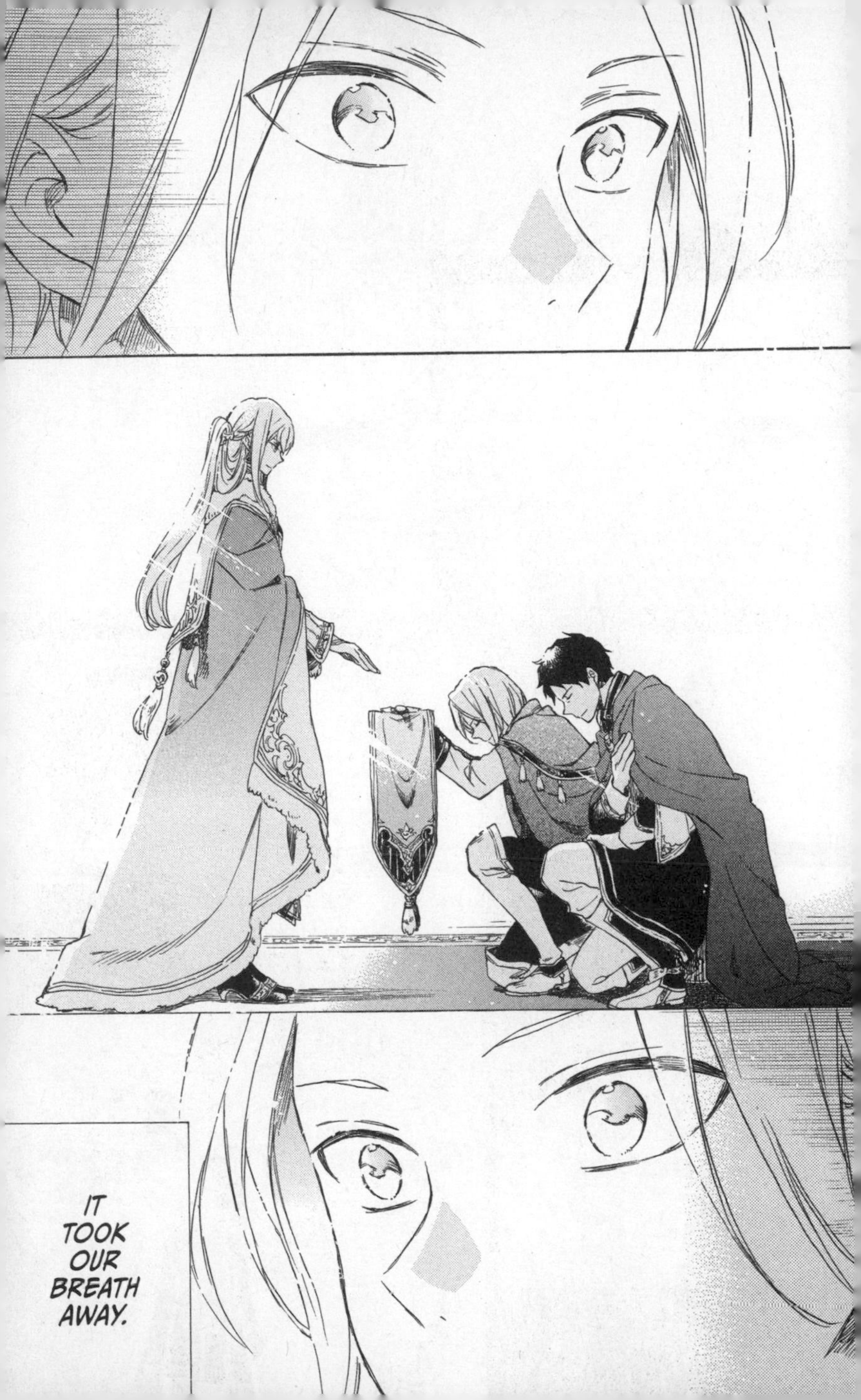
IT TOOK OUR BREATH AWAY.

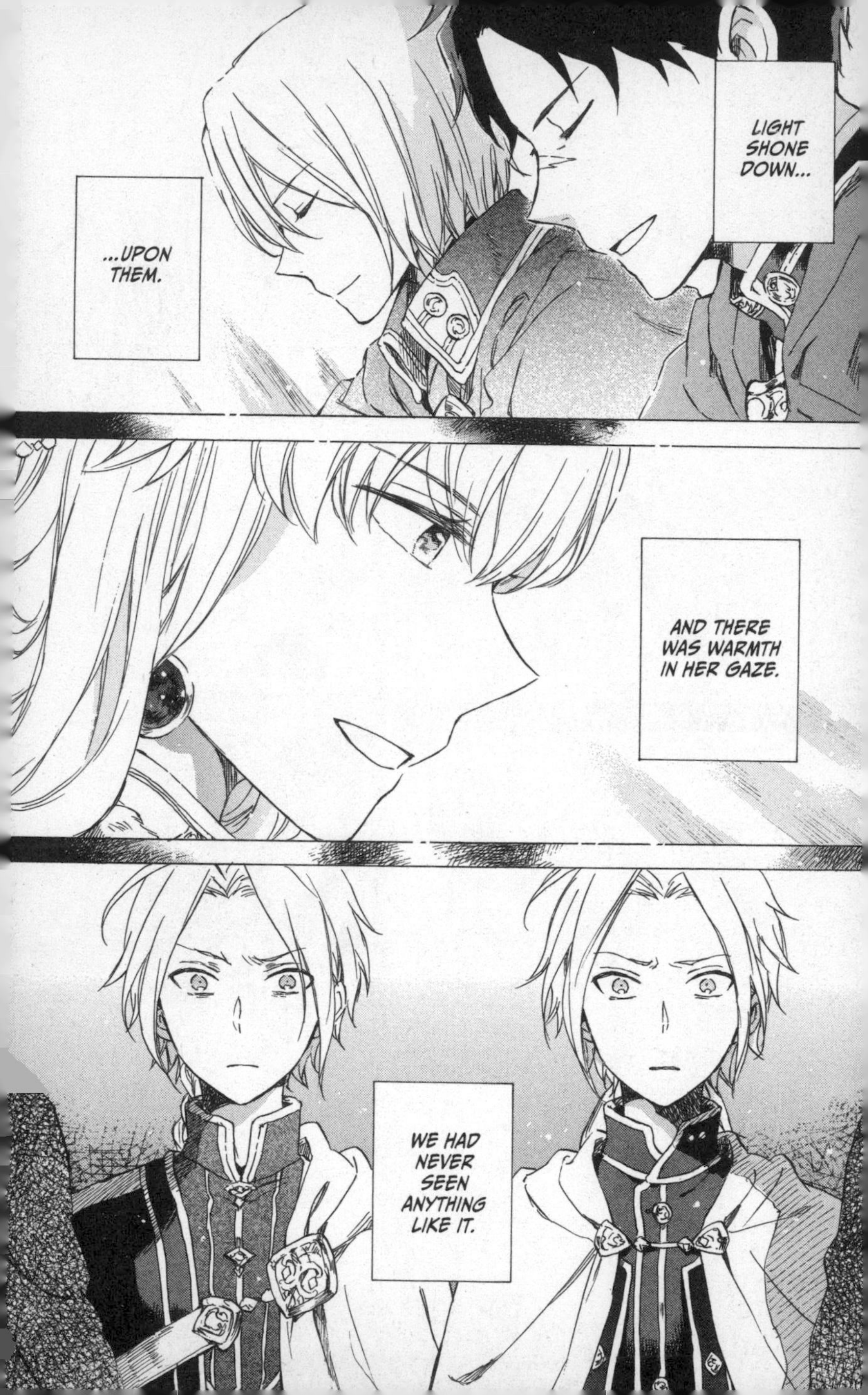
LIGHT SHONE DOWN...
...UPON THEM.
AND THERE WAS WARMTH IN HER GAZE.
WE HAD NEVER SEEN ANYTHING LIKE IT.

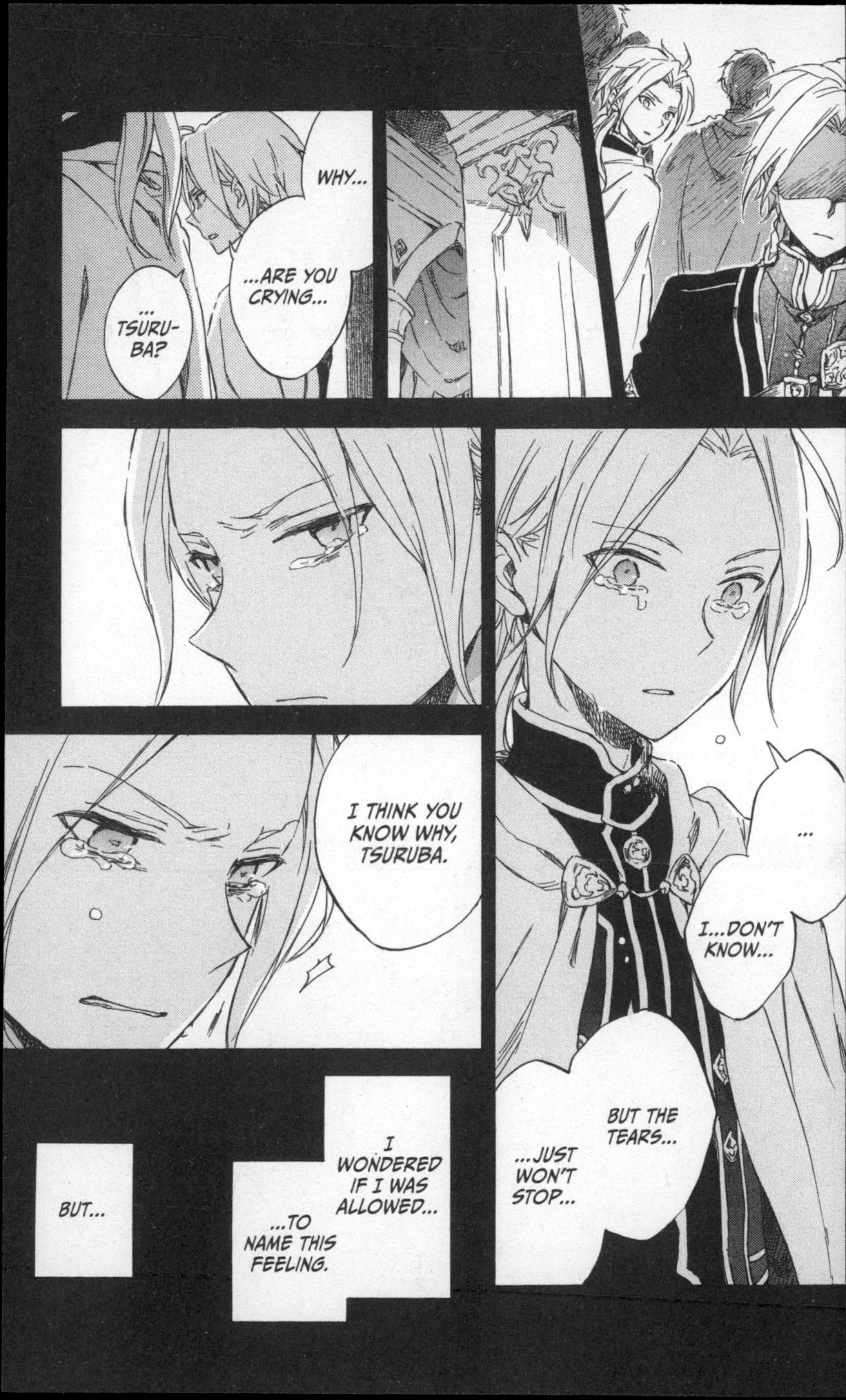
WHY...
...ARE YOU CRYING...
... TSURU-BA?
...
I...DON'T KNOW...
BUT THE TEARS...
...JUST WON'T STOP...
I THINK YOU KNOW WHY, TSURUBA.
I WONDERED IF I WAS ALLOWED...
...TO NAME THIS FEELING.
BUT...

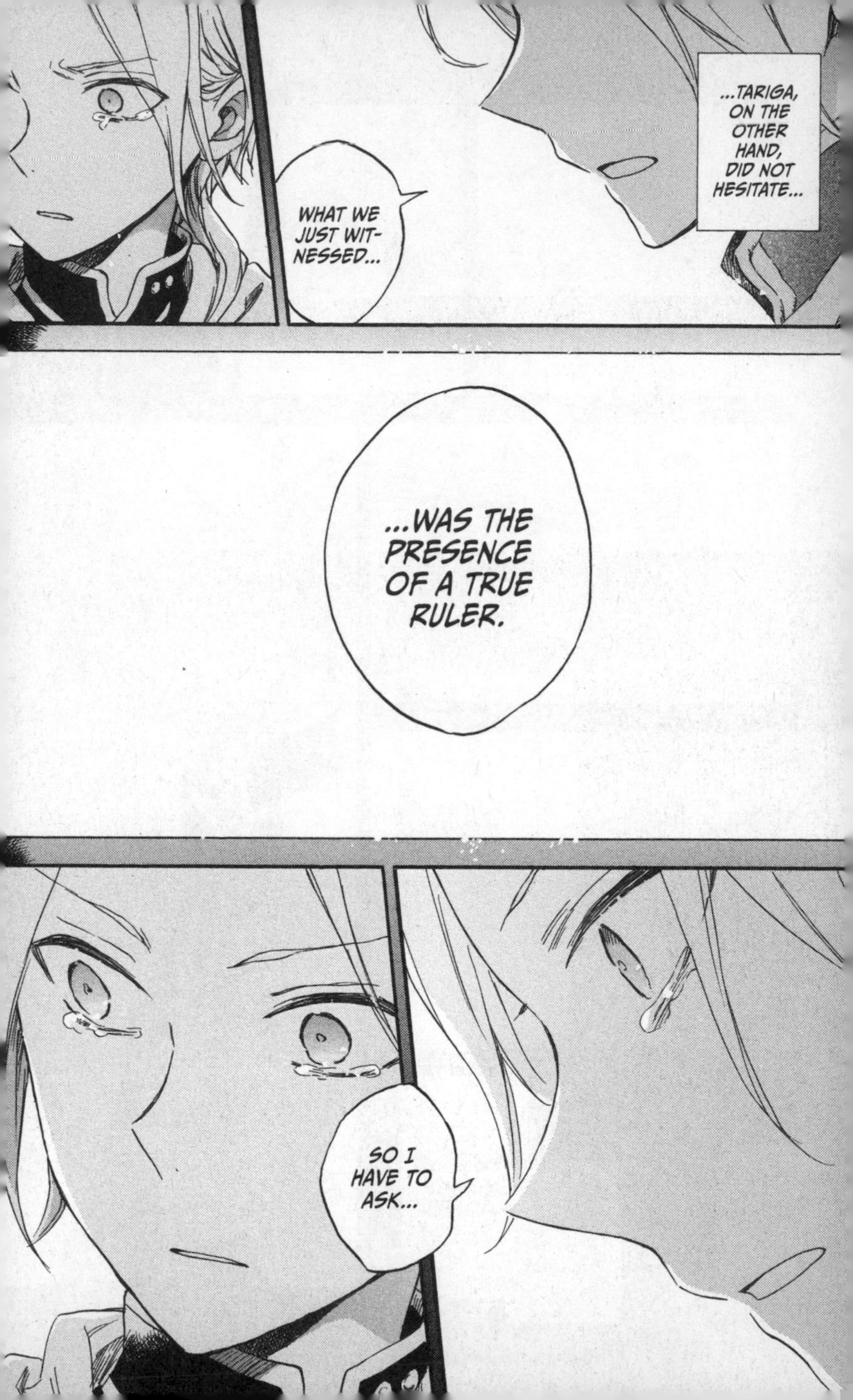
...TARIGA, ON THE OTHER HAND, DID NOT HESITATE...
WHAT WE JUST WITNESSED...
...WAS THE PRESENCE OF A TRUE RULER.
SO I HAVE TO ASK...

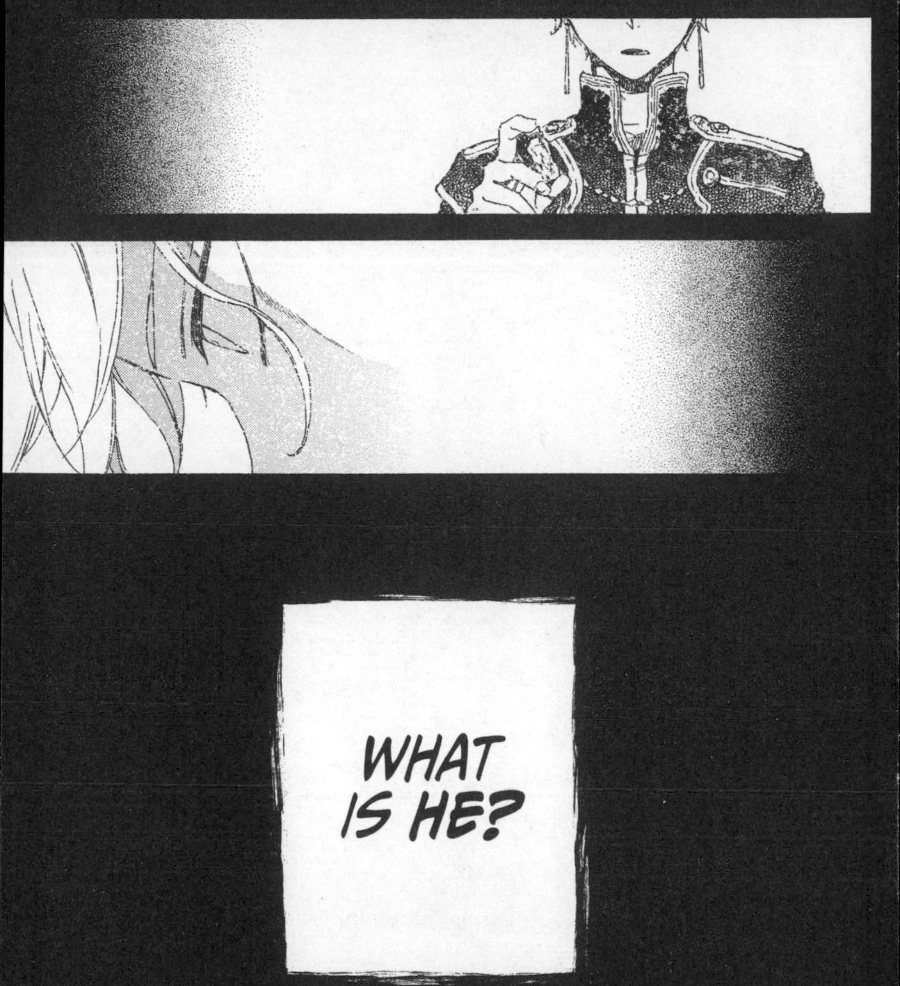
WHAT IS HE?

WE WOULD TURN
EVERYTHING
AROUND.

...THEN
WE...

IF BROTHER
WAS WAITING
FOR A CHANCE
TO SEIZE BACK
POWER FOR
HOUSE
BERGAT...

...WOULD
WAIT FOR A
CHANCE TO
STEAL THAT
POWER FROM
HIM.

HOW
INNOCENT.

HOW
NAIVE WE
WERE.

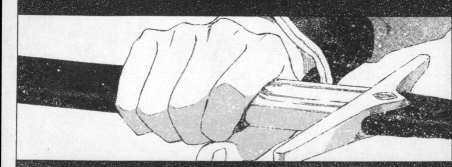

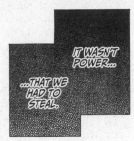

IT WASN'T POWER...
...THAT WE HAD TO STEAL.
CLOP CLOP
WHINNY
TMP
SHWNG

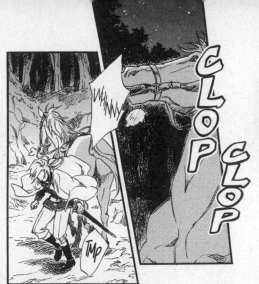

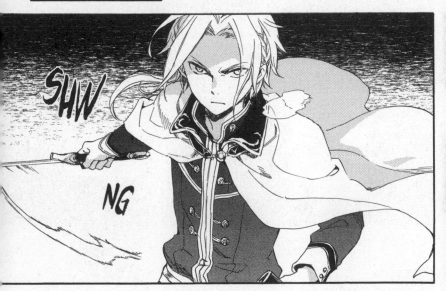

IT WAS OUR BROTHER'S VERY LIFE.

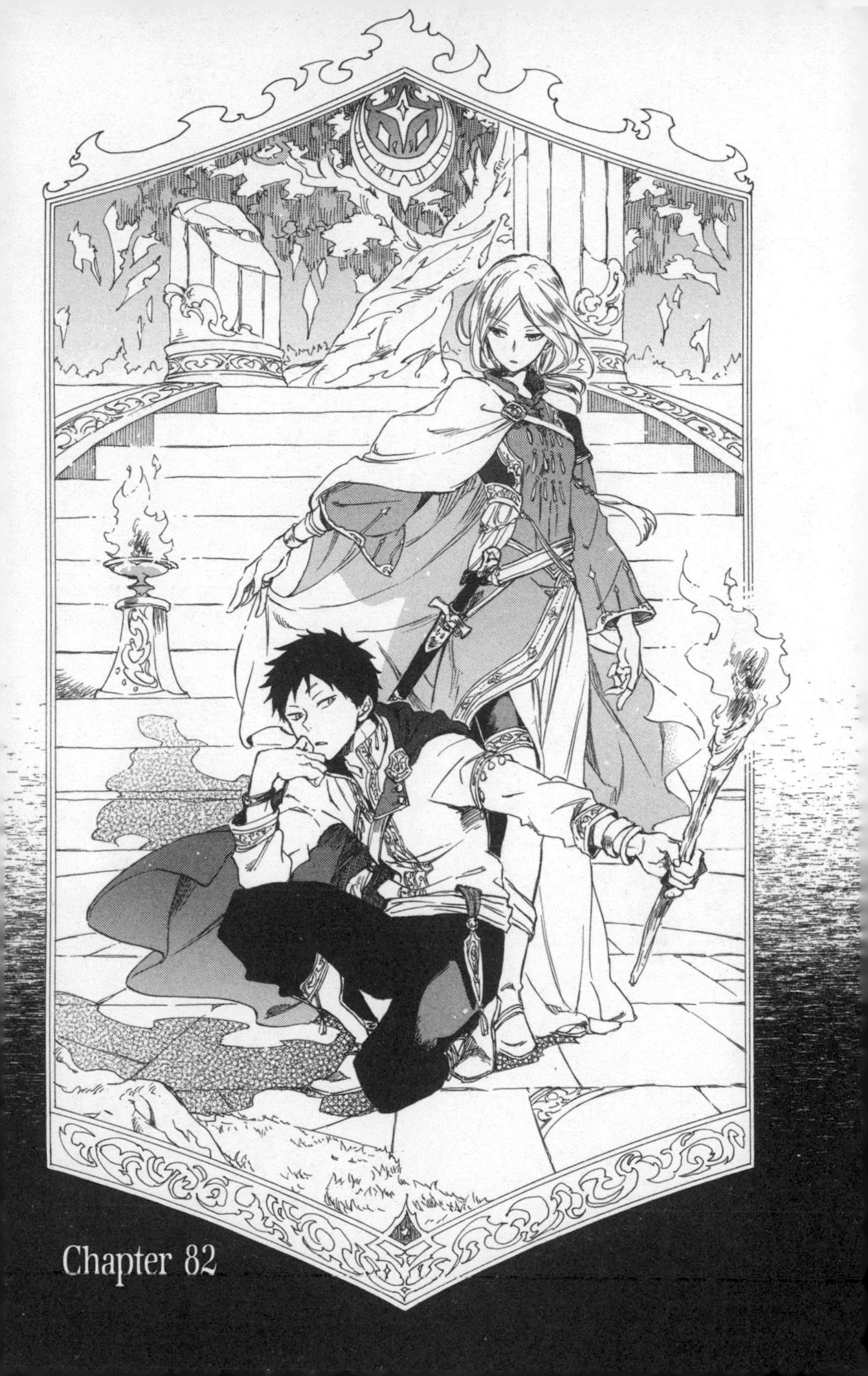
Chapter 82

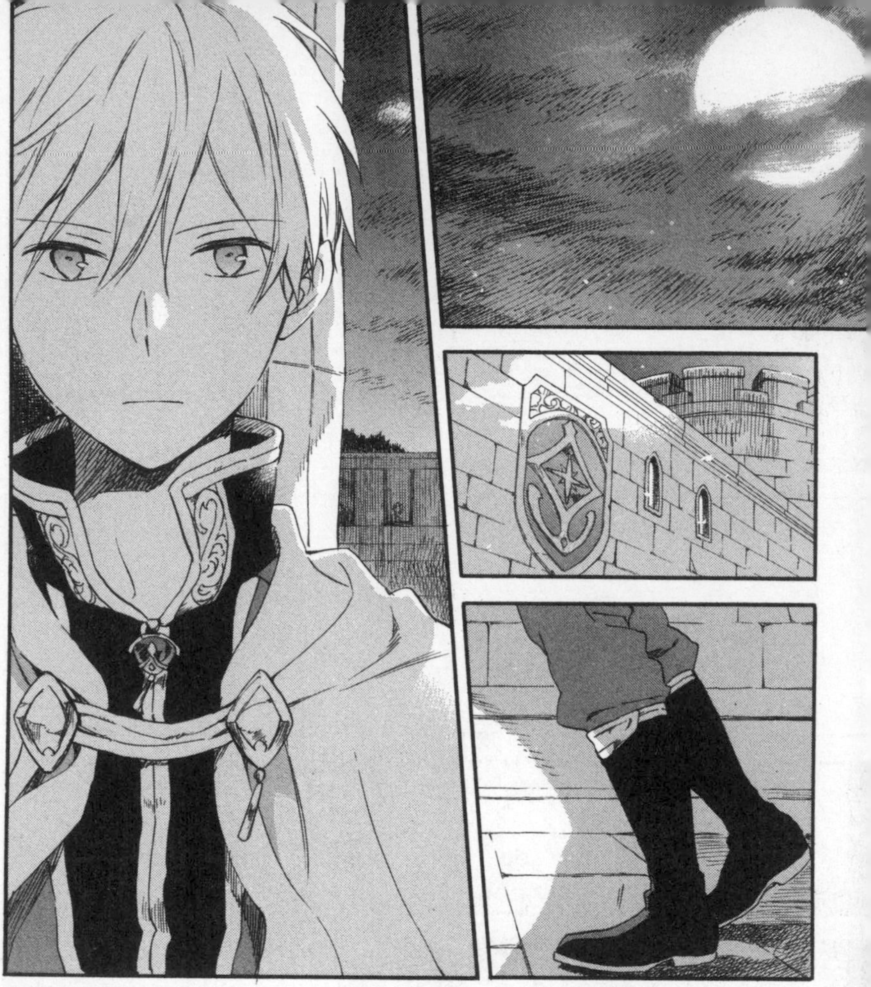

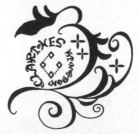

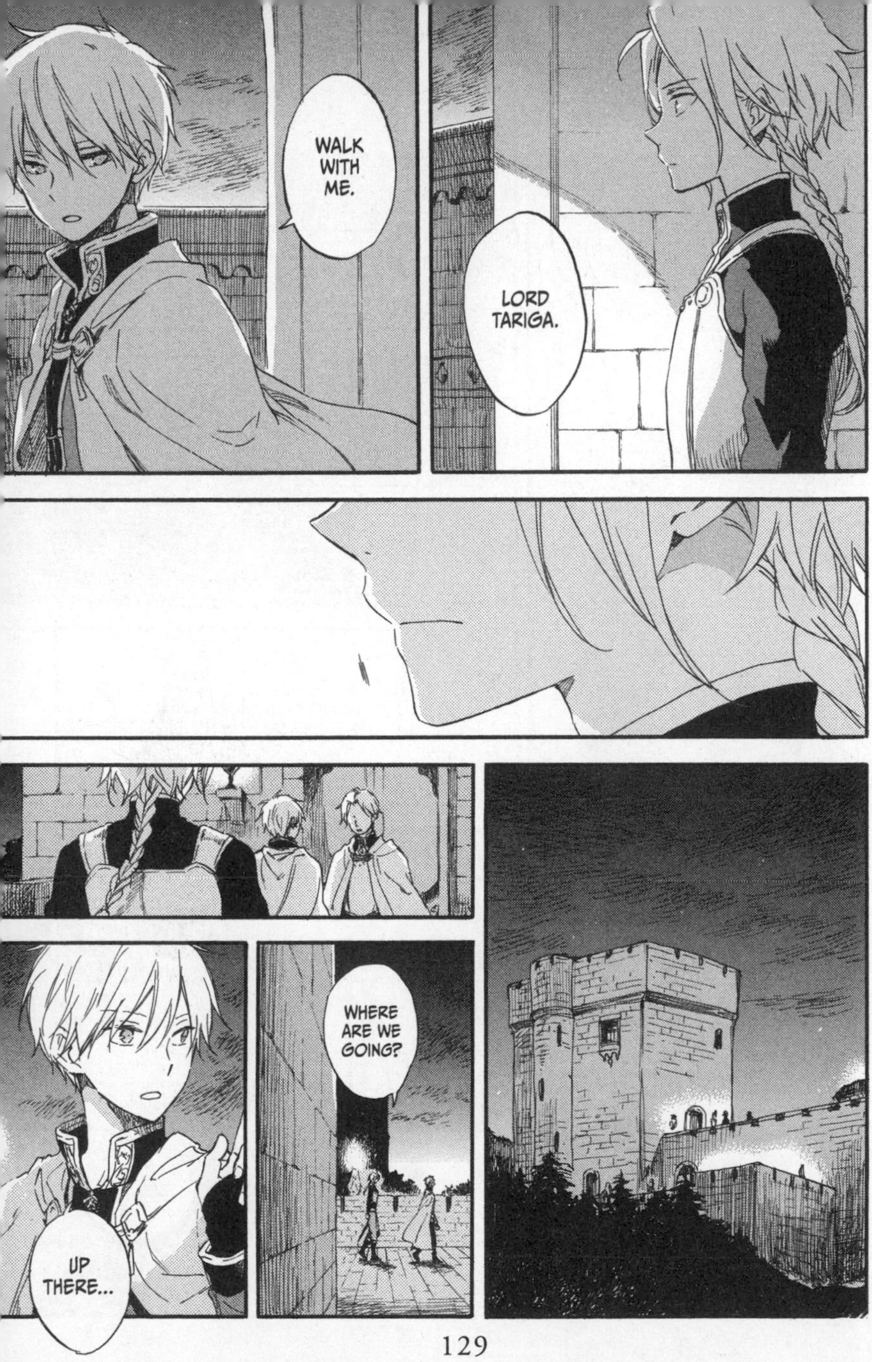
LORD TARIGA.
WALK WITH ME.
WHERE ARE WE GOING?
UP THERE...

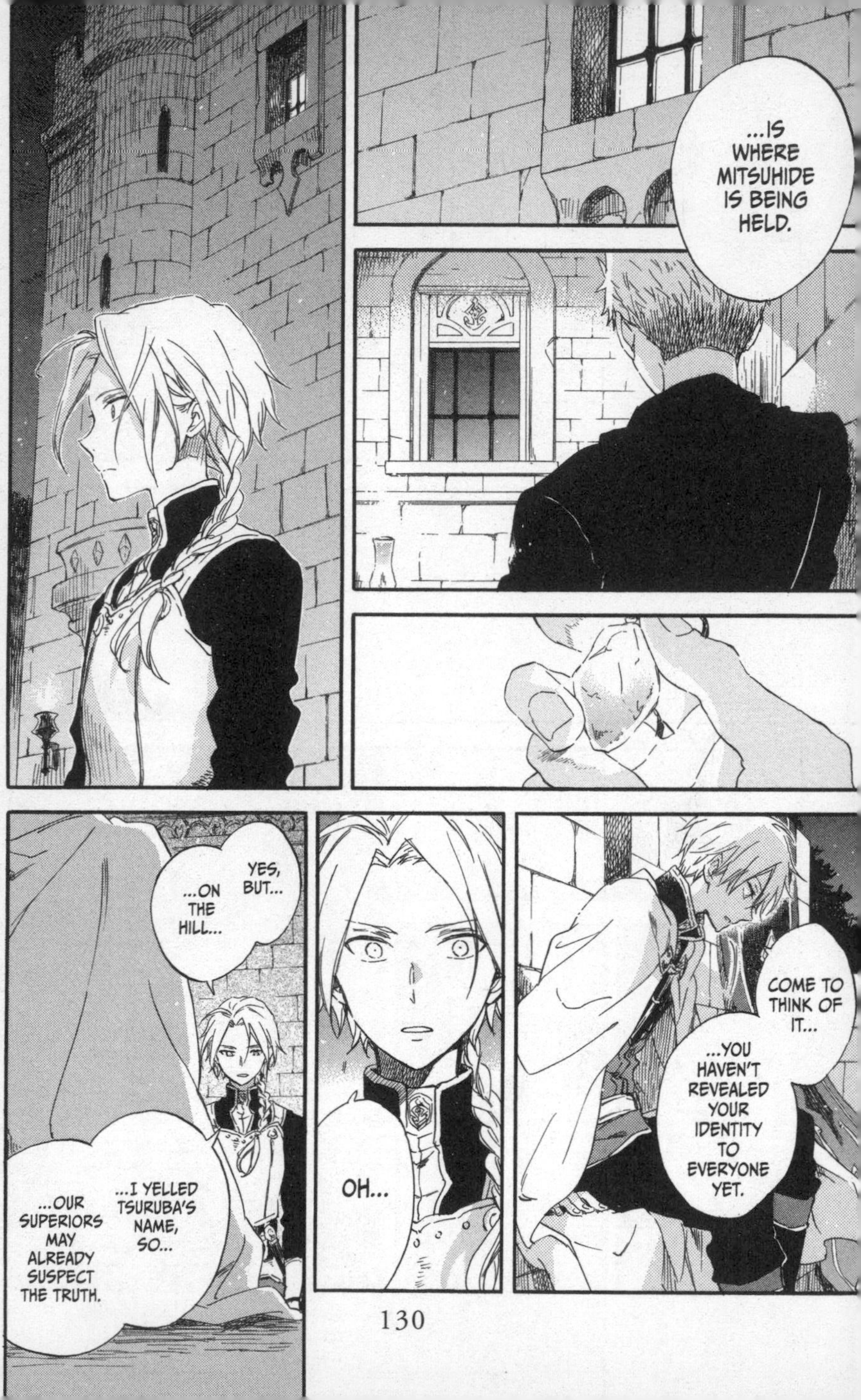
...IS WHERE MITSUHIDE IS BEING HELD.
COME TO THINK OF IT...
...YOU HAVEN'T REVEALED YOUR IDENTITY TO EVERYONE YET.
OH...
YES, BUT...
...ON THE HILL...
...I YELLED TSURUBA'S NAME, SO...
...OUR SUPERIORS MAY ALREADY SUSPECT THE TRUTH.

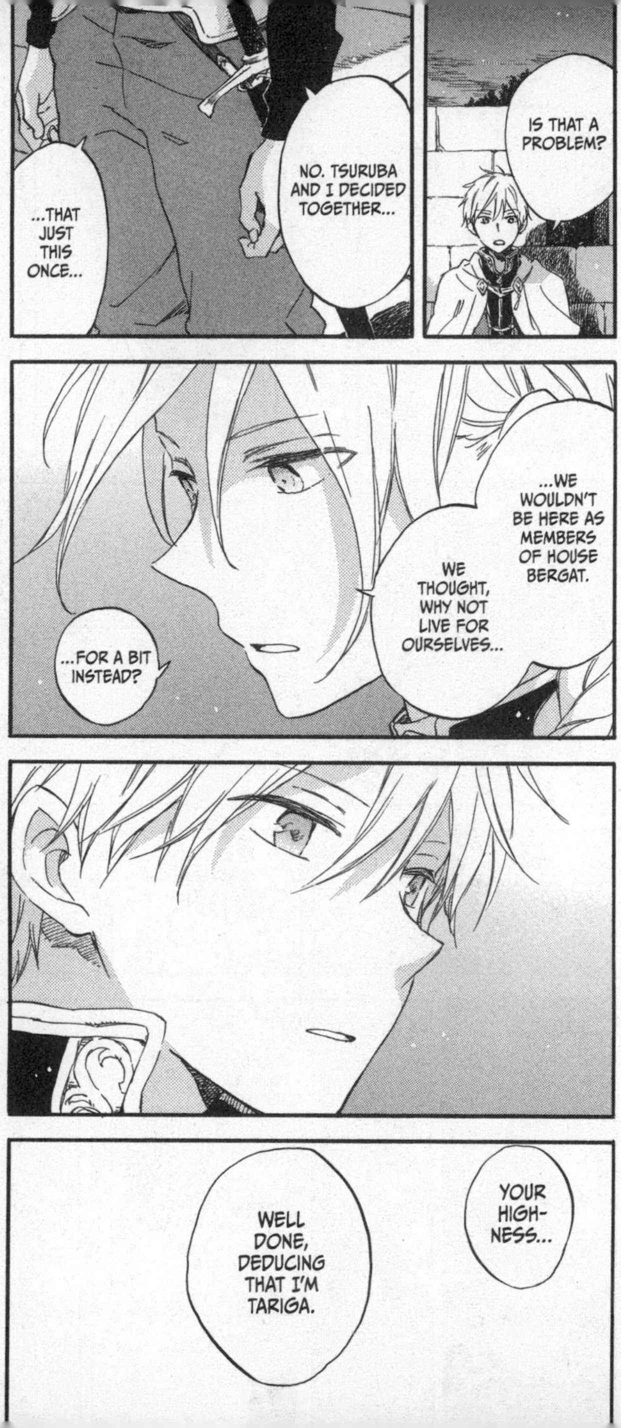
IS THAT A PROBLEM?
NO. TSURUBA AND I DECIDED TOGETHER...
...THAT JUST THIS ONCE...
...WE WOULDN'T BE HERE AS MEMBERS OF HOUSE BERGAT.
WE THOUGHT, WHY NOT LIVE FOR OURSELVES...
...FOR A BIT INSTEAD?
YOUR HIGH-NESS...
WELL DONE, DEDUCING THAT I'M TARIGA.

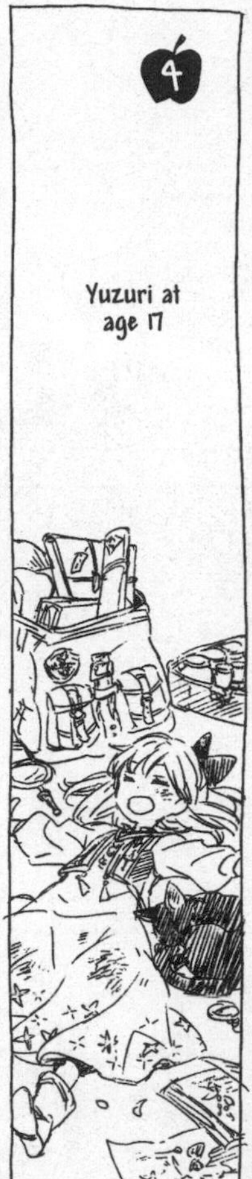
4
Yuzuri at age 17
I wanna do the same job as Dad!

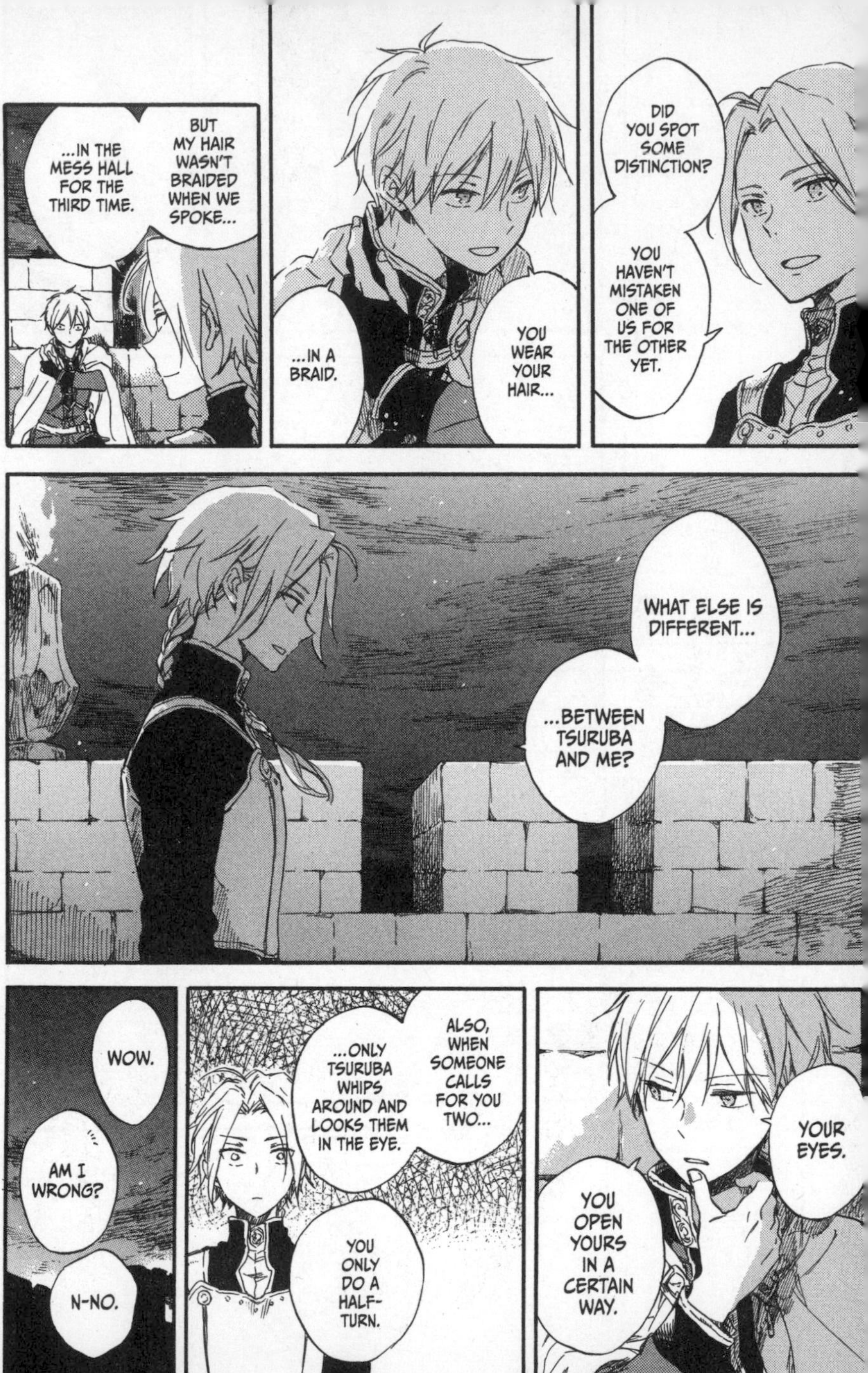
DID YOU SPOT SOME DISTINCTION?
YOU HAVEN'T MISTAKEN ONE OF US FOR THE OTHER YET.
YOU WEAR YOUR HAIR...
...IN A BRAID.
BUT MY HAIR WASN'T BRAIDED WHEN WE SPOKE...
...IN THE MESS HALL FOR THE THIRD TIME.
WHAT ELSE IS DIFFERENT...
...BETWEEN TSURUBA AND ME?
YOUR EYES.
YOU OPEN YOURS IN A CERTAIN WAY.
ALSO, WHEN SOMEONE CALLS FOR YOU TWO...
...ONLY TSURUBA WHIPS AROUND AND LOOKS THEM IN THE EYE.
YOU ONLY DO A HALF-TURN.
WOW.
AM I WRONG?
N-NO.

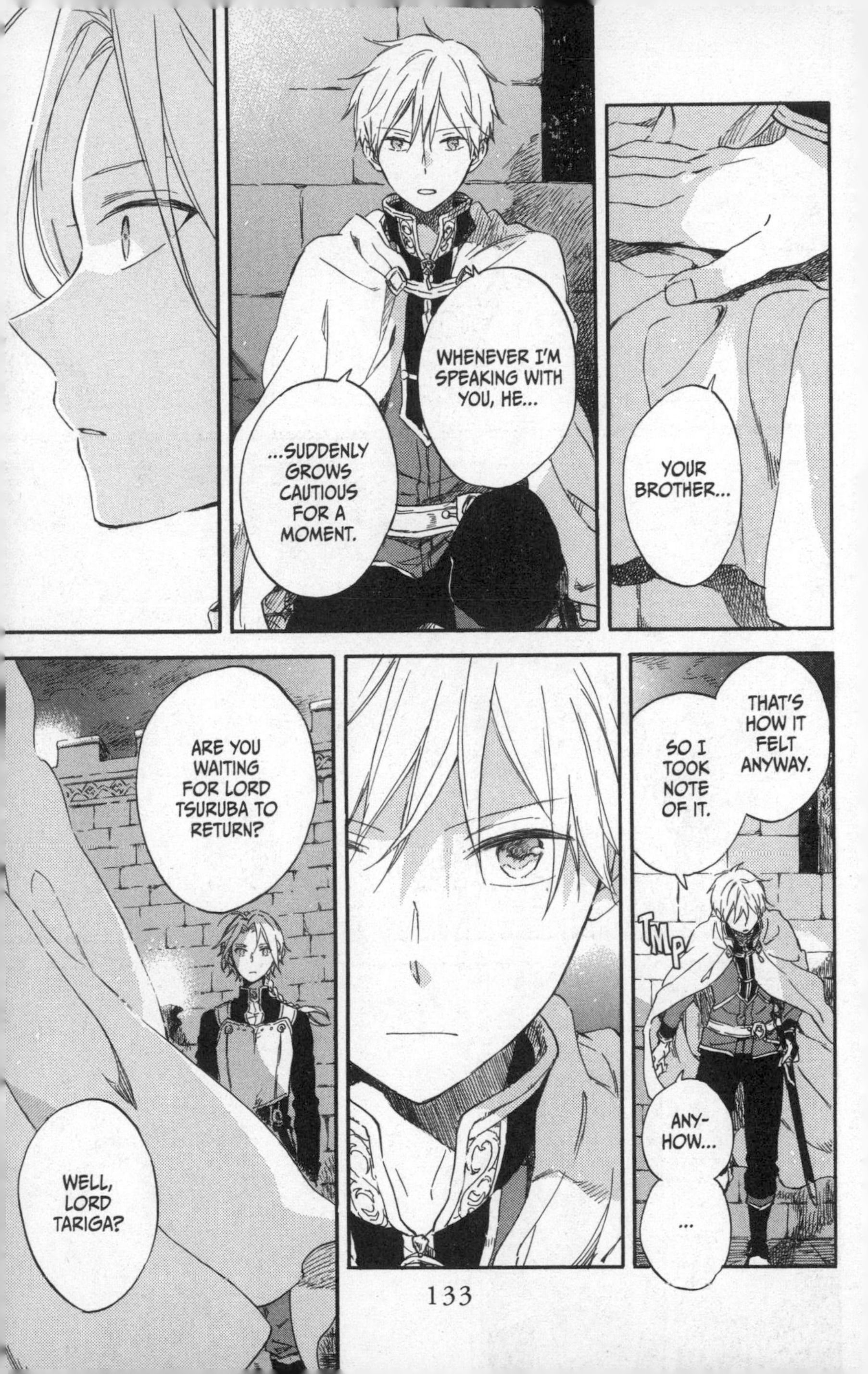
YOUR BROTHER...
WHENEVER I'M SPEAKING WITH YOU, HE...
...SUDDENLY GROWS CAUTIOUS FOR A MOMENT.
THAT'S HOW IT FELT ANYWAY.
SO I TOOK NOTE OF IT.
TMP
ANY-HOW...
...
ARE YOU WAITING FOR LORD TSURUBA TO RETURN?
WELL, LORD TARIGA?

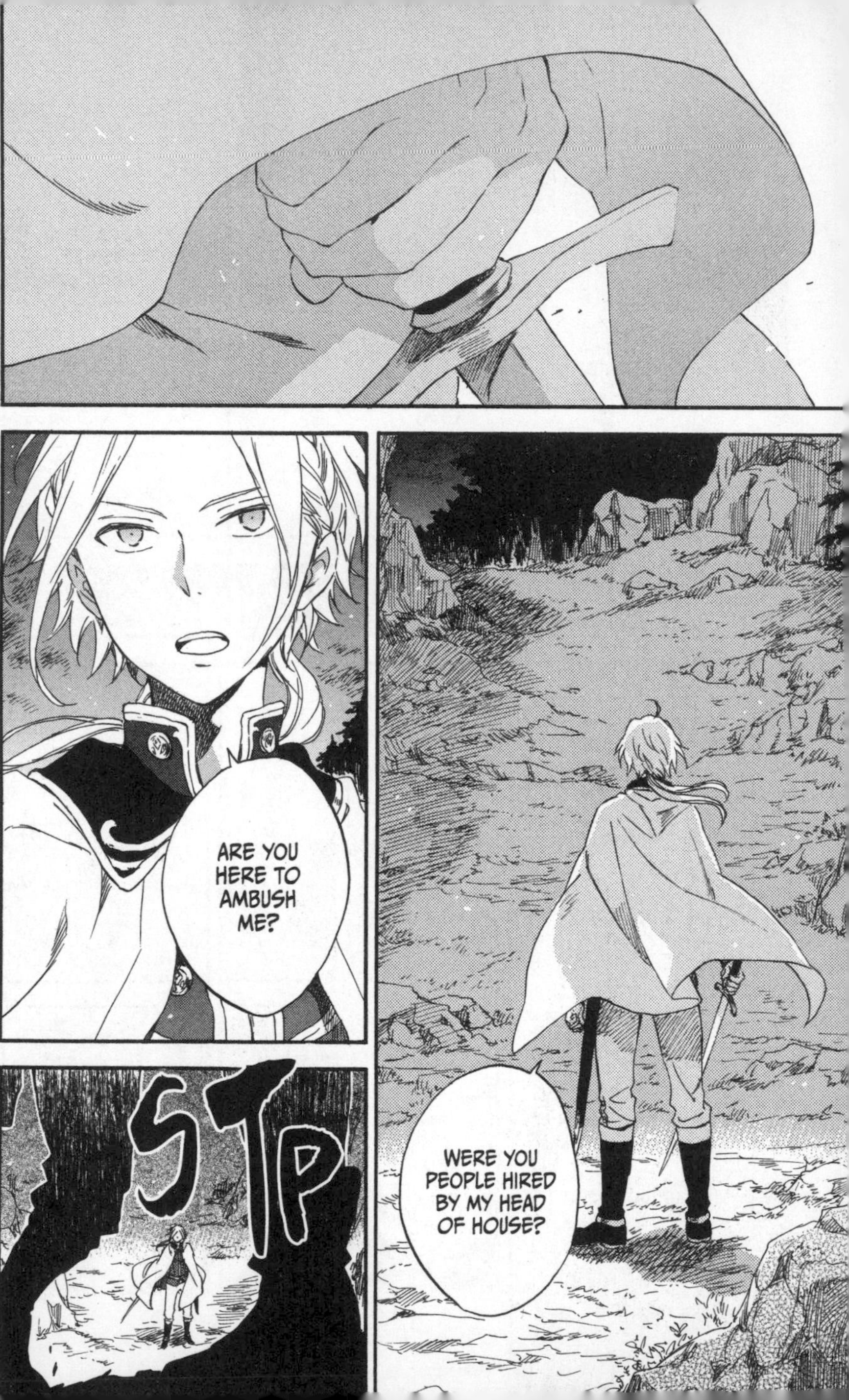
WERE YOU PEOPLE HIRED BY MY HEAD OF HOUSE?
ARE YOU HERE TO AMBUSH ME?
STP

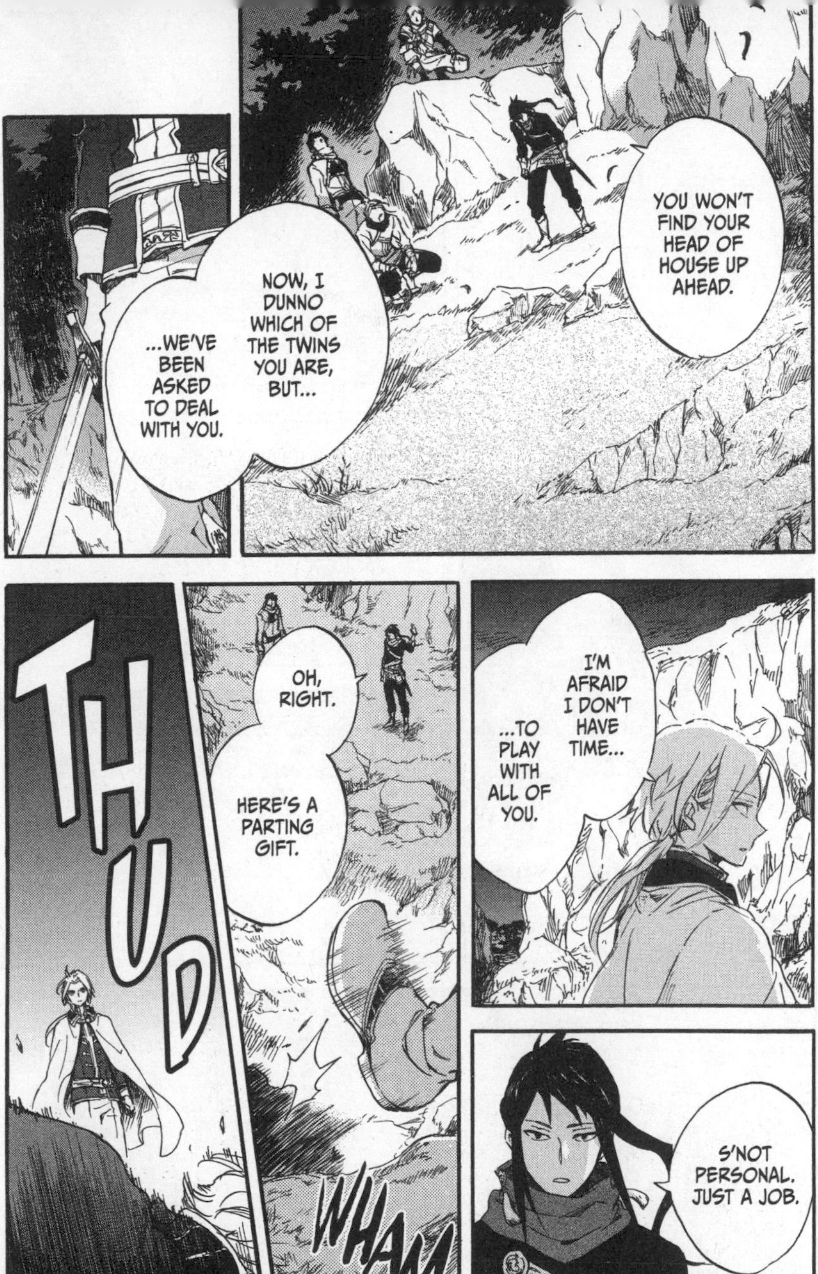
YOU WON'T FIND YOUR HEAD OF HOUSE UP AHEAD.
NOW, I DUNNO WHICH OF THE TWINS YOU ARE, BUT...
...WE'VE BEEN ASKED TO DEAL WITH YOU.
I'M AFRAID I DON'T HAVE TIME...
...TO PLAY WITH ALL OF YOU.
S'NOT PERSONAL. JUST A JOB.
OH, RIGHT.
HERE'S A PARTING GIFT.
WHAM
THUD

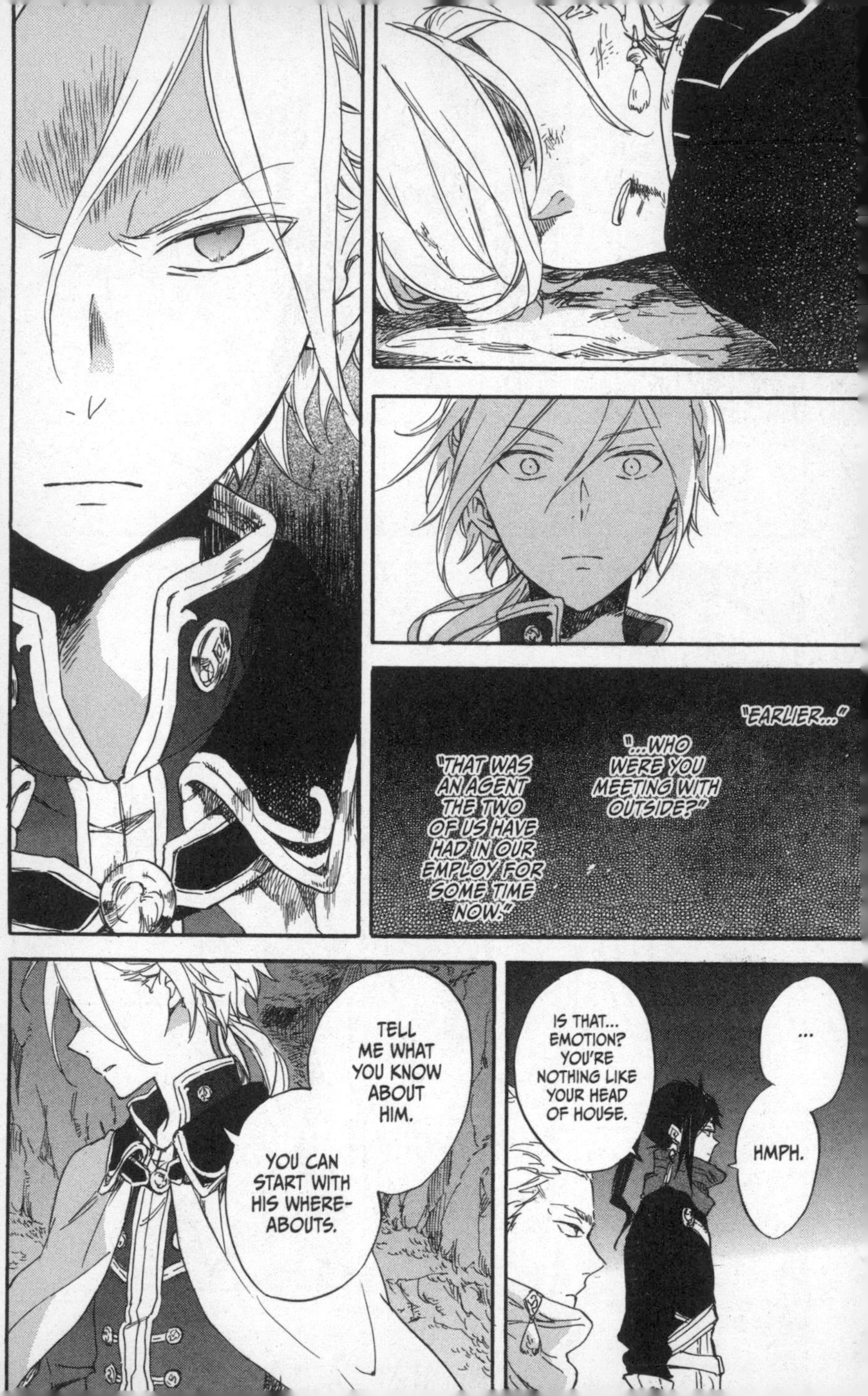
"EARLIER..."
"...WHO WERE YOU MEETING WITH OUTSIDE?"
"THAT WAS AN AGENT THE TWO OF US HAVE HAD IN OUR EMPLOY FOR SOME TIME NOW."
...
HMPH.
IS THAT... EMOTION? YOU'RE NOTHING LIKE YOUR HEAD OF HOUSE.
TELL ME WHAT YOU KNOW ABOUT HIM.
YOU CAN START WITH HIS WHERE-ABOUTS.

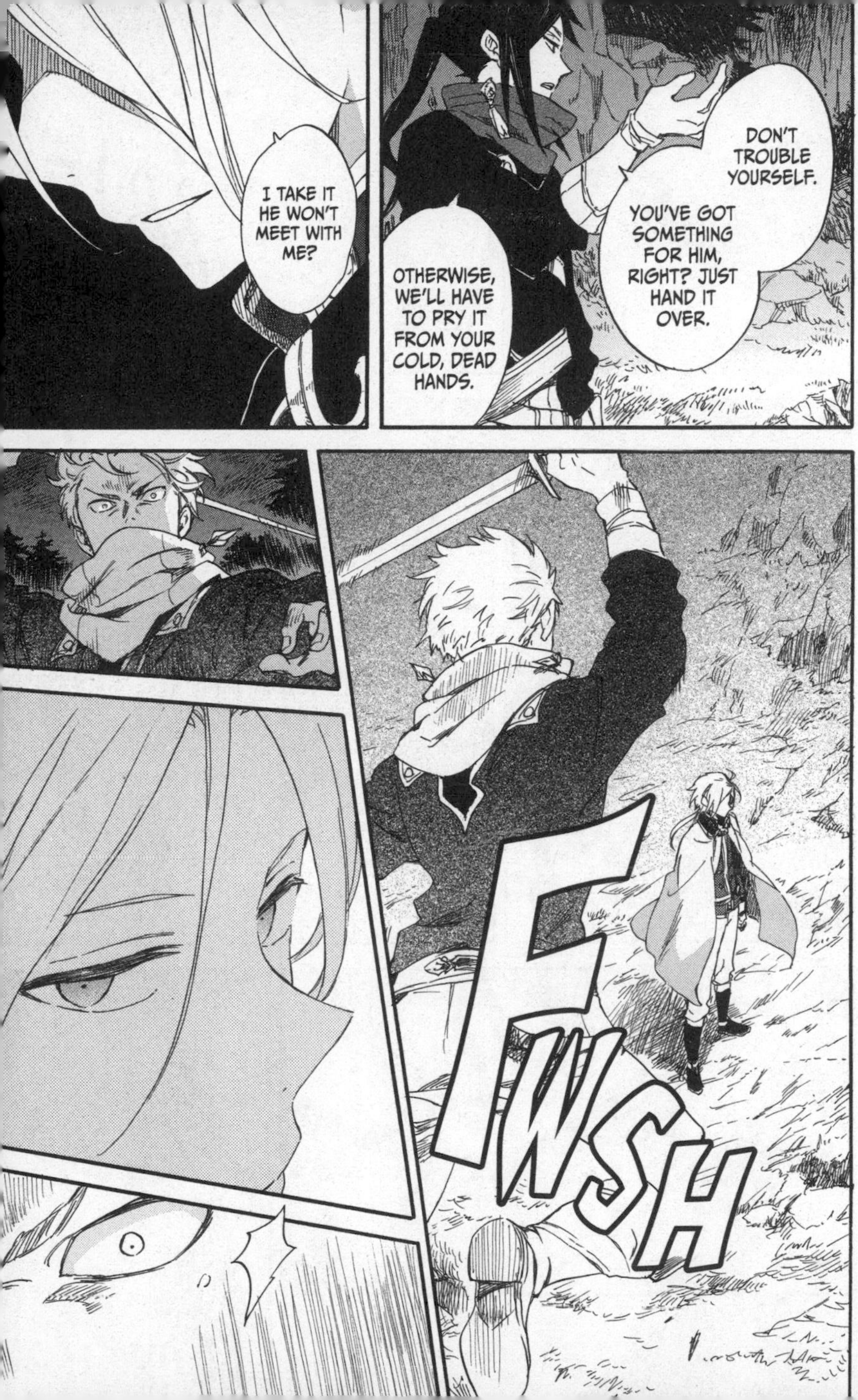
DON'T TROUBLE YOURSELF.
YOU'VE GOT SOMETHING FOR HIM, RIGHT? JUST HAND IT OVER.
OTHERWISE, WE'LL HAVE TO PRY IT FROM YOUR COLD, DEAD HANDS.
I TAKE IT HE WON'T MEET WITH ME?
FWSH

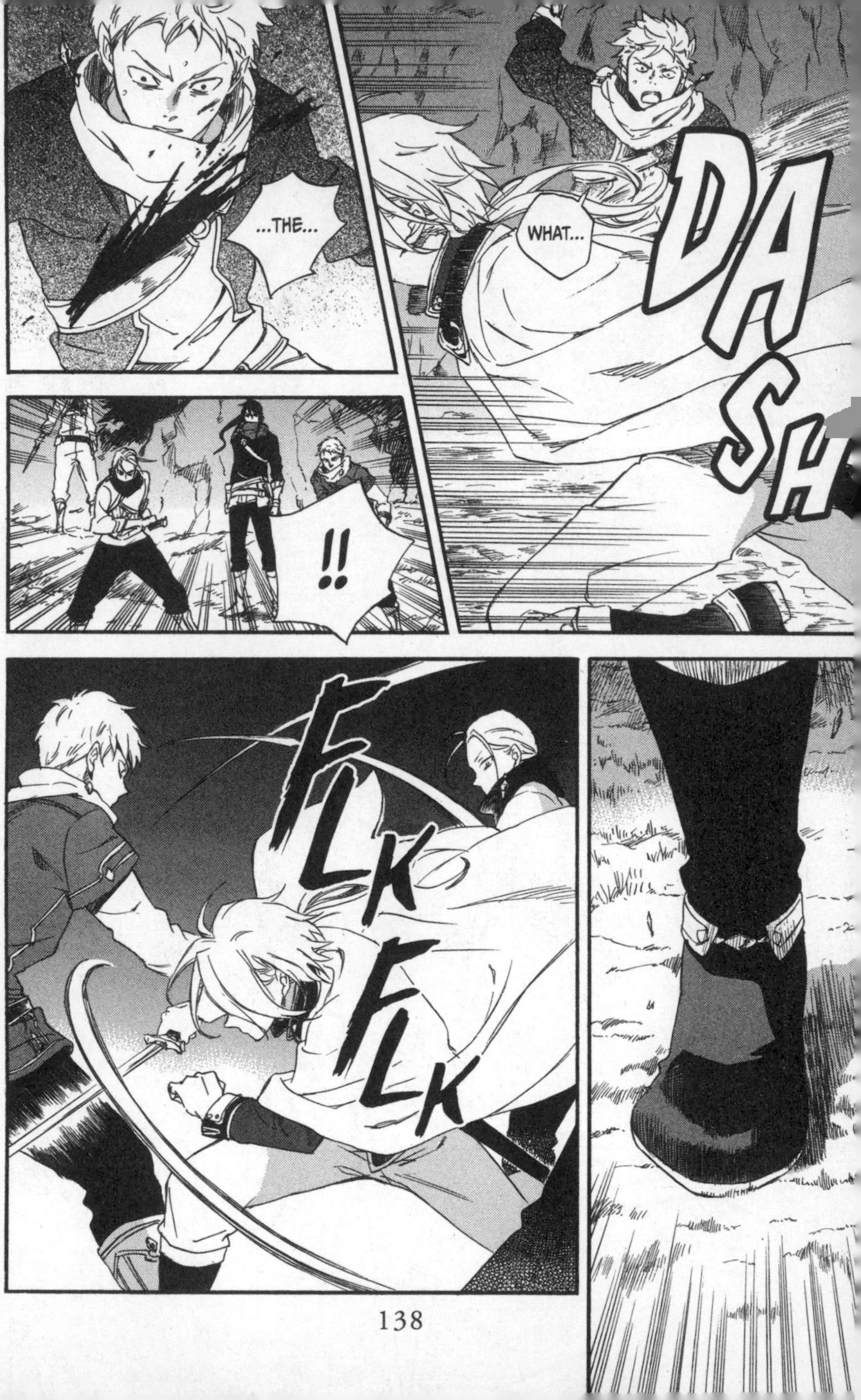
WHAT...
DASH
...THE...
!!
FLK
FLK

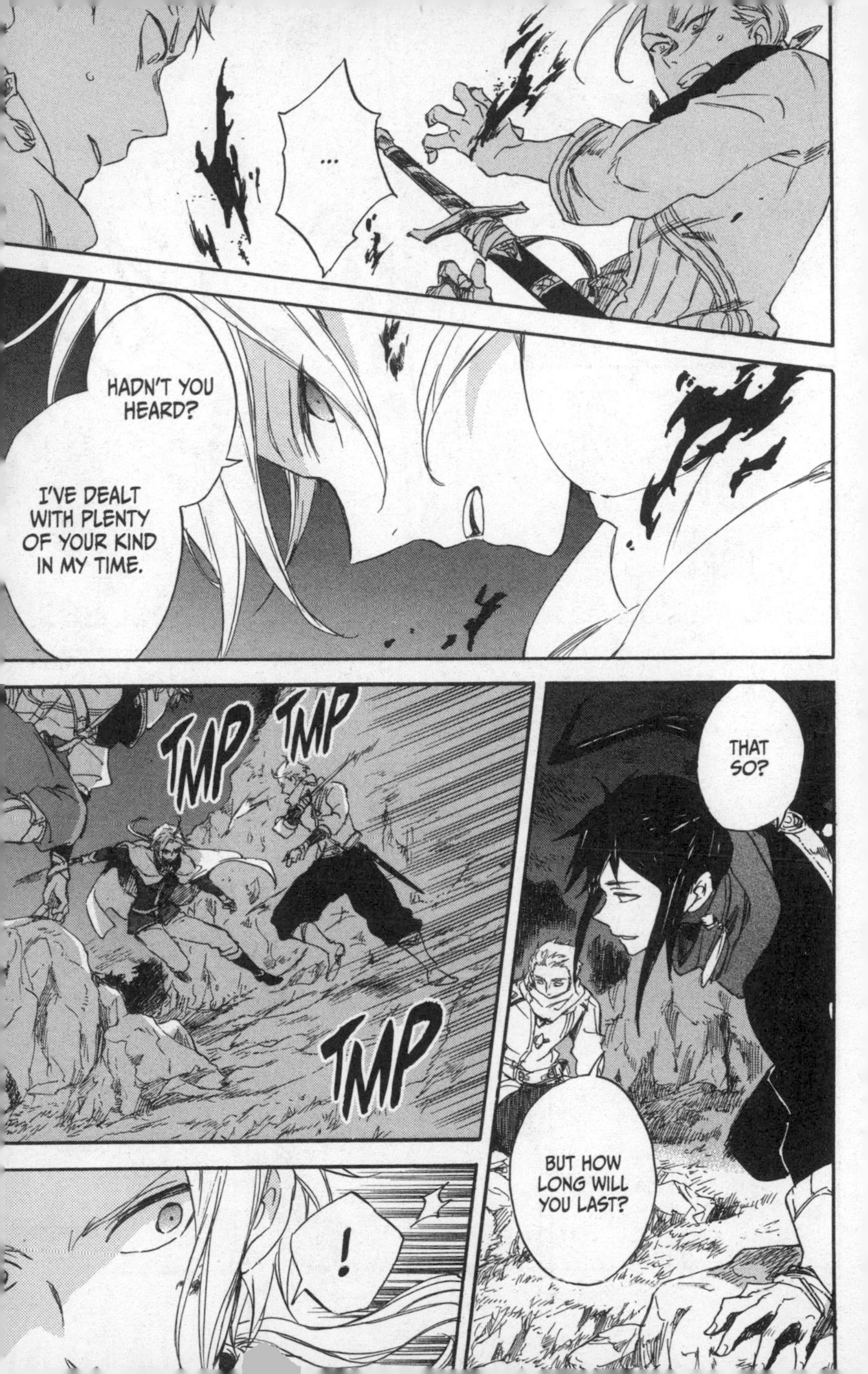
...
HADN'T YOU HEARD?
I'VE DEALT WITH PLENTY OF YOUR KIND IN MY TIME.
THAT SO?
BUT HOW LONG WILL YOU LAST?
TMP TMP
TMP
!

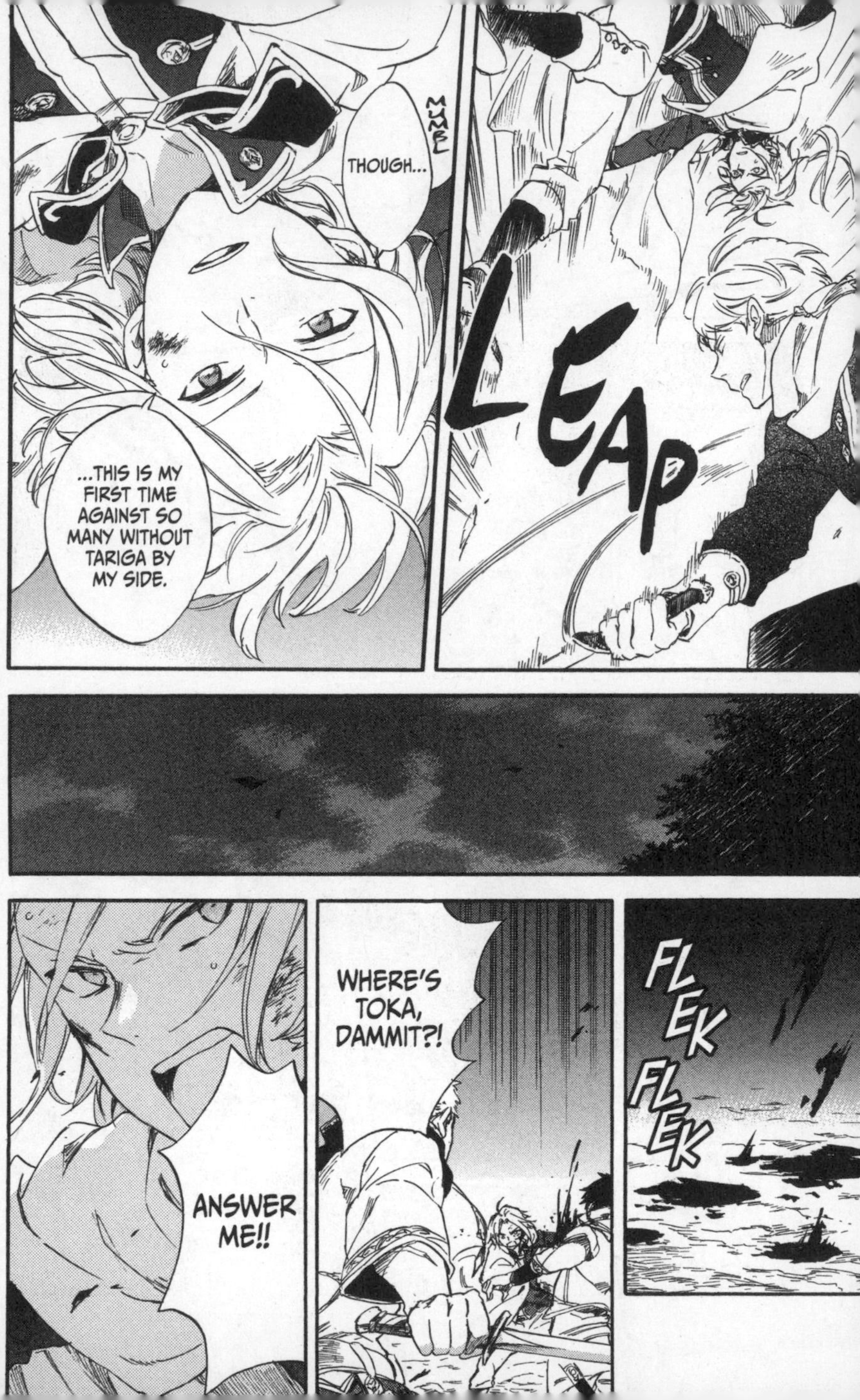
LEAP
MUMBL
THOUGH...
...THIS IS MY FIRST TIME AGAINST SO MANY WITHOUT TARIGA BY MY SIDE.
FLEK FLEK
WHERE'S TOKA, DAMMIT?!
ANSWER ME!!

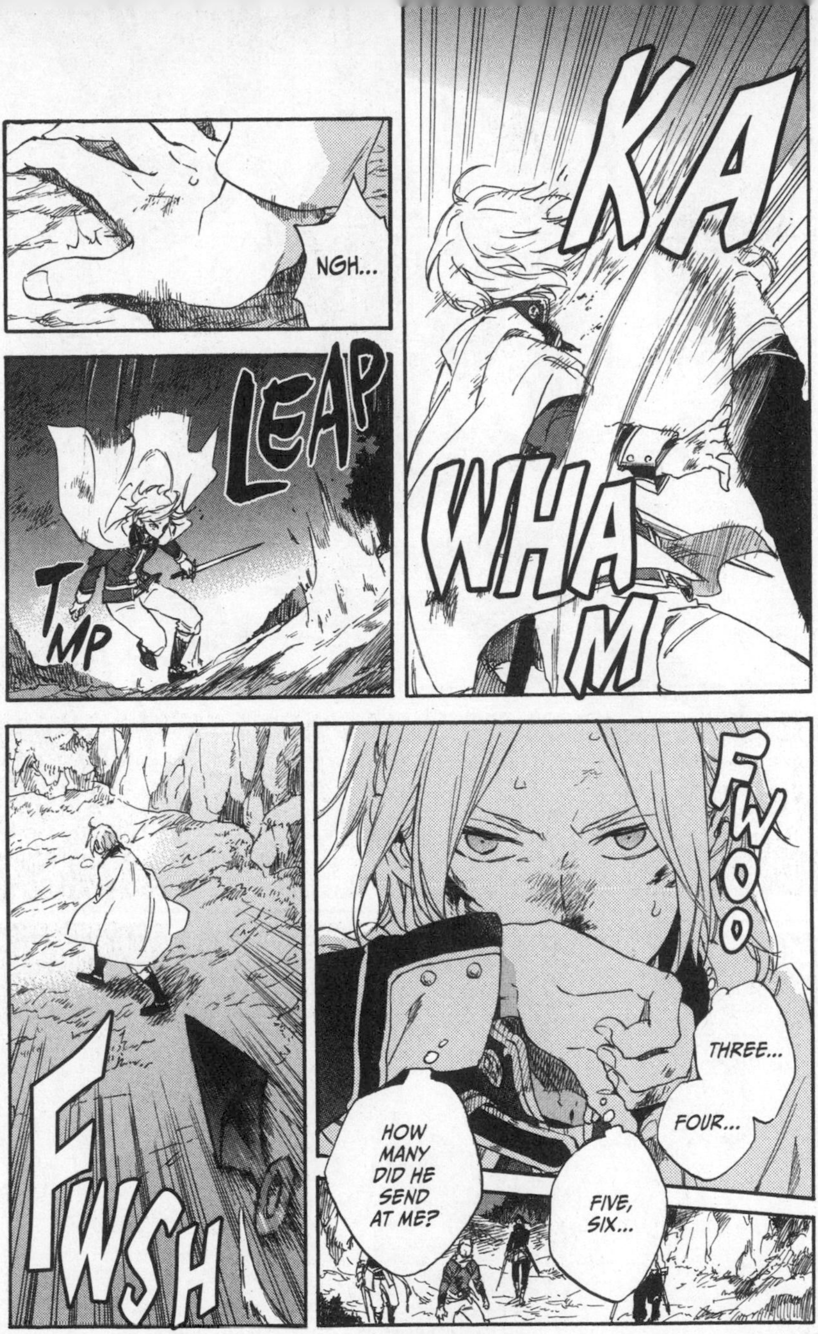
KA
WHAM
NGH...
LEAP
TMP
FWOO
THREE...
FOUR...
FIVE, SIX...
HOW MANY DID HE SEND AT ME?
FWSH

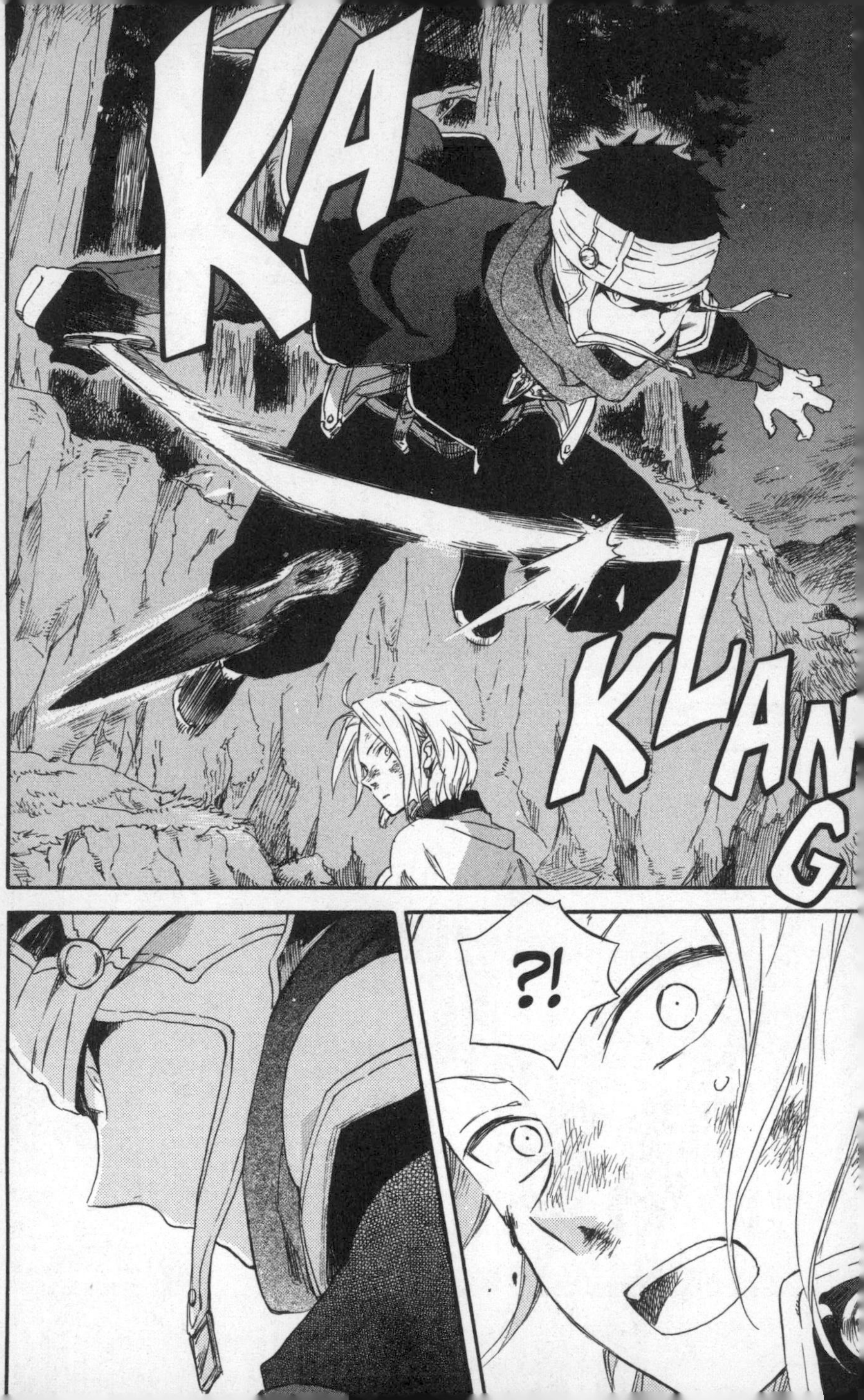
KA
KLANG
?!

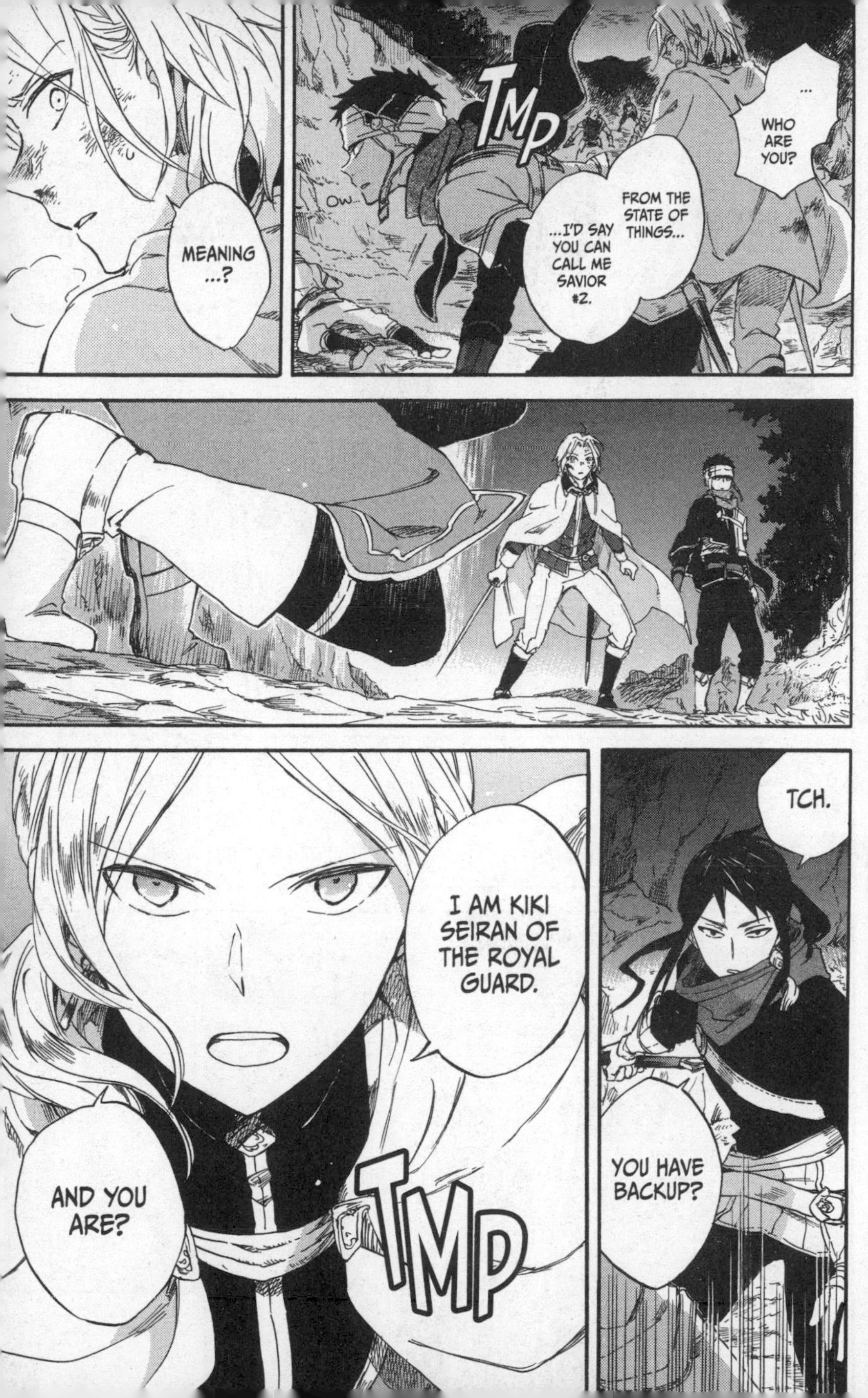
... WHO ARE YOU?
TMP
FROM THE STATE OF THINGS...
...I'D SAY YOU CAN CALL ME SAVIOR #2.
OW
MEANING ...?
TCH.
YOU HAVE BACKUP?
I AM KIKI SEIRAN OF THE ROYAL GUARD.
TMP
AND YOU ARE?

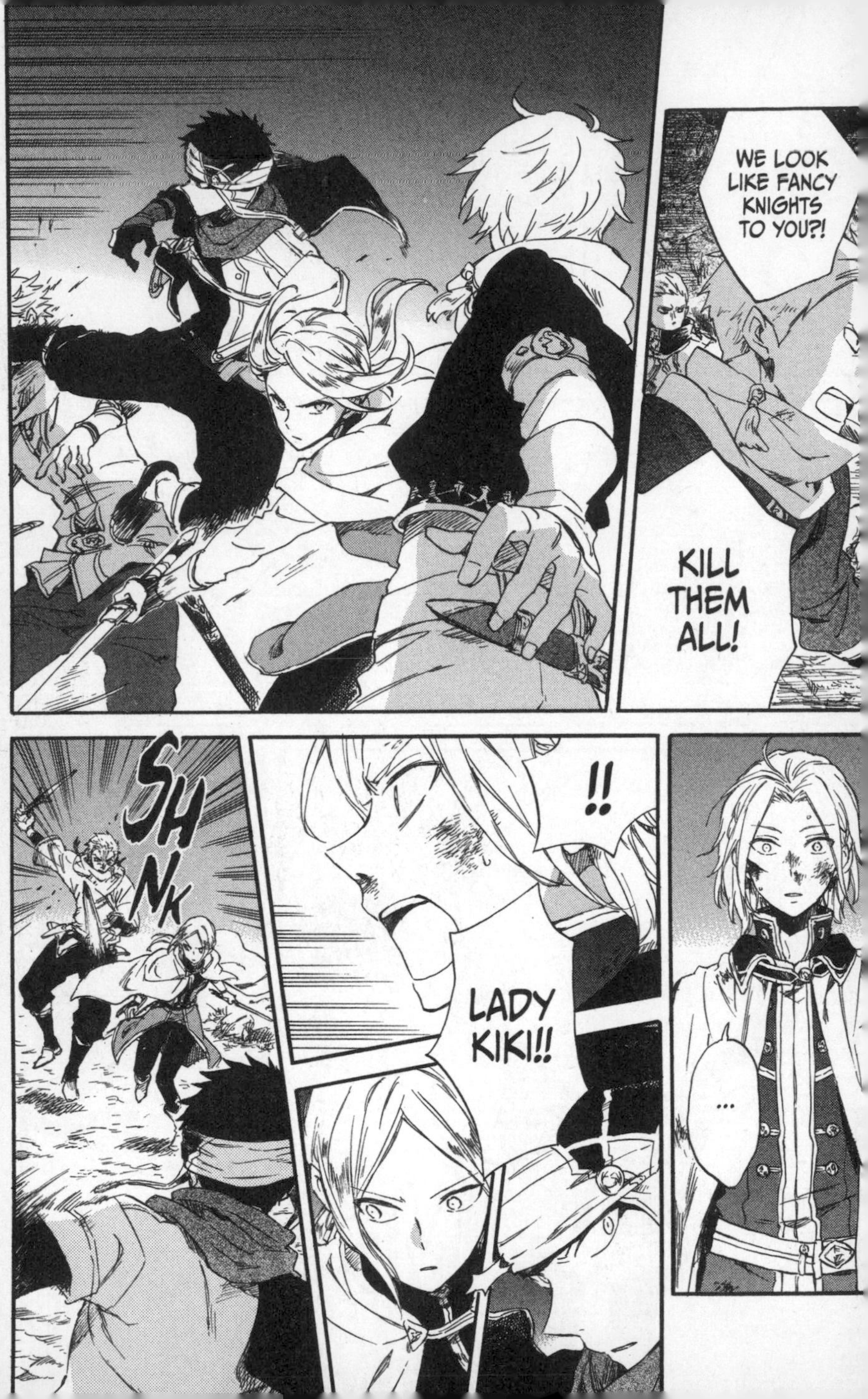
WE LOOK LIKE FANCY KNIGHTS TO YOU?!
KILL THEM ALL!
...
!!
LADY KIKI!!
SHNK

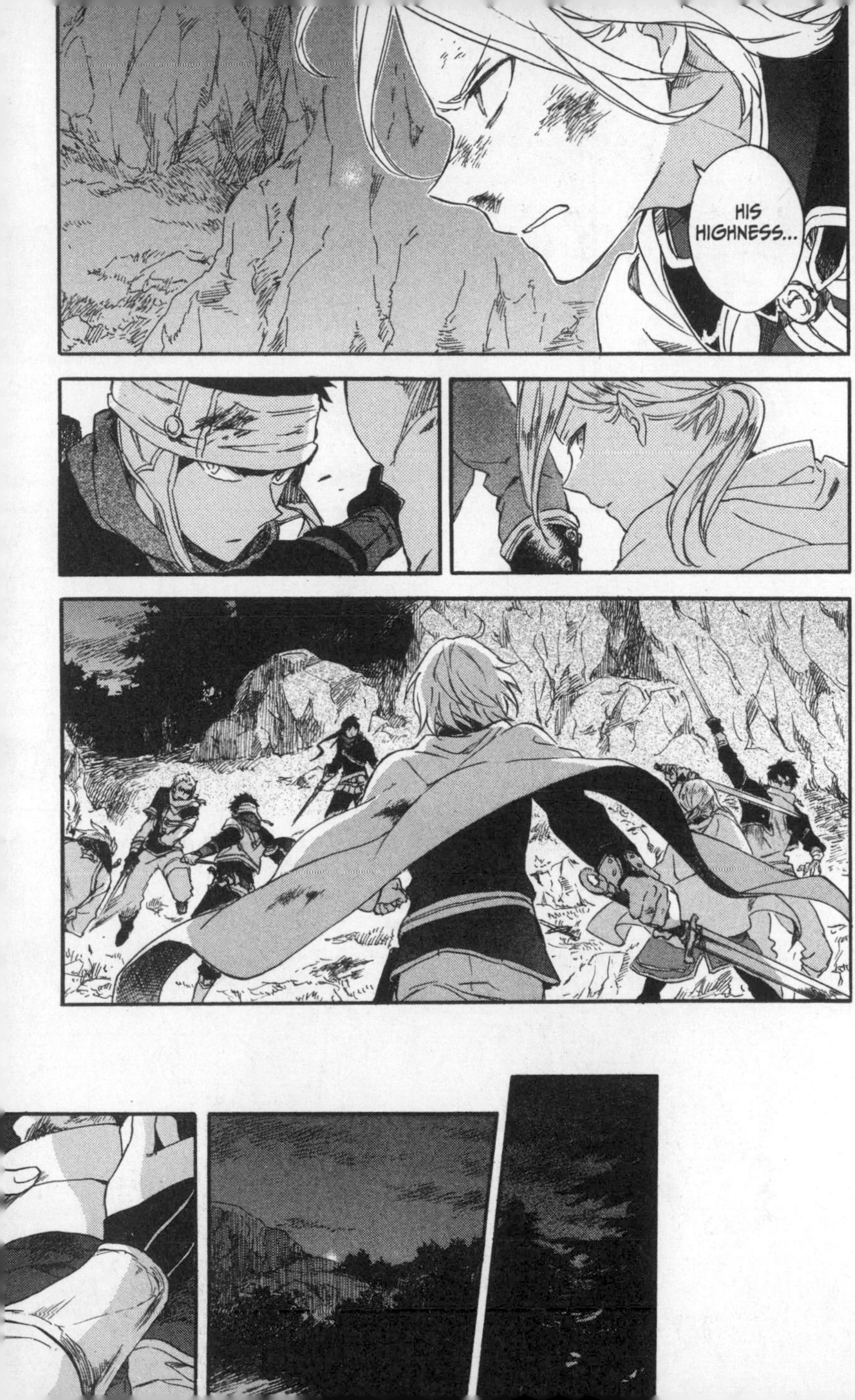
HIS HIGHNESS...

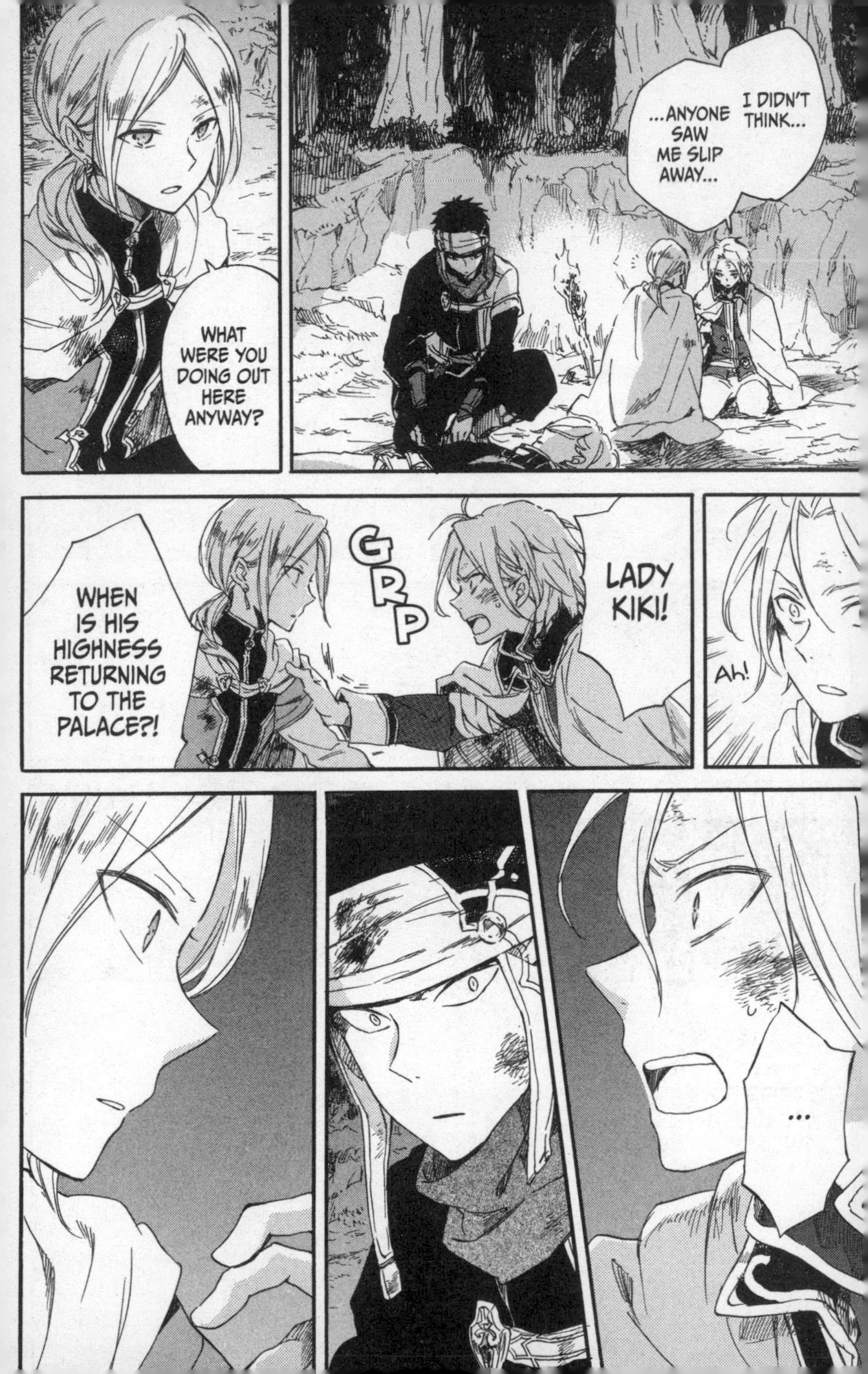
I DIDN'T THINK...
...ANYONE SAW ME SLIP AWAY...
WHAT WERE YOU DOING OUT HERE ANYWAY?
Ah!
LADY KIKI!
GRP
WHEN IS HIS HIGHNESS RETURNING TO THE PALACE?!
...

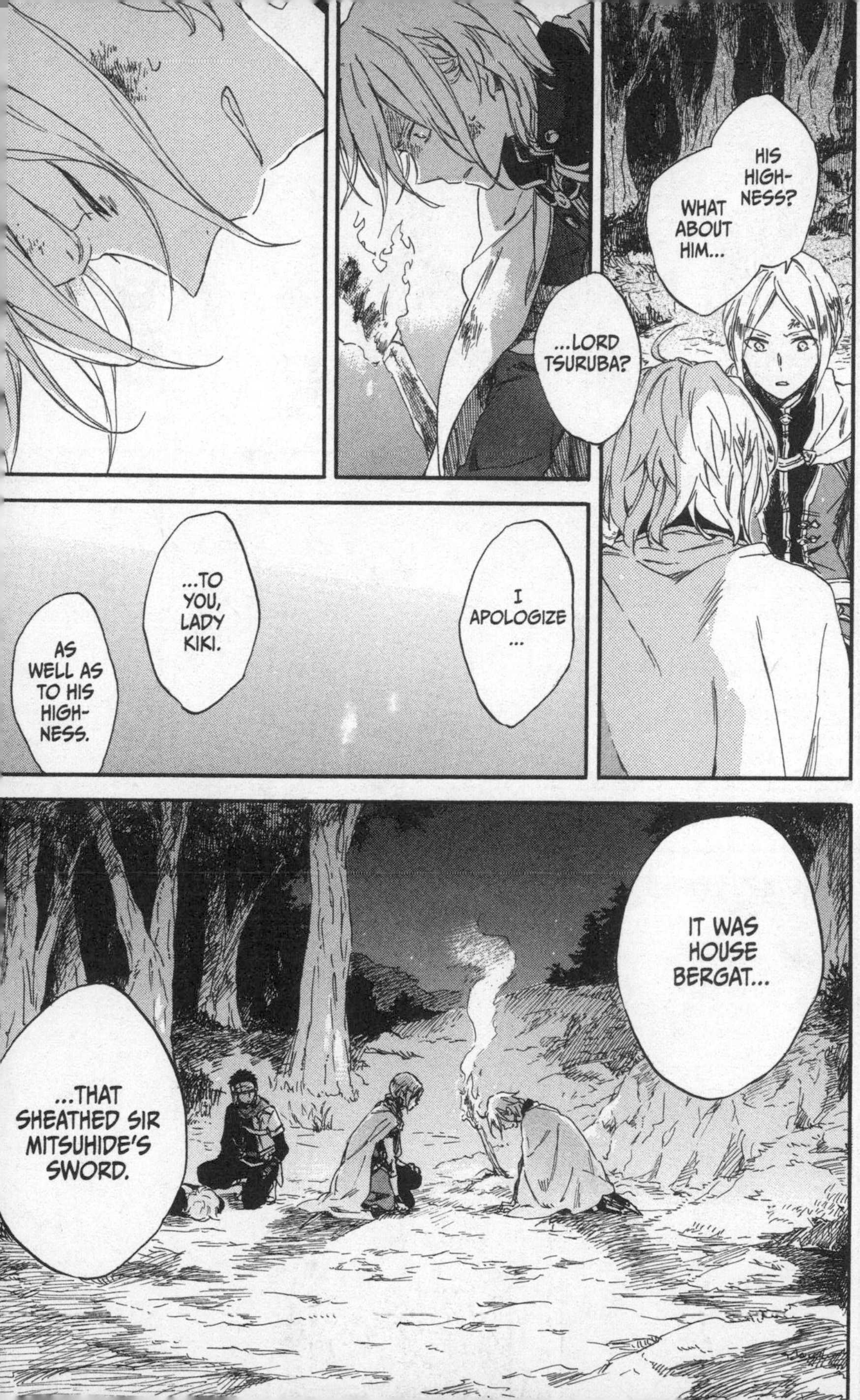
HIS HIGHNESS? WHAT ABOUT HIM...
...LORD TSURUBA?
I APOLOGIZE...
...TO YOU, LADY KIKI.
AS WELL AS TO HIS HIGHNESS.
IT WAS HOUSE BERGAT...
...THAT SHEATHED SIR MITSUHIDE'S SWORD.

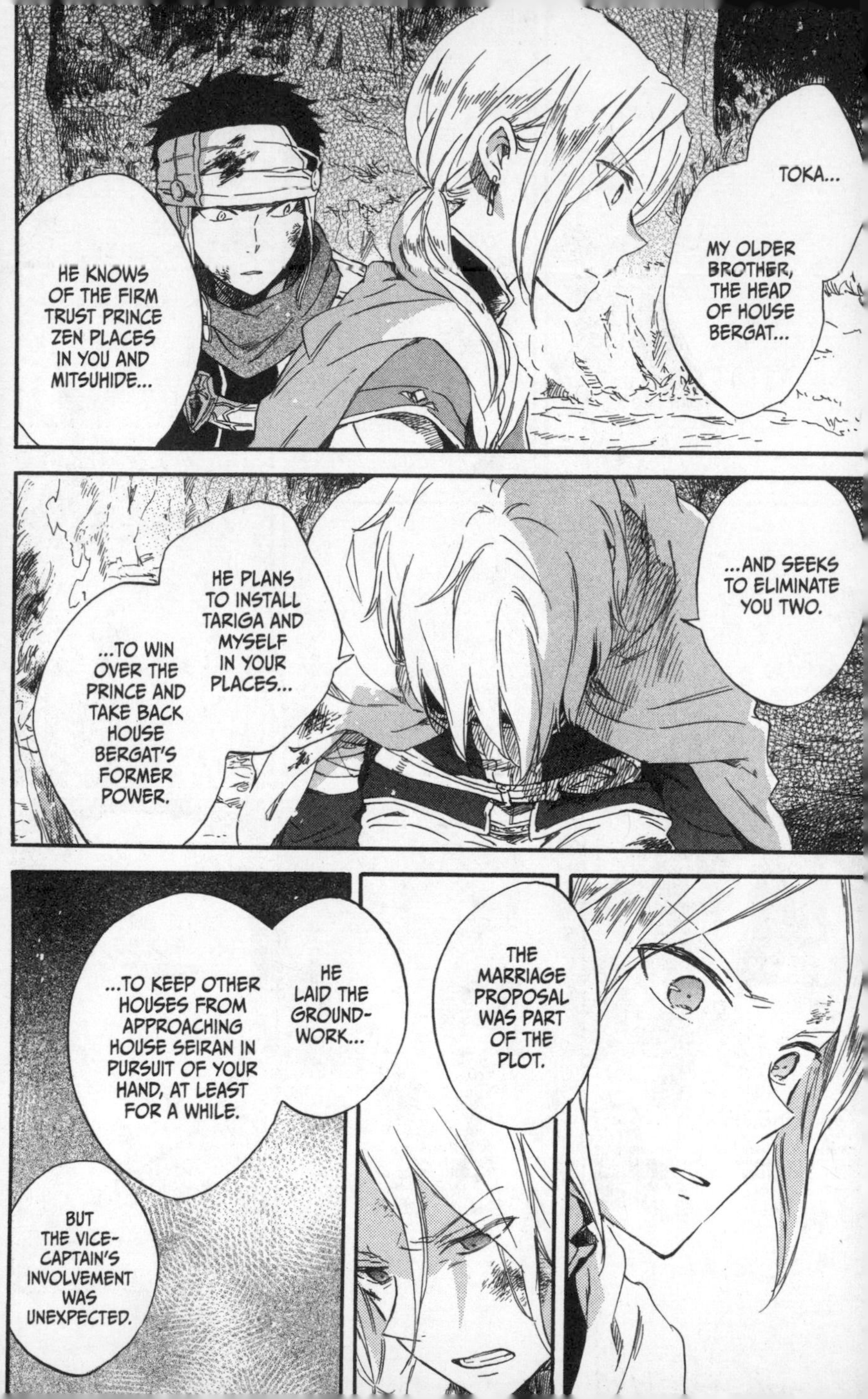
TOKA...
MY OLDER BROTHER, THE HEAD OF HOUSE BERGAT...
HE KNOWS OF THE FIRM TRUST PRINCE ZEN PLACES IN YOU AND MITSUHIDE...
...AND SEEKS TO ELIMINATE YOU TWO.
HE PLANS TO INSTALL TARIGA AND MYSELF IN YOUR PLACES...
...TO WIN OVER THE PRINCE AND TAKE BACK HOUSE BERGAT'S FORMER POWER.
THE MARRIAGE PROPOSAL WAS PART OF THE PLOT.
HE LAID THE GROUND-WORK...
...TO KEEP OTHER HOUSES FROM APPROACHING HOUSE SEIRAN IN PURSUIT OF YOUR HAND, AT LEAST FOR A WHILE.
BUT THE VICE-CAPTAIN'S INVOLVEMENT WAS UNEXPECTED.

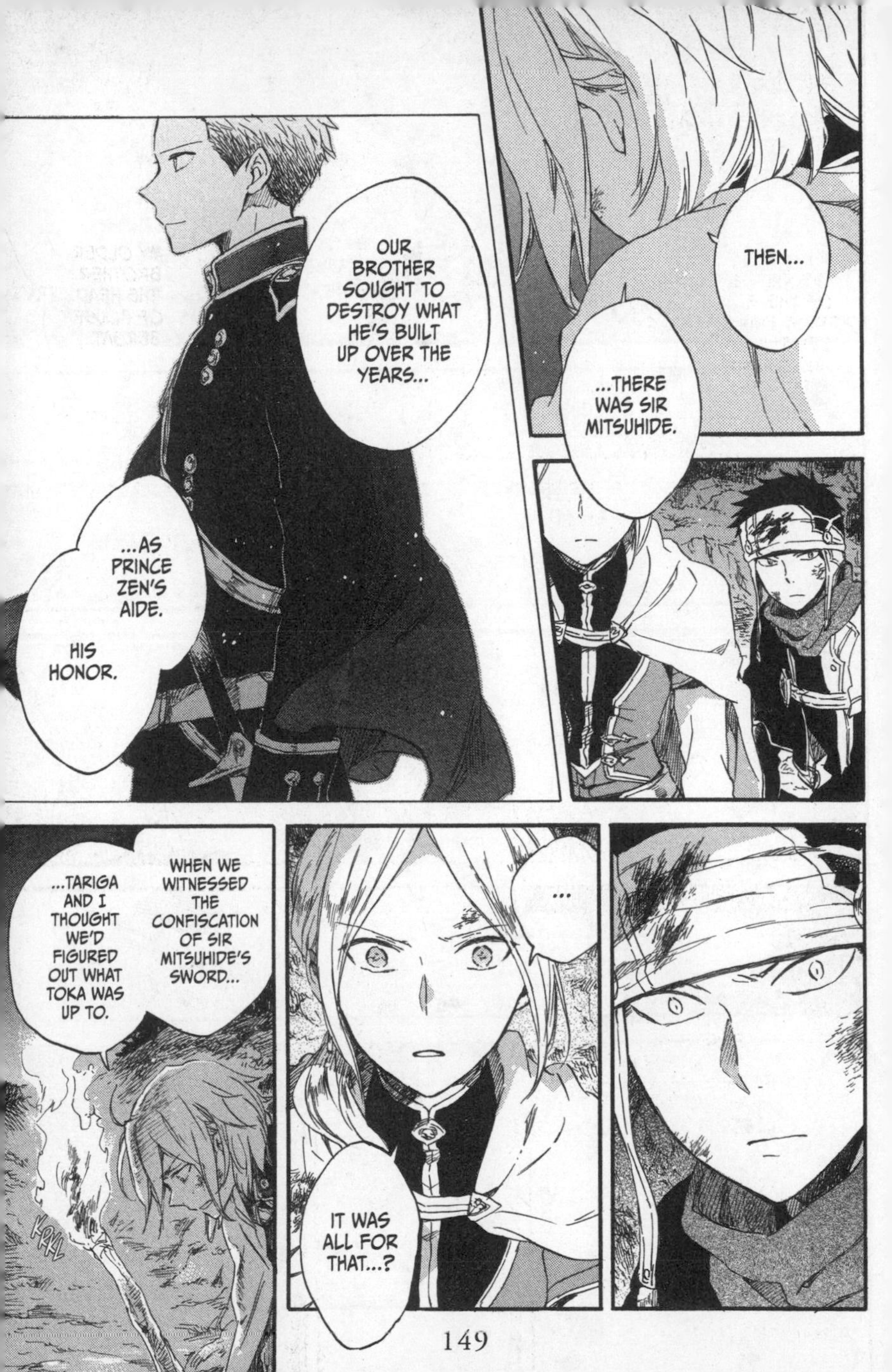
THEN...
...THERE WAS SIR MITSUHIDE.
OUR BROTHER SOUGHT TO DESTROY WHAT HE'S BUILT UP OVER THE YEARS...
...AS PRINCE ZEN'S AIDE.
HIS HONOR.
...
IT WAS ALL FOR THAT...?
WHEN WE WITNESSED THE CONFISCATION OF SIR MITSUHIDE'S SWORD...
...TARIGA AND I THOUGHT WE'D FIGURED OUT WHAT TOKA WAS UP TO.
KRKL

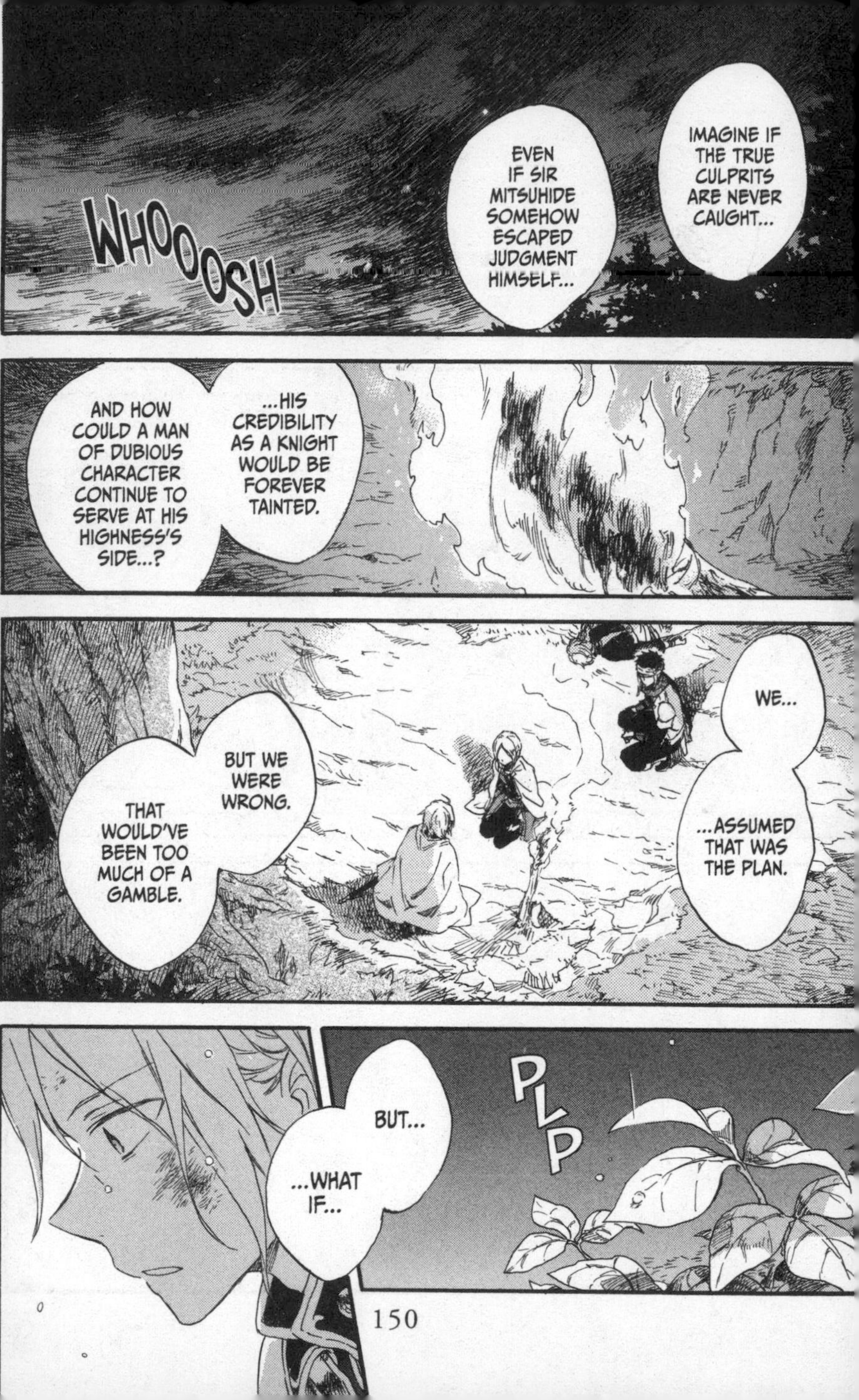
IMAGINE IF THE TRUE CULPRITS ARE NEVER CAUGHT...
EVEN IF SIR MITSUHIDE SOMEHOW ESCAPED JUDGMENT HIMSELF...
WHOOOSH
...HIS CREDIBILITY AS A KNIGHT WOULD BE FOREVER TAINTED.
AND HOW COULD A MAN OF DUBIOUS CHARACTER CONTINUE TO SERVE AT HIS HIGHNESS'S SIDE...?
WE...
...ASSUMED THAT WAS THE PLAN.
BUT WE WERE WRONG.
THAT WOULD'VE BEEN TOO MUCH OF A GAMBLE.
PLP
BUT...
...WHAT IF...

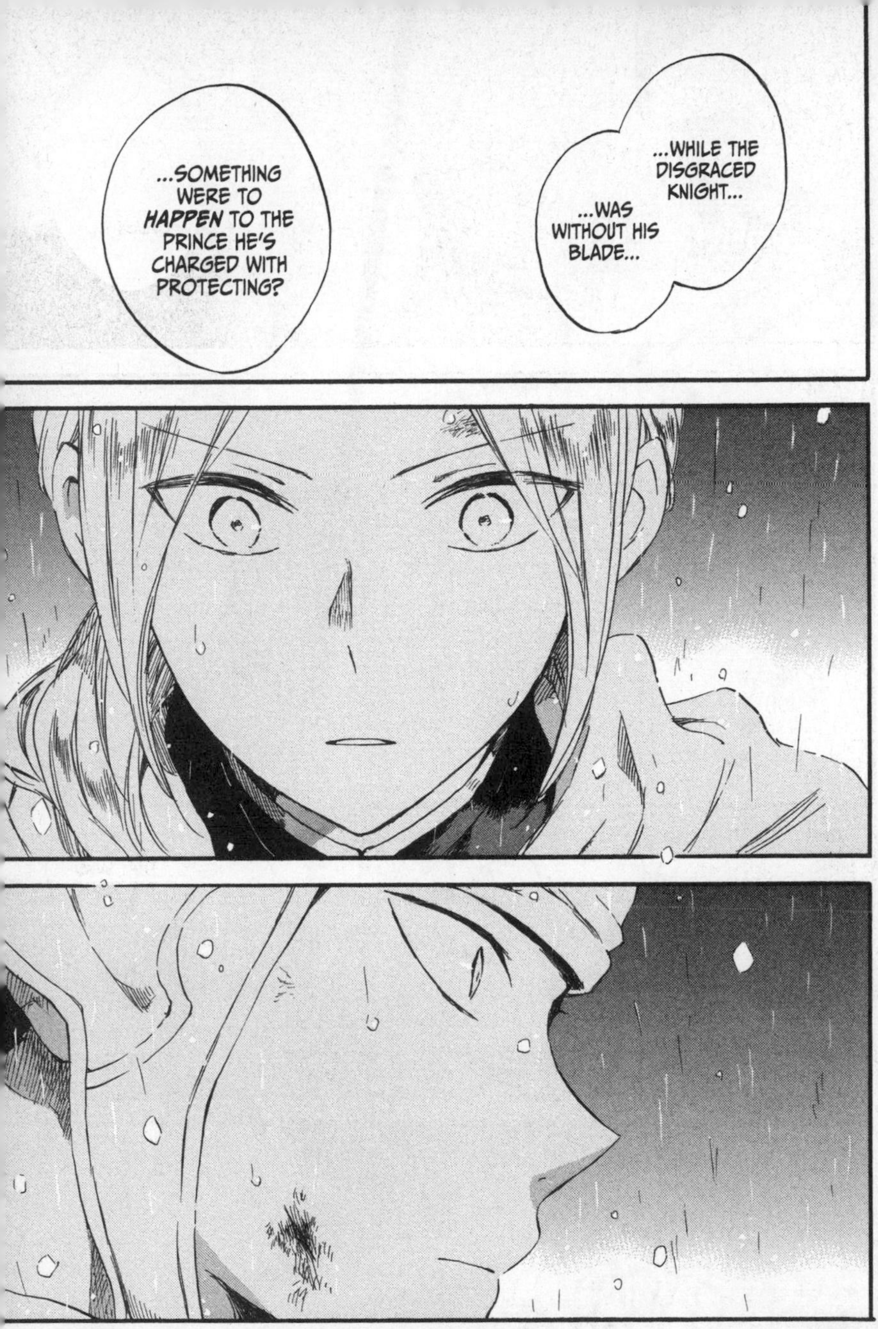
...WHILE THE DISGRACED KNIGHT...
...WAS WITHOUT HIS BLADE...
...SOMETHING WERE TO *HAPPEN* TO THE PRINCE HE'S CHARGED WITH PROTECTING?

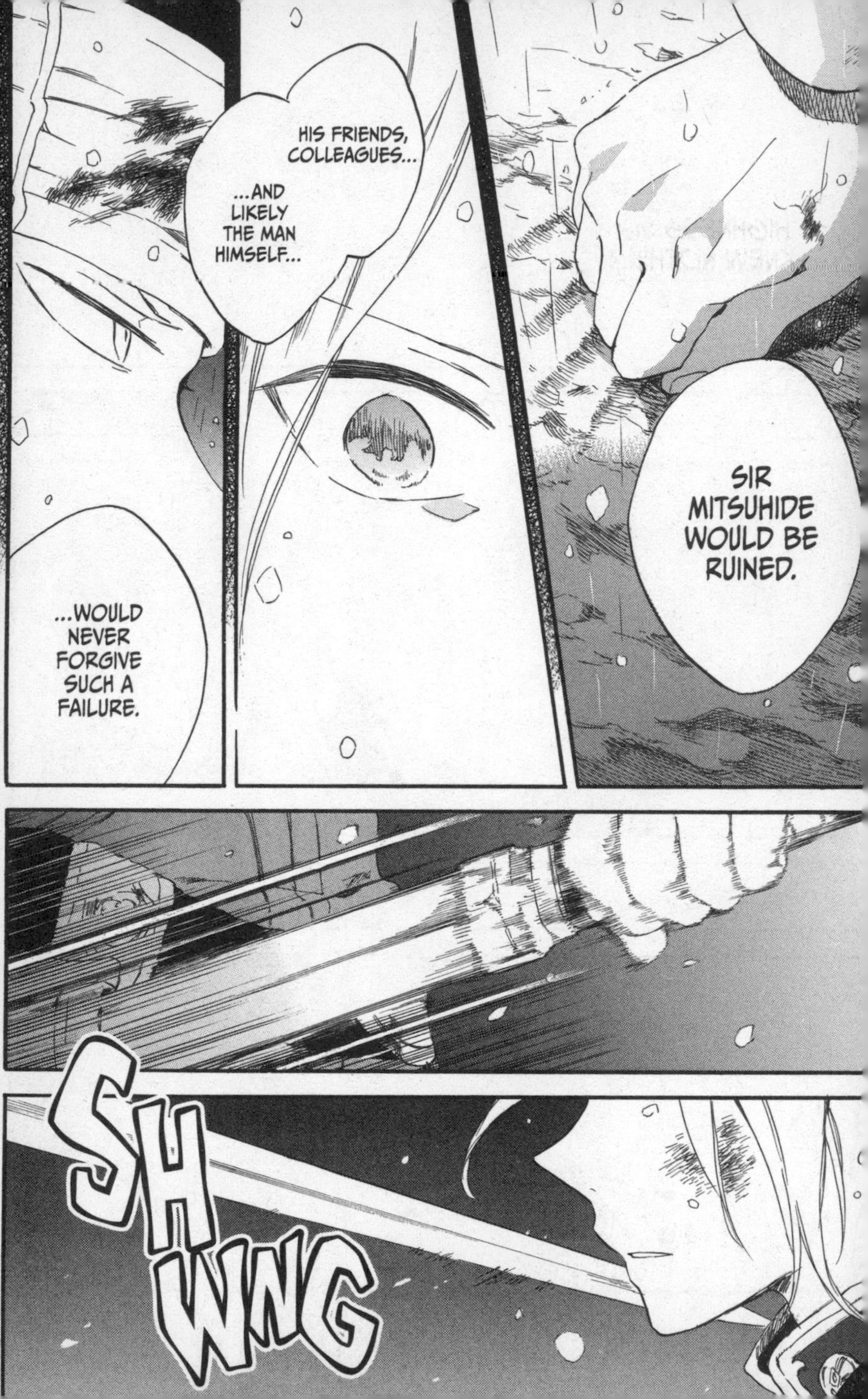
SIR MITSUHIDE WOULD BE RUINED.
HIS FRIENDS, COLLEAGUES...
...AND LIKELY THE MAN HIMSELF...
...WOULD NEVER FORGIVE SUCH A FAILURE.
SHWNG

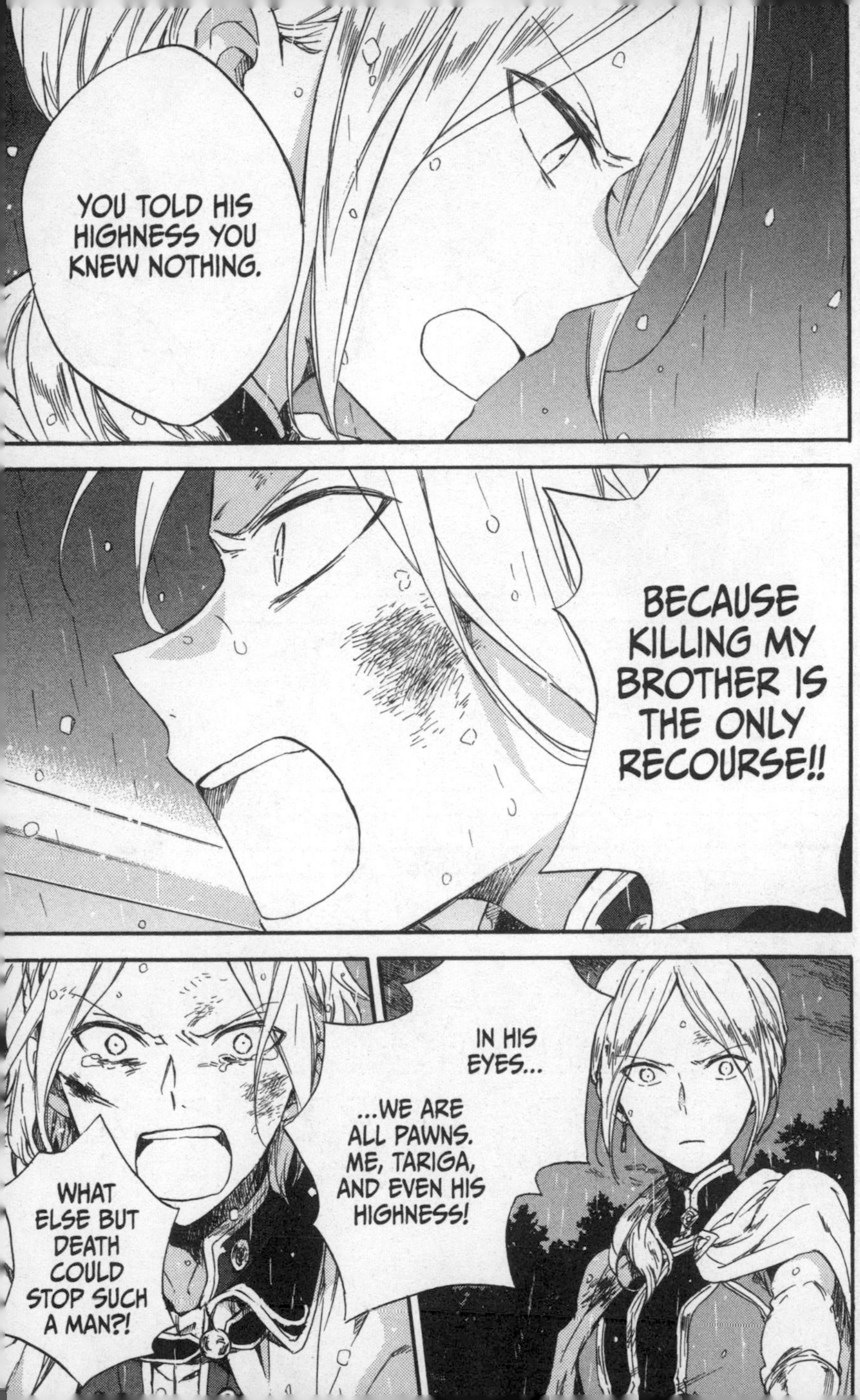
YOU TOLD HIS HIGHNESS YOU KNEW NOTHING.
BECAUSE KILLING MY BROTHER IS THE ONLY RECOURSE!!
IN HIS EYES...
...WE ARE ALL PAWNS. ME, TARIGA, AND EVEN HIS HIGHNESS!
WHAT ELSE BUT DEATH COULD STOP SUCH A MAN?!

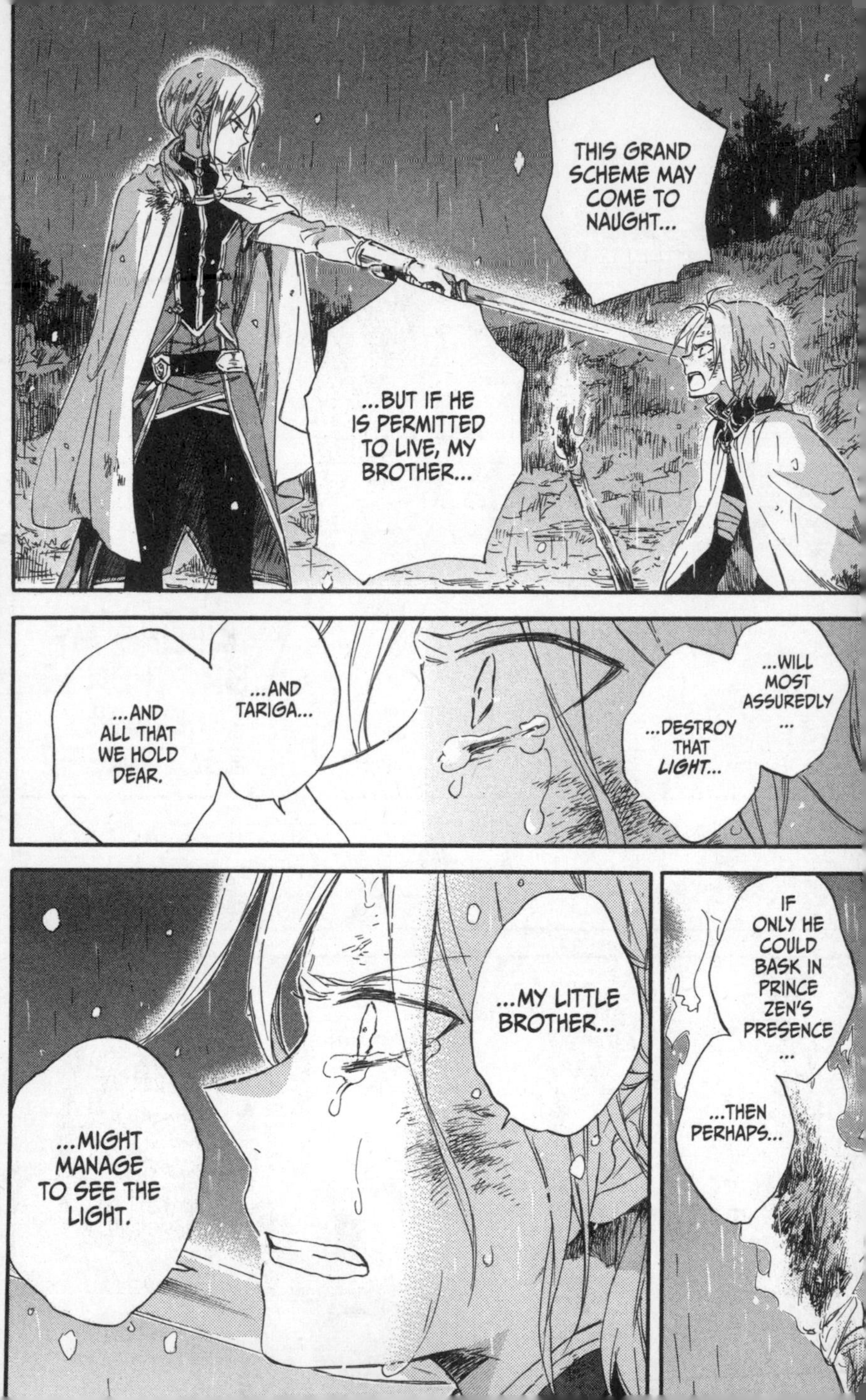
THIS GRAND SCHEME MAY COME TO NAUGHT...
...BUT IF HE IS PERMITTED TO LIVE, MY BROTHER...
...WILL MOST ASSUREDLY ...
...DESTROY THAT *LIGHT*...
...AND TARIGA...
...AND ALL THAT WE HOLD DEAR.
IF ONLY HE COULD BASK IN PRINCE ZEN'S PRESENCE ...
...THEN PERHAPS...
...MY LITTLE BROTHER...
...MIGHT MANAGE TO SEE THE LIGHT.

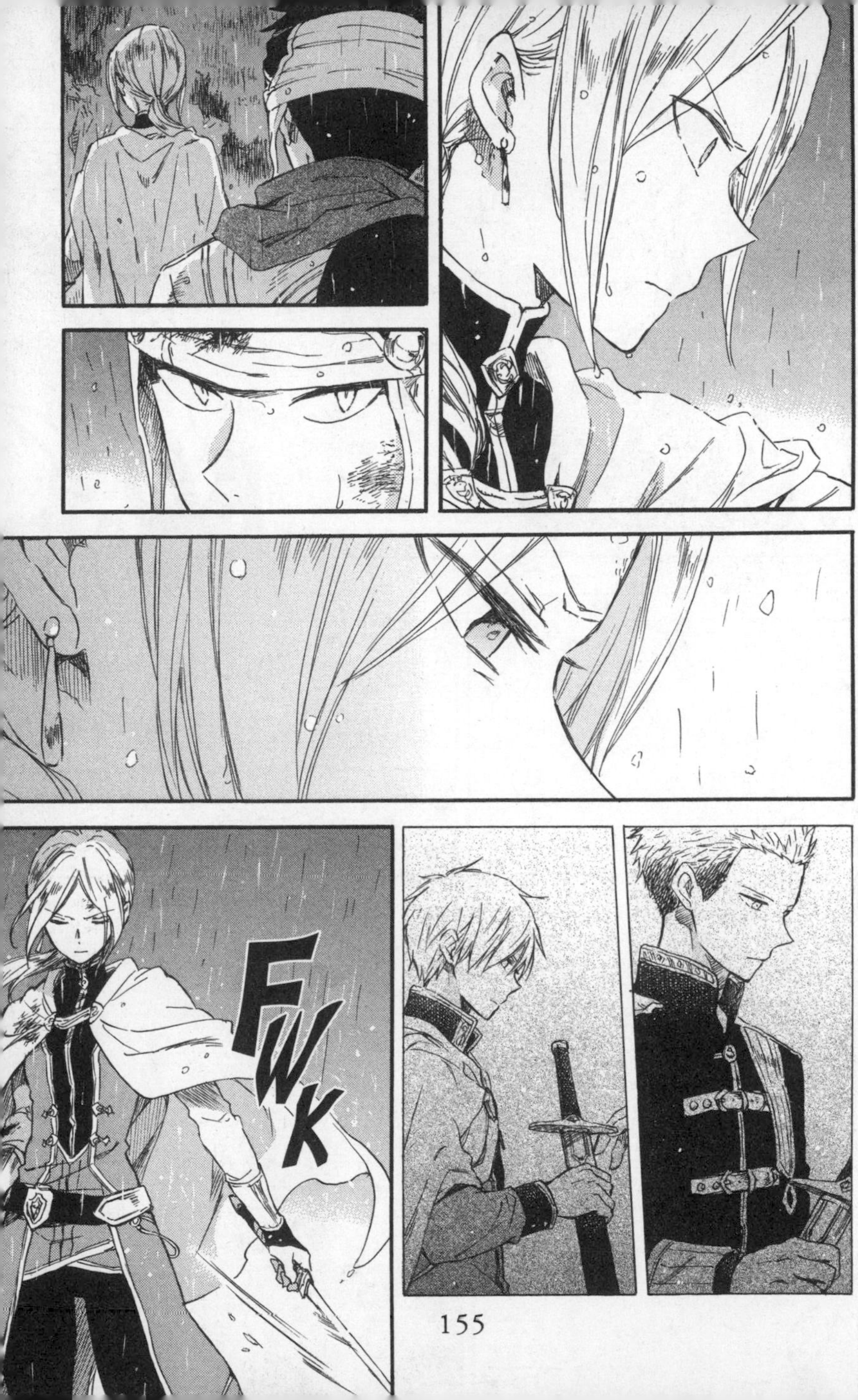
FWK

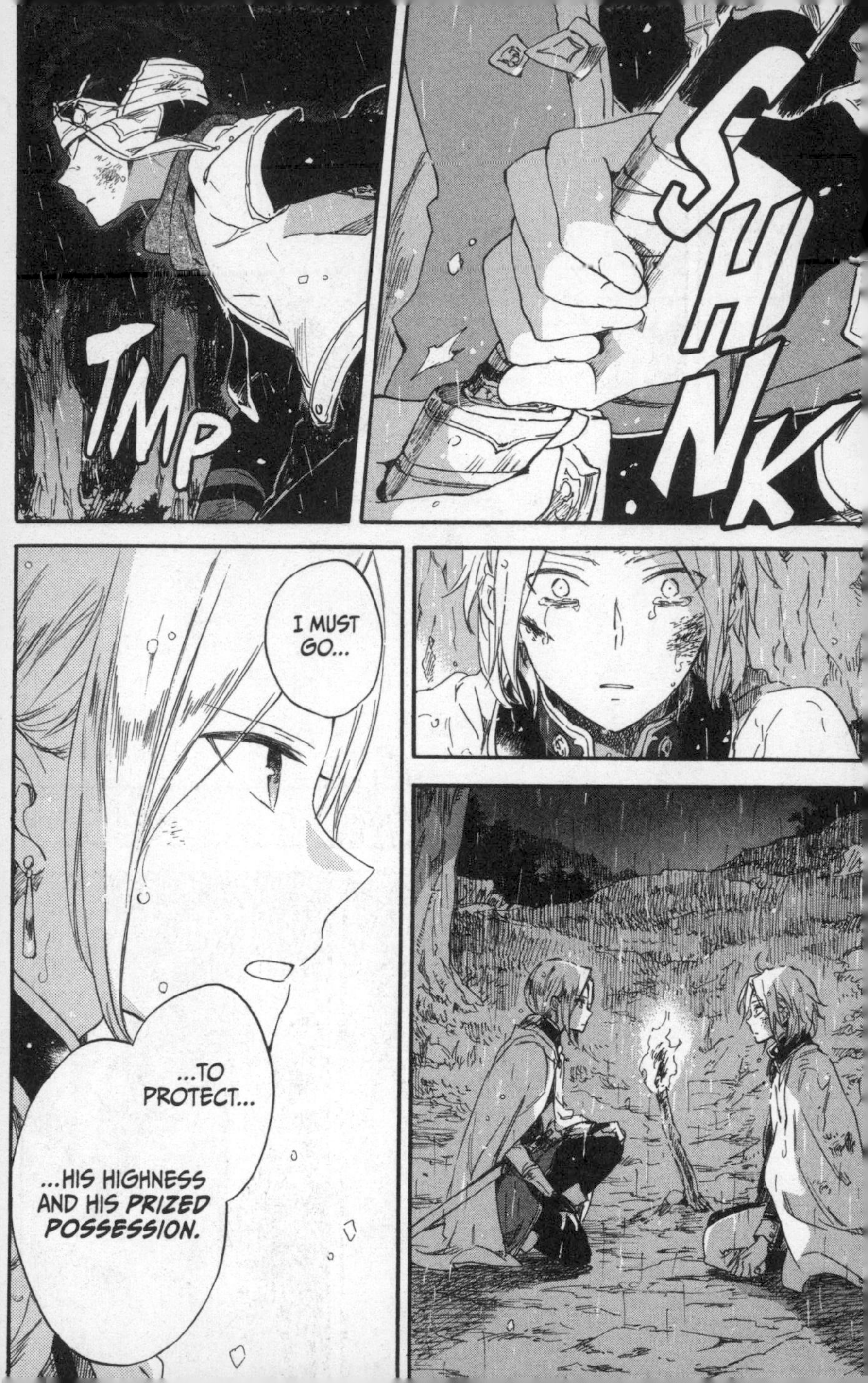
SHUNK
TMP
I MUST GO...
...TO PROTECT...
...HIS HIGHNESS AND HIS *PRIZED* POSSESSION.

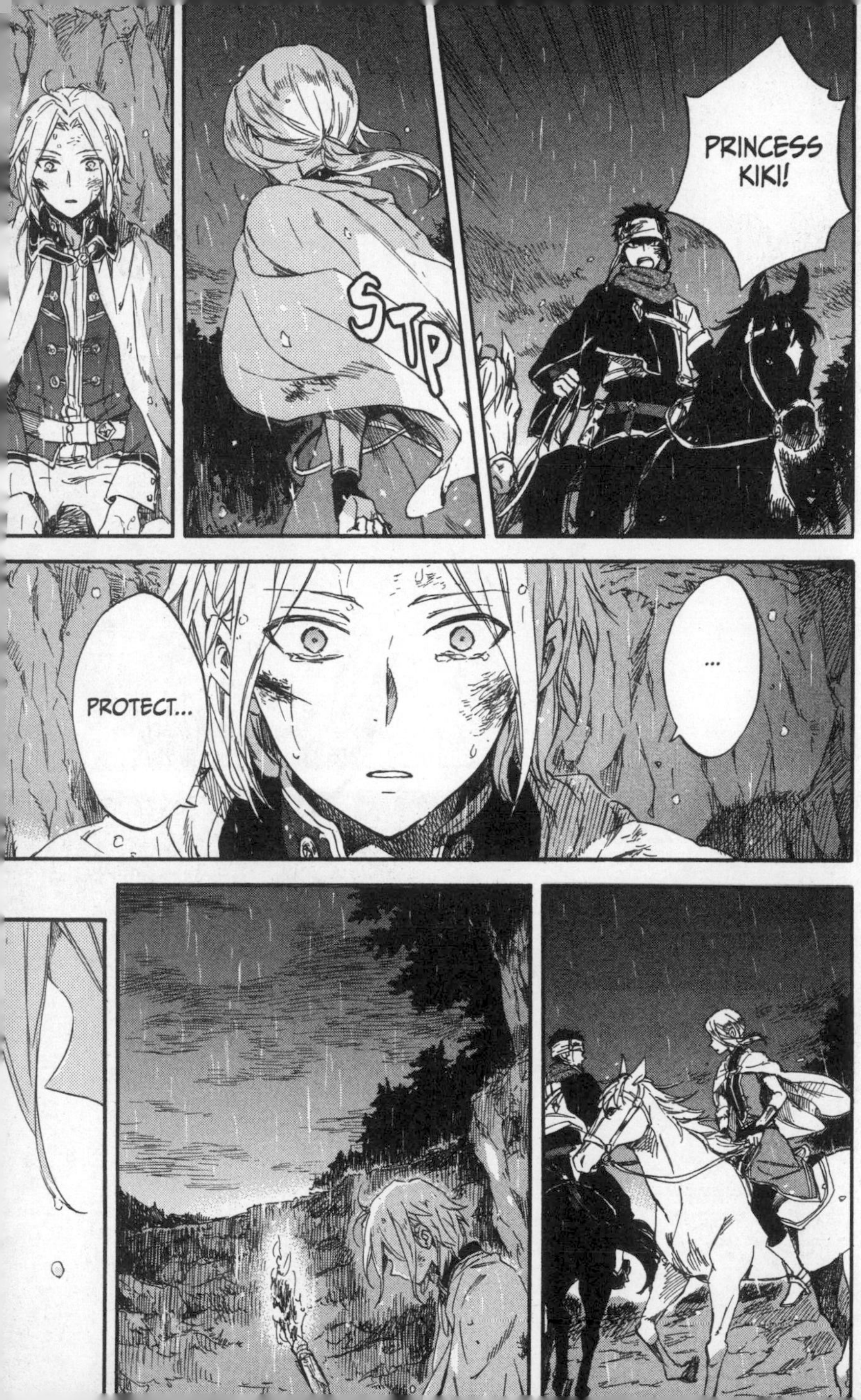
PRINCESS KIKI!
STP
...
PROTECT...

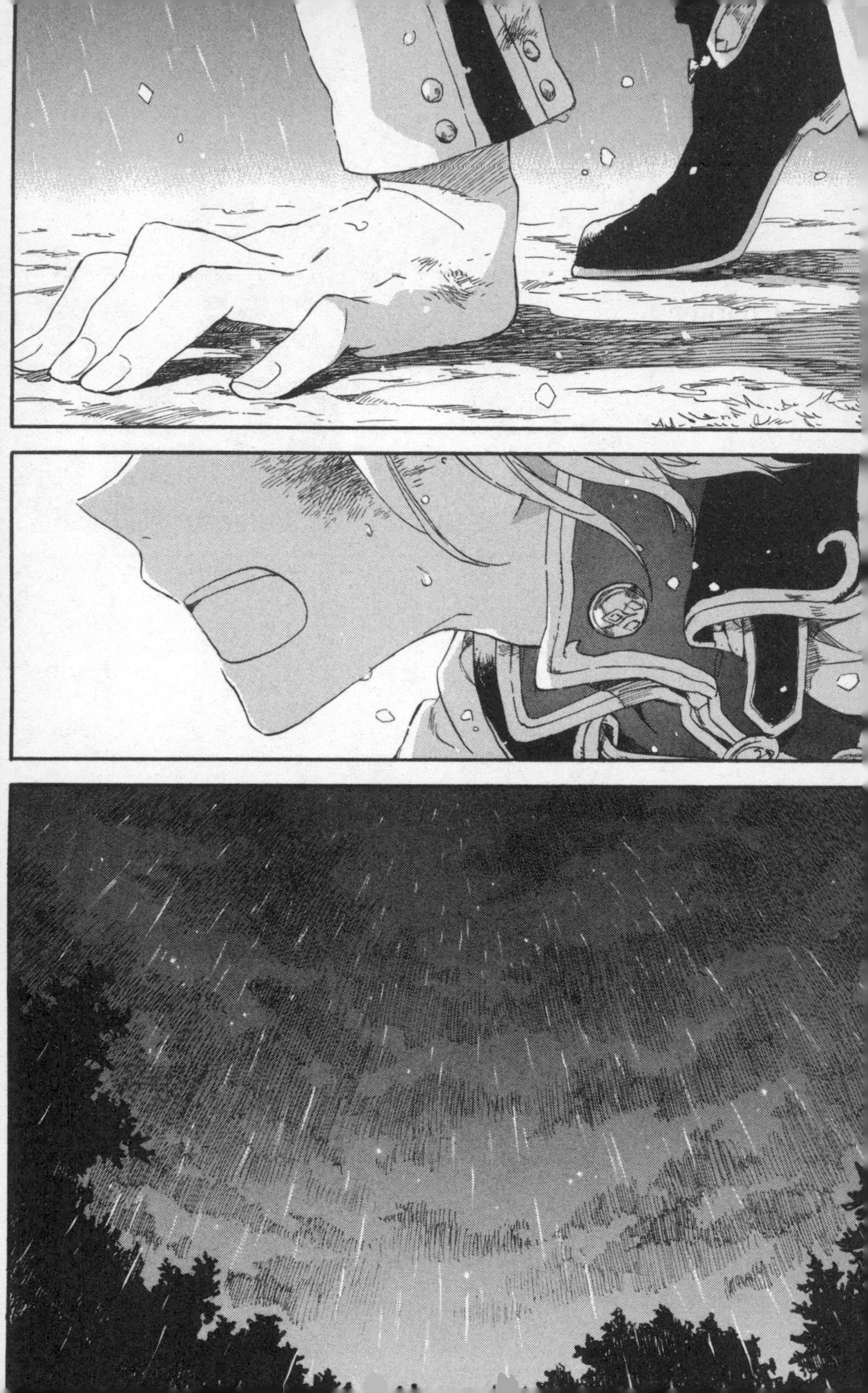

Chapter 83

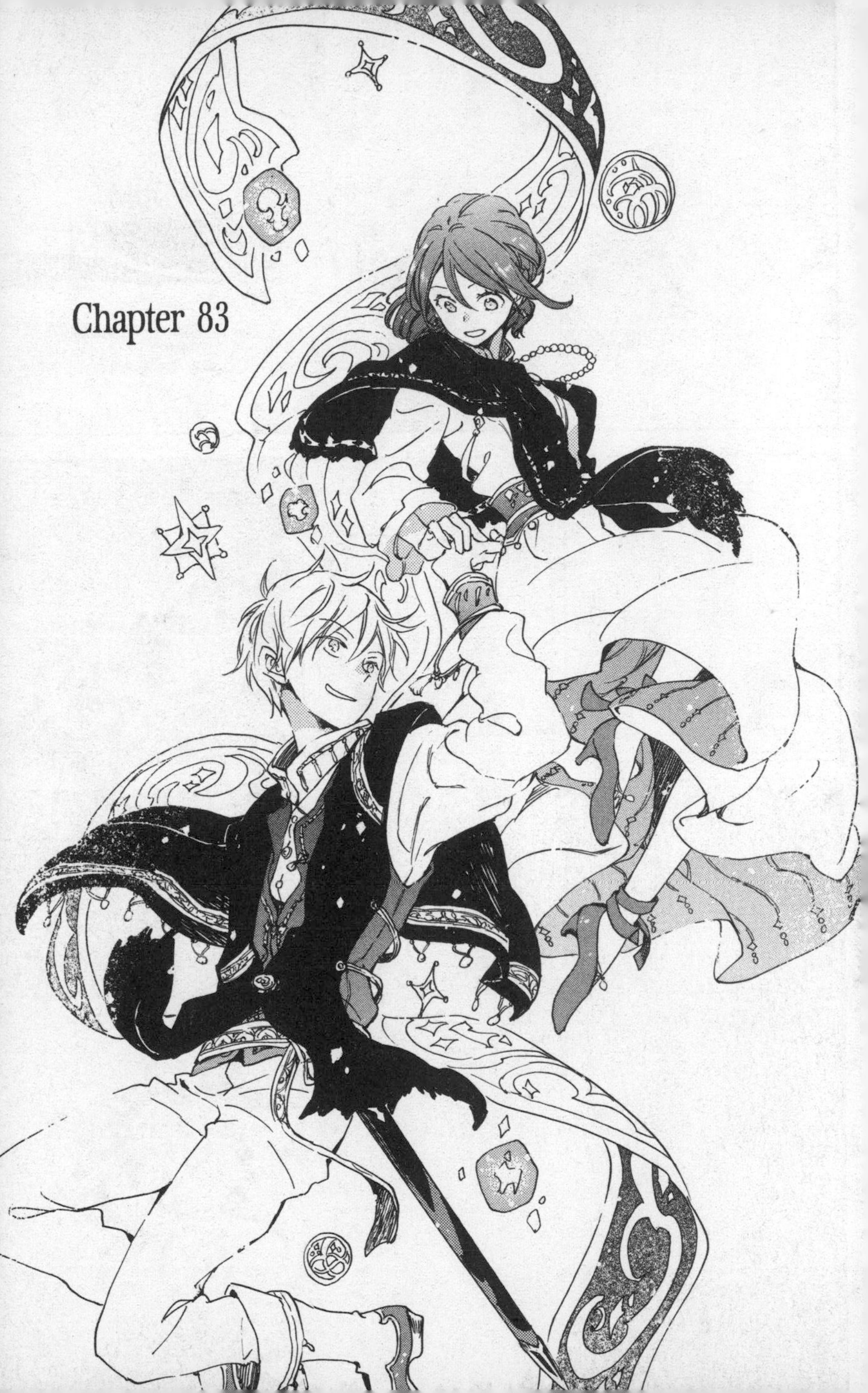

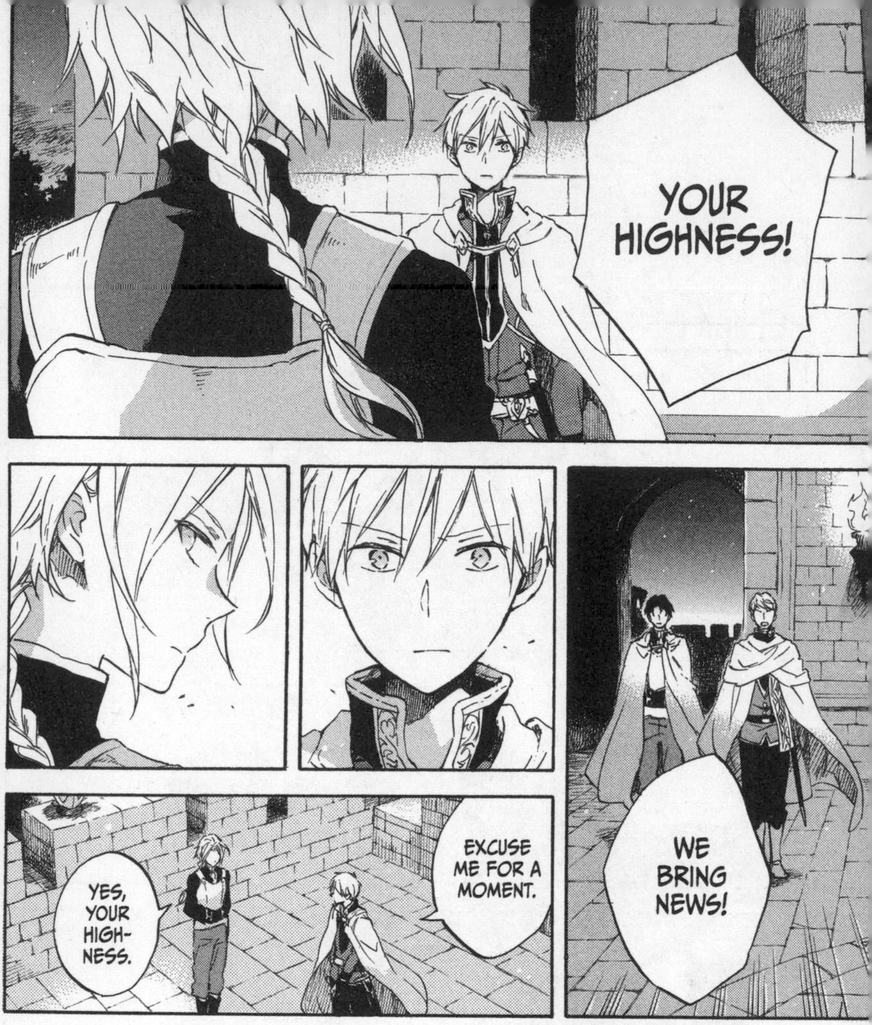
YOUR HIGHNESS!
WE BRING NEWS!
EXCUSE ME FOR A MOMENT.
YES, YOUR HIGH-NESS.

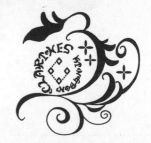

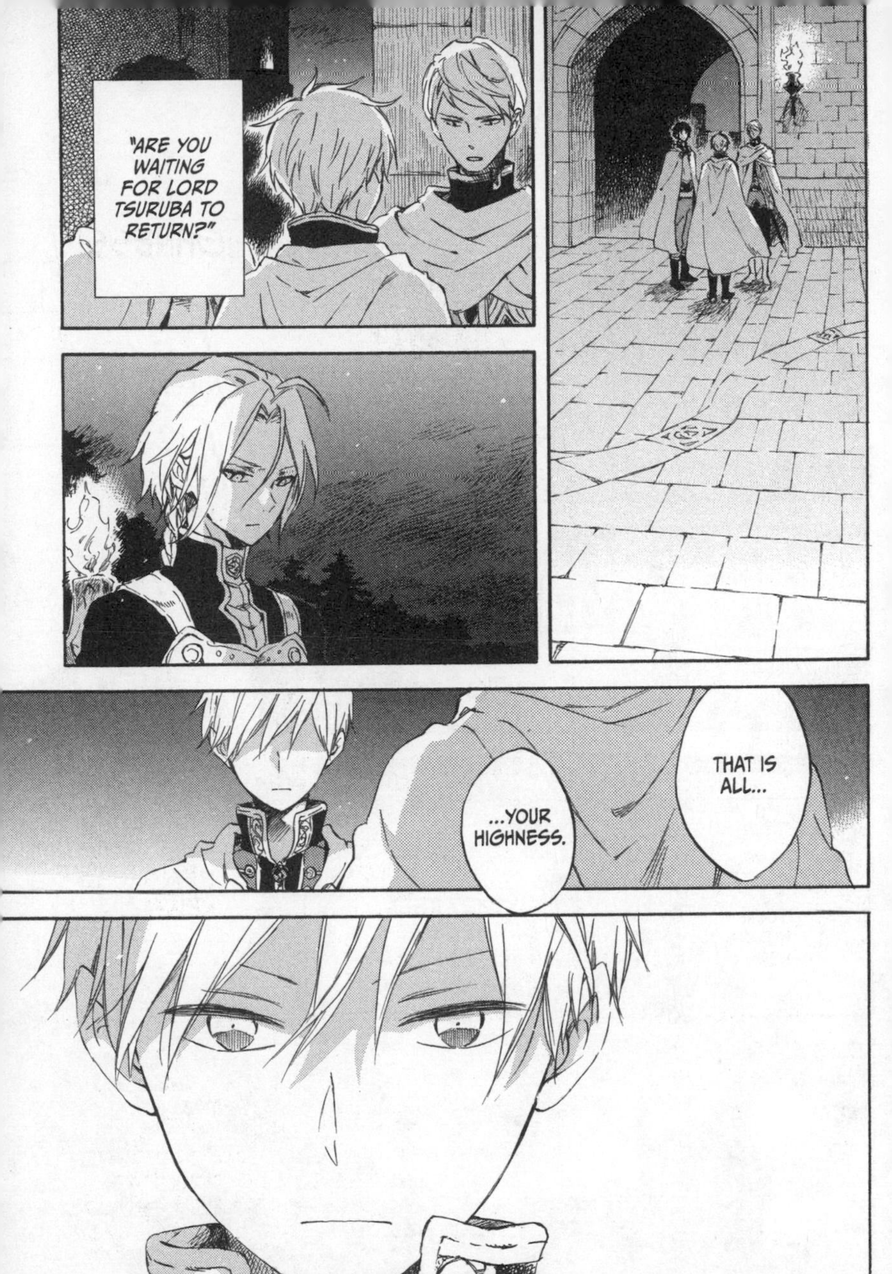
"ARE YOU WAITING FOR LORD TSURUBA TO RETURN?"
THAT IS ALL...
...YOUR HIGHNESS.

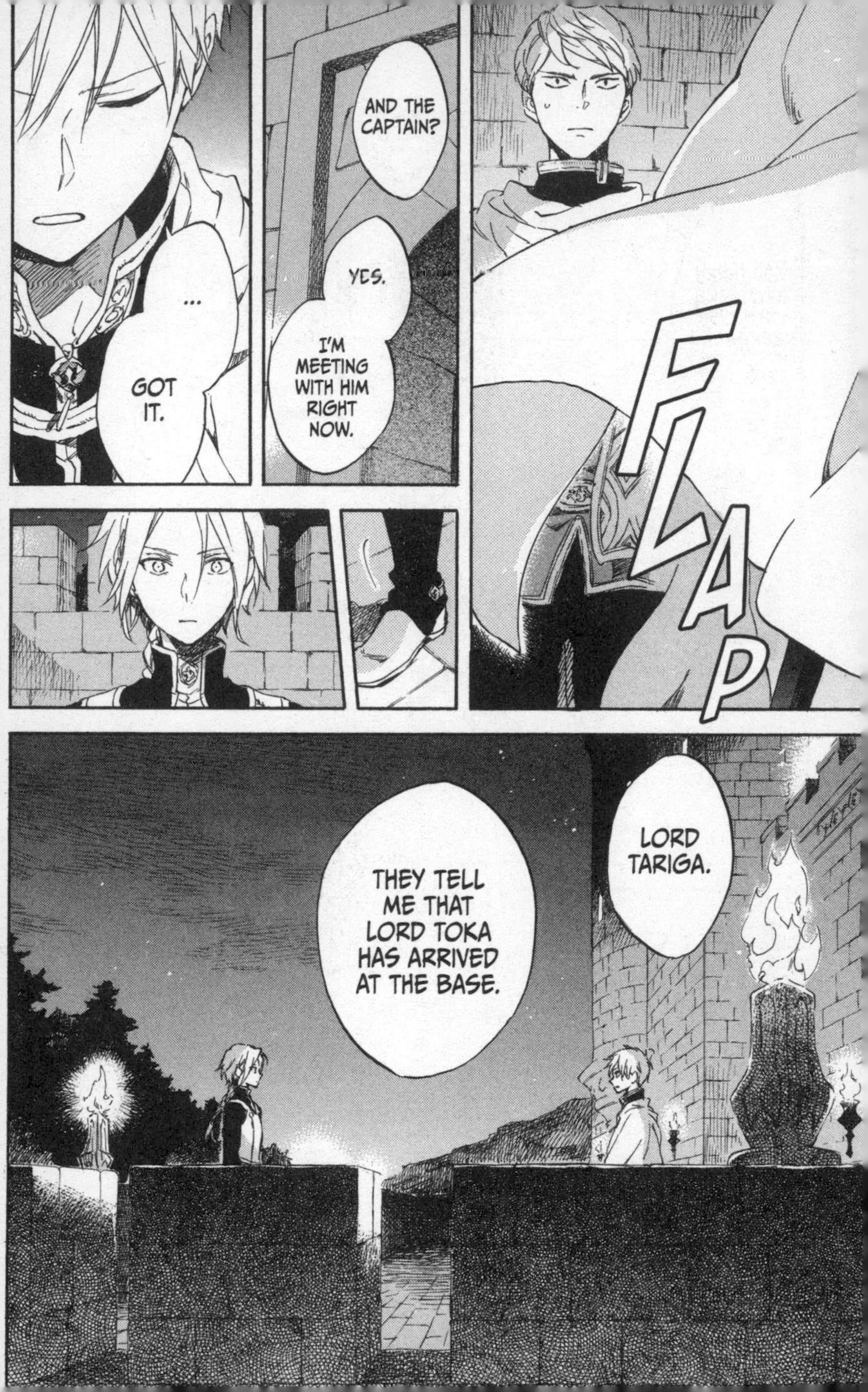
FLAP
AND THE CAPTAIN?
YES.
I'M MEETING WITH HIM RIGHT NOW.
...
GOT IT.
LORD TARIGA.
THEY TELL ME THAT LORD TOKA HAS ARRIVED AT THE BASE.

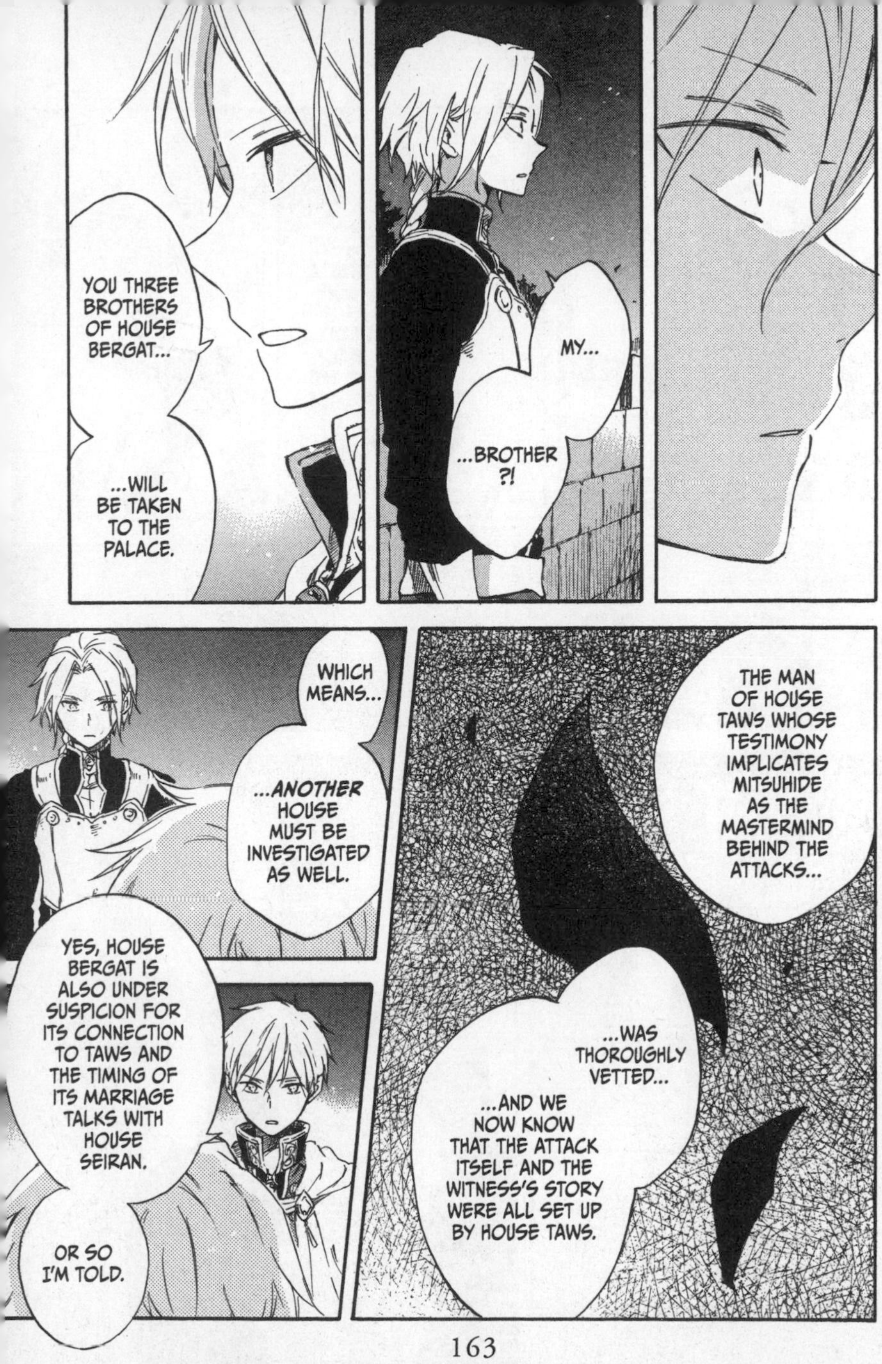
MY...
...BROTHER ?!
YOU THREE BROTHERS OF HOUSE BERGAT...
...WILL BE TAKEN TO THE PALACE.
THE MAN OF HOUSE TAWS WHOSE TESTIMONY IMPLICATES MITSUHIDE AS THE MASTERMIND BEHIND THE ATTACKS...
...WAS THOROUGHLY VETTED...
...AND WE NOW KNOW THAT THE ATTACK ITSELF AND THE WITNESS'S STORY WERE ALL SET UP BY HOUSE TAWS.
WHICH MEANS...
...*ANOTHER* HOUSE MUST BE INVESTIGATED AS WELL.
YES, HOUSE BERGAT IS ALSO UNDER SUSPICION FOR ITS CONNECTION TO TAWS AND THE TIMING OF ITS MARRIAGE TALKS WITH HOUSE SEIRAN.
OR SO I'M TOLD.

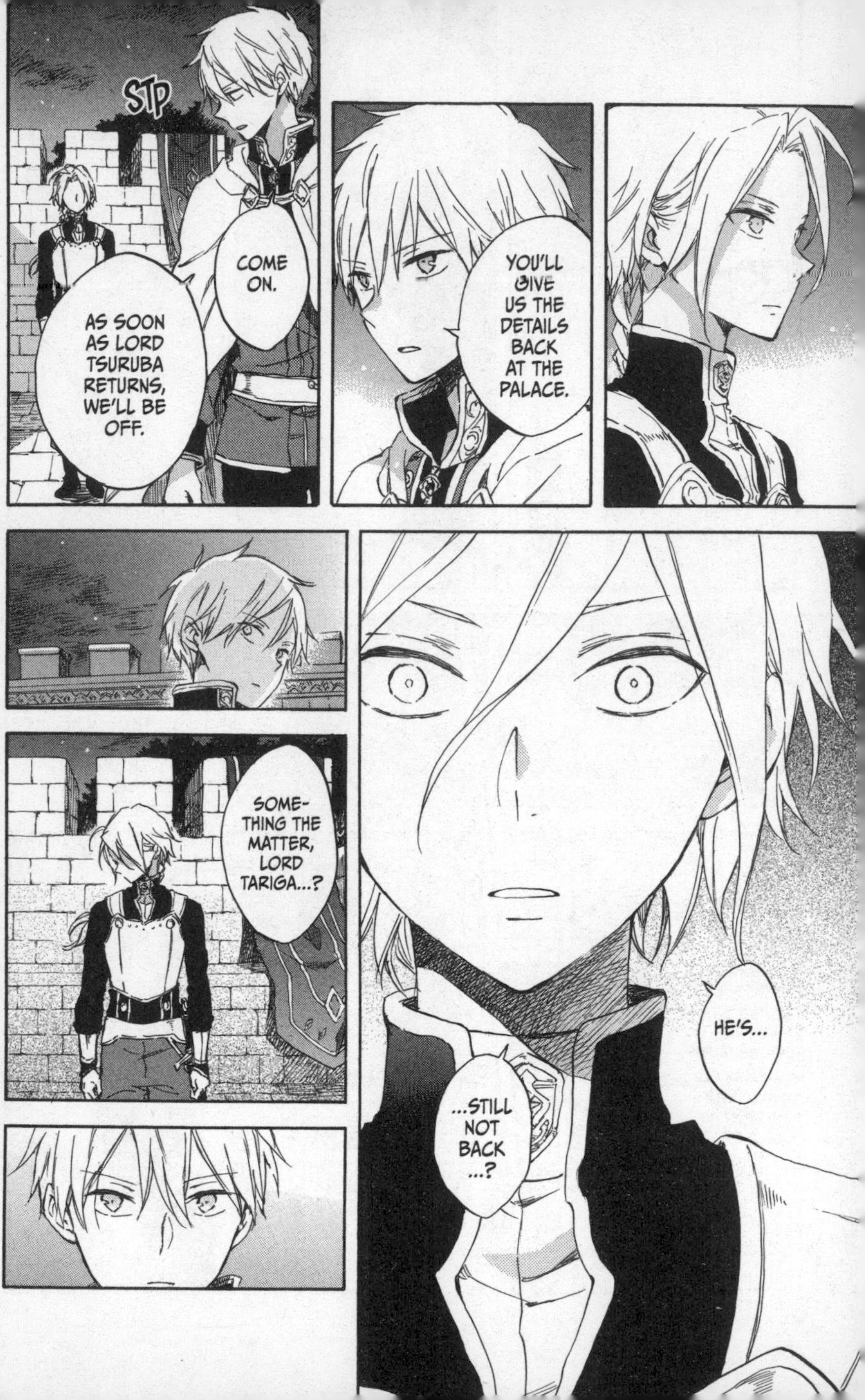
YOU'LL GIVE US THE DETAILS BACK AT THE PALACE.
STP
COME ON.
AS SOON AS LORD TSURUBA RETURNS, WE'LL BE OFF.
HE'S...
...STILL NOT BACK ...?
SOME-THING THE MATTER, LORD TARIGA...?

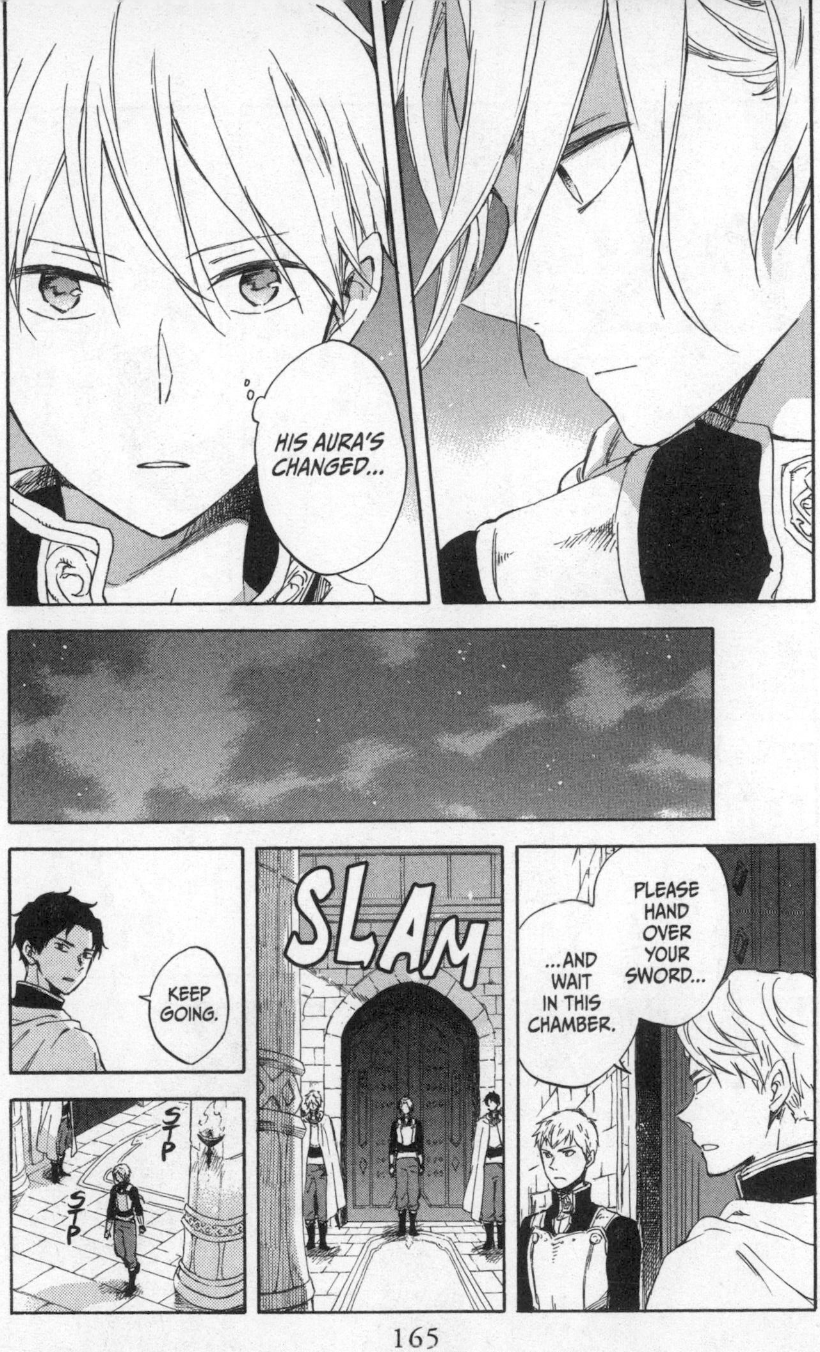

HIS AURA'S CHANGED...
SLAM
KEEP GOING.
PLEASE HAND OVER YOUR SWORD...
...AND WAIT IN THIS CHAMBER.
STP
STP

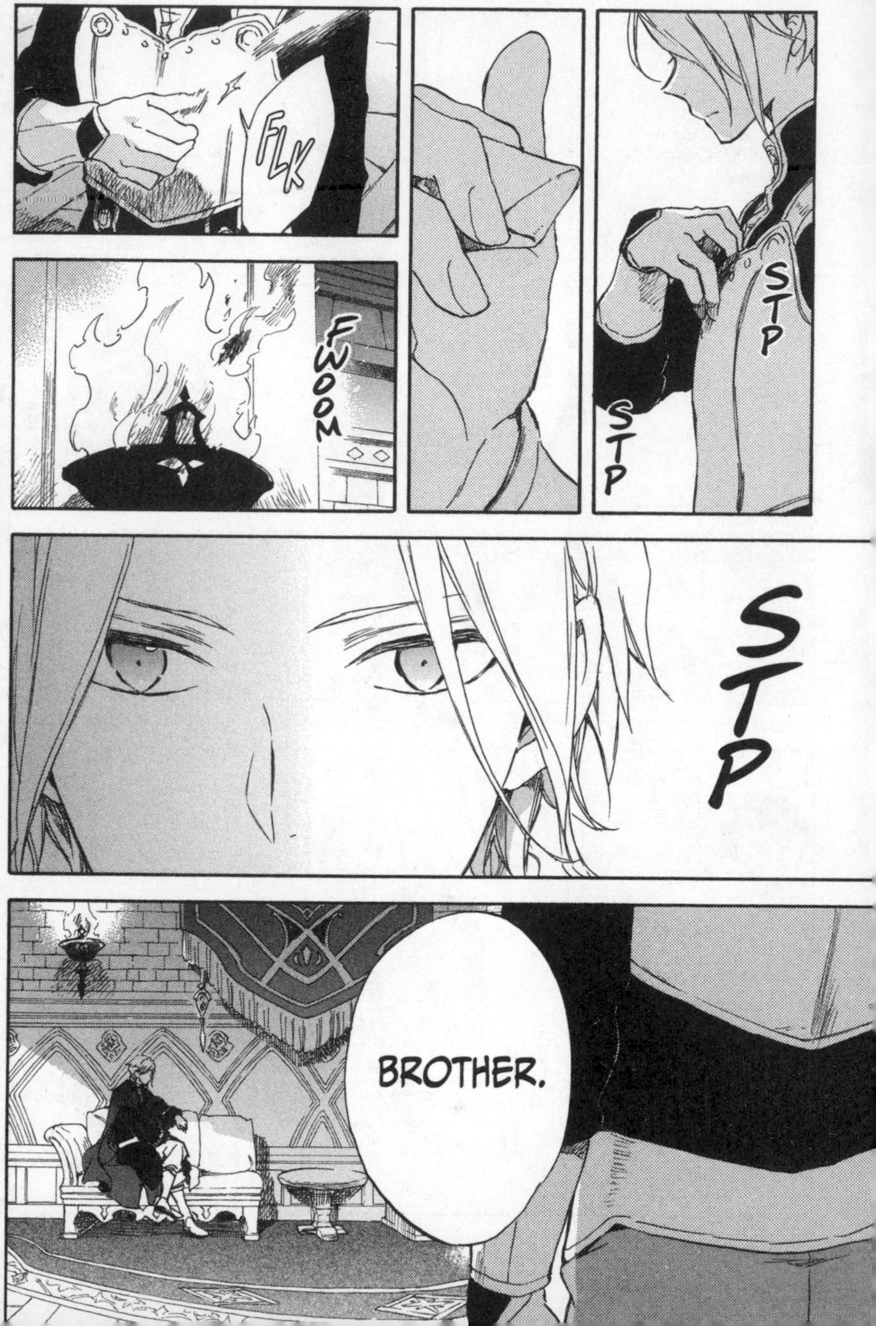
STP
STP
FLK
FWOOM
STP
BROTHER.

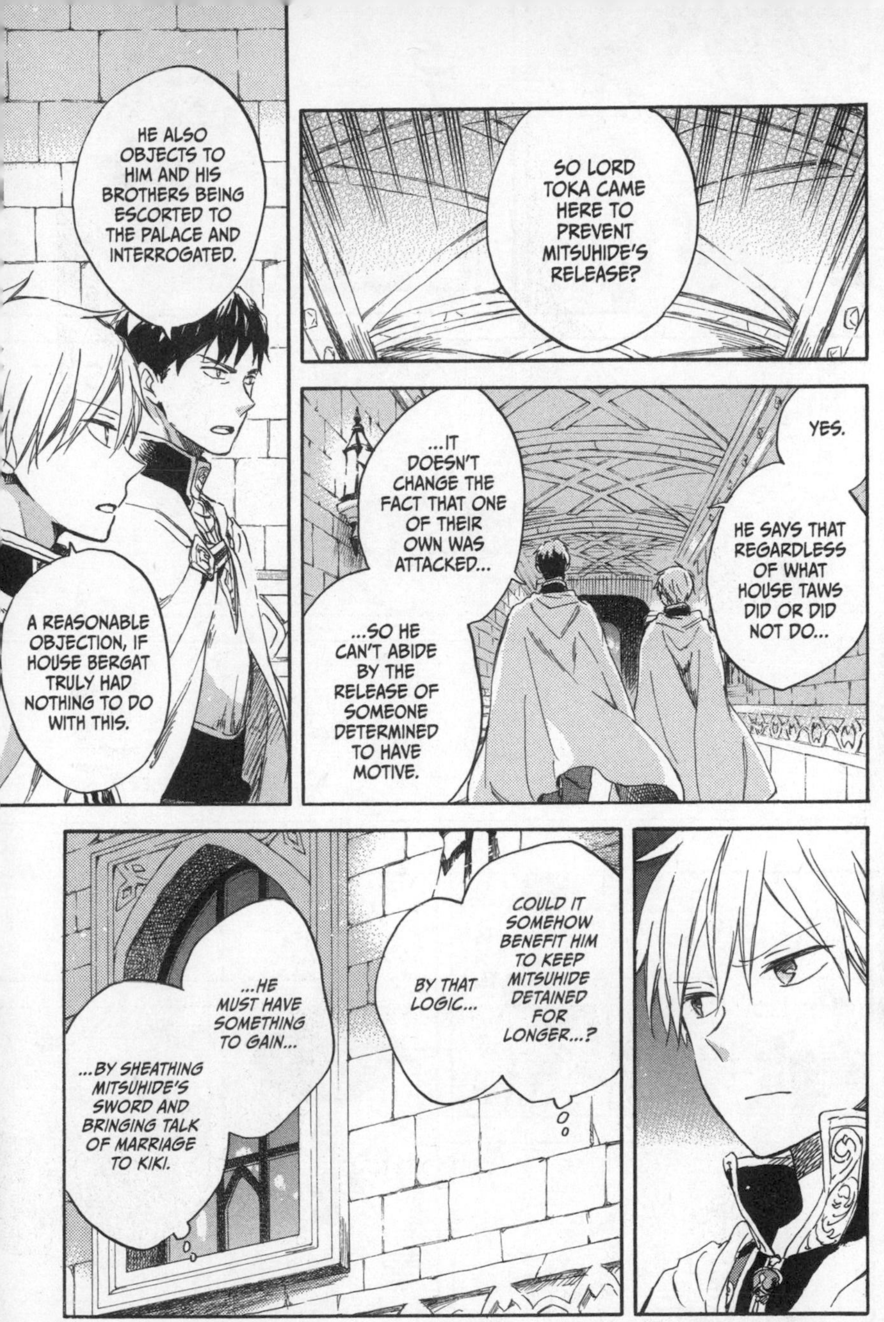
SO LORD TOKA CAME HERE TO PREVENT MITSUHIDE'S RELEASE?
YES.
HE SAYS THAT REGARDLESS OF WHAT HOUSE TAWS DID OR DID NOT DO...
...IT DOESN'T CHANGE THE FACT THAT ONE OF THEIR OWN WAS ATTACKED...
...SO HE CAN'T ABIDE BY THE RELEASE OF SOMEONE DETERMINED TO HAVE MOTIVE.
HE ALSO OBJECTS TO HIM AND HIS BROTHERS BEING ESCORTED TO THE PALACE AND INTERROGATED.
A REASONABLE OBJECTION, IF HOUSE BERGAT TRULY HAD NOTHING TO DO WITH THIS.
COULD IT SOMEHOW BENEFIT HIM TO KEEP MITSUHIDE DETAINED FOR LONGER...?
BY THAT LOGIC...
...HE MUST HAVE SOMETHING TO GAIN...
...BY SHEATHING MITSUHIDE'S SWORD AND BRINGING TALK OF MARRIAGE TO KIKI.

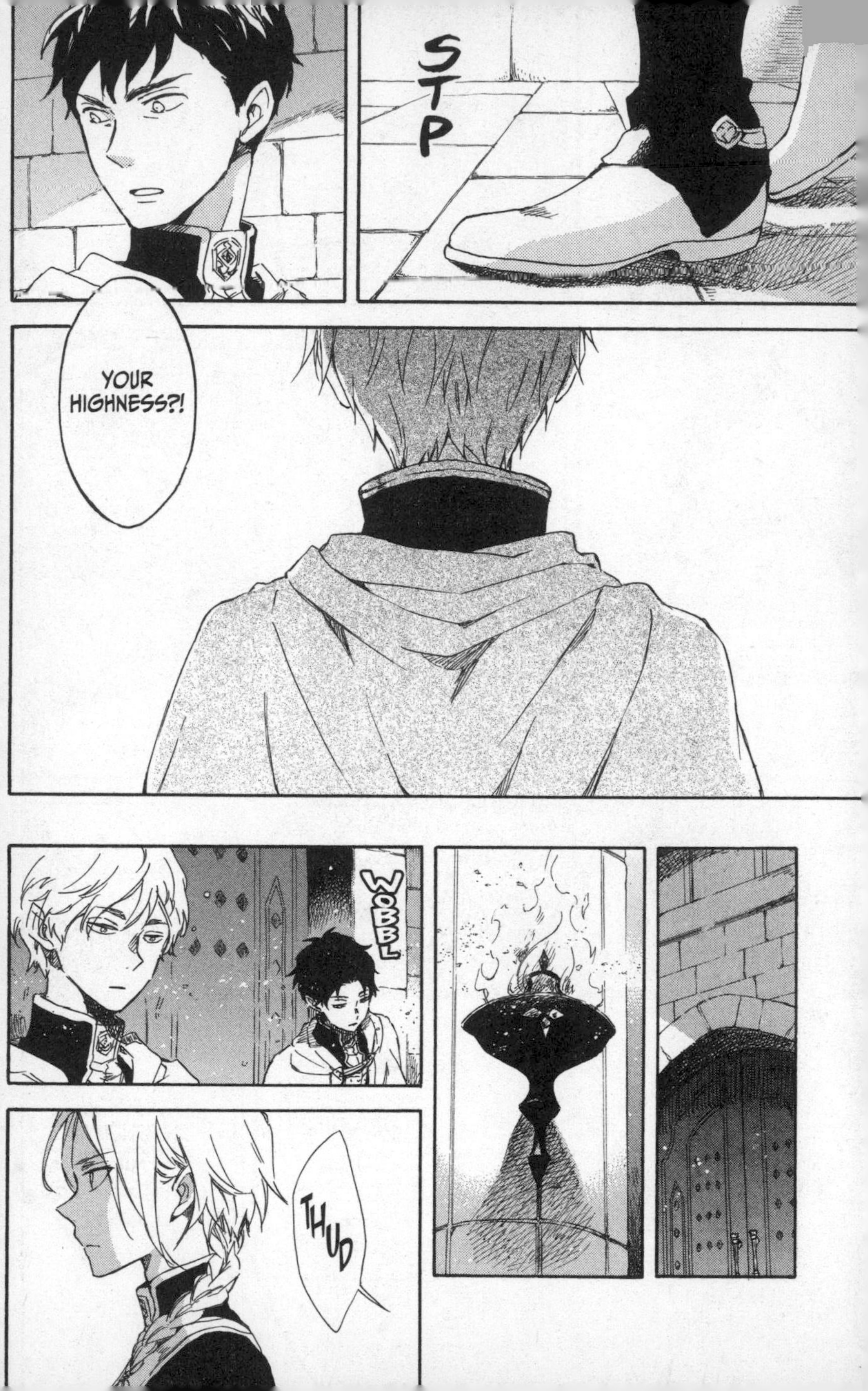
STP
YOUR HIGHNESS?!
WOBBL
THUD

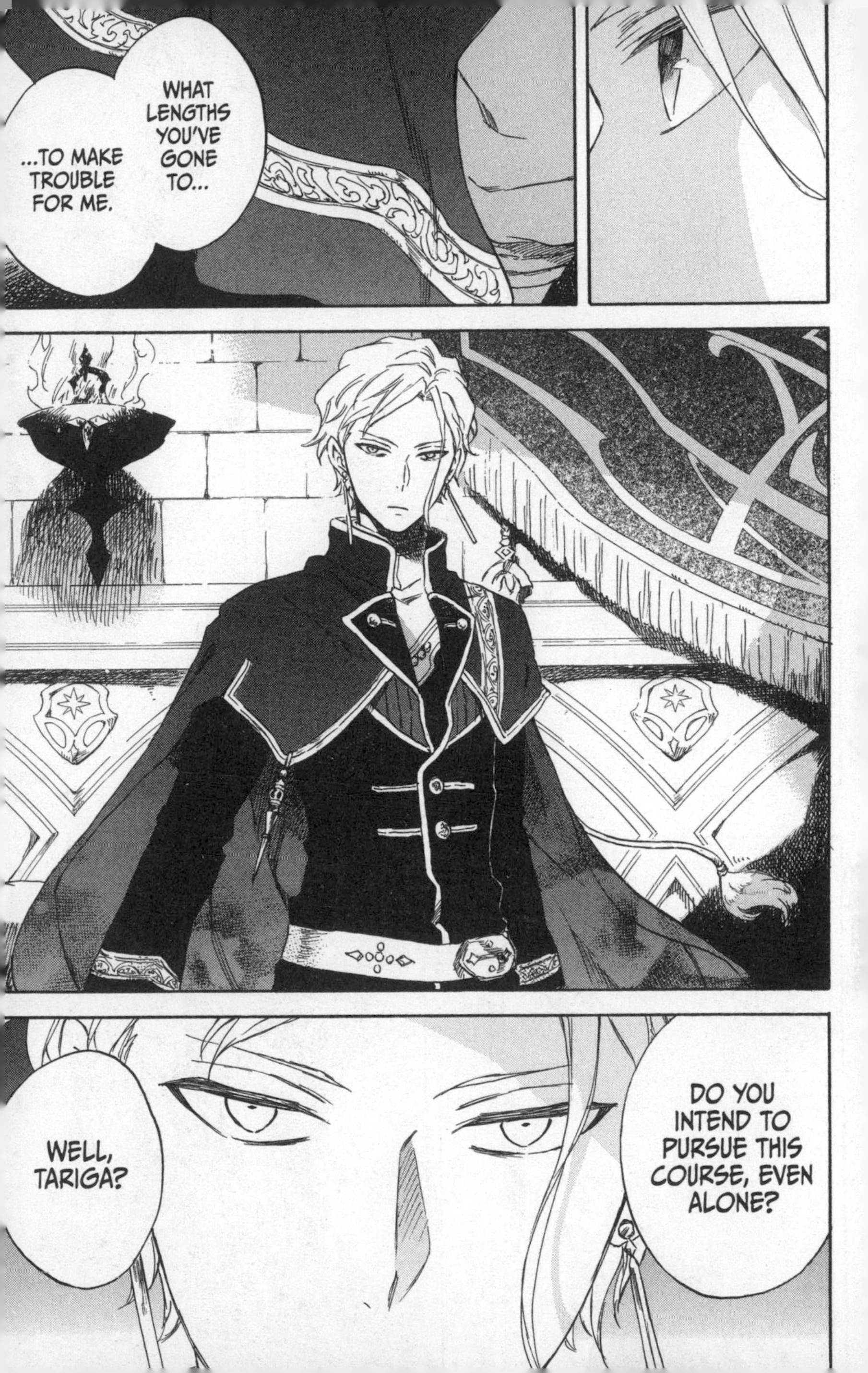
WHAT LENGTHS YOU'VE GONE TO...
...TO MAKE TROUBLE FOR ME.
DO YOU INTEND TO PURSUE THIS COURSE, EVEN ALONE?
WELL, TARIGA?

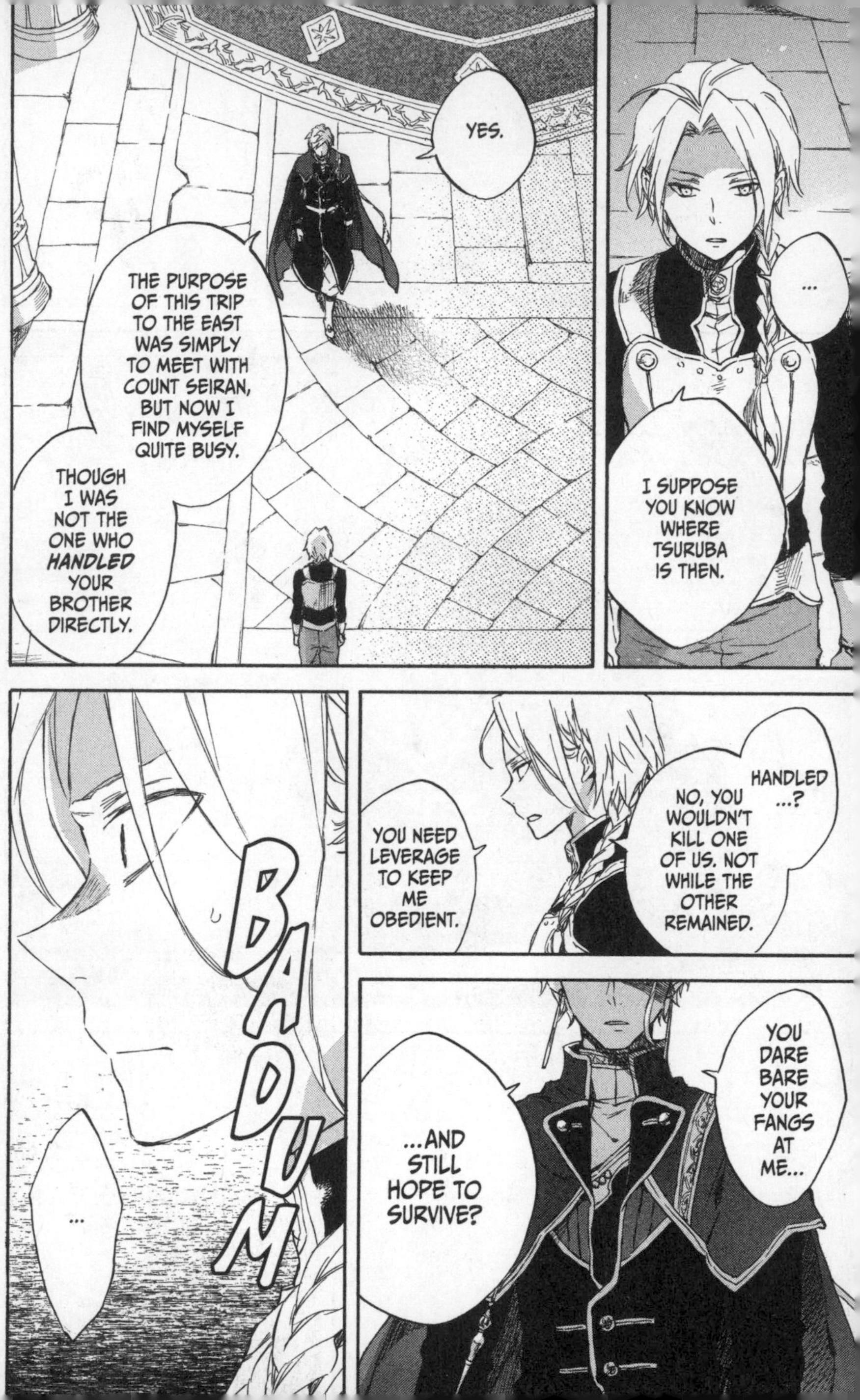
...
I SUPPOSE YOU KNOW WHERE TSURUBA IS THEN.
YES.
THE PURPOSE OF THIS TRIP TO THE EAST WAS SIMPLY TO MEET WITH COUNT SEIRAN, BUT NOW I FIND MYSELF QUITE BUSY.
THOUGH I WAS NOT THE ONE WHO *HANDLED* YOUR BROTHER DIRECTLY.
HANDLED ...?
NO, YOU WOULDN'T KILL ONE OF US. NOT WHILE THE OTHER REMAINED.
YOU NEED LEVERAGE TO KEEP ME OBEDIENT.
YOU DARE BARE YOUR FANGS AT ME...
...AND STILL HOPE TO SURVIVE?
BADUM
...

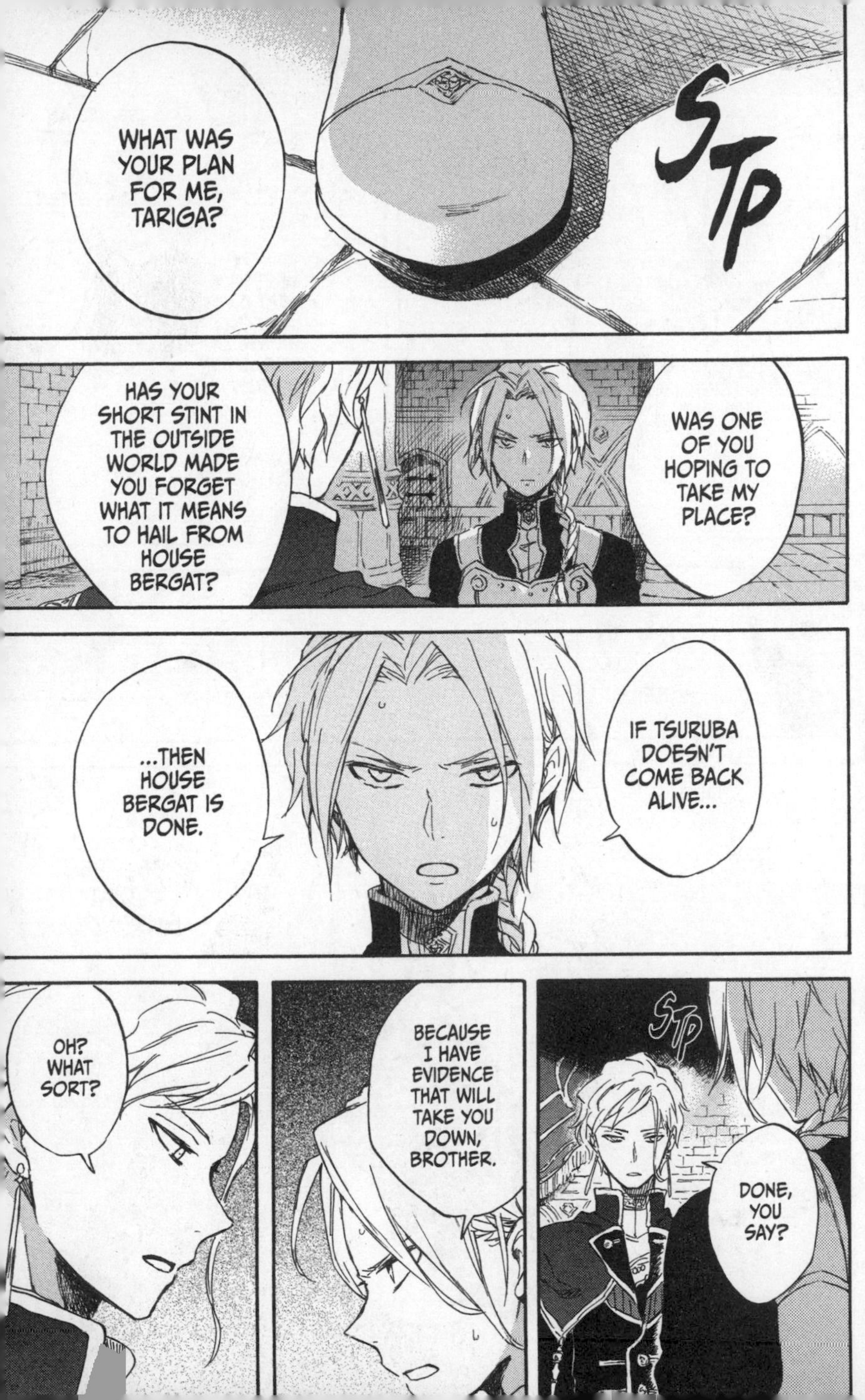
STP
WHAT WAS YOUR PLAN FOR ME, TARIGA?
WAS ONE OF YOU HOPING TO TAKE MY PLACE?
HAS YOUR SHORT STINT IN THE OUTSIDE WORLD MADE YOU FORGET WHAT IT MEANS TO HAIL FROM HOUSE BERGAT?
IF TSURUBA DOESN'T COME BACK ALIVE...
...THEN HOUSE BERGAT IS DONE.
STP
DONE, YOU SAY?
BECAUSE I HAVE EVIDENCE THAT WILL TAKE YOU DOWN, BROTHER.
OH? WHAT SORT?

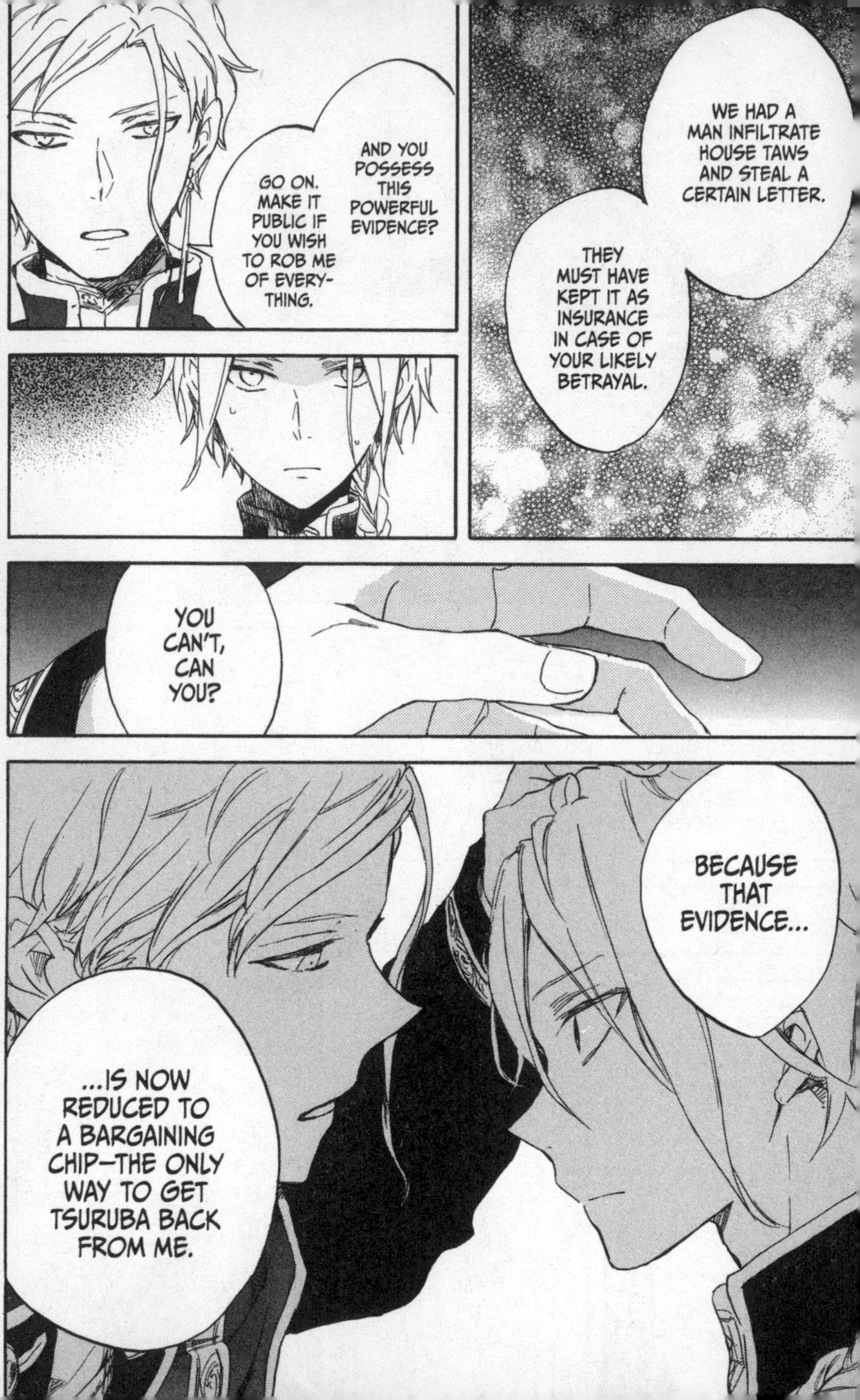
WE HAD A MAN INFILTRATE HOUSE TAWS AND STEAL A CERTAIN LETTER.
THEY MUST HAVE KEPT IT AS INSURANCE IN CASE OF YOUR LIKELY BETRAYAL.
AND YOU POSSESS THIS POWERFUL EVIDENCE?
GO ON. MAKE IT PUBLIC IF YOU WISH TO ROB ME OF EVERY-THING.
YOU CAN'T, CAN YOU?
BECAUSE THAT EVIDENCE...
...IS NOW REDUCED TO A BARGAINING CHIP—THE ONLY WAY TO GET TSURUBA BACK FROM ME.

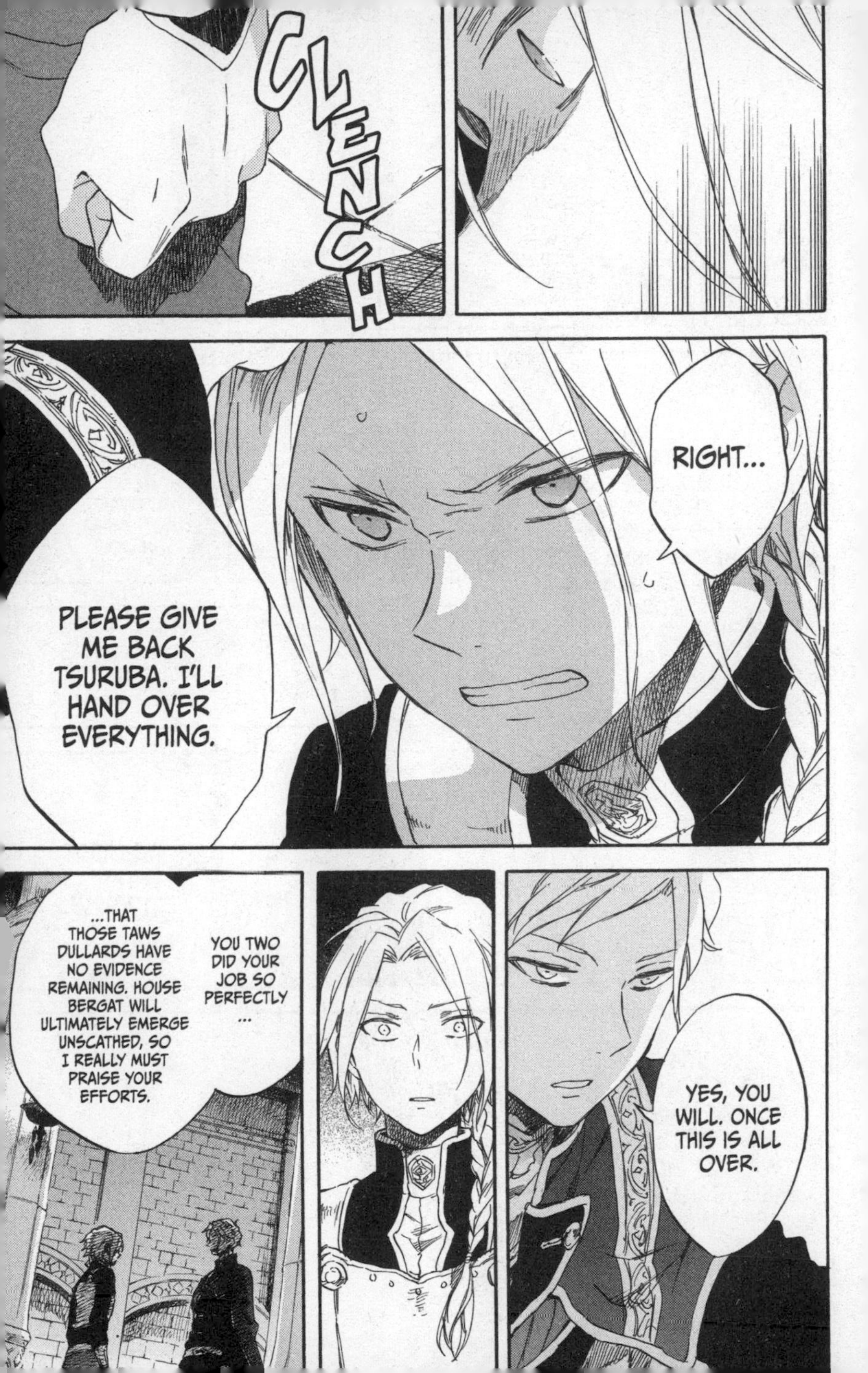
CLENCH
RIGHT...
PLEASE GIVE ME BACK TSURUBA. I'LL HAND OVER EVERYTHING.
YES, YOU WILL. ONCE THIS IS ALL OVER.
YOU TWO DID YOUR JOB SO PERFECTLY...
...THAT THOSE TAWS DULLARDS HAVE NO EVIDENCE REMAINING. HOUSE BERGAT WILL ULTIMATELY EMERGE UNSCATHED, SO I REALLY MUST PRAISE YOUR EFFORTS.

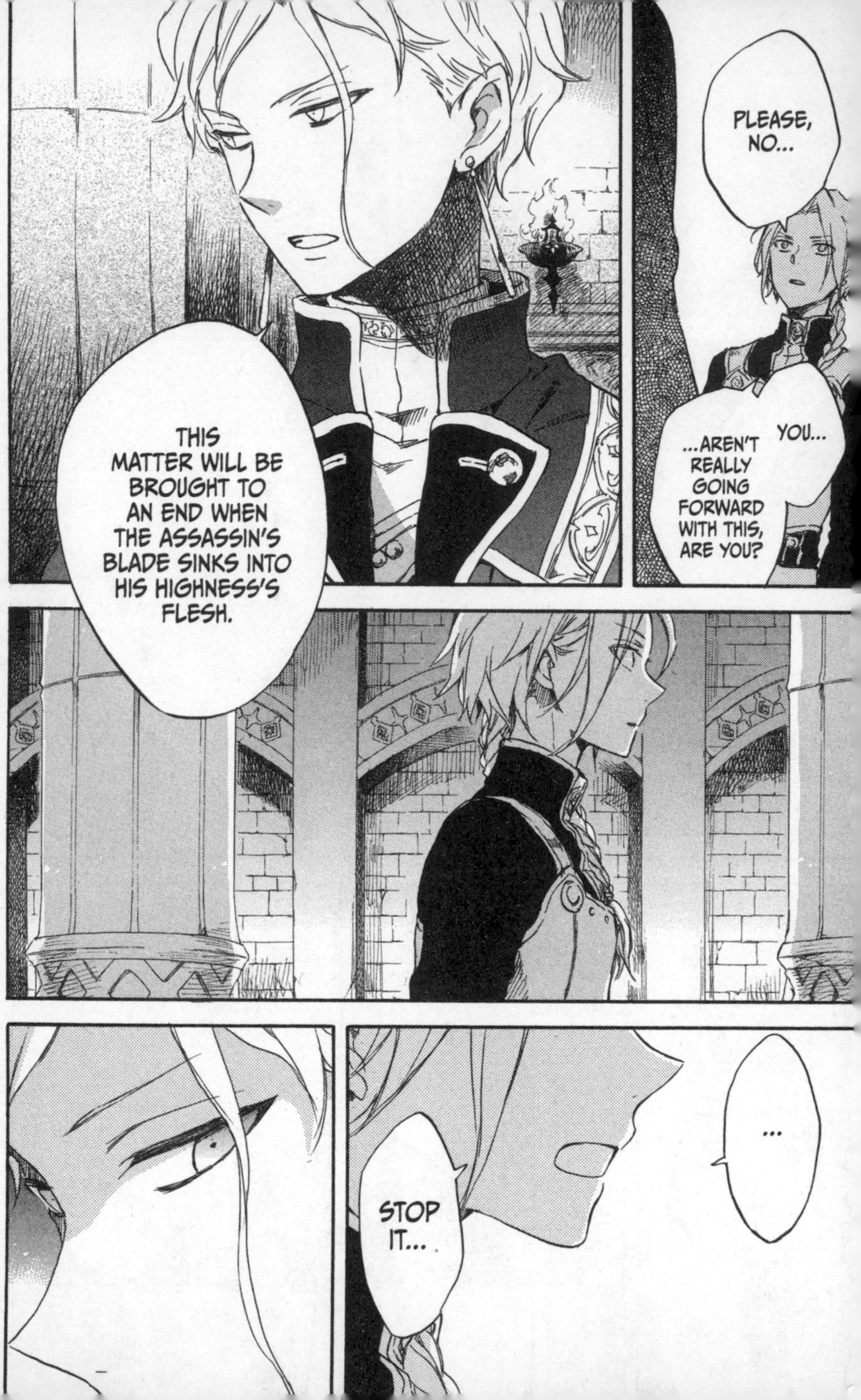
PLEASE, NO...
YOU...
...AREN'T REALLY GOING FORWARD WITH THIS, ARE YOU?
THIS MATTER WILL BE BROUGHT TO AN END WHEN THE ASSASSIN'S BLADE SINKS INTO HIS HIGHNESS'S FLESH.
...
STOP IT...

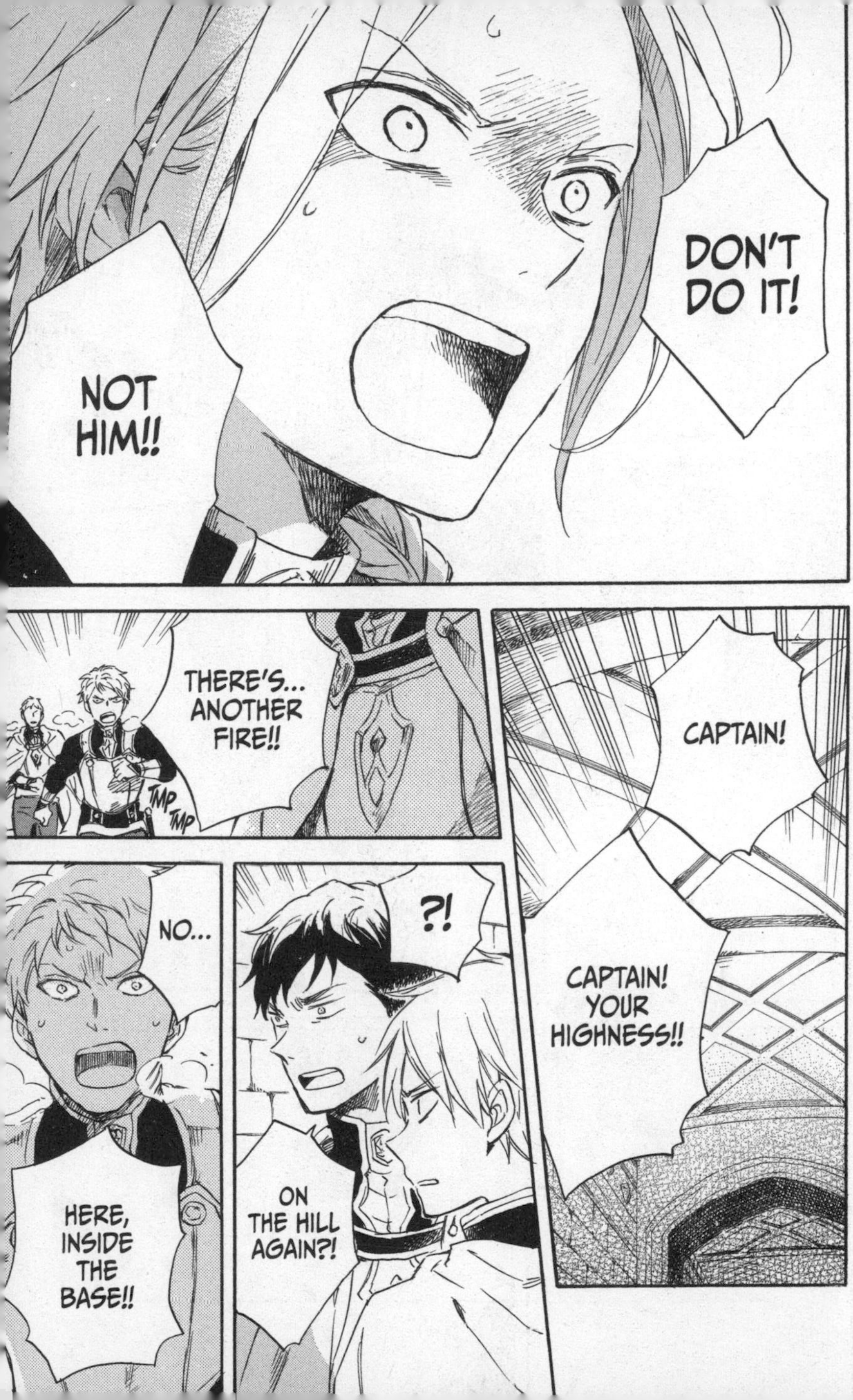
DON'T DO IT!
NOT HIM!!
CAPTAIN!
CAPTAIN! YOUR HIGHNESS!!
THERE'S... ANOTHER FIRE!!
TMP TMP
?!
ON THE HILL AGAIN?!
NO...
HERE, INSIDE THE BASE!!

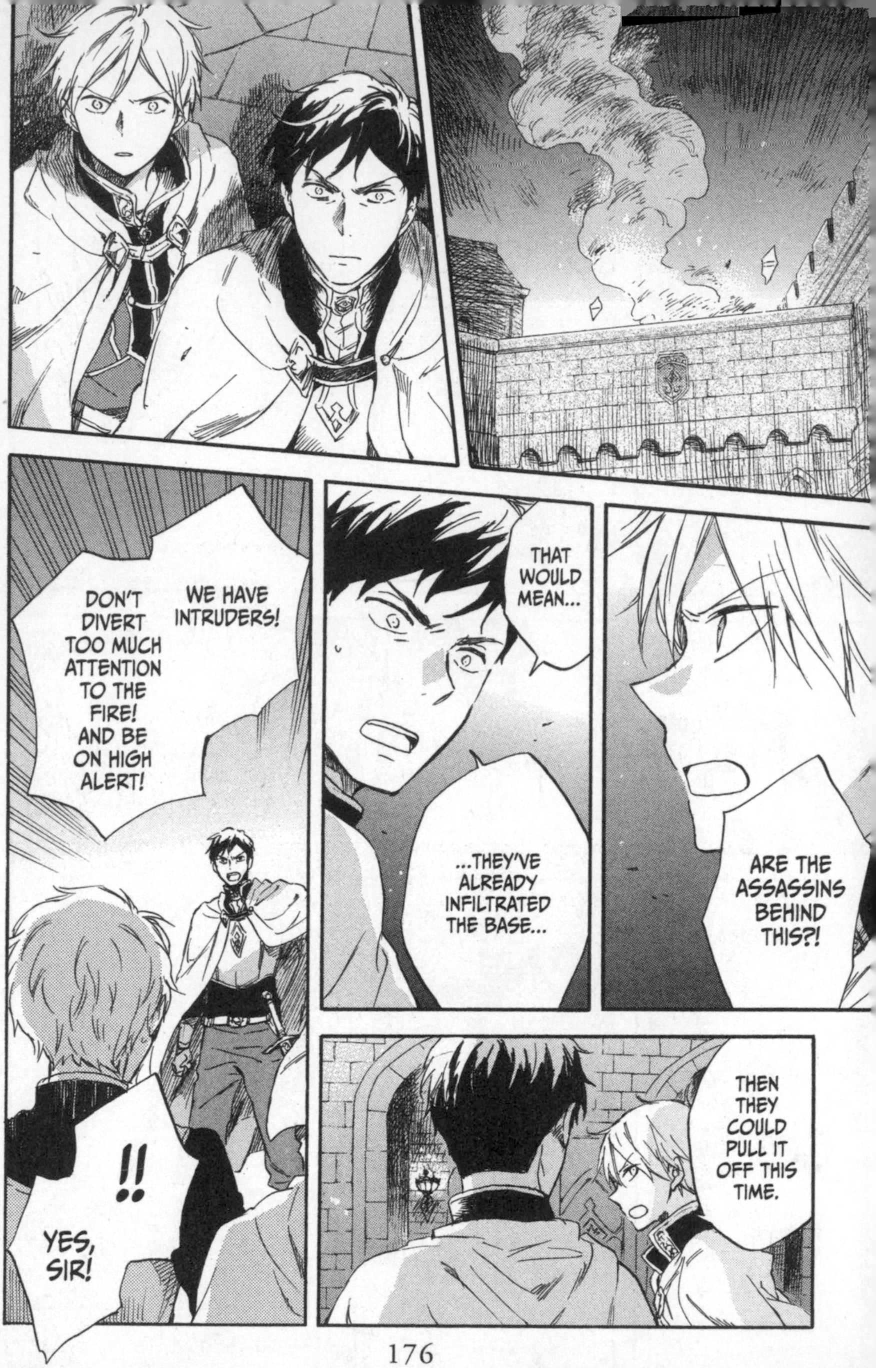
ARE THE ASSASSINS BEHIND THIS?!
THAT WOULD MEAN...
...THEY'VE ALREADY INFILTRATED THE BASE...
THEN THEY COULD PULL IT OFF THIS TIME.
WE HAVE INTRUDERS!
DON'T DIVERT TOO MUCH ATTENTION TO THE FIRE! AND BE ON HIGH ALERT!
!!
YES, SIR!

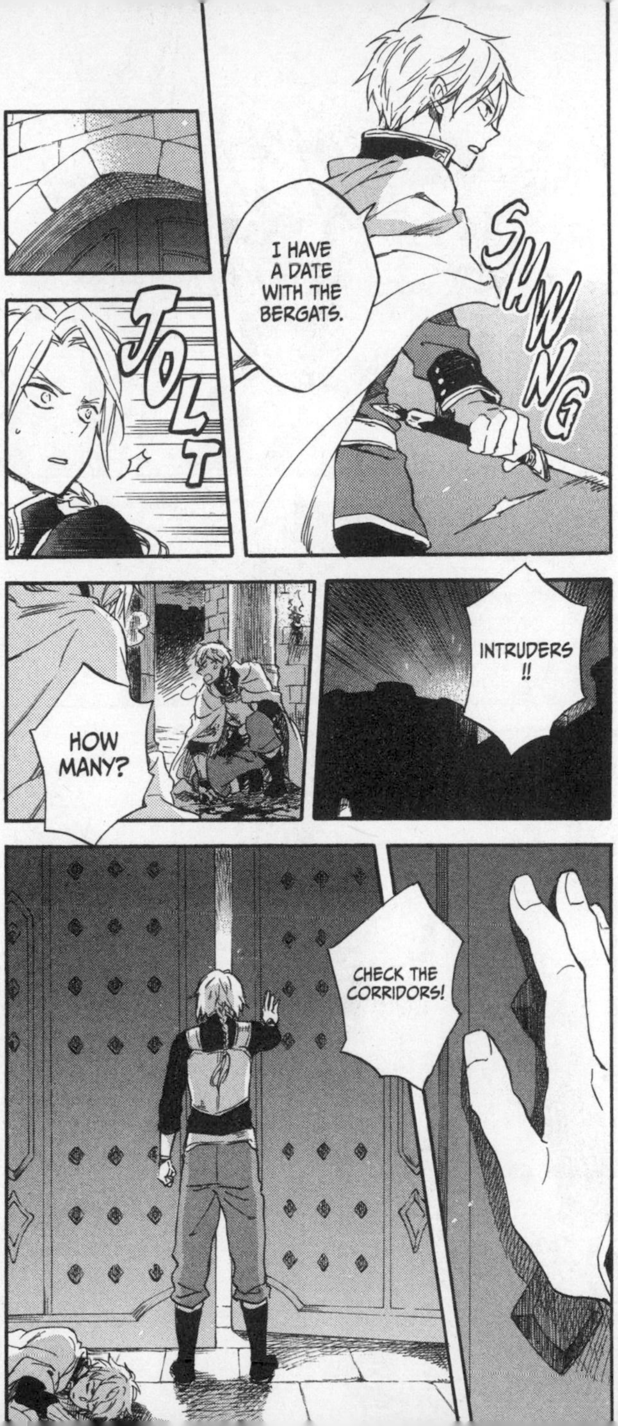
I HAVE A DATE WITH THE BERGATS.
SHWNG
JOLT
INTRUDERS !!
HOW MANY?
CHECK THE CORRIDORS!

5

Suzu at age 11

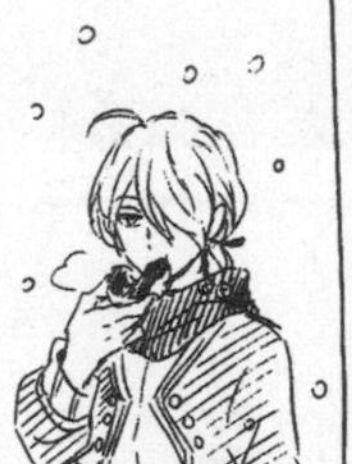

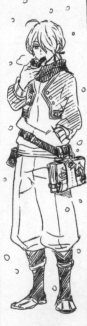

He spent two months experimenting with the hypothesis that covering one of his eyes with his bangs would make him more appealing to the ladies.

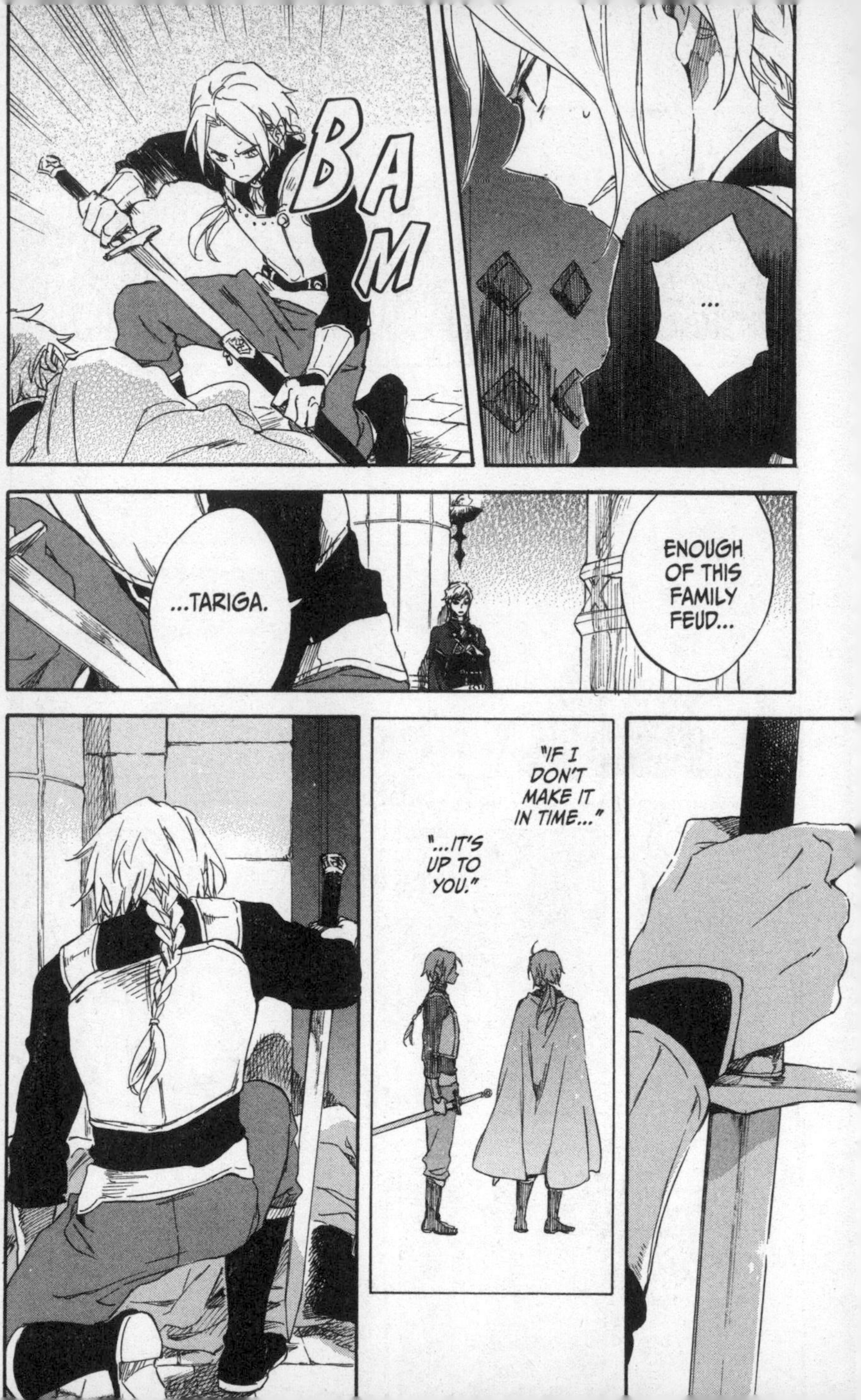
...
BAM
ENOUGH OF THIS FAMILY FEUD...
...TARIGA.
"IF I DON'T MAKE IT IN TIME..."
"...IT'S UP TO YOU."

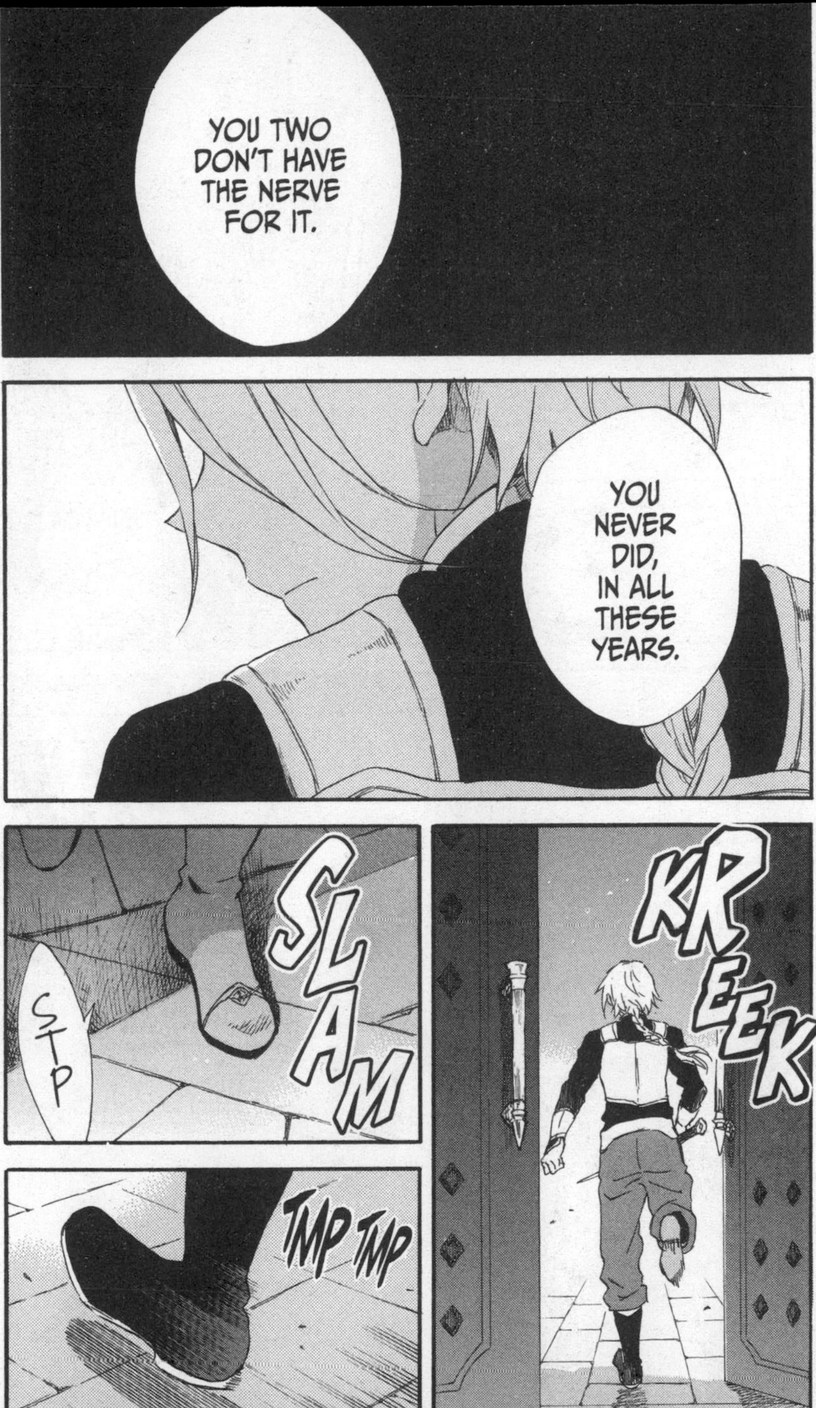
YOU TWO DON'T HAVE THE NERVE FOR IT.
YOU NEVER DID, IN ALL THESE YEARS.
KREEK
SLAM
STP
TMP TMP

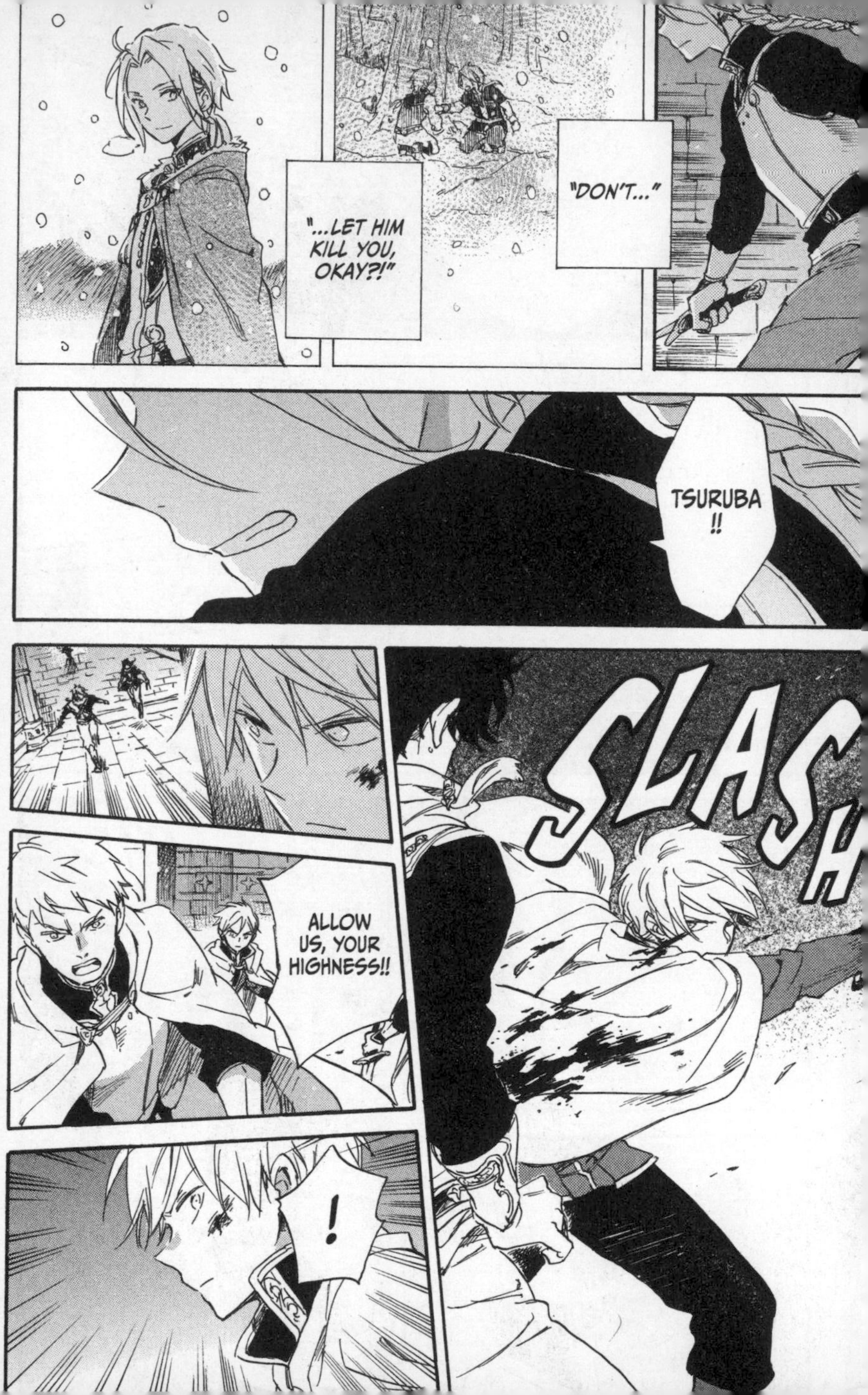
"DON'T..."
"...LET HIM KILL YOU, OKAY?!"
TSURUBA!!
SLASH
ALLOW US, YOUR HIGHNESS!!
!

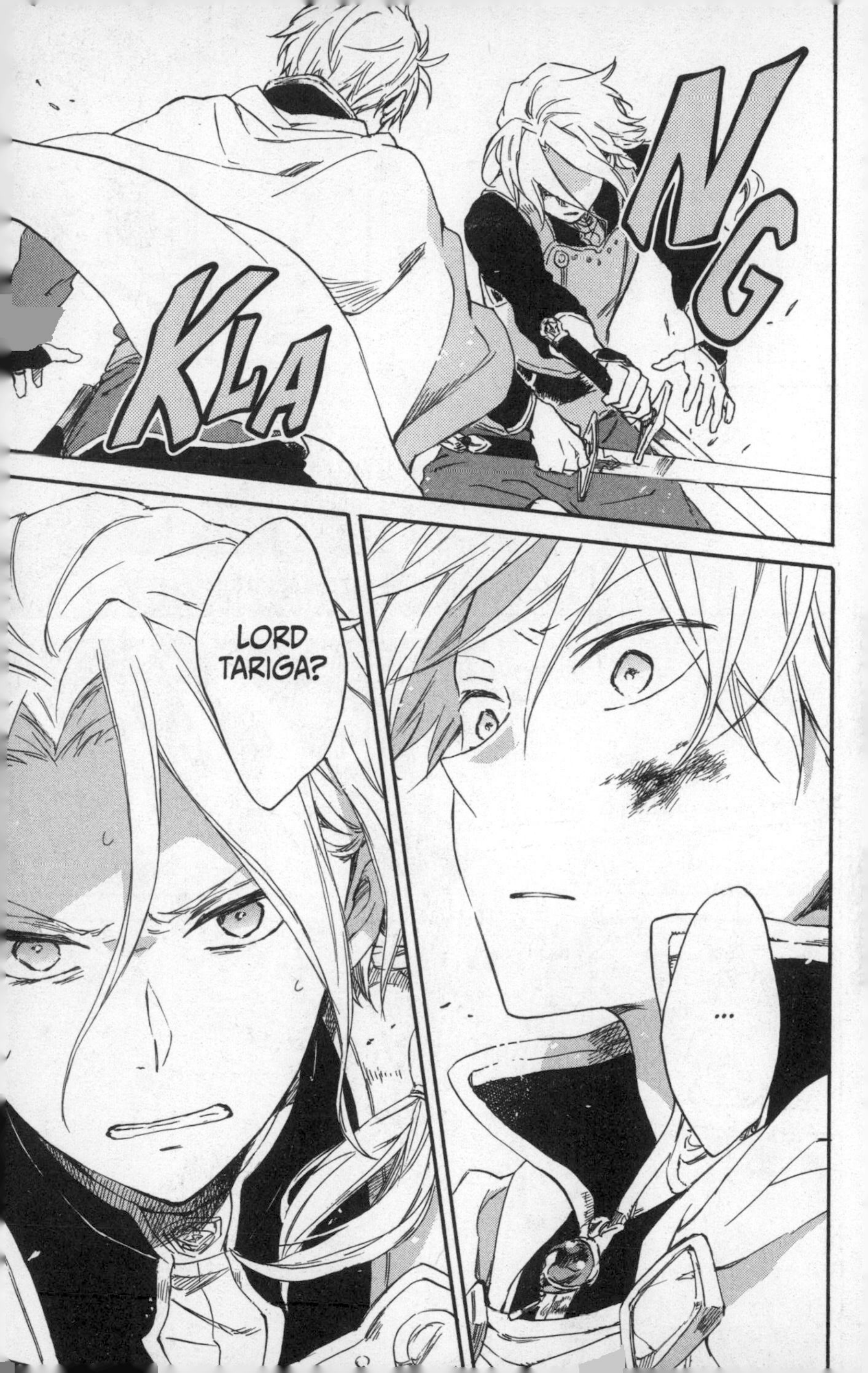
KLA
NG
...
LORD TARIGA?

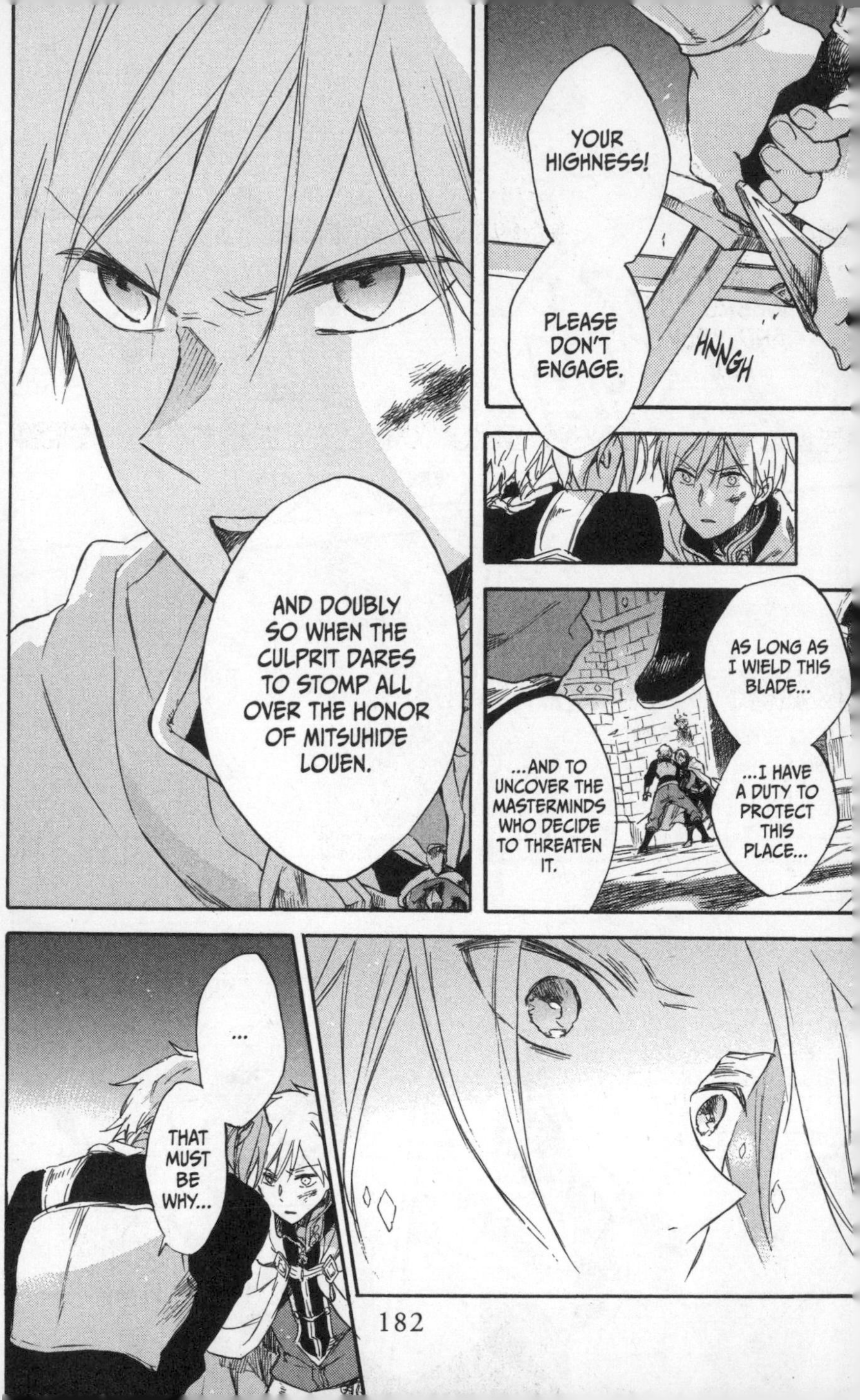
YOUR HIGHNESS!
PLEASE DON'T ENGAGE.
HNNGH
AS LONG AS I WIELD THIS BLADE...
...I HAVE A DUTY TO PROTECT THIS PLACE...
...AND TO UNCOVER THE MASTERMINDS WHO DECIDE TO THREATEN IT.
AND DOUBLY SO WHEN THE CULPRIT DARES TO STOMP ALL OVER THE HONOR OF MITSUHIDE LOUEN.
...
THAT MUST BE WHY...

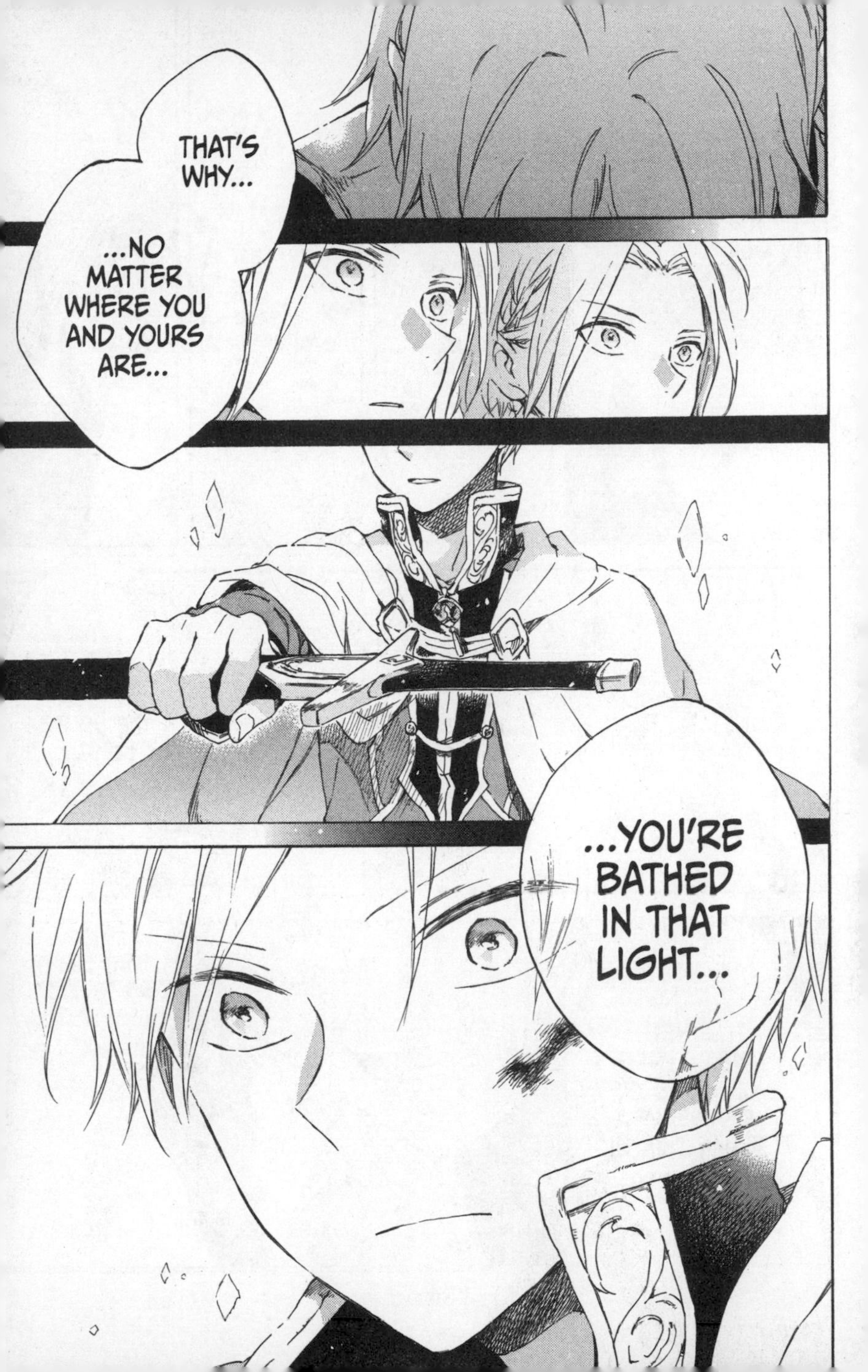
THAT'S WHY...
...NO MATTER WHERE YOU AND YOURS ARE...
...YOU'RE BATHED IN THAT LIGHT...

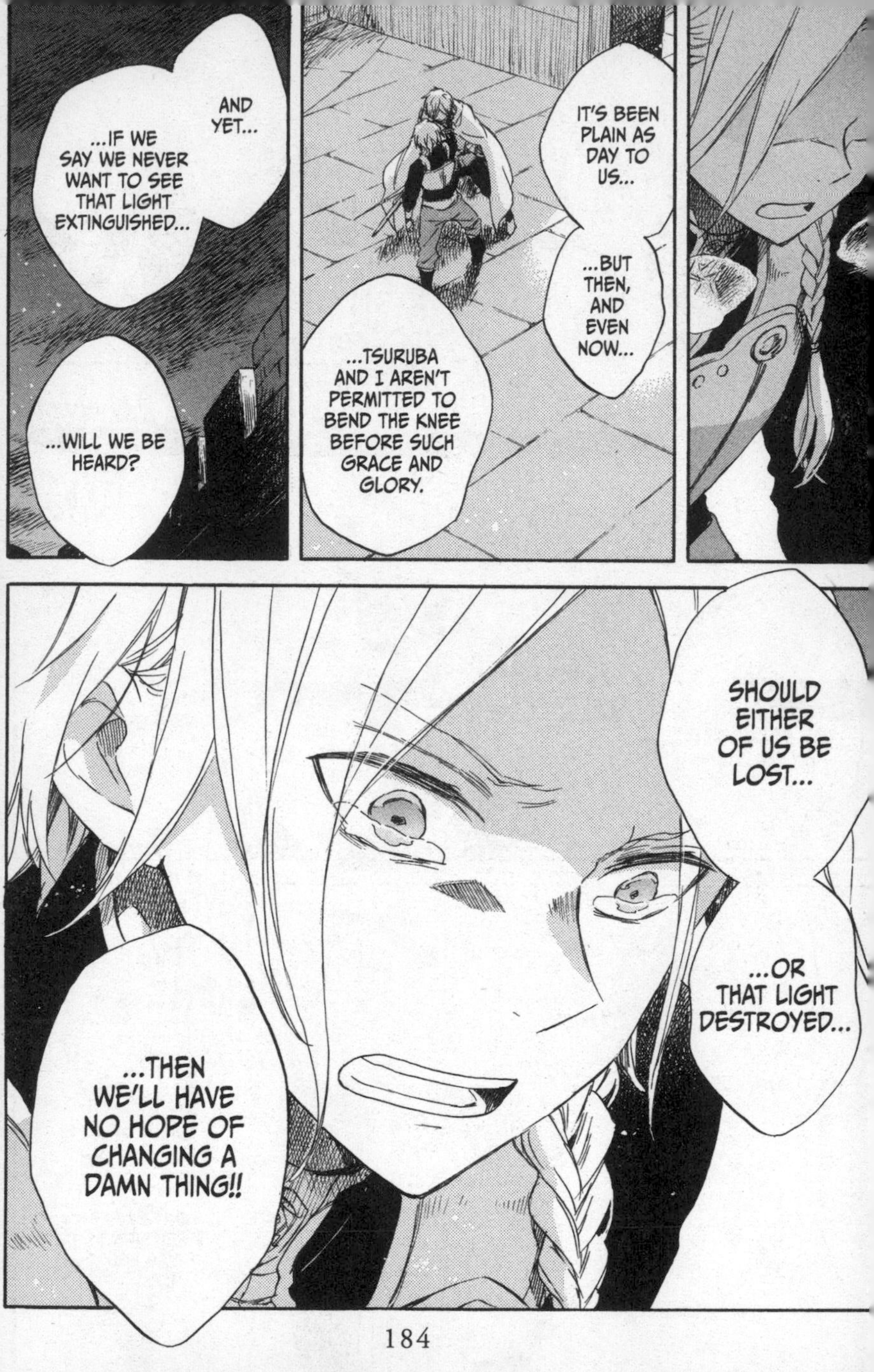
IT'S BEEN PLAIN AS DAY TO US...
...BUT THEN, AND EVEN NOW...
...TSURUBA AND I AREN'T PERMITTED TO BEND THE KNEE BEFORE SUCH GRACE AND GLORY.
AND YET...
...IF WE SAY WE NEVER WANT TO SEE THAT LIGHT EXTINGUISHED...
...WILL WE BE HEARD?
SHOULD EITHER OF US BE LOST...
...OR THAT LIGHT DESTROYED...
...THEN WE'LL HAVE NO HOPE OF CHANGING A DAMN THING!!

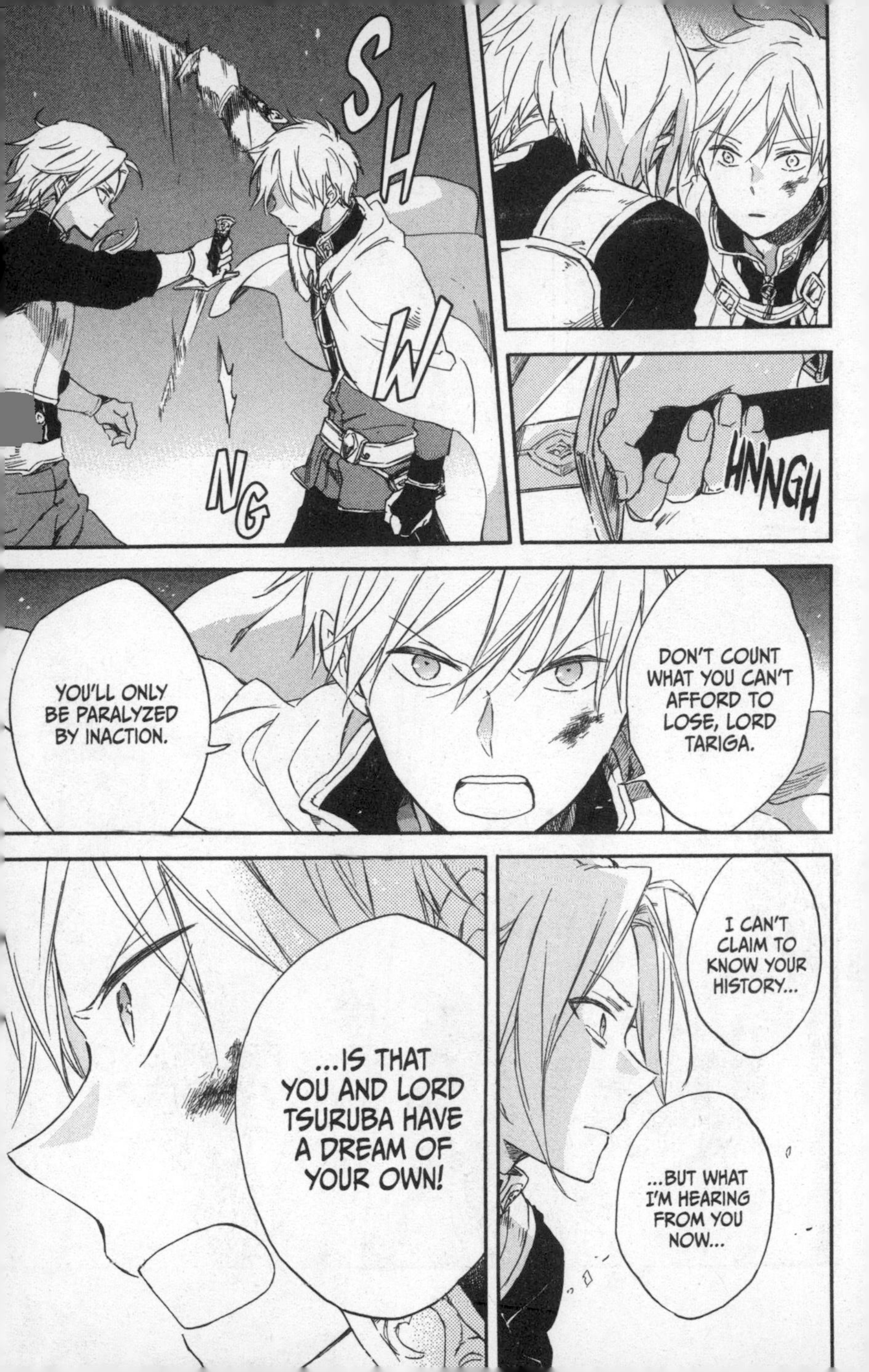
HNNGH
SHWNG
DON'T COUNT WHAT YOU CAN'T AFFORD TO LOSE, LORD TARIGA.
YOU'LL ONLY BE PARALYZED BY INACTION.
I CAN'T CLAIM TO KNOW YOUR HISTORY...
...BUT WHAT I'M HEARING FROM YOU NOW...
...IS THAT YOU AND LORD TSURUBA HAVE A DREAM OF YOUR OWN!

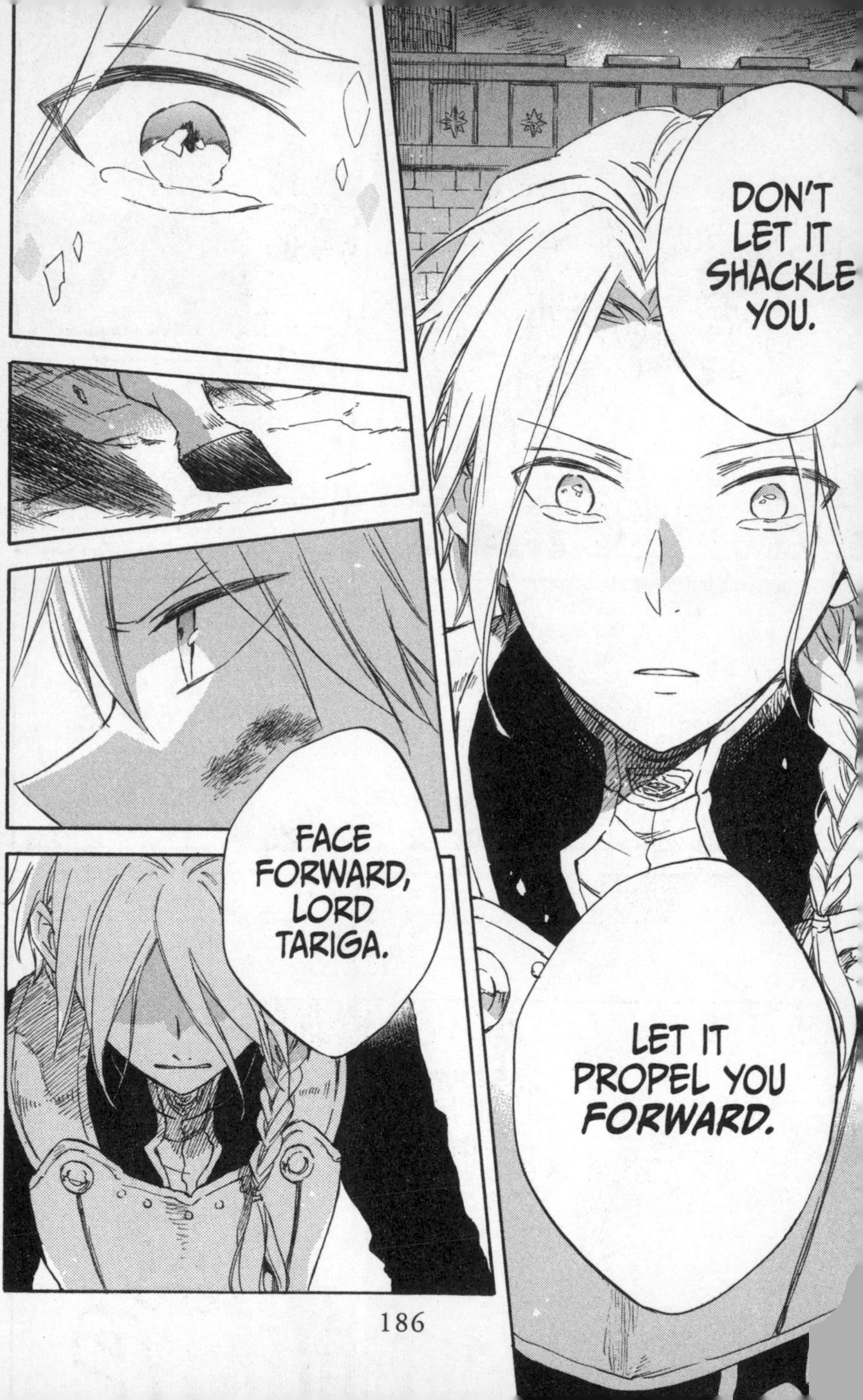
DON'T LET IT SHACKLE YOU.
LET IT PROPEL YOU FORWARD.
FACE FORWARD, LORD TARIGA.

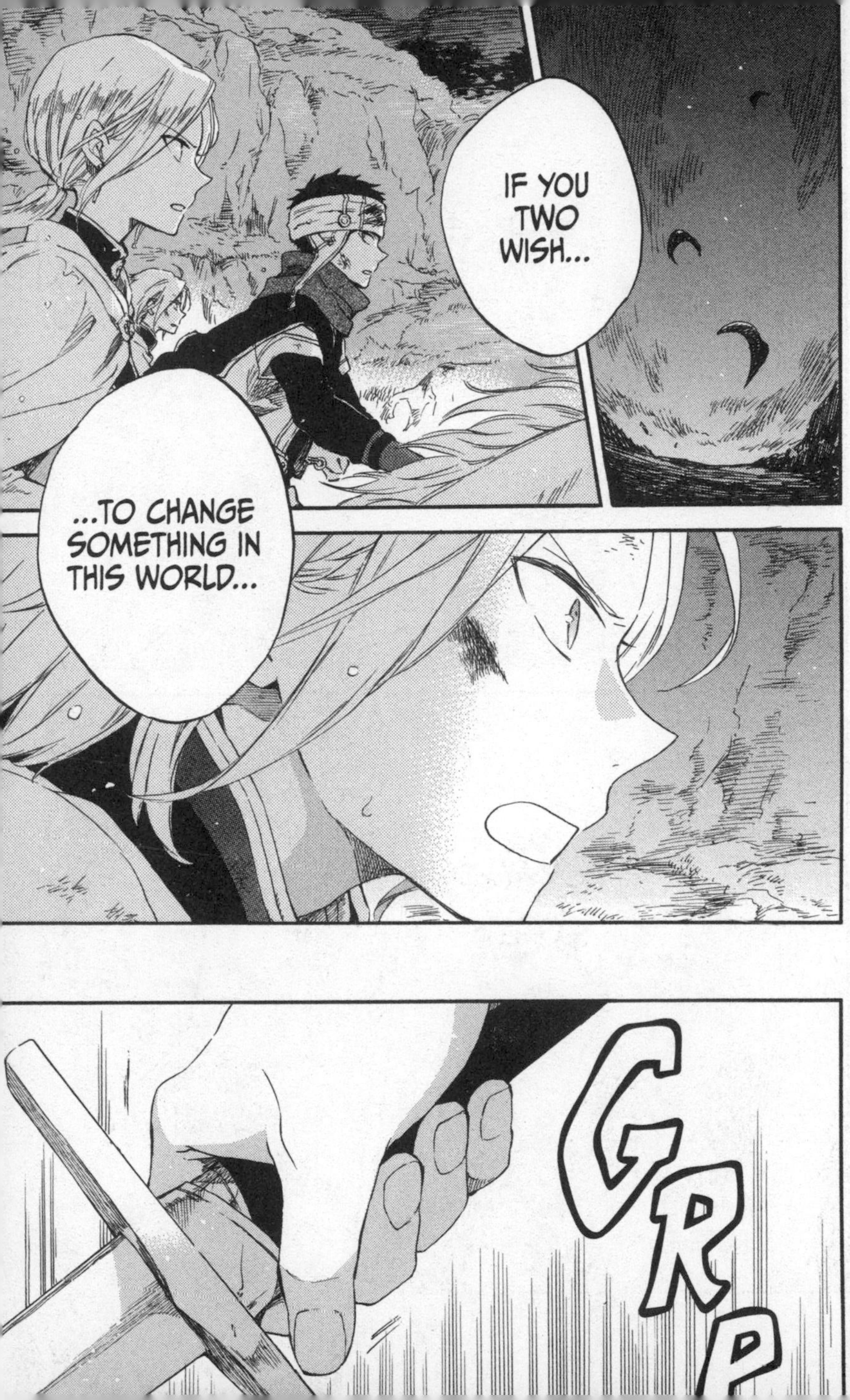
IF YOU TWO WISH...
...TO CHANGE SOMETHING IN THIS WORLD...
GRP

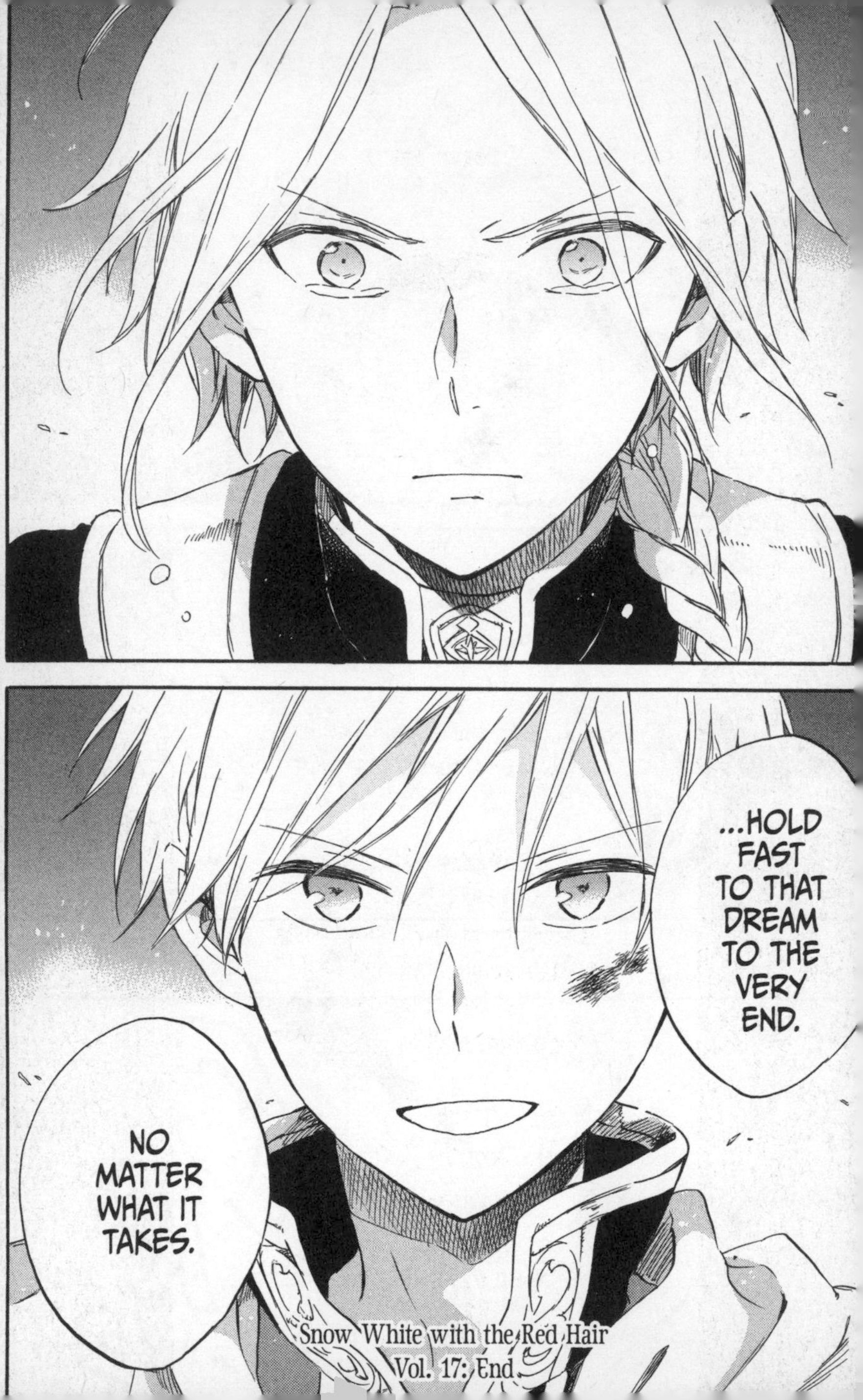
...HOLD FAST TO THAT DREAM TO THE VERY END.
NO MATTER WHAT IT TAKES.
Snow White with the Red Hair
Vol. 17: End

YOU'RE READING THE WRONG WAY!

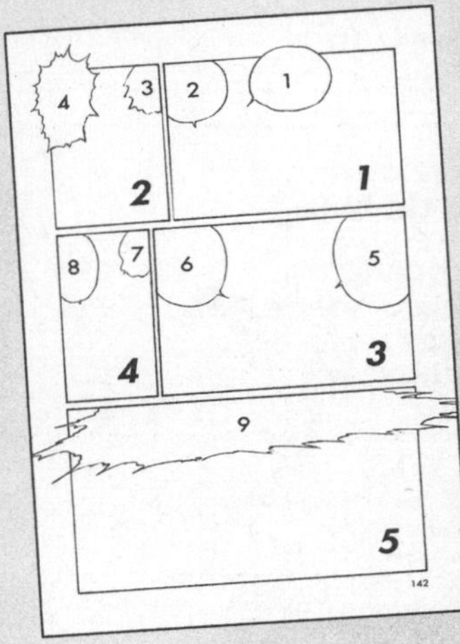
1
2
3
4
5
6
7
8
9
1
2
3
4
5
142

Snow White with the Red Hair reads from right to left, starting in the upper-right corner. Japanese is read from right to left, meaning that action, sound effects, and word-balloon order are completely reversed from English order.

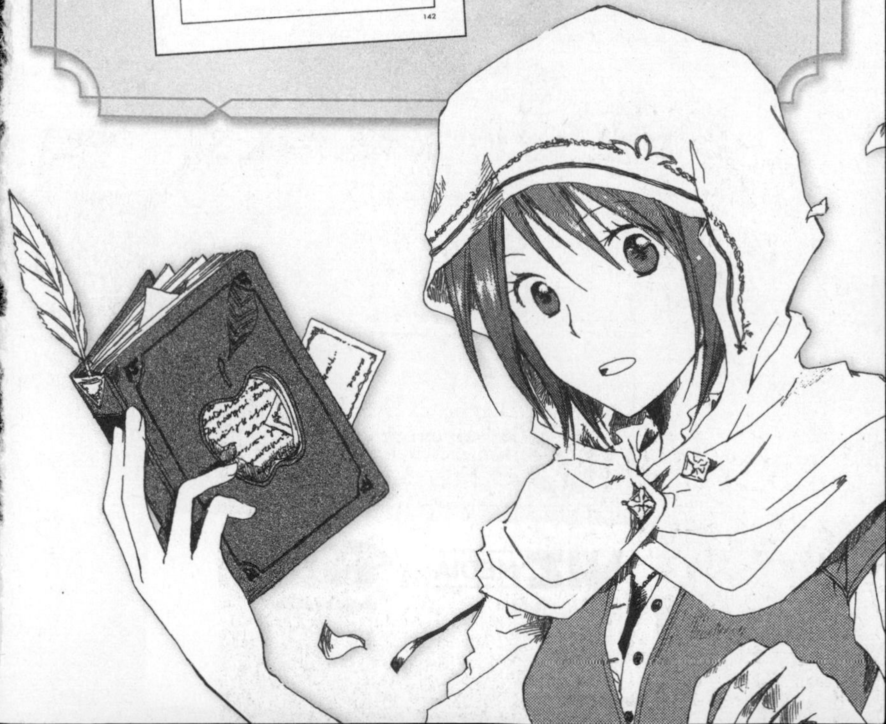

Snow White
with the Red Hair

SHOJO BEAT EDITION

STORY AND ART BY
Sorata Akiduki

TRANSLATION **Caleb Cook**
TOUCH-UP ART & LETTERING **Brandon Bovia**
DESIGN **Alice Lewis**
EDITOR **Karla Clark**

Akagami no Shirayukihime by Sorata Akiduki
© Sorata Akiduki 2017
All rights reserved.
First published in Japan in 2017 by HAKUSENSHA, Inc., Tokyo.
English language translation rights arranged with HAKUSENSHA, Inc., Tokyo.

The stories, characters, and incidents mentioned
in this publication are entirely fictional.

Printed in Canada

Published by VIZ Media, LLC
P.O. Box 77010
San Francisco, CA 94107

10 9 8 7 6 5 4 3 2 1
First printing, January 2022

Sorata Akiduki was born on March 21 and is an accomplished shojo manga author. She made her debut in January 2002 with a one-shot titled "Utopia." Her previous works include *Vahlia no Hanamuko* (Vahlia's Bridegroom), *Seishun Kouryakubon* (Youth Strategy Guide), and *Natsu Yasumi Zero Zero Nichime* (00 Days of Summer Vacation). *Snow White with the Red Hair* began serialization in August 2006 in *LaLa DX* in Japan and has since moved to *LaLa*.

Obi at age 12

Kinda cramped in there

✦ ✦ ✦ ✦ ✦ Special Thanks! ✦ ✦ ✦ ✦ ✦

Nakajima-sama, Iwakiri-sama,
Ide-sama, Yamashita-sama

-The editorial staff at *LaLa*
-Noro-sama
-Everyone in Publishing/Sales
-The anime staff and cast
-Kaneda-sama
-My sister, mother, and father

and You!!
—Sorata Akiduki
March 2017